KLaiR

A Man, A Monkey, And A Motorcycle Adventure To The End Of The Earth

By Adventurer:
Kix Marshall

Table of Contents

Guatemala **BANG-BANG!**	5
Canada **Talking Shit Or Taking Action?**	7
Talking Shit **The $107,000 Departure Challenge**	10
Canada **Taking Action**	13
USA **X's & A Nation Trump'd**	15
Mexico **Strippers For Christmas**	20
Mexico **Hemorrhoids & Jorge**	30
Mexico **Death On The Doorstep**	37
Mexico **Green Angels. Black & Blue Motorbikes**	41
Belize **$0 Beers. $8 Kraft Dinner**	46
Guatemala **Shitting In The Yard & Sleeping With Grandma**	48
Guatemala **Begging To Death**	57
Guatemala **A 10 Year Road Trip**	62
El Salvador **Converting Of A Coffee Atheist**	71
El Salvador **The Bourbon Jungle**	81
El Salvador **Grinding It Out In Coffee School**	86
El Salvador **Ransoms & Machine Gun Escorts**	90
Honduras **Kiss The Cook**	95
Managua **Bribery 101**	100
Nicaragua **Body Boxes & Toothpaste Rations**	105
Canada **The Backstory**	114
Costa Rica **Assault Weapons & Soup Pots**	117
Story Break **Why You Can't Escape Yourself**	122
Panama **From Police Detention To Police Escort**	127
Panama **The Dump Truck Of Death**	132
Colombia **HaMerotz LaMillion**	138
Colombia **Streeeeeeeetching**	143
Colombia **Problems In The Mirror Are Closer Than They Appear**	147
Colombia **Coffee's Poster Child, Juan Valdez or Kix Marshall?**	154
Venezuela **Oil Corruption & Salon Sacrifices**	159
Colombia **Emerald Tears**	164
Colombia **Desert Rains & KLaiR Strains**	171
Ecuador **Criminal Or Adventurer?**	180
Ecuador **Life & Death In The Amazon**	186
Ecuador **Motorcycling To The Highest Point From Center Earth**	202

Peru **The Girl**	206
Peru **Smashu Picchu**	213
Peru **From Life To Lunch**	219
Peru **Mental Shifts**	224
Peru **What Lies In The Rainbow Mountains?**	232
Bolivia **Black Markets & Bribes**	237
Bolivia **Blindsided By The Police**	241
Bolivia **Motorcycle Maintenance?**	250
Bolivia **Monumental Moments Never Talked About**	256
Bolivia **Teaching KLaiR To Swim**	266
Bolivia **Jungle People**	273
Mental Shifts **You Never Forget The First $7 You Made Online**	283
Paraguay **Umm, Sort Of...**	286
Brazil **Motorcycle Smuggling Take 3**	294
Brazil **Would You Do It?**	299
Brazil **Amazon Rainforest. The Most Amazing & Disappointing Place On The Planet**	304
Gil Serique **Alcoholic, Drama Queen, & Most Hospitable Man On The Planet.**	313
Brazil **What Is Ayahuasca?**	328
Brazil **The Lead Up To The Day**	331
Brazil **The Ayahuasca Experiment**	335
Brazil / Bolivia / Chile **The Race To The Girl**	348
Bolivia **Salar de Uyuni. Pass The Salt Please**	353
Chile **W.T.F.! & Other Swear Words Screamed Inside A Helmet**	357
Chile / Argentina **Feening For Friends**	362
Argentina **The Asador**	367
Argentina **Francis Mallmann**	374
Chile **Japanese Running Shoes**	377
Chile / Argentina **Screaming At Sunrise**	380
Argentina **61,264kms. The End Of The Earth**	385
Tears & Tattoos **PanAm's Final Chapter**	391
The Bonus Chapter **I Wasn't Going To Write**	405
Motorcycle Crash **Back To Whose Reality?**	406
Bonus Stories **Trip Stats, And Other Notable People**	415
I couldn't resist contacting this guy.	416
Writers Notes:	433

Guatemala
BANG-BANG!

"How long should a story be?"
- Mrs. Elworthy to my grade 9 English class
"Just like a woman's skirt. Short enough to keep your attention and long enough to cover the goods."
- Reply from the colorful kid at the back of the class

Day One Guatemala, 2 pm

Jose then picks up the gun and presses it into my hands. He explains how he'd smuggled this 9mm handgun out of California and into Guatemala when he left America. I'm 34, and this was the first time I'd ever held a handgun. It felt like I was holding a two-pound hard-on about to go off. The whole thing gave me a false sense of power like I now held some sort of control over things around me, a feeling I was sure was shared by every handgun-toting delusionist who thrives off this self-invented power.

Day One Guatemala, 3 am

BANG-BANG!

My eyes burst open to the point I feared they would begin to illuminate inside the darkness of my tent and give away my location. Without moving a muscle, I scanned the interior of the thin tent walls looking for glimmers of starlight that might appear through bullet holes hoping to detect the direction of the shooter. I then, very slowly, slide my hands up to hold my rushing heart thinking it might muffle the sound of its intense beating.

I lay there for what felt like an eternity, taking slow, shallow breaths trying to calm myself back to silence so I would not be detected. Would I die inside this twenty-dollar tent?

I had only just made it into Central America, and I was already being shot at.

Had Jose's safety meeting with me been a ruse? Were we under attack? Was he going to save my life? Was the day's earlier story a foreshadowing for him to make me disappear on his property in the darkness? My mind was racing uncontrollably down a dark tunnel of death in the Central American night…

But that's Guatemala and this story starts further north in Canada.

Canada
Talking Shit Or Taking Action?

"The Dream Is Free. The Hustle Is Sold Separately"
- Steve Harvey

The Plan.

People, like say, my concerned parents, sometimes need to know what *"The Plan"* is. So here's the bullshit one line answer I put together;

Drive across the Americas on my motorcycle.

Pretty straight forward really. It seemed that the goal of reaching Ushuaia Argentina, the most southerly city in the world from my home in Canada would be a worthy goal. Aside from marking a few tourist points on a map, like where to drink wine or find manta rays, I hadn't put much thought into where I might go or what I was looking to accomplish along the way. I just needed to go, and I wasn't clear with myself as to why.

I'd watched a popular motorcycle documentary on a plane ride from New Zealand to Canada years earlier about two movie stars who'd driven, arguably, around the world. They had support vehicles, motorcycle sponsors, pre-arranged fixers to help them cross borders, and even a doctor traveling with them!

The documentary had made the journey feel possible and based on their trip I figured I could replicate it in my own way. Naturally, I should have a traveling motorcycle show. So I shot a pilot episode for a television show, tried to raise $200,000, and pitched the show to major networks like National Geographic, Discovery Channel, The Travel Channel and a few others. As you might imagine, they did not instantly send a film crew and a sponsorship cheque to my house. After a year or two, the grand idea of a rockstar-road trip fell flat, zero dollars were raised and so, I started over.

The new plan looked nothing like the well-funded movie star trip I hoped to recreate. Instead, I had a 7-year-old used motorcycle I'd bought for $4000 that came with the helmet I was wearing. A $20 tent I bought on clearance, some second-hand motorcycle gear that was too big for me, and a host of motorcycle equipment I'd acquired for free by buying and selling motorbikes and stripping the needed equipment off the bikes before reselling them. My entire set up including electronics didn't exceed $6000. I wasn't convinced the $194,000 budget cut was a great idea, but I was further along in my goal than I was when the budget was $200,000.

The most fruitful efforts were buying and selling the motorbikes. At one point I had three KLR 650's in my yard. From the bike flipping, I gained an aftermarket Corbin seat, oversized windscreen, knobby rear tire, SW-Motech crash bars, luggage mounts, Pelican Case luggage, and an Arai helmet, all for zero dollars. I then kept one bike and sold all the others for the original purchase price and began to build my adventure machine.

By the fall I was converting a 10-foot x 10-foot shed behind my house into a workshop to use in the cold winter months. In the shed, I glued insulation boards to the tin walls, ran some lighting with an extension cord to my house, and placed a questionable propane heater inside to keep the ice out. I was hoping the holes in the tin shed would allow just enough airflow to keep me alive, and hold in just enough heat to keep me from freezing.

This fabricated tin box of death had a roof with a peak in the middle, just tall enough to stand up in. Of course, the catch was that if I stood in the very middle the CO_2 from my heat source, the burning propane tank, was more likely to kill me than the cold air was. I spent hours upon hours that winter in the tin box of death teaching myself anything I could about the mechanics of the motorcycle. This was, in fact, the second motorbike I'd ever properly owned with the intention to ride, and the first one I'd done any type of maintenance on.

They say it's easier to learn things with the mind of a child, and in the world of mechanics and motorcycling, I was no more qualified than a kid on his first tricycle.

My mechanical success that winter varied between staying alive in the tin box of death with aerosol lubricants canisters on the floor and gasoline-filled motorcycle all heated by the open flame propane heater and not losing focus on my goal while taking the bike apart and realizing how ridiculous this rickety, under-budget plan was.

Over time I would be rewarded with hints of success. The first highlight was when I removed the front brake pads and successfully mounted a new set. After several months of YouTube tutorial videos, I had one day managed to strip the bike to the engine and put most of the pieces back where they belonged. The results of this success felt like I'd just completed my first open-heart surgery and my patient was still alive!

I relayed my success to my then-girlfriend. A girl who never let you savor the moment long before moving the bar higher. She looked my excitement square in the face and said. *"Now, try doing it again with a sandstorm blowing in the desert".* Her point was alarmingly valid, but I wasn't excited to hear it.

Talking Shit
The $107,000 Departure Challenge

"How You Do Anything Is How You Do Everything"
- Tony Robbins

Having driven myself out of the world of business and into the tin box behind my house. I was feeling caught between feeling sorry for myself and feeling that I'd created my own reality. As winter set in I was still dealing with the previous years' business insolvency, coupled with the looming deadline of my girlfriend and her kids moving to France. Another opportunity I'd let pass me by while focusing on my *End Of The World* goal.

I'd spent the previous eight or so years turning a vacant space in a corner strip mall into a globally-inspired burger and pizza joint with the help of my father and various other friends & family. From there we'd taken a closed cafeteria in a large industrial factory and turned it into a steady food-business along with a blossoming catering company. Then, if I wasn't losing enough sleep already, my father had noticed a new space becoming available in the central bus station in our city. The following year we built a convenience store in what appeared to be the busiest foot traffic location in the city. Before my 30th birthday, I was on track to open my fourth small business and own my first property. I was allowing my inflated ego to believe that I had the golden touch.

By my 34th birthday, I would have nearly lost it all and was selling off the final piece of my micro-conglomerate and turning the proceeds over to my landlord to help pay down my outstanding debts. Then, one by one, I had laid off the incredibly loyal staff and executed the most difficult task of my entire life. Alone in my office while my Dad worked away at the till just outside the door, where he had for days on end, nights on end, and years on end. Helping his son to realize his goals.

I sat there drafting a formal letter that would mark his official layoff from my company. I wrote the letter, signed my name, folded it into three, then took a deep breath and walked out the door to reluctantly give it to him. The man who had once again let the course of his life be altered by his children was now being laid off by his youngest child. I'm happy to say my parents are alive and well, and aside from writing a speech for either of their funerals I could think of nothing worse in the world than handing over this letter. I would have rather it been my funeral that day. I would have rather died than walked out that door to give him that letter, but I did, and indeed a small piece of me died inside.

Soon it all became unbearably overwhelming and I eventually snapped. On the steps of my girlfriend's house one sunny summer afternoon, I melted into an emotional mess of tears and truth as everything around was crashing down faster than I could catch it.

The girlfriend was moving continents and I opted not to join. My father, who was not quite at retirement age but too old to be handing out resumes, was about to be unemployed at the hands of his son. I owed roughly $100,000 to friends, family, and suppliers, and I was liquidating everything in my life to stay ahead of bill collectors. Every day for exactly one month I cried continually throughout the day and into my pillow at night. If ever I could have imagined a low-point in my life, a moment where I felt like a massive failure, like curling up in a dark corner hoping to die, the nightmare of it was unfolding around me right now. I thought I was building a dream, instead I had built a prison and my sentence would get worse before it got better.

During the month of tears, I had sunk myself deep into the distraction of running. I was still crying while I ran, but at least I could hide behind sunglasses and people might assume it was sweat. Considering I don't recall crying much outside of funerals and breakups, the 30-days of tears was a completely new way to deal with problems than my preferred method of sweeping them under the rug. Finally, on this fateful 30th day of tears, I looked myself in the mirror and chose to make a new plan. I decided to start another company, take a job from a friend, and devise a plan on how I would pay down the $100,000 balance. No options were off the table, and almost everything I owned was for sale.

Life had become less glamorous than ever before as I watched my vehicle, personal belongings, business, and equipment slowly liquidate out the door. The job I'd taken was from a friend and former supplier, unbeknownst to him, the wage I was earning from him was going right into a line of credit I'd used to pay off a five-figure bill I had with his company. If I thought I'd been hustling in the previous 8-years, I would be compounding all of that into the year to come.

My new set of goals read off like an impossible checklist. I thought they would either kill me or take me to another failure.

November 2014:
- Pay off $100,000 of debt.
- Start a profitable side business.
- Leave for Ushuaia by motorcycle by October 2016 with money in the bank.
- Run a full marathon.

The list felt more like I was listing my own demise again. I'd never earned anywhere near a six-figure income in my life. I'd only started riding motorcycles a couple of summers earlier. My previous business was a failure, and my running experience had included a 5km fun run that ended in beer, and a half marathon that rendered me bedridden for several days a few years prior. When it came to talking shit, I was off to a pretty good start.

Canada
Taking Action

"...any budding adventurer knows, once you've mouthed off to all your friends, you have to go."

- Chris Scott, Adventure Motorcycling Handbook

With no ego and no sacred cows, I had rented out my basement as well as a room on the main floor of my half-duplex. I worked doing sales for my friends company/former supplier whose paycheques I would turn around and use to pay down my bill balance with them. I bought, cleaned, and sold cars, trucks & motorcycles. I sold my orange with orange and white leather interior imported Japanese VW mini bus and now drove this old beat-up catering van that looked like it was used to rob banks. I hauled scrap metal. I laid flooring. I drove around with $25,000 in twenty-dollar bills in a backpack plugging ATMs in gas stations and sketchy bars to collect a commission. I ran six days a week for a year. I worked more effectively than I ever had in my life.

To be able to leave I first needed to pay off the $100,000 in debts I had, and I was hoping to depart with $20,000 in the bank to fund my travels to the end of the world. By rough calculations, I figured the whole trip would take about 18-months to complete and would bring me back to Canada in the springtime. With $20,000 in the bank, I'd be one zero short of my original budget and would now have a little less than $40/day for food, fuel, bike parts, and all other travel expenses. I thought this was a bit tight, but I could make it work.

By October 29th, 2016 it had all come together, sort of. I'd paid off my $100,000 in debts, went to France to see my girlfriend and her two small children get settled in, completed a 42-kilometer marathon in just over four hours, managed to keep from losing my home, and saved $7,000 of travel money. $13,000 less than I was hoping to depart with, but considerably more than where I was a year earlier. I resolved to now make the $7,000 or close to $12/day budget work, and headed South from Canada in light snow and frigid temperatures to the loving goodbyes of friends and family.

Ok, it wasn't all smooth. I planned a small media event at a local motorcycle shop, Turple Brothers. Owned by an avid biker Glen Turple who was nearly 90-years-old at the time. Glen still worked at the shop 4-days a week, mostly doing sales and rode a trike to work year-round, in a place that has winter 6-months of the year. This was the kind of stamina I needed to leave with. Glen had also spent a good many years riding motorbikes with my grandfather & I wanted to leave from his shop to memorialize the event. The night before departure I'd changed the bike oil at my friend Andrew's, where I'd been living. Realizing in the morning I had put in too much oil, I needed to drain some before finally setting off. I showed up late to my own going away party, got some press photos, kissed a few babies, and was off.

Late October in Canada comes with pre-winter temperatures that aren't known for their enjoyable motorcycle riding. I was wearing layers of clothing, biker gear, and a full rain suit to try and stay warm. I'd stopped for a pee an hour after departure and dropped my overloaded bike facing downhill in a ditch. With fuel leaking everywhere, I looked like a yellow beached-whale struggling to get a motorcycle that weighed considerably more than its original weight backward up a hill. The overweight bike and an underprepared rider would set the stage for adventures to follow.

Departure photo in the local newspaper. *photo credit Red Deer Advocate

USA
X's & A Nation Trump'd

"The root cause of relationship conflict is unresolved trauma"
- Headline of an online clickbait article

Riding from Canada into America, I hit an unusually warm patch of weather for November 1st and managed to miss the typical snowfall at this time of year. That first night I spent the evening CouchSurfing in rural Montana. Then off to Utah for another night of CouchSurfing where I was taken on a city tour to see the Mormon world through the disgruntled eyes of a non-believer. From one extreme to the next, I was then off to Las Vegas for a few days with a girl I'd met earlier that year. With three free stays behind me, I was well on budget for sleeping expenditures.

I'd met this girl while volunteering for a fundraiser at a hockey game about 6-months before taking off. Despite being out of my league she seemed to keep laughing at my lame jokes and we hit it off, for now. I was sure I'd never see her again once I left and made the effort to keep her at arm's length during our time together. As a going-away gift, she'd given me a little plastic monkey to take on the trip in case I needed a friend. He was cute and had this big shit-eating perma-grin on his face so I named him Stanley and zip-tied him by the neck to the handlebars where he was now smiling back at me.

The girl was meant to be at a work conference in Portland the week after I left. However, by some stroke of budget-biker luck, her conference had been swapped to Las Vegas which was directly on my route, and I was now Couchsurfing in a premium suite at the four star LINQ Hotel right on the strip. Several nights in Vegas with my summer fling, then we again said goodbye for the final time before I headed back to biker life on the open road.

Just before leaving Vegas, I'd gotten a call from my x-girlfriend and her kids from France. They wished me well and sounded like they were mildly concerned if I'd survive the trip. With all of these previous relationship good-byes, it only seemed fitting that I stop in to see a former love of my life who happened to be in San Diego and staying at the house of her current love interest. Really, what could go wrong with this picture?

Rolling down the I-15 and into California, it was the final days of the Trump/Clinton election and each fuel stop led to conversations about who was going to be worse for the country. A potential first-ever female president dubbed a criminal by the opposition and his supporters or, a racist narcissist who seemed to be fueling the country's political fire before his plans to burn the well-being of the country to the ground. These same people were continually warning me about the political instability of the countries of Central and South America and how unsafe it would all be, but they had blindly overlooked their own backyard and its unbridled chaos.

Passing through rural Nevada I was treated to signs that read *"Vote Trump Or Die".* I could feel both the intensity of the country around me and the intensity within myself as I got closer to a girl I hadn't seen in years. This particular x-girlfriend and I had parted on less than settling terms after an incredibly intense five-year-relationship that took us around the globe together and into our first adventures in the world of business.

We met at 19 and 23 years old. I had returned to Canada after living in Europe on the back of several years of living in Toronto. The plan was to see my family for a few months then make my way back to Europe. Plans changed and several months later I'd be on a road trip across Canada to pick up a Mexican friend whom I once had a small catering and taco business with in Toronto.

At the time, Alberta, Canada where I was living was in the midst of an incredible oil boom and I had convinced my Mexican amigo to leave the Spanish comforts of Toronto and live in rednecks-ville with me to open a restaurant. I'd fallen for this blonde-haired, blue-eyed girl who was now keeping me in Canada and he'd fallen for my business proposal that would bring him west to Alberta. By the time we were back from Toronto my new girlfriend had moved us into an apartment and thrown a few parties to break our new place in.

With my very close friend, the incredibly talented chef Jorge, and my ambitious and beautiful girlfriend Jill, the idea of filling our restaurant bank account with oil money seemed too easy. I felt at the top of the world. Me at 23, the Mexican at 22, and the blonde at 20, we opened a casual dining restaurant in a small town to a full house. However, within a year I'd completely fallen out with my Mexican amigo on terribly bad terms. I bought out his half of the business, we parted ways, and I never spoke to him again.

Jill and I would eventually close up shop, road trip from Canada to Guatemala in an old Ford camper van, then later move to Thailand with the blind hopes of opening "The Pink Guitar Bar & Hostel". We lived fast, worked hard, and traveled like the world was ending. We'd lived more in 5-years than a lot of people do in a lifetime, but eventually I'd leave her standing at an airport in New Zealand to pursue another dream of mine.

Our unresolved break-up would have been a therapist's dream. The joys of peeling back layers from the onion of life to find out why the center had rotted. It had now been close to a decade since I'd had a substantial conversation with her. Before the day was over I'd be arriving at the house of my potential replacement where she was staying to "catch up" before continuing on.

I'd stopped at least five times on the way to her house. Maybe I needed a drink, maybe now was a good time to get fuel, maybe I'd stop and take some photos, perhaps I should show up with a bottle of wine? I was surely stalling. The wine turned out to be a good idea as I certainly needed a drink upon arrival. Eventually, I felt my balls were big enough to show up on the doorstep of this guy's house, and I nervously rang the doorbell.

I'm not sure either of us knew what was going to happen. Would we have the useless surface chatter I tried to pull off with her before? Would we settle back into the comforts of old lovers? Would we fight? Would we kiss? Would we have sex? I had no idea what to expect, but in my man's mind, I was hoping we'd continue to sweep things under the carpet, get drunk and make out. I clearly hadn't changed at all, had she?

We drank the wine, we talked about life, I confirmed that my potential replacement was out of town and we even discussed making out like it was some sort of business arrangement. To my disappointment, no arrangement was made.

When it comes to the heart of who someone really is, Jill could dive deep into your soul. She's a self-established life-coach, has a gifted understanding of people, is soulfully deep, and with the right Peruvian attire, you'd think she was a shaman.

We talked like we'd never talked before. We talked about life and where we were headed. We talked about the book she'd just contributed to. We talked about the crazy businesses we'd started and the dreams we'd chased across the planet at such a young age. Then we talked about ourselves. I'd never dealt with what was once us. For nearly a decade now, thirty-something me had been looking back at twenty-something me and realizing how much I pushed and pushed on a girl that pulled and pulled. It was a 5-year emotional tug-of-war where her heartstrings and patience eventually broke.

I'd refused to deal with what was once us, and the more we talked the more I realized it had been grinding on me for nearly a decade. I assumed she felt the same. To my shock and amazement, she had forgotten all the times I'd pushed at her while she tried to pull me closer. She'd forgiven me for my wrongdoings and the unforgivable moments of our relationship. She even forgave me for leaving her at the airport in New Zealand and attributed it to making her a better person! I couldn't believe she had dealt with it, mentally forgiven me, and moved on with life. What the hell had I been doing all this time?

Now here I was on the couch of my replacements place, a couple of bottles of wine down, meddling in their relationship while trying to deal with my relationship from a decade ago, that Jill had long since dealt with. Cue the daytime talk show spot; *Yes Dr. Phil I know I should not have been drunk on his couch with her, but I needed a place to stay and it was on my route.*

Amid my unsettled distress, Jill told me to stop and be still. She then looked at me through the eyes of an adorning golden lab, drew a long deep breath like she was consuming all the emotional angst out of my lungs and into hers. Then, with the otherworldly concentration that only a deep-rooted shaman could have. She placed both of her hands on my right forearm, exhaled the purified air towards me, and told me everything would be ok.

Suddenly that area of my arm became incredibly hot. The type of hot that no human can produce with a mere touch. It was burning up. I was sure she'd placed a straightening iron on me in the hopes of distracting my attention from the dark hole of a broken past that it was focused on. But it was only her hands, the incredible heat of her hands firmly gripped around my forearm. How was this happening?

Instantly a dam holding back ten years of emotion and tears burst. This emotional bottling came uncorked like a magnum of champagne exploding across the room. All to the touch of a blonde-haired, blue-eyed shaman whose hands I hadn't felt on my skin in close to a decade. These hands were now relieving me of ten-years of emotional torment.

Jill then looked at me and said *"You're Free."*

I said nothing.

I sat and finished my glass of red wine and made my way to the bathroom where I also felt the tension of my bowels release. I took a shower and cried until the last of the warm water rinsed away the last of my tears. I was completely cleaned out. Physically and emotionally. I had no idea what had just happened.

My mind, body, and soul had just been released from the inner cage I had been holding them in. That night I slept like I'd never slept in my life. I slept like the lid of my casket had closed, the final shovel of dirt had been thrown in my hole, and my soul had been set free. If I had set off for the end of the earth by motorcycle in search of freedom, I was quickly finding my way.

Mexico
Strippers For Christmas

"Every man dies, not every man really lives"
- William Wallace, Braveheart

Having driven through Mexico once before in a van and part of it another time on a motorbike I was fully aware of the rules, "Don't drive at night". Not for the drug cartel reasons the media would make you assume the problem is. On Mexico's roadways, you'll find domestic cattle, wild donkeys, discarded tires, people walking, crops drying, roads that aren't finished, car-swallowing potholes, and often there is no shoulder. Once you mix all of these obstacles together, then take away sunlight, you've just created a recipe for a deadly disaster.

Following the driving rules, I spent the days roaming around the Baja and the nights camping under the stars on the beach. With all of the sites to explore, fishing, and settling into nomad life, what was meant to be 3-days down the Baja, was now 3-weeks. This extended stay led me to meeting back up with Jill where she lived in Cabo San Lucas and again meeting up with Angie who had flown in with some friends to spend a week at a resort in Cabo. The timing of meeting up with what was supposed to be a summer fling was becoming unusually perfect.

Angie extended her stay and opted to come beach camping with me for the week. That poor girl went from a 5-star resort sipping margaritas by the pool & seafood buffets, to nights of sand blowing around inside our tent eating pasta from a pot. Who was this girl who could hang up her holiday heels in exchange for flip-flops and tenting?

By now, my 3-day ride from Tijuana to Cabo had been completely distracted with ocean fishing, breakfast with dolphins, watching surfers ride the waves under the moonlight, chasing sea lions, making friends, and meeting up with the girl, the Baja ended up being an incredible 36-days of adventure before crossing over to mainland Mexico. The captivating Sea Of Cortez and the tranquility of Baja life were nearly impossible to leave.

With so much initial x-girlfriend and potential-girlfriend activity right from the start of this "escape", I decided the only girlfriend for the rest of the trip would be one who I couldn't get attached to. I opted to name the motorcycle KLaiR, as this seemed fitting for a KLR650, and proceeded to refer to her as my girlfriend whenever anyone asked who I was traveling with.

My mission for mainland Mexico was to meet with a friend who lived in Mexico City. Actually, I had absolutely no desire to drive into the traffic madness of a city whose population rivaled that of my entire country. However, the idea of having friends around for Christmas outweighed the traffic trauma I was dreading.

A couple of years previous I had met Ivan in Canada. A typically friendly Mexican guy about my height, or tall for a Mexican, quite fit, with a chest like a whiskey keg and arms like he carried around Canadian bikers for fun. We'd met in the convenience store I previously owned and quickly became friends. I took him snowboarding one day and watched him laugh and smile all while face-planting continuously for hours in the cold snow. I was sure Ivan was more Canadian than I was. He was just as friendly as all Mexican people I've met, and quickly found himself hanging out with my friends and family.

After a decade or so in Canada Ivan was now back in Mexico City. Ivan had been living the dream of migrating out of Mexico into the North American dream. A dream shared, but rarely realized by many Mexicans. I stopped by to see Ivan in his small Canadian apartment one day. He'd lived there for nearly 8-years, working a steady job, paying his bills, and living his Canadian dream. However, he'd overstayed his visa allotment and despite being a perfectly upstanding citizen, was deported to Mexico with 10-days notice. He instantly had everything he'd worked for taken away.

We moved a number of Ivan's belongings to my house where I then sold off his possessions at a steep discount and sent him the money. It was the reality of many immigrants. Having built up a life in a new world only to have it all taken away from them at a moment's notice. I brought him back some of his t-shirts as a reminder I hadn't forgotten about him.

On the way into Mexico City, I'd become a bit concerned about my obvious outsider-looking appearance and the possibility of being robbed. I typically wasn't concerned about being robbed, but Ivan kept telling me how dangerous it was going to be in this city. As I tried to navigate the busy roads with my GPS I continued to get lost in the maze of turns and traffic. As my wrong turns continued, suddenly my GPS died, then moments later my phone died too. I had no idea where I was and no way to contact Ivan, I was officially panicking. The sun had now faded to darkness and I ended up in a few back alleys where I would wave to the locals staring at me trying to pretend I knew exactly where I was. After my 7th or 8th attempt trying to find Ivan's street I heard him yell out my name from the 3rd floor of an apartment building. He had spotted me, and now the whole neighborhood knew I was here!

Ivan came out to greet me, but the greeting was short-lived. Ivan looked around and explained it wasn't safe for my motorcycle to be on the streets after dark for any reason. I was feeling even more tense than I was driving around lost for the last hour. Ivan insisted we get the bike indoors right away. Great, I thought, where is the storage area? He hadn't found a spot for the bike quite yet and instead opened the apartment door where we awkwardly maneuvered overloaded KLaiR, all of her luggage, and wide ass with Pelican cases strapped to each side through the narrow apartment entrance. We then pushed her down the hall, and rammed her in front of apartment door 101.

I was laughing and asked Ivan if we should really have my bike inside the apartment building blocking the door of someone we didn't know. He said that the bike could not be outside or it might go missing. Also, that once the people in the apartment saw a North American bike with all my gear tied to it, they would understand. I knew back in Canada they certainly would not understand why a motorcycle was inside an apartment blocking someone's home entry.

From here Ivan took me to various neighbors' homes and garages trying to find a good spot for the bike. Finally, we found a friend of his with a large gate, capped with military-style razor wire on all sides. Behind the wire was the home of some retirees who had a nice little yard and parking space. They were all too happy to look after KLaiR while I was with Ivan. We headed back to the apartment to dislodge her from the doorsteps of his neighbors, and then back to safety behind the large gate, protected by razor wire and retirees. So far Mexico City was exactly, and nothing like I was expecting.

Mexican people are like no other culture on the planet. If you ever wanted to show up anywhere and instantly feel like you are part of the family, hang out with Mexicans. Not that facade where they are paid to be your friend on a resort in Cancun and force a laugh at your appalling lack of interest in their language or personal lives. Actually show up almost anywhere, meet a local Mexican and within a couple of hours you'll probably find yourself back at their place for lunch or at the very least enjoying tacos at their favorite taqueria. It's an incredible culture where family comes before everything, a stark contrast from North America where work is typically placed before family.

I would be staying at Ivan's house. He was living with his retired parents, more for economic reasons than for the love of the family, but this is life in Mexico. The apartment was a small two-bedroom home with old family photos in black & white, handmade wooden furniture, plants growing up and over the tables, and the whole place well decorated for Christmas with a mix of traditional items from years gone by along with simply *"Feliz Navidad"* written on cards. The space felt warm and welcoming, like it had probably looked and felt for years.

Ivan's parents are like your favorite aunt and uncle. It was instantly hugs, kisses, and the; *Me Casa Su Casa,* kind of welcome everyone wishes for in a foreign place. Ivan's Mum is beautiful with deep caramel skin, curly dark hair, and a smile that could melt the most macho of men. She spent her youth in the arts appearing on a number of children's television shows. She's extremely animated when she speaks, with these dramatic expressions of excitement on her face and hands moving frantically to describe a scene. She's the type of person you could watch talking for hours, a lady who was clearly perfect for television.

Ivan's Dad, a man in his 70's, shorter than Ivan, but equally as fit, with jet black hair and handsome features that still shine through. It's obvious he was quite attractive in his younger years. Ivan had explained to me that his dad used to be a performance dancer, quickly followed up with *"but he's not gay"*. Mexican men are wildly proud of their machoism. His father performed at Compañía nacional de Danza (National Dance Company), taught at the Pachuca Hidalgo School Of Arts, was hired to work for a number of years as a performer in Houston Texas, and appeared in various television shows and movies in Mexico. Ivan would later take me to a theatrical museum and show me books that featured his father. Just to be in this house was amazing and the parents seemed genuinely delighted to have me as a guest.

Later in the week Ivan was interpreting between myself and his parents and he asked me; *"This adventure of yours sounds quite fun, but what is the point of your trip?"* I looked Ivan right in the eyes, and without skipping a beat I said to him and his family. *"Every man dies, but not every man really lives. I want to feel alive."* Feeling very William Wallace and having no idea where that stroke of inspirational commentary came from, I smiled and tried to contain my composure without laughing as though I spouted off inspirational shit like that all the time.

For the next week, I shared a room with Ivan on a sofa bed in the house with his parents. If there were any drawbacks to this scenario, it was that my Spanish was as good as my navigation. If I was lost driving around, I sure as hell had no idea where I was going once I opened my mouth.

Meeting Ivan's amigos was like revisiting old friends. They adopted me as their own, Spanish or no Spanish, especially one guy named Burgos. Burgos had a respectively well-paying job and liked to make sure I experienced everything and paid for nothing. I was basically Burgos' guest of honor. Some of Ivan's friends spoke English, some did not, but no one seemed to care. They talked to me like I knew Spanish and I answered back like they had any idea what I was talking about.

Over the week Ivan took me to some of the best taco stands eating street meat and crushing Coronas while Burgos took us to some of Mexico City's top restaurants where we drank rare Mezcales and ate some local delicacies like lemongrass-flavored ants turned into guacamole. We partied at clubs until the sun came up, we got drunk with the Mariachis and police in Garibaldi, we ate cow tongue tacos over tequila shooters in La Coyoacana until I was speaking like I knew the local language. It was amazing, but eventually, I had to stop asking what things were. If I did, Burgos would buy it for me or take me somewhere and pay for everything to explain the answer to my question. I was feeling a little guilty about the endless pampering, even if it was genuine.

Finally, Christmas came and I was entirely unprepared for Christmas in Mexico. For the Mexicans, the important date is December 24th. On this day Ivan took me around to family events. At each stop, we were greeted with tequila and mezcal, hugs, and handshakes. By 6 pm I was already slurring in bad Spanish.

By midnight I thought things were winding down for the day. I could not have been more wrong or less aware of what was coming. By 1 am we met with Burgos and about eight of Ivan's other friends at a swanky lounge in the heart of the city. We were greeted with cappuccinos, espressos, and coffees all with a touch of holiday liquor. Then a platter of well-crafted desserts was brought out where I was told to choose first. Then the rest of our motley crew soaked up the savory crème caramels and fancy flans along with a few more shots of holiday liquor. It was now 2 am and I was thinking that surely this holiday eve was coming to an end. Ahh, silly Canadian, we are in fucking Mexico City at Christmas, no one is going anywhere!

Just then one of the amigos suggested taking the gringo (me) to "Queens". Where I'm from there is a 50's diner called Queens, so in my head, I'm picturing a little diner stop for some fries and a beer before finally heading home to wait for Santa.

A couple of the amigos head home while the rest of us cram in Burgos' car. We drive deep into the city and park on what appears to be an empty street. Just then a questionable-looking man appears amongst the respectable-looking cars. Burgos gives the man some money and Ivan explains that this man will watch the car while we are in Queens.

A brief walk in the quiet darkness and suddenly we're met by a line of men pouring out the doors to the entrance of a place blaring obnoxious dance music while the sounds of party people come spilling out onto the streets. I think to myself, oh great, a dance club. It looks like I won't be getting home anytime soon.

One of our amigos asks the bouncer how long the wait was? Gauging by the response, apparently too long. Instead, Burgos talks to the bouncer, some money exchanges hands, and we're waved to the front of the line and ushered inside.

I'd heard a lot of Christmas tales over the years, but I was sure this one was about to turn out like no other. Queens, as I was about to discover, was a gentleman's club.

The inside was lit with flashing lights that bounced along with deep house music. Women were walking around in their underwear serving an array of equally as alluring cocktails. The entire place was wall to wall with men, a number of them with beautiful Mexican women on their laps as paid company. In the middle of all this madness was a small functional stage designed as the room's focal point. I was getting the eerie feeling that anything goes here, all you have to do is ask and pay. Happy Birthday Jesus, and welcome to Queens!

It was explained to me by Ivan that I was the guest of honor, could have anything I wanted, and was asked to pick a bottle of liquor for the table. Recalling the disastrous mess that Whiskey has played in my world on previous occasions, I looked across the bar, spotted a bottle of Johnnie Walker Red, and ordered one. Moments later an attractive Mexican señorita wearing a string bikini and a smile returned with several glasses, various mixes, and our good friend Johnnie.

Looking around it became clear that if you were a single, lonely, or a party-hardy male in Mexico City on Christmas Eve this is where you came. It also became clear that I was the only pale, white, gringo in the bar and I was starting to notice the eyes of other men in the room as well as the featured entertainment focusing on our table.

It wasn't like it was my first strip club. Actually, my first ever strip club experience was just outside the city limits of Cancun at my brother in laws stag party. On that occasion, I was greeted at the part strip club, part brothel, by large men with machine guns. As opposed to here where we were greeted by a well-dressed Johnnie and the underdressed host. I was just 16 at the time and had been instructed by my older brother to pull my chair in as close as I could to the table and not to touch the entertainment. Here I was being instructed to do the exact opposite and to enjoy watching these Christmas gifts unwrap themselves.

Even though I'd had enough Christmas cocktails to tranquilize a rhino, the attention I was getting from the eyes of everyone in here was keeping me a little tense. The locals weren't looking to make me feel uncomfortable, I was just the one thing that looked most out of place in a bar where many things should look out of place.

Over the next hour, I'd seen more fake body parts coming down the production line than you would at a Barbie factory. Some girls had incredibly well-crafted breasts while others had breasts that looked like paper mache that hadn't finished drying. Some asses shook to the music while other asses couldn't move no matter how much they shook. A few girls had scars that ran up under their breasts from surgeries that had clearly gone wrong. Some girls had long sets of staple scars that ran the length of their torsos. Others had lips so swollen they looked more like an allergic reaction than a Botox touch up. No one seemed phased or surprised by the looks of these ladies, but the ladies did seem surprised by the looks of our table.

Burgos then asked what else I wanted? I knew what he meant, and replied in bad Spanish that the cocktails were good enough thank you. He looked at me like I misunderstood him because of my poor Spanish. Occasionally a girl would walk by in her underwear slide her ass across the lap of whoever was most accessible then mix them a drink and slide away. This would get some excited whoo-hoos from our table while the girl would continue her ass-slide and drink mixing around the room. If nothing else, the service was top notch.

Finally, Burgos flagged down one of the more beautiful and full-figured ladies making the ass-slide drink-mixing rounds and said a few things in her ear. She then began to make her way directly towards me. I rarely feel uncomfortable in any situation. I mean unless you want me to talk about my feelings that is, and I was sure this girl didn't want to talk about my feelings.

This beautiful Mexican woman eyed me like a lion going after a baby gazelle. Probably the same eyes that are often imposed on her. I instantly froze and immediately shut down like it was my first therapy session. My legs closed, my hands went in my lap, and I began to look straight ahead. I was again the 16-year-old in the Mexican strip club with his older brother staring at dancing Mexican girls for the first time. If anything was going to save me now it's that I didn't know Spanish.

The nearly naked, full-figured Mexican woman came and sat next to me. I sat looking straight ahead unable to answer any of the questions from my hired companion. My Amigos looked overwhelmingly unimpressed. I then learned you should never underestimate the good deed of a Mexican or the ability of an enterprising dancer to get things done. Having dealt with this English speaking problem before, my full-figured companion got up, slid her ass across my lap, topped up my drink, and went and whispered in the ear of Burgos with her well-formed ass staring me right in the face. He smiled with delight and off she went. I relaxed a bit and the show, drinks, hollering, and stares continued on as they had before.

Quickly the full-figured host returned with two glasses of champagne and a friend. Our table and the one next to us lit up with whoops and hollers. The friend was built like the chiseled statue of an Olympic champion. Short, toned to the point of a six-pack, and thighs that looked like she spent her mornings deadlifting. She had long beautiful brown hair, an inviting smile and looked at me more like a mate than a meal. She looked nothing like any of the other girls working the room. She had the sexy librarian look as opposed to the bush-meat look.

I thought to myself what the fuck is going on, it's Christmas! If my parents knew where I was they would surely die.

This new girl, let's call her Myrrh, could speak flawless English. Shit, my plan of playing dumb as I didn't know Spanish was coming unraveled! Again I clammed up like the room temperature had dropped 20-degrees, and again this girl proceeded to drape herself across me like wet blanket. I got the feeling that she wasn't your average working girl.

Myrrh told me to relax, and poured me another drink. I told her this wasn't really my thing. She said no problem, she would take care of me. I continued to look ahead while she asked me questions about what kind of fun I was looking to have and if I liked to party. Finally, after 10-minutes of me playing ice cube, Myrrh realized I wasn't here looking for the same paid attention as most in the room and she settled back into her seat a little.

Myrrh then asked me some personal questions about my life and I told her about my trip and my friends and asked her the same. Myrrh told me about her job as a performer in the circus, how she was going to school to be a lawyer, and that the dancing and circus was paying for all her education. I think we're becoming friends.

To the disappointment of my amigos, we were having a pretty casual chat about life and not about how much per song to have her dance for me.

They were appalled that I had been given two pre-paid girls to enjoy and refused to put a hand on either. Finally, Myrrh explained she didn't make tips by chatting but enjoyed our talk. Ivan asked for her phone number and said we'd call her if she wanted to hang out in the city.

Myrrh got up to leave, and Ivan asked if he could see her stomach before she went off. Myrrh flexed her Cirque du Soleil abs, gave a quick flash of her leg and arm muscles to our wide-eyed table, and wished us happy holidays. I had officially let down the entire bar with my lackluster performance. I don't think I'll be invited back to Queens.

We drank, we laughed, Myrrh winked at me when she got on stage, and eventually, we would stumble our way through the door greeted by Ivan's parents for Christmas breakfast shortly after 9 am. It wasn't Christmas carols with three wise men, but it certainly felt like of all the traditional gifts that could have been given to Mary & Joseph, Myrrh would have been the most memorable.

(Ivan's Dad on stage as a young man)   (Ivan's Mum on television as a young girl)

(Christmas with Ivan & his parents. I got them Tim Hortons, they got me socks!)

Mexico
Hemorrhoids & Jorge

"Every Thought We Think Is Creating Our Future"
- Louise Hay

I sat staring, lost in deep thought at the message on my phone for nearly ten minutes. Despite only being a few lines long I felt it impossible to decide on whether I should send it or not.

"Hola hombre. How are you, are you still living in Veracruz?".

It took me ten years to write that message and the ten minutes I'd taken fretting over whether or not to hit send felt like another ten years. I didn't know what to do. If I hit send I might be opening up a wound I wasn't sure I was going to be able to stop the bleeding on. Such is the cycle of life.

I met Jorge in my early twenties when I moved to Toronto. We'd both arrived there not knowing anyone and looking to make our mark on the world. At the time, I was working as a Sous Chef and Catering manager at a restaurant on King Street near the core of the city. Jorge was working as a cook at a cafeteria run by the same people I was working for. The cafeteria was built to feed all of the creatives who were working on an upcoming Disney movie. Even though Jorge was scooping and serving pre-cooked food, to a bunch of underappreciative computer geeks, he was actually a very skilled chef that was being held back by very unskilled English.

We met, became friends, started our own catering business, then a taco stand on the side of our other jobs and for the next several years proceeded to party together like we might not see tomorrow. I'd seen more drinks, drugs, drag queens and dancing girls pass through the doors of mine or Jorge's house than at any point in my life combined. It was an incredibly exciting time in our lives, and one of us was rarely seen stumbling around a party without the other. We worked together, partied together, and did business side by side. We were literally inseparable. But the last time I'd spoken to him was in an argument on my & Jill's doorstep at 4 am over 10-years ago.

A decade had passed since Me, Jorge, and Jill had spent all of our days together. Having recently cleaned things up with Jill, now I was sweating it out and staring at the send button on my phone as to whether or not I'd contact Jorge and try to do the same. Fuck, it had been such a wild ride with the two of us. We had fed off each other's strengths and weaknesses flawlessly, at such a vulnerable time in our lives. Coming from nothing to selling tacos for beers, to owning our first restaurant together in our early twenties. It's true, there can be too many cooks in the kitchen. We'd done and learned and experienced so much together in such a short time. Then, at the peak of it all, we'd come crashing down. In an instant, it was over and I hadn't spoken to him since.

I knew I had to contact him, but I was being a pussy about it. I was in Mexico City and if Jorge was back where he grew up in the state of Veracruz I knew I was going to be riding right past his doorstep. I figured that on such short notice and around the holidays that it was likely he wouldn't reply or wouldn't have time to see me. I figured I'd send my two-line message and if he declined, then at least I could say I tried before moving on with life. I could feel justified with the fact that he was too busy for me.

With sweat building around my forehead and a hefty heart beating in my chest, I finally sent the message. I was as nervous as I was relieved. I was sitting alone in the bedroom of Ivan's house. He'd left for Cancun to meet a friend where he'd then fly to Germany for a couple of weeks. I got up and grabbed a drink from the fridge then made my way back to the bedroom. My phone lit up, there was a Facebook message. I picked it up and sure enough, it was Jorge.

"Hey man, how are you? It's really good to hear from you. I am living in a small city in the state of Veracruz with my family, not far from Xalapa. Where are you? It would be nice to talk to you."

The reply was fast, the words sincere and the English was remarkably better than when I used to hang out with him. I sent back a message about where I was and what I was up to. Without hesitation, he invited me to spend New Years' with him and his family.

I thought about it, became nervously flustered about the idea of not only talking to Jorge but actually seeing him and being in his home as a guest. I bit the bullet and decided to jump right in with both feet just like we used to. I replied that I'd get on my motorcycle and arrive in two days.

I said goodbye to Ivan's parents, sprung KLaiR from behind the security fence where she was stored, and headed to Veracruz. It felt like I'd been through an ugly divorce and was now driving two-days to go on a date in the hopes of getting back together. This was by far the most nervous I'd been on a date with an EX.

I met Jorge on the patio of a Starbucks, he came up and in nearly perfect English said *"Hey Kixy boy, how are ya!"* and gave me one of those dramatic handshakes that lead into a big hug. I was amazed, his English was maybe 50% - 60% understandable when we hung out. Now, aside from a colorful Mexican accent, it was nearly perfect. Jorge didn't seem anxious at all. If anything he seemed excited and happy I was there. We had a brief chat and headed back to his house.

Behind a large gate, not unusual for Mexico, in a suburban neighborhood like that of any other small city, I parked my KLR650 next to his new BMW650. It would appear that things had gone alright for Jorge back in Mexico. Inside I met his young daughter and beautiful wife, and before I knew it, one night suddenly turned into 10-days and I'd also meet his mother who had heard a lot about me over the years. She hugged me like I was her other son and explained how grateful she was to finally meet me as though I was some biblical Saint. I was feeling incredibly welcome.

Had Jorge not told her about our messy breakup? Had he not mentioned how the last time I'd seen him I was basically throwing him out of the house at 4 am? Had he not told her how much of an asshole I was or that we hadn't spoken in over a decade?

I was getting the impression that most of the bitterness built up inside my head was not the same inside Jorge's head, perhaps he too wasn't losing that much sleep over me. Then, one night, he finally told me what had happened to him after our break up. Before coming to Canada he had gone to culinary school to become a chef and had excelled with incredible talent and cooking ability. Part chef, part artist, Jorge could alchemize the most melancholy of melons, plain potatoes, and unexciting eggs into a 5-star Huevos Rancheros with Poblano Potatoes and Candy-Coated Swan centerpiece that would drop your jaw and stuff your stomach. To prove it, he did just that one afternoon in a cooking competition we were part of in Toronto, and we took the gold.

He loved cooking, he loved entertaining, he loved to be in the kitchen at home and at work. We both shared this passion and it drove us to each other. After leaving behind everything in Toronto to come to Alberta, he had sold me his half of the business, our friendship had dissolved, and he returned to Toronto where he took a job doing construction before eventually returning to Mexico. He said he never stepped foot inside another commercial kitchen after that day. It hurt too much. It crushed him. I crushed him.

I felt awful, I felt like a failure. I felt like I had taken someone's dream, helped them build it up, then when they were most proud, I had taken it all away from them in front of the whole world. Now here I was in his home, with his family, finally hearing the rest of the story. He'd forgiven me, I'd forgiven him, but he'd never try to realize his dream again. I did not want to hear this story. This was not how I wanted this fairy tail to end. This was the slap in the face he had kept hidden from me, the kick in the balls I knew was out there waiting for me that I'd been avoiding for 10-years. With the full force of a steel-toed boot to the groin, I could now feel it. I felt like an asshole.

* * *

During my stay, Jorge took me to local restaurants hidden deep in Mexico where the food is still smoked over wood stoves, salsa crushed in wooden mortar & pestle, and tortillas handmade from corn harvested from the maize fields behind the restaurant. He took me to the tiny town where he grew up to take me swimming where he'd always swam in the rocky outcrops of the ocean since he was a kid. He took me to parties with his friends and lunch with his family. It was like we hadn't skipped a beat, let alone a lifetime. He even helped me out with a little medical problem, the way only friends will.

My Spanish was still pretty bad and I needed some assistance from the pharmacy. When it came to ordering meals I could usually blunder my way through the menu and if I get the wrong thing I'd still eat it. At the pharmacy, I wasn't interested in getting my order wrong.

Shortly before leaving on this adventure, I'd been jogging one night and my ass had gotten unusually sweaty. When I got back I was shocked to see my boxers had blood on them, blood from my ass. I had no idea why and hoped it wasn't some life-threatening disease that might threaten my trip. I hoped it went away. Then it happened again, and again, and subsequently my ass was quite sore. I had no idea what was going on and booked myself in for a doctor's appointment just days before leaving.

The doctor wasn't entirely sure what the problem was or if it was related to heavy running or lots of time in the seat of my motorbike, however, he gave me some cream for my sore ass and sent me on my way. Once I finally set off on the bike the problem finally went away and I was happy that this little cream did the trick.

Now here I was in Mexico and the day before meeting Jorge it had happened again. After some self-diagnostic Googling, I finally realized I'd had hemorrhoids. It wasn't a side effect of too much time in the saddle or too much running, it was fucking hemorrhoids! I thought hemorrhoids were something you got when you were over 50 and spent too much time in cold chairs. How did a man in his early 30's in warm weather have hemorrhoids?

That day I explained to Jorge what the problem was and that I would need his help at the pharmacy to buy some cream for what I'd previously thought was a cream for chafing from my running. He laughed and told me that after we'd parted ways and he was living back in Toronto he was fighting with the idea of moving from Canada back to Mexico. Just before he left, the same thing had happened to him. This got me thinking there was more to hemorrhoids than just running, cold seats, or bad timing.

I did some more Googling and learned that a lot of women who are pregnant get hemorrhoids. This time instead of seeking out any more answers from modern medicine to solve my problem I looked for solutions from Louise Hay, the author of You Can Heal Your Life.

Louise had cured herself of cancer and eventually discovered that your body is a reflection of your thoughts. In short, the book outlines what might be happening in your environment and that your thoughts are a reflection of what is happening to your body. I'd referenced Louise Hay plenty of times in the past with great results and was looking for her advice again. These days I'm a firm believer in my thoughts reflecting my wellbeing and have found a world of evidence to support my theory.

The book stated that hemorrhoids were a result of *"Fear of deadlines. Anger of the past. Afraid to let go. Feeling burdened."*

Holy fuck I almost fell off my chair!

I was experiencing all of these emotions right now, all in abnormally large amounts, and the same was happening just before I'd left on this trip. It seemed like Jorge was experiencing something similar just before returning to Mexico from Canada. It was shocking to see the blatant accuracy of this happening and burning up my ass again.

I had Jorge get me some cream from the pharmacy in the hopes that I could use the meds and the thoughts together to help speed up the resolve. Standing in the pharmacy I tried to describe the problem with my body actions to the pharmacists while Jorge translated. All of us giggled. It was an entertaining show for everyone in the shop that day. Once I got the cream I then proceeded to use Louise's mantras to change my thoughts. Whether modern medicine, mantras, or putting the current situation behind me, magically the hemorrhoids went away and never returned.

With the past buried, the friendship rekindled, and all of the problems that had been creating pain in my ass resolved. I hugged Jorge and his family goodbye, breathed an incredible sigh of relief, and headed further south in Mexico.

As I rode on the country was now teetering on the brink of a civil war. The government was trying to get Mexico off of fixed fuel prices and onto the floating market to stop from continually bleeding money in the form of fuel subsidies. Cities were rioting, fuel trucks were being stolen and government buildings were being burnt to the ground. I wasn't sure how far I'd make it without roadblocks or fuel shortages, but I set off with a clean conscience and a new friend rather than an old foe.

When I was planning this motorcycle adventure, I had pictured days sunning myself on a beach, getting lost in the wilderness of the world, and partying until dawn with the locals. Somehow as the route wound further on it was becoming the Kix Marshall dealing with your demons tour and less and less of the glossy fun in the sun brochure I'd sold myself on before departure. The whole thing was feeling less like a road trip and more like a therapy trip.

(Camping on the Baja. The abandoned house I slept in and the oceanside sand dunes.)
*Dune photo credit Angie

Mexico
Death On The Doorstep

"The future is uncertain, but the end is always near."
– Jim Morrison

As I wound my way further south following the beautiful Gulf Of Mexico the news that flashed on television screens at local fuel stations and inside tiny roadside eateries confirmed that things were getting worse, not better.

The locals were stepping up their protests against Mexico's corrupt government and blocking a number of major driving routes, crippling the supply of fuel and food. The outrage towards the government was building more and more as the people rioted, and it appeared that the local police were doing little to stop the madness. Many believed that the police, who were also underpaid and treated poorly by the government, supported what was going on. Though I do enjoy a nice dramatic photo or two for my social media posts, I was hoping to avoid becoming part of the protests and tried to follow the dusty backroads that wound through southern Mexico's farmland.

I spent a few nights on beaches, camped out in farmers' fields, and eventually discovered my first cenote. These magical openings in the earth's crust reveal pools of freshwater hidden below. The water is often so clear you need to drop a pebble to see the water ripple to know it even exists. The cenotes can have stalagmites hanging from the roof, small fish swimming below, and are often connected to a series of waterways or other cenotes via underground rivers. These once Mayan locations of sacrifice are like a resort spa for the dusty biker looking for a place to swim and stay.

For the brochure-toting tourist you can often find large cenotes closer to the resort areas of Cancun and Playa Del Carmen where you are crammed onto a tour bus, given a life jacket, and made to "relax" around dozens of other tourists. Some of us on the other hand, happen to get lost on their motorbike and stumble onto a wooden sign near the gate of a farmer's house with the faded words "Cenote" written in cheap spray paint. You can pull in, give the farmer 50-pesos and spend a couple of nights near the maize fields swimming and sunning yourself.

It's here I met one of a number of families I'd meet along the way from France. In this family of four, the mother spoke English and I was able to hang out and share some of their impressive stash of French wine they had been carrying around for months in their European motorhome. The family was a bit unimpressed that being from a country whose second language is French, I could only read French food labels to know the ingredients but could barely pronounce a French word properly. Either way, they treated me like family, and the 12-year old boy & I got on just fine having cannonball competitions into the cenote for a couple of days.

Back on the road, I was headed to see the aunt of a friend who lived out the Canadian winters in Mexico. I am never one to let the promise of new friends and a place to sleep with a shower and flushing toilet pass him by. Aunt Ellen and I had met briefly while I was staying at her nephew Andrew's place just before leaving. She had offered me to come for a visit if I was ever passing by tiny Chan Chemuyil, a community that sits on the coastline between Playa Del Carmen and Tulum in southern Mexico.

Ellen is the kind of aunt that you could sense had lived life in her younger years like a streak of lightning. Not the running from the law type, but more likely that her name gets an honorable mention when reminiscing old party stories. I could see us getting along just fine.

Chan Chemuyil is an ungated community for mostly retired North Americans and some local Mexican families between two major tourist hubs. The first thing I passed when I rode through the community was a paper sign next to a gravel parking lot that translated to say "Cock Fights Today 40-Pesos". The feathery fight was just starting as I rode by. I could sense that the place was just far enough away to fend off tourists and just close enough that you're still part of the real Mexico.

I arrived at Ellen's and was greeted like I was part of the family. Her home was a single-level cement adobe with a small sitting area out front, a couple of bedrooms, and my spot on the couch in the air-conditioned living room. Compared to the tent, I felt like I was moving into the Four Seasons.

This quaint seaside community was incredible; it still felt authentic as it wasn't overrun with rule-making North Americans looking to defend their piece of property. As a little bonus, there were even tiny freshwater cenotes hidden inside the neighborhood.

At the house was Ellen and her visiting friend, Kathy. If I had to guess, I would put Ellen in her mid-60's and Kathy in her early-70's. Side by side, Ellen was definitely still the streak of lightning, and Kathy seemed a bit more settled into her retirement years. Kathy was delightful and friendly, she just moved a little slower than Ellen and it was clear that her health wasn't as good as Ellen's.

Lucky me, I would have these two beautiful ladies all to myself. However, I had grossly underestimated them. To the untrained eye, one would suspect that these two cute little retirees would be knitting on the porch in the morning and settling into a good crossword puzzle by 7 pm before going to bed.

With that assumption planted in my head, I did them the favor by taking a shower and rinsing off the day's biker sweat before we all set out for dinner at the local pub up the road. Upon arrival, we were greeted by twenty or so other retired expats out for a quiet dinner. If there is one lesson I continually forget to learn, it's to stop judging books by their cover, or in this case, their age.

By 7:30 pm we were having dinner, by 8:30 pm we were onto the fourth margarita. By 9:30 pm half of the retirees in the bar had found their way onto tables and were dancing to 70's American music remixes like this was a college house party! I was easily half the age of most everyone there, that meant nothing. I was also easily out-partied by all.

As the eclectic crowd ordered more rounds of margaritas and the dancing amplified along with the small crowd singing, I sat and enjoyed the action next to Kathy who seemed a bit off. I wasn't sure if Kathy had maybe had a couple too many tequilas, though I didn't remember seeing her have anything other than fresh juice. She wasn't making sense when she spoke and some of her words would come out backward. Each time she went to stand up she always seemed a bit dizzy. Maybe she did have a few beers and I didn't notice? Either way, she seemed delighted to be out having fun and offered to pay for my and Ellen's dinner. Overall the double date with the beautiful ladies was going great!

I spent the week going from one event to another with the ladies and each night no matter if we had one drink or none, Kathy always seemed a bit dizzy and continued to mix up her sentences. On a few occasions mid-day, I found Kathy exhausted and sleeping in a hammock on the patio. Other times I'd see her acting a bit confused about where we were going or what time of day it was. She explained to Ellen that she'd been watching her medication to ensure she didn't miss anything and I'd assumed that maybe the heat or the change of pace was getting to her.

One night with the ladies turned into two nights, then two nights turned into a week. I ended up befriending a retired Kat in the community. A colorful lady who always had a drink in her hand and a smile on her face. She had a positive attitude about the world and I interviewed her on camera about why she was so damn positive! She could hold a one-sided conversation like no one else and I had to eventually stop recording before I ran out of memory on the camera.

After a week we finally parted ways with some hugs and those motherly reminders from Ellen and Kathy to be safe. The next day I began to make my way towards the border with Belize and received a message from Andrew, Ellen's nephew back in Canada. It seemed that the exhaustion and confusion of Kathy throughout the week were not unfounded or without dire effects. Kathy had passed away in her sleep the night I left. It was a shocking reminder to enjoy my time doing what I liked on this planet and with those you enjoy being around. I was lucky to have said my goodbyes to Kathy before she had said her final ones.

(Laundry day!)

(BBQ fish tacos on the beach)

Mexico
Green Angels. Black & Blue Motorbikes

"I had to sell the kids for medical experiments just so I could ride a BMW"

- Jorge a.k.a Rubber Cow.
Posted in ADVRider.com when asked for a BMW Quote

It had been two days since the passing of Kathy, and KLaiR & I were en route to exit Mexico and cross into Belize. For me, this felt like the official start to the adventure. On this and previous road trips I'd driven through Mexico and Guatemala. Belize however, was going to be unchartered territory and I was excitedly nervous about exploring the unknown.

Mexico is such a mix of good and bad decisions. It is beautiful beaches that are overrun with pollution and tourists or incredible people that are forced to do unimaginable things for bad people just to earn a living. The government is no different. For the most part, they are a bunch of corrupt criminals who bleed the citizens dry until there is nothing left to take. Just look at Javier Duarte, the x-governor of Veracruz who stole millions from the state for his financial gain and ruined the local economy. However, for all the mismanagement that Mexico's government creates in their country, they do some remarkable things to look out for road traveling tourists.

Roughly 100-kilometers before the Belize border I passed one of the country's Green Angels, parked off the road, tucked into the shady bushes. The Green Angels are a fleet of pickup trucks and other autos painted in green and white that roam the roads of Mexico looking to aid stranded foreign travelers with vehicle breakdowns. The drivers of this fleet are typically skilled mechanics with a minimum grasp of the English language. Considering Mexico's roads get such a bad rap for crime, the Angels are sent to get a broken down vehicle back on the road as soon as possible to avoid criminal attacks or any problems in general.

The Angels are equipped with spare fuel, car parts, and tools to change a flat tyre. If you need to call on one of these heaven-sent Angels you just enter a 3-digit code (078) on your phone, explain your location, and someone is sent out to help, free of charge. The whole system is unbelievably remarkable, when it works.

I passed this particular Angel in the scorching heat of mid-day, southern Mexico, it looked like he had his eyes closed and was resting his wings. He had backed his truck just off the road and into the shade, with his seat back and appeared to be mid-siesta. I thought nothing of it and continued on 45-minutes up the road. Then things changed.

Here, on the edge of a dusty small town on the cusp of Belize, I passed a motorcycle traveler on a BMW 650GS. The rider was peering into the motor of his bike. The type of peering you do when you're searching for a problem, but have no idea what you are looking for. I passed him with a long gaze to see if I could catch his eye. I then stopped, swung back around, and pulled over to see if I could help.

The man was a Swiss traveler who'd come from the far end of the world. He was riding the opposite route to me, from South to North America. I looked at his worn riding gear, sun-faded and beaten-up like your favorite baseball glove. His motorbike plastics were covered in a wealth of souvenir stickers from the countries he'd passed through. Then there was the bike itself. The bike looked like some of those stickers were helping to hold it together. I'd rarely seen a BMW motorcycle that wasn't fresh from garage storage and sparkling clean. BMW motorcycle riders are easy to poke fun at, as they typically have all the best gear, luggage, and accessories every ADV rider envies, but their bikes never see life off-road. This guy was proving my conceptions of a BMW rider all wrong. His bike was a mix of memorable scrapes and scratches that might suggest it had spent most of its life off-road as opposed to the garage princess bikes I was used to seeing.

The combination of the worn man and the battered machine looked like they had been on the road for some time. He looked back at me through reddened, tired eyes. That rugged look that only the open road, relentless sun, and dwindling budget can provide you with. I wondered what I looked like to him? I hadn't even put on my jacket since Nevada & just spent the week in a retirement community sleeping in the air conditioning while enjoying regular siestas. Maybe he thought of me, what I used to think of him.

I got off my bike and asked if I could help? Through a colorful Swiss accent, he explained he had a sensor problem and the bike wasn't running properly. He then went to put the kickstand up to push the bike into the shade to show me the issue. As he did, one of the sub-frame bolts finally broke, and the center of his bike buckled into itself. The BMW looked like an empty beer can that had been stepped on in the middle. While my mouth dropped, the man seemed entirely unphased by this.

He braced the bike with his leg and went to put the kickstand back down. Well fuck, then the bolt on the kickstand either broke or finally gave way and the BMW collapsed towards the guy. This time he caught the bike like he was awkwardly cradling a baby elephant. My eyes bugged out with great concern as we found a large rock to slide under the skid plate and support the motorbike from further collapse.

The dusty man on the decaying bike said he was trying to sort out how to get the Beemer from where we were in the southern reaches of Mexico another 400kms up to Cancun where he could find a BMW dealer to source parts. As he'd just arrived in the country and likely wasn't aware, I proudly explained the Green Angels like I was the country's ambassador, and how they could help him to get the bike up the coast.

The man explained he was Swiss and had a Swiss phone that would work anywhere in the world and attempted to call the 078 number for assistance. The lady who answered said there was a separate number for the very south of Mexico and that 078 was for the rest of Mexico. Two different Angel numbers, who knew? I didn't speak Spanish, but the Swiss guy seemed confident that what she said was true. The guy then called the other number. It didn't work. Not that either of us was surprised that Mexico would have a perfectly good service that you weren't able to use.

I explained that I'd seen one of these Angels sleeping in the bushes 45-minutes back and I would go to get him. The Swiss guy said not to worry he'd ask around for a truck or just sleep here. I felt obligated to help him out, and so I went looking for the sleeping Angel.

I backtracked the 45-minutes until I found the Green Angel. Sure enough, he was still sleeping in the bushes. I went up and banged on his window, the Angel awoke, surprised to see a gringo at the window. In my extremely poor Spanish and extremely dramatic hand signals, I tried to explain the situation. He must have got the gist of it and told me that south of this point wasn't his territory. Then he told me about the other number to call. I was shocked, the helper Angel wasn't willing to help.

I told him to call the number as I clearly couldn't speak Spanish. He called, the number didn't work. He said south of here was too far and he wouldn't be moving. I explained it was only 45-minutes and that he had to help. He refused.

Now I can probably count the number of times I've lost my cool, sober, on one hand. That number was about to increase by one.

{In a Broadway-level display of dramatic theatrics combined with yelling, utilizing the Spanish verb for work (trabajar) and the Spanish verb for help (ayudar), along with some swear words I'd learned years ago.}

I then proceeded to act out a very visual display of what the Angel looked like sleeping, what he looked like not helping, then what a motorcycle traveler looked like in distress. For anyone who may have driven by at that point, it would have made for an excellent video. I sensed a standing ovation in my future.

I'm sure my chaotic babbling and theatrics were scaring the hell out of this Angel who had been sleeping only moments earlier. Perhaps he thought he was still sleeping. I wouldn't leave the guy alone, actually, I got more dramatic. My hands waved faster, my tone got louder and I continued to insist he come.

The Angel then started his truck, great I thought I finally convinced him to come. He then closed the door to keep me out of the truck. Wait, he wasn't coming, he was leaving! I began to yell louder and my hands began to move faster. I banged on the door. He put the truck in drive. I yelled louder.

He drove away. I kept yelling. There, in a cloud of dust, I stood looking and feeling like the Angels had failed me and I had failed the Swiss guy.

It was roughly 2-hours between the round-trip driving and Angel-yelling by the time I came back to add more bad news to the Swiss guys' situation. He seemed unphased and said he'd spend the night here by the roadside and find someone with a truck to drive him where he needed to go. I was impressed with his lack of concern for an immediate solution and the fact that he planned to camp in a parking lot on the edge of this tiny town completely exposed to those passing by.

We shook hands, parted ways, and I left with the penetrating image of this man's motorcycle crumbling below him. KLaiR and I were loaded down, polished up, and running like a well-oiled machine. Would this be the fate of us, crumbling on the roadside into a pile of battered nuts and bolts? Certainly not, this man must have been recklessly abusing his BMW. Not me, I don't drive like that. Like day one of Navy Seal training, I grossly underestimated what would lie ahead for us...

Belize
$0 Beers. $8 Kraft Dinner

"Why Fit In When You Were Born To Stand Out?"
- Dr. Seuss

Belize is like the Japanese macaque. Everyone loves to see them, they're fun, it's great to go and visit them, but how in the hell did primates end up in the snow? In this case, how did a country of spirited black people who speak English end up in Central America? The world is a very interesting place.

Belize is surrounded by caramel-colored, mainly Spanish speakers of various native and cultural descent. In Mexico and Guatemala, there are the Maya people, the Aztecs, a host of other native descent, and you have some Spanish blood mixed in from a conquest or two. Then boom, you cross an imaginary line on the ground and suddenly you are taken into what looks like central Africa! However, if you close your eyes and listen it feels more like a European colony of English speakers with thick, nearly inaudible accents. It's an incredible mind-fuck that without knowing the country's history would be nearly impossible to piece together.

Here on the border of Mexico & Guatemala is this tiny landmass of just under 23,000 sq kms with a total population of around 400,000 people, less than most mid-sized cities. The people are a mix of Mestizo, Creole, Maya, Garifuna, European, Asian Indian, and East Indian people. In the late 1700's the British brought thousands of slaves to Belize from Africa. Over time, cultures mixed giving way to the Creole language and a mix of people with light and dark skin. To fly from an English-speaking country to here is one thing, but to be immersed in the Spanish countries that surround it and then arrive in Belize throws you for a real loop.

I met loads of people, mostly American expats who loved Belize. They loved it so much they sold their homes to retire here and soak up the stunning weather and stunning locals. For me, Belize wasn't a memorable stop on the route south. If you like diving and island pubs it's likely exciting. Compared to cheap as chips Mexico with all its cultural diversity, Belize felt to me more like a 5-star menu with 3-star results. So much so I resorted to buying the cheapest "meal" sold at the local grocery store, $8 Kraft Dinner. Belize is not a budget-friendly stop on the road south. As for motorbiking, the limited roads don't allow for much off-road exploration. An hour one way or the other and you've maxed out the day's excitement.

My time here was mostly spent CouchSurfing with an incredibly hospitable retiree from the U.S. who takes in all kinds of misfits like myself at his Belizean home. There were three of us at his house that week, spread across spare rooms and couches. Uncle Joe, as I started calling him, seemed to like the company so much that he was building a smaller house behind his house to pack in even more Couchsurfers!

Uncle Joe took us to every happy hour on the peninsula and paid for everything but the tip, we covered that. His hospitality was shocking. Even more shocking was the neighbor across the road. He had a massive RV, the type you move into when you're 75-years old and drive around North America from horseshoe tournament to bocce ball game spending your kids' inheritance on diesel fuel.

This particular RV had Alberta, Canada license plates. The guy had in turn spotted my Alberta plates. He yelled from across the road and came over for a chat. It turns out he wasn't 75 at all. He was more like 50, had an attractive 20-something-year-old girlfriend, a restaurant he hated, and a life he loved. He was from Alberta and had made a small fortune during the previous oil boom.

He'd first ridden his Harley down to Belize to test things out. He loved it here and went back to Canada to pick up this luxury home on wheels and drive it down. He was here to stay. To sum up our meet and greet, I would say the man was a "colorful character".

After my days of $0 beers and $8 Kraft Dinner, I set off for a sweltering night camping by the ocean, then headed for Guatemala. Sorry Belize, you just didn't get my heart pounding enough. Maybe I'm still too young for you...

Guatemala
Shitting In The Yard & Sleeping With Grandma

"Guatemala has the sixth highest rate of chronic malnutrition in the world and the highest in Latin America and the Caribbean"

- Worldbank.org

Entering Guatemala I was hit with another flood of memorable moments. In another life, Guatemala would be the final country of discovery when Jill & I had fled the insanity of young entrepreneurialism and the mental claustrophobia of small-town Canada. It was crazy to think of where life had gone since those days nearly 14-years earlier.

At the time we'd purchased the 69 Ford Super Van for $1800. To acquire this van of van's, wasn't your usual car purchase. The owner spent 3-hours telling us heartfelt travel stories and gave us a full bumper-to-bumper explanation about the quirky features of this living time machine. It was a full adoption process.

The man who owned the red & white Super Van resembling a Canada flag on wheels, actually had three camping vans. One newer model modified Mercedes van, one 80's model modified family van, and this 60's model camping van. It was to the wife's delight that two young transitioning hippies were potentially buying a van that mainly ran on dreams & blind faith and that we would keep the wheels and dreams rolling. Upon purchase, the parting gift was a file folder of every single maintenance record for the van, including the original purchase document, hand signed by Ford from 1969. We were officially the 3rd owners in nearly four decades.

The two of us were leaving behind 18-hour workdays, crushing relationships, infidelity, and one hell of a learning experience. We traded all of this for another steep learning curve that would take us down literal and figurative roads of life we never could have imagined. This type of immersive travel had seeped into my veins in my late teens and early twenties and I was clearly addicted to it.

Just before departure from Canada south, we had stopped to see my sister in law who had been cleaning out a library at the local school. She found a Lonely Planet guidebook to Mexico that was about 10-years old. She gave it to us assuming it would be a nice addition to our collection of books, GPS, and whatever else we had packed. To her and possibly our surprise, we had packed nothing that might give us even the slightest bit of insight about where we were headed. In actuality, we had no plan of any kind, and as a result, took nothing to plan with.

If you were looking for a visual explanation of the word "freedom," you could have taken a photo of that van putting down an empty desert road in Mexico, each of us having one sun tanned arm hanging out the window, headed to nowhere.

Now, 14-years older, on the back of another restaurant disaster, with Jill again in my mirror, and I was again looking to rediscover myself. If anyone was looking for evidence that history might repeat itself, here I was living out my soul-searching reality, again. Had I changed, had I stayed the same, who the hell was I and why was I going where I was going this time?

Having covered a large part of the western and central part of Guatemala in that van, this time I was only looking to see the eastern side and decided on a route that would skim along Belize and the Caribbean Sea before dipping into El Salvador.

My courage from traveling alone on the bike was building, but I was still mainly using established places to sleep, like hostels, and the homes of people I knew or met online. Wild camping was still an option, but it would need to be calculated so I knew exactly what to expect when I arrived.

I'd found a posting on the CouchSurfing website for a local family where they would offer you a local experience, a place to stay in a village not far from the culturally famous Tikal, and a meal for the equivalent of about

$10. This wasn't exactly how CouchSurfing was meant to work, but it was relatively cheap and the experience sounded amazing.

I contacted the family a couple of days before my arrival and the man who responded said he'd meet me in the square of a small town on the day of my arrival. Sure enough in the mid-afternoon a couple of days later I was met by Aldolfo. Aldolfo and his family would completely change the way I chose to experience the local culture for the rest of my trip.

Aldolfo was in his late 20's, about the same build as me with wonderfully caramel-colored Guatemalan skin, short dark hair, and a captivating white smile. He'd ridden his squeaky old bicycle about 5-kilometers from his house in the countryside to meet me. Aldolfo didn't know a drop of English and my Spanish was basic at best. We exchanged hellos and in first gear, fluttering my clutch, I slowly followed him on the bicycle back to his countryside home.

The home was built on the intersecting corners of two dusty dirt roads. To one side was a lightly forested area made up of mostly lush jungle scrub. The other side of the road was charred, black ground, with little puffs of fresh smoke still smoldering here and there. I presumed it was once a jungle-forest like the other side of the road. The home was a tiny, one-level structure with a wooden exterior, earth floors, and the interior of the kitchen was painted in bubblegum pink.

The doors to the home looked as though they were never closed, the dirt floors were hardened from years of foot traffic along with small ducks, chickens, and rabbits that casually passed through like they owned the place. In the yard were some small fruit trees and a small structure roughly four feet, by four feet and eight feet tall surrounded by a battered black tarp on all sides.

I was greeted by Adolfo's wife, a beautiful woman with a smile like Aldolfos who knew enough English to explain basic things to me. Together they had several children of various ages and on this day there were some other children at the house playing. I was having a hard time sorting out who was related and who wasn't. It all looked like one big happy family.

The oldest kid was a delightful 10-year-old who loved to talk. So much so he'd managed to learn English in a school in Belize. Aldolfo had gone to Belize for several years to work an illegal job for extremely low pay so his son could attend one of the local schools. In Belize, the English education was better than in Guatemala and Aldolfo wanted a better future for his children so badly he was willing to sacrifice whatever it took to get it for them.

The family was delightful and showed me around the property. Well, mainly the 10-year-old showed me around the property as I could understand him the best. After a brief tour of the home, he then took me to the backyard to explain the black-tarped box. This black box was precariously placed in the middle of the yard. Maybe it was a greenhouse, maybe it was a shed, I wasn't sure but I was interested to find out.

He took me over, pulled open the tarp, and revealed a small wooden box on the ground painted in the same bubblegum pink as the kitchen. In the top of the wooden box was a hole with some wear marks on each side of the hole and little wet marks in front of it.

Next to the box was a roll of toilet paper. My face scrunched up a little and I could feel my brain piecing the puzzle together. It finally hit me. The hole was for the toilet, the wear marks on the seat were from the natural oils on your skin that would eventually penetrate the wood as various bums sat on the box, and the little wet spots in front were little pee dribbles from the boys. There was no water to flush here, just a hole and the bubblegum pink box.

Overall this was your standard house with four walls, bedrooms, and a kitchen. However, this was 2017 and I didn't know anyone who had an outhouse as their main or only toilet. I'd definitely gone to the bathroom in worse places, but every day like this? I wasn't too sure how I felt about shitting in the family's yard. I smiled at my tiny tour guide like this was just like the toilets in Canada and the tour continued.

As the day wound down we had a nice family dinner and it was explained that I would stay in a different house a few hundred feet away with the grandmother and an older boy. The family issued me a tiny flashlight and the kid walked me over to neighboring Grandma's house. If I thought the main house was rustic, Grandma's house was the base, rustic model.

Grandma had no power on her property, no bedroom walls, and no bathroom. The family shared the bubblegum pink toilet in their yard. However, there was a shower and the shower was pretty cool. It was set in the garden and closed in on three sides by scrap wood and the fourth side was living plants. You could literally shower amongst plants and flowers. The bedrooms in the house were sectioned off by old bed sheets as opposed to walls. On two sides I had the exterior walls of the house and on the other side between me and grandma was a hanging bed sheet. Across the room was the teenage boy with his exterior walls and his room dividing bed sheets. Inside my sheet room was a wooden dresser and a small bed with a mattress and some blankets on it. It wasn't quite dank, but was flirting with that adjective.

I took off my biker gear and piled it on top of the dresser in the event anything came scurrying across the floor in the night. As I crawled into the tiny bed I almost sunk out of sight. With a series of giant creaks, I was swallowed up in the center by a bed whose springs had given way many many sleeps earlier. I felt like I was laying in a Venus flytrap with a springy mattress mouth. Each time I moved to try and break free from this trap the bed squeaked like an old train taking off. I had done plenty of camping, but even tent life with a blow-up air mattress felt higher end than this. I wasn't sure if the plush life I'd come from in North America was going to transition well here.

Sometime between dealing with the creaks and fighting from being eaten by the mattress flytrap, I finally fell asleep. This was short-lived and was soon awoken by something making noise under the bed. As predicted, something came scurrying inside. It was a cat. It sounded like he'd captured some sort of dinner and was treating me to his late night dining experience. Likely a giant moth or jungle bug was on the menu. As the cat wrestled to get the night's meal down his throat, I could hear each echoing crunch as the corpse disappeared. 10-20 minutes of crunching and wrestling later and we would both fall asleep.

After a restless night with the crunching cat and creaking bed, I awoke to the sunrise making its way through the endless cracks in the exterior of the home. As I looked around in the light of the morning the design of the house was finally brought to life. The one thing this home had over the other was cement floors. The exterior had no advantages though. It was made entirely of scrap wood and old road signs. Literally, it was painted boards from other homes, road signs that were either acquired or "borrowed", and bits of mismatched wood pieces from all types of old buildings strung together to make four walls. It felt like a fort, the type you might build on a zero-dollar budget as a kid.

Like most mornings, I awoke feeling like I was about to pee the bed. I quickly ran into the backyard in my underwear and biker boots, then remembered there was no bathroom. I hadn't heard anyone else awake so I thought I could take an emergency pee in the garden. Halfway into my emergency garden pee, I heard someone come out into the makeshift box with the hose surrounded by plants that made up the shower. It was Grandma!

Here I was, a guest in Grandma's house, and the first time she would meet me was peeing in her garden in my underwear. I finished up and when the shower turned on I thought I'd sneak past. No chance. Grandma said hello to me on my way by and I sheepishly muttered hello in Spanish back to her, then retreated behind my curtain to put my pants on.

I wasn't sure I was transitioning well into this life as an outsider and decided I would depart after breakfast. I met the family in the bubblegum pink house for the morning meal and they asked me my plans for the day. I said I would leave after breakfast. All at once, the whole family looked surprised and a little upset about my early departure. Then the 10-year-old piped up in English and begged me to stay, literally begging, he said there was so much to show me. Just then all the kids got on my lap, looked me in the eyes, and started to ask why I was leaving. With their cute smiles, sad eyes, and frowning faces, they each attempted to say "stay-stay" in English. I got the impression they had used this tactic to get what they wanted before. It was working fantastically well.

Aldolfo had his son translate to me that he wanted me to stay for lunch so he could show me around the property a little more. I buckled under the abundant friendliness and agreed to stay for lunch before getting back on the road. That day Aldolfo showed me around the property and took me back into the forest across the road. Here in the scrubby jungle, he showed me a shallow pond he had dug and explained that he was growing tilapia fish that they were planning to sell at the market.

Once he made enough money from these tilapia he could pay to have another hole dug to grow more fish. There was no credit here; you pay for the job and then it gets done. Next on the tour he took me across the road and showed me his tiny maize farm where he grew the hardy corn-like vegetable to eat and sell. Next, the proud farmer who was supporting his family explained to me they had cleared away the jungle next to this maize field and burnt it to the ground so they could grow more maize in the hopes of generating more income. The conversation was entirely in Spanish, but Aldolfo's slow Guatemalan speech and dramatic explanation for my benefit made it so I could grasp the idea.

After my years of learning in school how destructive slash and burn farming in the jungle was for the environment I was now witnessing it live. I was torn. I knew from what I'd learned that the ground would probably only have a few years of production before the soil's nutrients would dissipate and burning it to the ground would have irreversible effects on the jungle, its plants, and the wildlife that originally called this area home.

Now with a local man touring me around, I was understanding why they resorted to this method. The locals needed to feed their families. If they could slash the jungle and burn what's left to a blackened char, they would yield 2-3 years of harvest from it. This would buy 2-3 years while they worked on the next solution to feed the family. If your choice was no years of feeding your family or 2-3 years of feeding your family, what would you choose? My western education and real-life situation were at a moral crossroads.

After the tour, I then made a decision. This decision would affect how I traveled for the rest of this trip. I decided if living in a shack made from reclaimed road signs, eating maize from the slash and burn field next door, and pooping behind a black tarp in the yard was how the locals lived every day, then I could do it for a few days or as long as I needed too. I was starting to get a deeper understanding of life from the locals' perspective.

Each day following, the family and I would sit down for breakfast. And each day I would see at least one of the children drinking from a red mug with "Nestle" written on the side. I jokingly said one day that it looked like the child was drinking coffee. The mum said to me quite casually that the kids were drinking coffee, instant coffee. What, why is your 5-year old drinking instant coffee?

Without hesitation, the mother explained to me that when the kids are really little there often isn't money to supplement their diet with baby formula. Instead, the kids are fed instant coffee because it fills them up and keeps them feeling full. I could feel my heart drop and my eyes begin to gloss, I tried to hide this shock and sadness from showing through. I'd never heard anything like this in my life. A family searching for any solution to keep their kids feeling full when money and local resources could not provide a solution. I could not imagine having to make a decision like this for my child.

I spent five more days with the family and over the week they took me to their local Evangelical church and prayed for me and my journey. Not your average prayer mind you. Aldolfo, who was one of the leaders of the church, would kneel at the base of a statue of Jesus and pray for nearly an hour during the service. With music blasting out the windows and everyone singing loudly, he just kept praying. Longer than any of the other 20-30 people there. I was surprised to learn they went to church every day. The kid even questioned me about why I didn't talk to Jesus like everyone else when we went to the Church? He explained that Jesus was my friend and I could talk to him about anything. I said Jesus and I were friends, we just didn't talk that much. I could sense his skepticism in my response.

The mum taught me to cook tamales in banana leaves over an open flame with her friends. They toured me around to meet all their neighbors. The kids colored me photos and showed me local life in rural Guatemala. It was just living, but it wasn't living like I was used to. If it hadn't been for Aldolfo and his family I would have probably spent the next 2-years traveling south like other scared tourists inside hostels and hotels taking photos of the locals from a distance and never really letting them penetrate my soul. It was an incredible change to take the side roads into the life of the locals rather than passing them by on the highway of life I had been riding down.

I tried my little part to give back to the family by taking Aldolfo to the local market the day I left and told him to pick out whatever he wanted and I would buy it for his family. Aldolfo wasn't sure where to draw the line so he placed a small bag of rice into a basket. I said to Aldolfo,"No, get whatever you need." He didn't grab anything.

I started to throw things on top of his rice and then waited to see how he reacted. Aldolfo just smiled and said thank you. We left with a mix of sugar, flour, pasta, rice, and some treats for the kids. I certainly gave less monetarily than he did culturally and I could tell he was unsure that there needed to be any exchange at all.

I also attempted to deal with a technical issue they were having. Another traveler they'd met from Germany had set them up with the CouchSurfing account where I'd found them, but the listing was a little confusing as it had been translated from Spanish by a German then to English. Other travelers had arrived expecting a hotel of sorts and this family to pamper their every need and entertain them. One of the reviewers was appalled that the family couldn't speak English and that they were expected to stay in their home. Not entirely the fault of Aldolfo, he had no idea what the post said. He just knew that tourists would message him on occasion and spend the night for the equivalent of a $10 donation.

Not entirely the fault of the travelers, they were just reading what was written and were looking for a cheap local experience. Maybe I was too, I just got more out of it than I was expecting. I updated their ad to explain the sleeping accommodations, the bathroom, and how rich of an experience this was and that you would need to have an open mind to stay here.

5-days and a complete change of mental direction later and I was on my way south again.

(Inside the pink home with the dirt floors)   (Slash & Burn, who it's feeding)

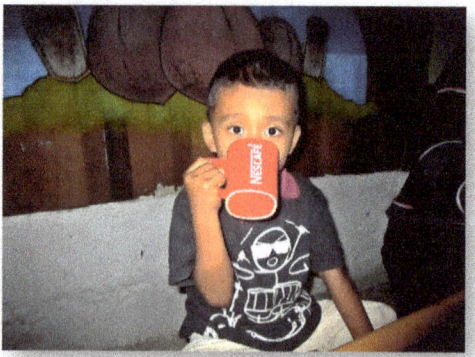

(The Nescafe cup)

Guatemala
Begging To Death

"AISH (Assured Income for the Severely Handicapped) provides a maximum monthly living allowance of $1,685 to assist clients living in the community."

- Humanservices.ca .
A Canadian assistance program for the mentally handicapped.

I rode south through the sweltering tropics along crumbling roads built without shoulders and potholes that could swallow up a motorcycle then spit its suspension out the other side. I would pass some of the most beautiful and some of the most heartbreaking sites that will forever be etched in my mind.

The economy of Guatemala is impoverished in the best of locations. I would ride past people selling bananas from the jungle, juice from local fruits, meals made of maize, and offering various services for tyre repair or some type of mechanics, all for next to nothing. I got the impression that if you couldn't invent some kind of income-producing job, you likely wouldn't eat. But what if you couldn't work, couldn't invent your own job, were not able to be part of the working class, then how would you eat? How would you survive? Does the government look after these people? My polished, positive outlook on the world was about to get a negative scuff on it.

As one crisscrosses the Americas you'll find that before each town and at many random locations for no reason at all, there are large cement humps in the road known as *topes,* a.k.a., a speed bump. The reality of the road is no one respects speed limits or road signs and the only chance a community has of getting drivers to slow down is with these large shock-devouring topes placed at the entrance and exits of each town. If a driver wants to come ripping through and ignore the reduced speed limit, it's their choice. However, it might cost them their front suspension.

This particular day as KLaiR, Stanley, and I rode along on the decaying asphalt past lush jungle and scrappy roadside villages, the traffic would continually slow to a turtle's pace as large trucks and automobiles on the brink of collapse slowed down for one of the dozens of topes along the way. I was roughly eight vehicles behind a tope that was 300-feet or so from the upcoming village. The heat was stifling and with no breeze against my open helmet to cool me down, I reached for my bottle of warm water strapped to the handlebars for a quick refreshment.

As we inched closer to the stop I saw someone sat off to the side of the road and something else sitting right near the tope. It was quite common to meet the local entrepreneurs selling their nuts and bananas for a few cents at these slow points. This particular point was a bit different though, I didn't see people coming up to drivers windows with nuts and fruits.

As I got closer I noticed it was a person sitting near the tope. A man sat awkwardly on a piece of scrap cardboard, perched in the middle of this highway right where the cars, bikes, and large trucks were passing. They would slow down for the tope, then let out bellowing smoky exhaust to get them back up to speed and carry on. The man sat right in the heat of the relentless Guatemalan sun on top of the hot tarmac.

The man looked oddly out of place. I wasn't sure what he was selling and why he was sitting so low where he would be unable to reach the windows of those slowing down. It seemed like some poor sales and marketing on his behalf, why was he just sitting there?

I was behind one of these large, smoky trucks that had been retired from service in the USA, then retired from service in Mexico, and were now living out their 3rd, final life in Guatemala. As the driver slowed to get each set of his 18-wheels over the bumps and avoid hitting the man on the ground I realized what the man was doing down there, he was not selling anything.

The man on the bump was not an entrepreneur, he was not selling fruits or juices, he was not offering nuts or any type of service. He was handicapped and from the vacant look across his face, he appeared to have a severe mental disability. As the daydreaming in my head went from thinking about fresh roadside coconut juice for $0.25 that would quench my dry throat, it quickly flipped to seeing this man in his most vulnerable state sitting awkwardly on the road. I was entirely caught off guard from my daydreaming.

He had a leg tucked to one side and the other sort of sat out in front of him to keep his balance. He was wearing old blue sweatpants dirtied from crawling or possibly being dragged across the highway. His eyes were rolling back and forth from side to side trying to focus on those driving past. His mouth hung open with a bit of saliva continually running down his chin and onto his shirt. He did not look like someone who should be left sitting in the middle of a highway on a hump in the heat. He did not look like someone who should be left anywhere alone.

The weather was easily over 30oC with blistering humidity. Even as I rode in my t-shirt and shorts sweat was streaming out from under every bit of clothing. Now here was this mentally disabled man, dragged out into the middle of the highway on a speed bump with an old bucket, the size of a paint can, sitting in front of him. I then realized he was trying to beg for change from drivers as they passed him by.

To the right, I noticed that next to the road was a very old woman in the shade in a chair. She had a tiny fan made from the thick jungle grass and looked like she was exhausting the last of her energy to cool herself. I assume she was with him, there was no one else around. Maybe a mother or grandmother who could not work herself to support either of them. Maybe a family member assigned to him to make sure he was safe in the blazing heat while he was trying to beg for survival through the cloudy outlook of a damaged or underdeveloped brain.

I had come across so many people selling things by the roadside I had gotten into the routine of ignoring them unless I needed something. It was like riding past the continual advertisements on North American billboards or media ads. After seeing enough signs you don't even notice what they are advertising anymore.

I can honestly say this display of helplessness by the man whose eyes rolled around, propped up with awkward legs in the blistering heat of the highway had caught me so off guard that I was unsure what to do. I was blank. I stared like you inquisitively stare at art in a museum trying to understand why the artist created it. Next came my turn to pass over the speed bump with this man's eyes rolling towards me and saliva rolling off of his chin while the old woman sat staring at me and my large, otherworldly motorcycle from across the road.

To the man in the tattered sweatpants trying to focus his eyes and mind simultaneously, I'm sure I was just another motorized sound passing by his existence here on the road. To her, I was probably a wealthy motorcycle rider from Guatemala city on a holiday. An ATM on wheels.

I glanced at him, I glanced at her, I rolled over the bump. I felt like the large landslide of reality had let go and came crashing down from where it was perched up in the mountains of perfection where I usually lived. The scene poured over me and smothered my picture-perfect view of the world. I was stunned by the stark contrast between the life I had come from to the one this guy was living here on the highway.

I continued on with the motions that were happening around me. I didn't shift, I didn't speed up, I didn't slow down. I did nothing. I just froze mentally while my hands continued to control the bike at a slow steady pace in what felt like time standing still.

Nothing, I did absolutely nothing.

For miles and miles to come all I could do was think about this man, his life of muted struggles, and the easy life in Canada that I had left behind. If this situation had played out in its exact setting in Canada this man's life would be national news. A disabled man on the side of the highway in tattered blue sweatpants sitting on an old piece of cardboard begging for change. You would have seen it on the front of every paper in the country.

His caretaker would probably go to prison if they were of sound mind. He would be hailed a hero for having to slide out to that perch each day hoping to survive. His elderly grandmother would be cradled by the government until a local organization stepped in to care for her and their lives would be made as comfortable as possible while they were living them.

Not here, not in Guatemala. Here everyone works to survive. Even if your underdeveloped or damaged brain has no idea what you are doing or why. There was no local help and no free rides.

That moment sat heavily on me, I felt guilty that I did nothing. I felt guilty that this was the man's life. I felt guilty that my life was so easy. I felt concerned that this reality would appear more often and I would do nothing. I thought about every time I waited in a line for a drink and a sandwich while listening to myself and those around me complain about how long it took to get an $11 sandwich and $7 coffee. Fuck your $7 coffee! I felt guilty for coming from the land of easy living and taking it all for granted.

That moment sat with me very heavily, and it still does.

Guatemala
A 10 Year Road Trip

"Ferdinand Magellan (1480–1521) was a Portuguese explorer who is credited with masterminding the first expedition to circumnavigate the world."

- rmg.co.uk

I was camping on an expansive property on a river in rural Guatemala. To get here I had followed a crumbling roadway where most of my attention was spent focusing on the endless potholes and chunks of asphalt that were scattered across the road of what once may have been considered pavement. The directions to my destination noted that I should watch for a small sign on the edge of the roadway depicting a painted river with the words "Baños" written on it, the Spanish word often used to mark a swimming area.

After several hours of riding, I finally caught a glimpse of the sign I'd been hunting for while riding past it. I stopped and turned around before making my way down a one-way gravel road. While kicking up plumes of dry Central American dust, I cautiously rode past a series of farmers who stare blankly at what is the calamity of my overloaded and poorly packed motorbike. I'm not convinced I'm going in the right direction and the farmers aren't making me feel like a lot of tourists come down this road. Eventually, I arrived at the Baños in the midday heat to a small house in a large green field.

I'm greeted by a smiley male staff member who speaks slow Guatemalan Spanish and shows me where to camp. The man recommended that I set up my tent near the ebbing river to enjoy the surroundings, but still be as close to the house as possible. A few hours after settling in a different man arrives, his name is Jose.

Jose is incredibly friendly, speaks remarkably good English, and invites me on what becomes a two-hour interactive walking tour. Jose beams with pride as he explains the assortment of herbs, fruits, vegetables, and some exotic mushrooms that grow on his property. Jose kept drilling into me how easily I could live off the land if I knew what foods I was looking for. He then noted that because I continually answered "*no*" when he asked if I knew what each flower, fruit, and herb was on the tour, that I would probably die here without a supermarket. So much for the grand adventurer I thought I was.

Jose tells me how he'd previously lived in California for over a decade. This explains his nearly flawless English spoken through his thick Guatemalan accent. The entire tour he talks and talks with a constant smile on his face, he's so proud of this place. Saving the best for last, Jose's tour follows the stunning river back to my tent.

The water along Jose's property is incredibly vibrant; it feels almost unnatural and the water is clear to the point I can see rocks and swaying plants along the bottom. It looks like a highly photoshopped Instagram post to promote camping products for sale. Jose stops me to point out dozens of small turtles living in the water and the tiny fish they eat as they come swimming by. He explained that he loves it when people come camping here or spend the weekend fishing and jumping into the water from the wooden platforms built into the trees. The whole place is a living paradise plucked right from the Land Before Time movie.

Back at the picnic table next to my tent, things suddenly change from talking about life to talking about death. Jose now wants to discuss my safety. As we sit down, his voice lowers and takes on a sterner, more direct tone. Jose then reaches down and promptly pulls a large handgun from the front of his pants, the warm mood turns to ice in an instant. Jose puts the gun on the table in front of me. It lands on the wooden top with a disturbing thud, a thud that echoes in the back of my throat. The weapon had been concealed by his shirt during our friendly walking tour, I'd never once noticed it

Jose then leans in closer, uncomfortably closer. I could smell the spices from his lunch as his breath wafts across my face. Jose wanted to capture my full attention, and he had it.

Jose then locked in on my eyes and began to explain that we were sitting on what was originally his parents' property, and now in his 50's, he had returned to Guatemala to help assist them in their final years. They had since both passed away and he had inherited the property. Now he would look after it for the rest of his life until it became the property of his children. He then noted that in all the years he'd ever lived here, despite all of Guatemala's conflicts and civil wars, he had never fallen victim to any conflicts on the property. No one had ever come to cause problems here, and no one had ever threatened the life of him or his family. Even the money that would stack up during weekend-long sporting events and the income from his small store had never been robbed.

Well, I thought, if everything is so great around here then why are you breathing spicy bbq chicken in my face, with only a handgun dividing the space between us? You just want to explain how wonderfully tranquil things are over a 9mm?

To reassure me that my safety was his number one priority while in his home, Jose then added that he was good friends with a division of the military that patrolled this part of the country, and if for any reason he were to have any problems with anyone, he could simply call the military and these problems would instantly disappear.

All of this safety, money, military, guns, and disappearing problems talk wasn't leaving me with the calm secure feeling I think Jose was hoping to instill in me. Either way, I wasn't about to get up and leave.

Jose then picks up the gun and presses it into my hands. He explains how he'd smuggled this 9mm handgun out of California and into Guatemala when he left. I'm 34, and this was the first time I'd ever held a handgun. It felt like I was holding a 2-pound hard-on about to go off. The whole thing gave me a false sense of power like I now held some sort of control over things around me, a feeling I was sure was shared by every handgun-toting delusionist who thrives off this self-invented power.

* * *

Bang-Bang!

Now, here I am, at 3-o'clock in the morning, lying on the ground with my eyes glowing, scanning the tent, holding onto my heart, as the sound from the day's earlier gun lesson had come blasting to life in the middle of the night just outside my tent.

Had Jose's safety meeting with me been a ruse? Were we under attack? Was he going to save my life? Was the day's earlier story a foreshadowing for him to make me disappear on his property in the darkness? My mind was racing uncontrollably down a dark tunnel of death in the Central American night.

As I lay here quietly, suddenly a hushed-flurry of Spanish is exchanged between two people just outside my tent. In the empty darkness, I can feel my blood rushing through my body and my senses amplifying. I try to focus on where the voices are coming from and start to get my bearings on the location of the men outside my tent.

I then hear the chickens and ducks near Jose's house squawking with hysteria. Just then another gunshot rings out from the area where the voices were coming. Then I hear a splash in the turtle-river across from my camp. Then, a quick exchange of Spanish whispers, then more commotion from the animals. Suddenly a light passes through my tent as it makes its way steadily across the property like a lighthouse beacon patrolling the sea. Then, like the final performance at a stage theater, the lights drop, bringing with them the black curtain of night and everything falls silent.

For the next thirty minutes, I lay motionless. I'm breathing in shallow bursts, still trying to calm myself. From what was total calamity, I now hear nothing. I close my eyes and wish that I was invisible. I reach down and slide my wallet into my motorcycle pants then reach up and pull my cell phone down into my sleeping bag as the thought of being robbed seeps into my mind. As a solo traveler in a foreign land who awoke to the scream of gunshots outside his twenty-dollar tent in the middle of the night, the imaginative possibilities of what just happened were running rampant through my mind.

An hour passes without me moving, and now that I've calmed down and my nerves have settled I need to pee. I don't know what to do. Trying to make the feeling of needing to pee go away is impossible, it only makes me want to pee more and the rushing river nearby is not helping.

I devise a plan to ever so slowly make my way to the tent door, gently open part of the zipper, slide my penis outside the tent, and pee in the entranceway. I'm hoping to do this while maintaining my invisible status and without making a sound.

I now imagine I am a giant snail trying to slide along without making a sound as I slowly inch my way towards the tent opening. I reach the edge of the tent and painfully slow, tooth by tooth, in what feels like zipper opening eternity, I open the zip creating a 3-inch opening in the tent. Delicately removing my sleeping bag from around me, I continue my stealth snail moves and invisible capabilities while I work my pelvis towards the opening. I then slide my penis out from my boxer shorts and out through the zipper opening of the tent. With a nervous sense of relief, I begin to pee. I'm hoping that I'm slightly uphill so the pee will run away and not into my tent. Having peed multiple times a day for 34-years, trying to remain quiet, still, and invisible while I was peeing was the most challenging pee to date.

After the invisible-mute-pee, I lie awake in the darkness for another hour while the warm, stank odor of stale pee hangs onto the humid tropical air inside my tent. The entire time I'm intently listening for even the faintest sound of whatever fell in the river to come back to life and start walking towards my tent. Would Jose hear it first and come to my rescue? Had he been killed? Was I alone or surrounded? The big tough adventurer in me was fading to a timid turtle hiding in the shell of his tent.

Eventually, I fall asleep and awake a short time later to the sun heating up my tent shell and the pee next to it, it's shortly after 7 am. I opened the zipper and made my way over the invisible-mute-pee spot and into the warm Guatemalan sun. I then try and casually make my breakfast as though the night before had been like any other. I was also hoping to spot Jose alive and have him come over to provide an explanation of the previous nights' events.

Twenty minutes or so pass and Jose appears across the yard. He smiles at me, waves, and makes his way over to my camp. I try to keep up my casual disposition, but I'm dying to know why my life had been in danger the night before.

Jose goes first.

Hey Kix, did you hear the sounds last night?

What…, yes of course I did. Jose, what the hell went on last night?

Kix, do you know this thing that is kind of like a rat but bigger than a rat? Sometimes in the night, they come to eat the chickens. Last night the caretaker heard one of these rat things and came outside to try and sneak up on it from behind your tent. I heard him and came out to help.

The rat thing went up into a tree near the river and we both shot at it with our guns. Then with the flashlight, we found it up in a tree and shot at it again. I hit it and it fell right in the river!

I exhaled a monumental breath of relief and rolled my eyes in disbelief of what all had happened outside my tent last night, compared to what all had happened inside my mind.

Just then Jose looked up as several large military trucks painted in desert camo with machine guns mounted to them came rolling into his yard. He jumped up, smiled, and said; *Hey there are my friends!*

I sank into the bench relieved and exhausted. As more and larger guns made their way into the yard, I wondered where this road trip was headed next.

* * *

After the night of gunshots and muted pees at Jose's, I was back on the road south. As each day passed it seemed like the roads got worse. I found my pace continually slowing down to avoid the bike-swallowing potholes as well as slowing to match the lifestyle of the locals. One day after several hours of riding I realized I hadn't even looked up to see what was around me since setting off in the morning. The fear of landing in one of the potholes and getting ejected out the other side kept my eyes focused on the road, it felt like if I didn't stop I would never see the country.

The culture of Guatemalans is extremely laid back by North American standards. The locals grow up in a world where the bus is likely late or doesn't come at all. Where you need to wait for the fruits to grow before you can harvest them, and where economics mean you are more likely to wait for the cheapest option to get things done, rather than the fastest. The language was dialed back to a slow, audible pace where even if you were a Spanish-speaking beginner, the locals enunciated words so soft and slow that I could typically understand what people were saying. Coming from Mexico where the people spoke like machine guns, in Guatemala, the words came out more like a musket, one by one.

By now I was using a relatively new app called iOverlander pretty constantly to get information from other Overlanding travelers about highlights along the way. One discovery led me to a set of hot waterfalls near a small town that rests on the edge of a water inlet fed by Amatique Bay, part of the Caribbean Sea. Here, the town Rio Dulce, is split into two sides of the inlet and connected on either side by a bridge that acts as the only road to shuttle people and goods from Northeastern Guatemala & Belize to Southeastern Guatemala and Honduras/El Salvador.

The strategic location also serviced water travelers from country to country and seemed to be a prime smuggling point for getting people into or out of Belize undetected as well as a stopping point for foreigners sailing the Caribbean and Gulf of Mexico. The waters' edge had a couple of small, western-style pubs where you might find questionable expats who fit the look of someone you might expect to see hiding out from one thing or another. All enjoying hamburgers, Coors Light, and watching English Football. It seemed as out of place in this dusty port town as Belize did in Central America.

I pulled into a hostel on the edge of the river that sat perched atop the water just enough that I thought the whole place might be set afloat in the rainy season. The hostels' premise was that the room charge supported a local orphanage while employing the locals. The rate was $3/night for a dorm bed and included a place to park the motorcycle. How far would $3 go that it could cover wages, hotel overheads, and still support a local orphanage? A bottle of water was $3 at home, let alone a room and parking. I was happy with the setup and hopefully, they were too.

Here in the most bizarre of situations, I found myself watching the Super Bowl and drinking beer with a German girl backpacking, a guy from

Denmark driving an SUV, and a German guy riding a motorcycle. Not one of us knew anything about who was in the Super Bowl, but the hostel had the game on in the bar for tourists and it brought us all together.

I'd spotted the German guy's motorcycle near mine in the small parking area. It was a V-Twin Honda that looked like it had been through a tornado, though the speedometer only read something like 31,000kms, a few thousand less than KLaiR.

The more we talked the more I became hooked on the travel stories of this briefly connected table of travelers. It turned out the Honda had wrapped around the Speedometer once already and even broken for a brief period. If it read correctly, there would be a 1 at the beginning and another 8,000kms on it. Nearly 140,000kms! The German guy, Moritz, had been riding that motorcycle around the world for close to 5-years! My trip looked like a weekend outing compared to his.

I'd met another German, a kid in his twenties while staying next to an elephant watering hole in Botswana a few years earlier who was riding from Germany to South Africa. This had etched the idea of riding across Africa firmly into my mind. I just needed to get across the Americas first.

As for the Danish guy. Well, he took the road trip prize. He'd left Europe with the idea of Overlanding as far as he could make it. He ended up circumnavigating the planet in an old Land Rover and noted that he even ended up near my home in Canada in the middle of winter and his Land Rover didn't even have heat. He'd scrape the windshield with a credit card while he drove south searching for warmer weather. After he'd driven the planet once he still hadn't decided on what to do with his life, so he packed up and hit the road again. At this point, he'd been driving across the earth for 10-years! It felt like I was meeting heroes I never knew existed.

People drool over celebrities and lose their minds when they meet these mere mortals in person. I'd never really understood it. Now here I was with a guy who'd been crisscrossing the planet on a motorcycle for 5-years and another guy who'd driven around the planet twice over 10-years. I was officially losing my mind with envious excitement. I found it hard to contain myself. How were they doing this, did they have no family, did they have limitless supplies of cash?

The girl knew several languages and was able to pick up odd jobs in countries along the way. The Danish guy had worked a few days a week as an online accountant and turning his Euros into local currency was funding his travels. The German guy worked part-time in tech for a German company and used the same currency conversions to fund his travels. I wanted this endless nomad lifestyle so bad, I had so much to learn.

That night the heavens would let loose rain in biblical amounts that would rattle off the tin roof like it was raining rocks. I was sure the river was going to fill and wash us out to sea. Though my blood alcohol content left me feeling completely unconcerned as I passed out to the sound of a couple of travelers fucking in a bunk bed across from mine. Ahh, luxury hostel living.

The following day we found the spot where the cool murky waters of a river met the clear hot waters that boiled up from the earth's surface and flowed down over a cliff's edge to meet the river below in what was a marriage of unnaturally warm river water.

A local man explained where to jump from and land in the dark water in order to enter the river without being injured.

Being the tough guy that I am, I waited until this small European girl scaled the slippery waterfall of rocks and vines to find the place where the tree roots had been unearthed by others that reaffirmed the correct spot to jump into the waters below.

I walked a little upstream at the top of the falls to find a small, natural pool filled with hot water from the earth. This would mark my second hot bath of the trip. A hot bath, a death-defying jump, and a cool swim. What a way to enjoy the miracles of the planet all in one spot.

After sucking as much information as possible from the 5 & 10-year long travelers, we all parted ways. Next stop, El Salvador, the country that would change my life forever.

El Salvador
Converting Of A Coffee Atheist

Serendipity: The fact of something interesting or pleasant happening by chance.

- Oxford Dictionary.

Knowing my relationship with coffee was zero at best, my friend messaged me to ask; *"So are you now a converted coffee drinker?"*

My reply; *"Yes, so long as I know the farmer on a first name basis, have met the bean pickers, was in the truck when the beans were transported to the mill, personally roasted the beans, and watched the barista make the coffee."*

In my present situation, it was pretty easy to check off this list of requirements.

***

El Salvador is a tiny country only rivaling Belize for the smallest landmass in Central America. At this point, all I knew were the country's stats on robbery and murder from my guidebook. On average there were 90 reported robberies per 100,000 people per year and about 55 murders per 100,000 people per year. In comparison, the city I was from had nearly the same number of yearly robberies, and a rate of 0-3 murders per year. Somehow I was feeling a touch uneasy about El Salvador, yet had never felt unsafe in my city.

The roads I was on during the final section of Guatemala were just as relentlessly shitty as the ones I'd entered the country on. I was now rushing to get to the border with enough time to avoid crossing in the dark. Trying to avoid the potholes, it didn't look like I was going to make it.

Just to get up over 50km/h on these shit roads was a mission all its own. The roads were paved in the sense that someone had once paved them, but since that fateful day back who knows when, they had crumbled. If I was in my lane, and the car-sized pothole was in the other lane, whatever was in that lane was definitely coming into my lane to avoid driving into the hole.

Big transport trucks and chicken busses (a school bus that had retired from USA to Mexico, then been retired from Mexico to Guatemala that carried passengers and often livestock like chickens) would take the smoothest parts of the road and any other motorized vehicles were left to fight over the slices of pavement and stone that were left. By size, motorcycles were on the bottom of the right of way list.

At one point after dodging a bus followed by a truck that had come into my lane, where I was run right off the road. I stopped in the ditch and I yelled out to Guatemala from under my helmet that "I'm not very fucking impressed with the driving and shitty god damn pavement"! Then promptly got back on the highway only to get the hell out of the way of the next Chicken bus coming at me. At least the busses were easy to spot. Picture your standard yellow cheese wagon with a glimmering 21-color paint job, bedazzled in chrome, then stuffed full of people and farm animals, screaming down the road with all gas and no brakes. Look out!

I knew coming up to the border crossing that getting into and out of Central American countries can be an hours-long crapshoot with a tree-murdering amount of paperwork that requires anywhere from up to five copies each, of things like your drivers' license, passport, vehicle documents, paperwork proving you left the previous country, insurance for yourself and the vehicle, and vital documents you never knew existed.

The kicker is when you've finally run around in the circle of stamps from one window to another with the various requested forms to get them all stamped, you then see the nice border official writing by hand in a little ledger your name and license plate number! I'm sure the papers end up in a lake three months later, but it's the system, so you roll with it.

This need I always have to cross borders in the daylight was later affirmed in the trip when I would meet an arrogant American on a shiny BMW 1250GS Adventure bike who referred to himself as "That American Asshole." He chose to cross into Guatemala in the middle of the night, probably one of the dumbest things I'd heard, but listening to the guy I wasn't surprised. While he was inside the officials' office trying to get his paperwork done, border agents moved his bike behind a compound fence and made him pay them $100USD to get it back. If you walk into a lion's den with steaks in your pocket, something's going to take a bite out of your pants. I felt no sympathy for "That American Asshole."

On this day at the Valle Nuevo crossing into El Salvador I got stamped out of Guatemala, drove across a little bridge into El Salvador, handed over the requested document copies, got some more stamps, and in close to an hour, the border formalities were cleared. I was officially in country number five. To my delight, I still had a few hours of daylight to spare before getting to my assumed camping spot up the road in an hour or two. This speedy crossing felt like a small miracle compared to other multi-hour crossings I'd experienced.

I'd stopped in the city of Ahuachapán in El Salvador to get a cold sugary drink to help elevate what felt like a hard-boiled egg that had been cooking in the 30oC+ temperatures inside my black helmet. I found a shop and inhaled 1 yogurt drink, 1 sugary pop, 1 thing that looked like a Gatorade, a pack of something that looked like ham, some kind of cheese, and I was feeling less like a piece of dehydrated beef jerky and more like a sweaty hot dog who couldn't always handle the heat.

The plan from here was to head towards the hills of Apaneca and find a camp near a local hot spring. The road that runs through this area is known as "Ruta de las Flores", or The Route Of Flowers. Aptly named as the road is lined with an abundance of flowers in the blooming season and brings the road to an incredibly fragrant life. Or so the story was sold to me. However, since the locals caught onto this blossoming treasure, they started to pick the flowers and take them home or to the market to sell.

At this time of year, it was more like *The Route Of Fleeting Flowers*. Nonetheless, it's a pretty drive through the volcanic mountains, and watching the surrounding scenery, I became distracted and completely missed the area I was looking for with the hot spring and camping. I noticed this as I suddenly ran smack dab into a small village at the heart of these volcanic mountains. The town of my accidental discovery was Juayua, and it would forever change my life.

Lost, confused, and facing a setting sun, I found on my phone what seemed like a suitable cheap night's accommodation. I then entered the location into my fancy GPS and proceeded to follow the little pink line that digitally mapped my route. You would think in a village with only a few streets this would be a seemingly easy task.

My first stop landed me in a back alley, so I exited and tried again. My next attempt landed me a block over in another alley, this one with chickens sounding the alarm that an intruder was in their territory. My third attempt took me around the block and back to the original alley. It was taking me longer to ride around and get lost in alleys than it would have to walk across the entire village.

It was now bordering on darkness, and I kept driving by the same groups of people on my large motorcycle with expedition equipment clinging onto large boxes and was getting a little concerned that my look and obvious confusion would be noticed and I'd be an easy target for the 90/100,000 people robbery stats. Come on GPS don't fail me now!

I tried to act cool about the confusion and double-checked that my coordinates were right. Suddenly a man in a Tuk Tuk (small three-wheeled taxi) approached me and all the reading I'd previously done about murder, coupled with my confusion, exposed electronics, and the impending darkness hit me at once. I tried to pretend like the Tuk Tuk guy wasn't staring at me.

Tuk Tuk guy then yelled something at me. I tried to pretend that I didn't hear him.

He then pointed at my phone and said something in Spanish. I hid my phone.

Tuk Tuk guy looked at me confused, I looked back at him concerned.

Then he said "hotel?". I said yes.

I realized he was trying to help me find the hotel and promptly felt like a scared moron tourist who believes everything he reads.

Tuk Tuk guy pointed at my bike and made the motion of driving back and forth a few times and laughed. He'd seen me drive past him enough to know I was lost. I pulled my phone back out and showed him the hotel name I'd been looking for. He smiled and said "Hotel Anahuac", and motioned for me to follow him. Less than a minute following Tuk Tuk guy and he rolled up to the yellow exterior and opened wooden doors of the small hotel, honked, waved, and drove off. No handshake, no payment or tip requested. Seems he wasn't one of the murderous El Salvadorians I'd read about.

I was greeted at the entrance by a short stocky guy in his late 20's who only spoke Spanish, but had clearly dealt with enough of us gringo types to know what we needed. For $5 I had a dorm room and place to put my things for the night. Sadly he was unable to find a place for my motorcycle to park aside from the street, however, he assured me this little town was safe at night and he'd be sleeping in the laundry room right in front of where KLaiR would be parked. Not entirely convinced, I cleared most everything I could off KLaiR, locked the rest up in the laundry-guys room, then showered, and went to find some food before retiring for the night.

The next day I took to getting to know my surroundings in the beautiful setting. The hotel had roughly six rooms. Two of them were six-person dorms and the others were private double rooms. Everything sat around a small courtyard with fragrant flowers, small shrub-like trees, and a large bundle of freshly harvested green bananas about half the size of me, hanging by a rope. The bananas were meant for the guests' breakfasts, but the birds enjoyed them for breakfast too.

In the small foyer where I checked in was a make-shift coffee shop with a couple of small tables, and a reception desk about 8-feet long that had a large commercial coffee grinder on one end, with a series of scales and other tools that might be used for dealing drugs or in this case coffee.

Behind the counter on the back shelf were different glass jars wrapped in leather that looked like something a mad scientist might use to concoct an elixir. Then there were some smaller plastic containers with plungers and units of measurement on the side, and a series of cocktail glasses. Oddly, no coffee cups to be seen. On the shelf above were various clear containers with lids and filled partway with coffee beans.

Each container had numbers like 1200m, 1400m, 1600m, and some dried fruits that looked like half red grape peels that had been left to dry. The bean labeling and fruit system seemed bizarre and I thought maybe they were selling items like a bulk foods shop, just on a much smaller scale and maybe this was a price or pricing code.

Despite having previously owned several small businesses that sold coffee, having also sold coffee to hotels & restaurants, and having been the first person in my city to offer the Doi Chaang line of coffee that would later become a global brand retailed by 7-11 and Costco, I enjoyed nothing about coffee. I couldn't wrap my taste buds around the muddy taste, its ability to leave the user with lingering stagnant breath, and my limited knowledge only went as far as knowing the cost per cup for various commercial brands. I'm sure I drank no more than 3 cups of coffee in my entire life aside from milky iced coffee in places like Vietnam. To say I was about to be delightfully blindsided by coffee would be to say a Tsunami might get your pants wet.

Behind the coffee/reception counter that morning was a new face. This new guy had a thick bushy ponytail pulled back behind his head and a scruffy beard that grew thick but patchy like Che Guevara's did. He was shorter than me, thick like an out of season football player, and wore a long-sleeved plaid shirt, industrial blue jeans like a lumberjack, and sturdy boots that had seen some serious days in the field. He could pass for late 20's or late 30's, I wasn't sure. I didn't have time to think much about it as he greeted me in English with a thick Spanish accent that suggested he still wasn't fully comfortable with the English language.

With a warm smile on his face, he asked if I'd like a cup of coffee? I declined, citing my limited coffee experience as my excuse for not looking like a fool in this environment. Just then a little timer went off and the attention from my awkward decline quickly shifted to other matters.

The lumberjack then picked up one of the weird jars wrapped in leather from off a scale and swished it around like a large cocktail. He then brought the jar up to his face and inhaled a lung full of the thick coffee air, smiled excitedly, and poured himself some of the concoction into a clear cocktail glass that revealed the rich toffee-like colors of the brew. I had no idea what the hell was going on, but the smell of fresh coffee was permeating the air, and as much as I didn't enjoy the taste of coffee, I certainly enjoyed the smell and was happy to let him keep doing what he was doing.

After this little coffee ritual, the man introduced himself as Javier. Javier was a man of varied knowledge and if anything was an artist by trade. Javier told me that before working here, he was once living homeless in Guatemala City with a group of artists who would spray paint art in the streets of the city. At one time his art caught the eye of a local drug lord who had him decorate four walls in the room of his house differently to represent each of his four mistresses. The drug lord loved Javier's work and "looked after him well" making sure he enjoyed himself while he was in Guatemala City. A series of stories involving expensive cars, beautiful women, and the "untouchable life" would seep out during later conversations.

The natural progression from being a homeless artist was then to university in El Salvador studying to be a medical doctor for several years. Then he switched to chemistry where he had learned the process of making quality meth before abruptly abandoning it all to pursue a love of coffee. You might say Javier was a quick study.

From here he and a friend had opened up the well-positioned yet discrete coffee shop, Cadek Café in Santa Ana where he explained they were trying to educate the people of El Salvador about what excellent coffee they have here and get them to drink the coffee they deserve opposed to the instant Nescafe coffee they could usually afford. This in itself was a tall order.

As we chatted during this initial meeting, Javier asked what I was up to and if that was my motorcycle out front? After a quick chat, he explained he was going to roast some coffee up in the mountains today and would I like to come? I had never seen coffee roasted before, had only just met this man, and had no idea where we were going. The sales pitch of a new experience instantly hooked me and so I agreed. Javier said "*great*" and explained that we were leaving in 5-minutes. Shit! I ran and grabbed my day bag, helmet, some snacks, a drink and met him out front.

When I arrived a lady I'd recognized as sleeping across from me in the tiny dorm room the night before was there too. She had this big crazy hair that would make Sideshow Bob's curly mop look like a bad perm. With her dark features, round smiley face, and welcoming personality she addressed me in English and then Spanish.

I was still a bit reserved about going places with strangers and opted to follow them to the location on my bike. They jumped in the box of a shared pickup truck with more people than space where the bed of the truck was compressing down over the tyres. I followed them up a narrow winding road that could only be climbed as the driver ground the gears down into first without letting off the gas.

Five or six lurching volcanic mountain stops later the duo hopped out of what was now a half-empty truck box at the base of a steep entrance 85-feet or so up to a little farm. To welcome our arrival, several barking dogs and squawking chickens lit up with excitement. At the top of our hill climb was a simple home with coffee beans drying on a rack out front, and to the right of the home was a tiny wood cabin perched 8-feet off the ground. It looked like a hobbit home just big enough for one person to live in. Javier pulled from his blue jeans a set of keys, entered them in the lock, pulled open a wooden door, and unveiled what was inside. I was amazed to see it wasn't a cabin at all. Instead of household furniture, there was a long wooden bar table, a large cappuccino machine, big blue plastic bins, and a glistening coffee roaster.

Javier then unlocked the wooden window covers and exposed the glass panes behind them. My mouth dropped as I let in a slow gasp of excitement. Wow! The window looked directly over rows of coffee beans, cherries, and fruit trees growing in perfectly set rows on the volcanic soils below. You could see not only the endless rows of cherries, but also the peaks of the volcanic mountains across the valley that sat in an ocean of blue sky, gently hugged by light fluffy white clouds all hanging within reach of the lush vegetation below. I tapped on the glass to make sure the setting was real and not painted on the panes.

With a sense of disbelief in my voice, I asked if this is where they roasted the coffee? The Spanish duo and their equally crazy hair both laughed and asked if I liked the space. If this was El Salvador, and this is where coffee beans roast to life, I was delighted to be here. I was about to get a very hands-on, crash-course in the country and its beans.

As the day went on I learned Javier was the manager of the hotel I was staying at and he looked after all things coffee for the owner of the farm and hotel when he was away. His duties included overseeing the specialty coffee farm, taking tourists on coffee tours where they would bring groups to teach them about roasting beans and the business of coffee.

The apprentice was from Costa Rica and had been here for several months as a volunteer in exchange for learning everything about the coffee business and an intimate course in roasting. She was in her final days before setting off for the next stage of her coffee career path and I was in the middle of a sort of goodbye between the two of them and this experience.

My day here was spent unpacking green beans from large, clear plastic bags while they explained varieties, altitude growth, storage, and walked me through everything from the roasting to the brewing phase. The numbers that had been listed back on the bean display in the hotel coffee shop followed by the letter "m", matched up with the bags in the big bins. Ahh-ha! The "m's" were meters, and the beans were labeled to signify the altitude in meters of growth for each of these specialty beans.

Lesson One; The higher altitude a bean was grown in, the harder it had to work to become a bean. These higher altitude beans were denser and considered to be a higher quality bean. Right now we were hanging out somewhere around 1200m. I was getting the impression the learning curve was going to be as steep as the volcanic mountains to get here.

I ended up leaving just before the crazy-haired duo. They opted to walk back the 30-minutes to town as it was downhill and they could enjoy the views and spend some final moments together. I opted to ride KLaiR because we too enjoyed the views and spending time together.

That night back at the hotel Javier asked what my plans were in the coming weeks? I explained I was pretty free to do as I pleased and was only limited by the length of my visa and the amount of time I was allowed to stay in each country. He said if I wanted to stay in this little village for at least a few weeks and volunteer to help with coffee tours and around the hotel he'd teach me everything he knew about coffee.

I didn't know what to think. Yesterday I was leaving Guatemala en route to some hot springs in the hills to camp for one night before pressing on. Then I got lost, ended up here, and was now being propositioned with an apprenticeship in a field I cared nothing about.

Did I want to learn everything he knew about coffee? Could he handle the fact that I didn't know any Spanish? What would I do in this village? Where would I park KLaiR? For all this free spirit I prided myself on I sure didn't know how to handle it when new experiences landed in my lap.

I agreed to stay for two weeks. This way I had a two-week escape plan if it sucked. The next day I started my new position as Javiers' latest and least educated apprentice as a coffee tour host, barista, hotel receptionist, and laundry-folder.

El Salvador
The Bourbon Jungle

"97% of the world's coffee beans are non-organic and treated with pesticides, herbicides, fungicides, and other chemicals."

- naturalforce.com

On day three I was sitting around the hotel and met a guy named Sala, a local El Salvadorian who was in town for the yearly coffee expo being held just up the road. He had asked where I was from and when I said Canada, he proceeded to explain the various cell phone packages from national cell phone provider Telus.

I looked at him extremely confused while he recited my previous cell phone data plan, minutes package, and proposed what plans were the best option for me. As the look of confusion washed over my face he explained that Telus hired out some of their customer service calls to El Salvadorian workers and he had worked for them for a couple of years. His introduction was one of the best ones yet!

Once a year, after the bean harvest, farmers in the area bring the best of their beans to a very special auction. At the auction buyers from across the planet come to see what the season has bestowed on the area. If it's good, the buyers purchase part or all of the harvest directly from the farmers.

The cupping process (how to taste and judge the features of a coffee) is completely blind and you bid for your bean strictly on flavor. This way you are guaranteed to only buy based on preference and quality, not stories and marketing.

Sala was here to present several samples as well as one hundred pounds of premium green beans from his organic, boutique farm not far from here. He was hoping to impress with his product and find a long-term buyer. He explained that not every bean up for auction is purchased and he would be lucky to sell his for market rate, $2.50USD/ pound, if he sells any at all. I'd never seen coffee that was $2.50/ pound back in Canada, I felt the math wasn't adding up here.

Later, over beers in our garden patio, along with some Dutch girls Sala met at the event, he explained that his beans had found a home with a Swiss buyer who happily paid $3.50/ pound, or one dollar more per pound than the regular rate. Sala had reason to celebrate and all of us were happy to join in.

The following day I met up with Sala again when he was meant to be heading back to the farm to help his father with the relentless demands of the coffee crop. Noting a small window of opportunity to see my first coffee farm from the farmers' perspective rather than a rehearsed tour guide's perspective, I ask if I can come along? I'm not sure if he's as excited as I am, though thirty minutes later KLaiR and I are following his jeep back to the farm.

The route is a twisting mountainside road overlooking a lush valley that's home to various coffee entrepreneurs of various scales. The final push leads us up a short steep dirt road as we arrive at *The Bourbon Jungle*. Emerging from the bushes comes Salas' father, a smiling man that's lean like Sala whose skin is weathered from years outside in the fields. He's dawning the standard white, flat-brimmed style hat I've seen atop the heads of many of the local farmers and looks excited to see us.

The father is followed by his right-hand man, the head farmer who has dedicated 30-years of his life to this hillside crop of premium beans. He lives in a small shack near the entrance, literally living with the crop. The father and the farmer spend the days in this slower season walking the rows with machetes trimming back weeds and tending to the happiness of the crop.

I'm delighted as the father immediately greets me in English and rolls right into an explanation about the organic crop, the coffee buds, and some of the challenges they've faced since turning from a typical fertilized chemical crop to a fully organic crop. As we sat perched for lunch about halfway up this dormant volcano in the middle of their forty hectares, Sala's father explains the farm.

He had originally bought one hundred and sixty hectares back in the eighties during El Salvador's civil war from some successful farmers who needed to flee the country. Since then he had sold off one hundred and twenty hectares in the valley to pursue the best forty at the top of the volcano, a section that would produce a denser, more premium bean. This was his version of the 80/20 rule, where 20% of the production outweighs the 80% that takes more time than it's worth.

One fateful day about fifteen years earlier they had been farming away like most others, fertilizing with chemicals and churning out an impressive crop of around 300,000 pounds of beans each year. The coffee was good and a businessman from Oslo Norway was in South America buying beans to export home when someone had told him about the beans of this little El Salvadorian farm. The cup of black gold was supreme and he wanted to see the farm for himself. Sadly he was disappointed to learn of the fertilizer and chemicals used and disapproved of their focus more on profit and less on quality.

The foreigner began discussing the organic process with Sala's father en route to the farm. Upon arrival, this Norwegian was so amazed by the size and age of the coffee trees as well as the impressive layout of the farm that he began to hug the lush coffee bushes and their Bourbon beans like he'd just been reunited with a long lost lover. He instantly referred to the area as "The Bourbon Jungle". The name stuck, the farming method was completely swapped to 100% organic, and a steady buyer had made a deal with a happy grower eager to learn new methods.

The quality would rise as would the price of the bean. However, the same crop that used to pump out 300,000-pounds of chemically enhanced product quickly dropped to 160,000-pounds of beans. Over time, other challenges would arise such as mold and rust within the crop. Before these problems were easily fought off with chemicals, but now had to be fought with a mixture of copper or sulfur sprays that were considerably more expensive and couldn't do the job as effectively as chemicals.

Often they couldn't afford the ingredients to fight off the problems at all and would lose much of the crop. Such is the life of the farmer; you don't always get a good harvest and in El Salvador, the harvest is only once per year unlike multi-harvest crops of other regions in the world.

In 2011 the crops started to drop off significantly from the 300,000-pound peak in 2013. The worst year on record, the farm only managed to turn out 1400-pounds of usable beans, a mere fraction of what it once did. The family had considered uprooting the entire crop and its bushes that were in some cases 100-years old in the hopes of starting again. The father compared it to killing off part of his family to feed the rest. I could feel the pain in his voice.

The family became even more frustrated when their neighbors were able to bounce back from disaster faster with chemical enhancements while the humble organic boutique farmer would need to focus on crop attention and smartly organizing the fields to ensure a healthy future. Slowly, as time went on, the beans began making a promising comeback to the fruitful gems they were today.

Sala explained that the El Salvador harvest is roughly from November to March where they hire out local pickers to scale the steep volcanic landscape and harvest the flowering bounty by hand. He said that a typical picker would receive about $1.50USD per twenty-five-pound basket of the picked crop. However, they pay $2/ basket and regularly supply free lunch to the workers to ensure a good supply of returning help each season who understands their process. On an average day, a picker might bring in fifty to one hundred pounds of beans. Sala felt the laborers were still underpaid for their efforts as were most of the people in the country. I wondered what he was paid from Telus for his customer service work? Likely not a Canadian wage.

As we walked from the dissension near the peak of the volcano his father continued to divulge the details of the love for his farm and the intricate knowledge of what to look for in a bean, the leaf, and the nutrient-rich volcanic soil that blesses them on this farm. To see a man who has handcrafted his future through times of war, fruitless harvest, and the promise of enough good fortune to keep his dream sputtering along explain his love of the bean. You would think there is no place on earth as magical as these forty hectares and sharing that love, slow-roasted and freshly brewed with the world was the greatest gift one could give.

I'd looked at a lot of bags of coffee in my time, but I'd certainly never looked at them like this man did.

(Salas' father proudly showing off his crop. Spot the other farmer?)

(Sala, ready to road trip.)

El Salvador
Grinding It Out In Coffee School

"I want someone to look at me the way I look at coffee."
- Unknown

The setting and timing of my situation were impeccable. Each day was met with new coffee gurus or coffee celebrities of a sort. Caesar, the owner of the farm and hotel, was a tall skinny man with a peppering of spotty facial hair who drove an old yellow Land Rover with crank windows and the type of old school Landy suspension where your head bounce off the roof as the tyres bounced across the ground. It would make Jeepers salivate with excitement. I'm not sure if he was forty, but he regularly greeted people and slapped hands with staff like they were all teenagers at high school. If Caesar was in town he frequented the hotel chatting up guests and talking about coffee. If he was out of town he was cupping coffee around the Americas for a large coffee buyer.

The comings and goings of coffee junkies through the doors of this tiny hotel, in this tiny village, in this tiny country, during my six-week period were impressive. One day a member of 'Team Greece', the team responsible for once winning the IBBIK world coffee championship stopped by for advice. They were in town looking for inspiration straight from the source.

Another day a buyer from Japan stopped in, one day some buyers from Panama, another day some buyers from Europe. A publisher for a U.K. coffee publication of varying quality stopped in for a few days searching for a story while talking a bunch of shit about how great he was. There were always various other coffee who's who that flowed in and out looking for tips, advice, and where to go for the best beans. People from all over the planet stamped a path to this tiny yellow door that I couldn't find with GPS from just one block away!

I'd spend days running the reception, making coffees in the Chemex for guests and explaining the beans, folding laundry from the dorm bunks, helping with coffee tours at the farm and at the coffee drying & sorting facility. I spent the weeks shadowing personalized coffee tours hosted by Javier for Lechuza Café soaking up all things specialty coffee.

We covered the spectrum from bean development altitude and how the denser, strictly high altitude, or any bean growing over 1200 meters would typically yield a better, denser bean, like Lechuzas Finca Limon that grew at 1640m. Javier explained how the farm would specifically plant things like mango, oranges, and avocado, as shade for the bean and to uniquely influence the flavor. Often we'd go to the mill and unload organic beans to be dried in African beds with the cascara on for a honey finish that would sweeten the bean while it dried.

Other days I would help sort green beans for various selections from American to European to even a zero-defect coffee. We would literally be hand inspecting each fucking bean for the certain number of defects it was allowed per bag. The bean separation took place in a hot little cement room at the coffee warehouse that was dreadfully boring and not recommended while hungover. We were regularly sweating it out hungover staring blindly at tiny green beans looking for microscopic insect bites. Kill me now.

The beans we were handling were being hand planted, hand groomed, hand-picked, hand-dumped, and then hand-spread in the African bed to dry. From here they were hand-turned every hour during sunlight for roughly sixteen days until they reached a point of 12% humidity. Then run through a trilla by hand with a fan behind them to remove the cascara and parchment then picked through by hand (often mine) to ensure quality.

These same beans were then small-batch-roasted by hand, only to later be hand-brewed from 1-4 cups. This was by far the most carefully overseen process for quality I've ever been a part of in my life. Some of these beans would come from Lechuzas Jardin de Pacamara, the crop that won best espresso shot in the 2016 El Salvador Barista Championship.

I'd grown up believing that coffee farmers were a group of uneducated people living in poor countries working for pennies so we westerners could drink this cheap mud to keep our energy up for work. Aside from being paid poorly, the farmers were nothing like this. These were highly skilled individuals who loved these little beans and would literally sleep next to them to ensure a quality product that reflected their impeccable reputation. After seeing all of this, you would think it should be the farmer who was charging more per liter than jet-fuel, not the final brewer.

Later, during my time here, I would be explaining the roasting and growing process to tourists while on coffee tours. One of the funnier moments was during a coffee tour when an intrigued European traveler who seemed impressed with my knowledge of the area and the bean asked how many years I'd been living here? I laughed and said this was my third week! I then promptly credited Javier for my knowledge and said the brunt of the questions should be directed to him while I quietly brewed coffee in the background.

With some random regularity, a traveler or buyer would come bursting through the yellow doors of the hotel coffee shop with a zip lock bag of some sample roasted beans from god knows what little farm in the middle of nowhere. They had heard the beans had a taste profile of rich caramel & black licorice that was rounded out with burnt orange peel and we all needed to experience it.

At moments like these everyone at the hotel would stop what they were doing and gather in the small foyer while Javier got to work. Quickly a pot of purified water was brought to a boil and 440g of hot water was drizzled across 33g of fresh ground beans allowing it to bloom for 30-seconds before the remaining water was layered over the coffee through a pre-rinsed filter on the Chemex. The whole process took place on a scale to guarantee a precision pour while a digital timer tracked the seconds between bloom and brew. The water would claw away the flavors from the bean and you could see the pupils dilate in the eyes of the anxious coffeeholics awaiting their fix.

This day's particular coffee was dark and shimmery like the hair of Jasmine in Aladdin and crept across my taste buds nailing all the aforementioned flavors, right down to the burnt orange peel. Damn these guys were good! It was incredible to watch such enthusiastic excitement.

It was the $50/lb coffee that we were selling for $1/cup that took me by surprise. Some American tourists had requested the beans from a jar labeled *Finca San Nicolas*. As Javier brewed the beans each of us watched, astonished to see that rather than a black, brown, or caramel tinge, this brew came out reddish, looking more like a cup of fruity raspberry tea.

Somehow, during my initial weeks here Javier had forgotten to explain the origin of this brew. In 2013 at the Cup Of Excellence competition the beans from this same farm had been sampled and a buyer from Japan's UCC Ueshima Coffee Co. He was so impressed by the fragrant and light fruity flavors that they paid $50/lb for the beans and bought the entire crop, making these beans one of the top ten most expensive coffee beans in the world. A $90,000 payday for the farmer! Well, almost the entire crop. A few locals had snagged some bags for their personal stash and some of the beans from this farm were in the cup in front of me.

Armed with a great story and my newfound love of coffee, I bought the last pound the Lechuza coffee shop had for closer to $8 and stashed it in with my biker gear. This whole experience had me trading out the space I usually reserved for questionable liquor for premium beans.

(I admire the beans in the African beds while Javier gives the tour)

(A proud coffee farmer & his pets)
    (Hungover, sorting green beans by hand in a room with no ventilation)

El Salvador
Ransoms & Machine Gun Escorts

"Freedom is something that dies unless it's used."
- Hunter S. Thompson

I could see her, but I could not touch her. KLaiR was being held for ransom and all that separated us was a set of steel gates. She was enclosed in the lobby of a house under some old linens blowing on a clothesline just above her windscreen. I hadn't ridden her in weeks, and now I couldn't even get near her.

In this tiny town, there was no need to drive anywhere, and I currently had no place to go. Instead of leaving her out on the streets, one of Javier's friends suggested that I could park KLaiR at her house just up the road. These steel gates were meant to protect her, instead, they had captured her.

Now I finally had a day off from my coffee duties and wanted to ride down to the coastline and see the ocean, but this man I'd never met before was between KLaiR and I. He was claiming that I needed to pay a fee for using the space she was in. With my best level-1 Spanish, I tried to explain I was offered the spot for free. The man explained he was the uncle to the girl who had offered the space and did not care what I had been told. In short, direct sentences like an upset child making it clear he does not want to leave the park, the uncle continued to demand money, but of no set amount.

Each time he spoke I could smell cheap booze on his breath, a smell that seemed out of place this early in the day. His lunch hour booze breath combined with no clear ransom figure was making me feel like his request might be fabricated, either way, he had the keys to release KLaiR and I did not.

I was happy to offer something as the stay had been longer than I thought, but wasn't sure what to offer and to whom. I was pretty sure the uncle was just a resident in the home and not the homeowner and I didn't trust him enough to just hand over some cash.

Unable to leave with KLaiR, I quickly returned to the hotel and asked Javier & Caesar what to do? Javier called his friend and she said she felt terrible about the misunderstanding, but also didn't want to upset anyone in the house as she still had to live there after I left. Caesar suggested I give the man some money, but his request seemed ridiculous that should only give him $5 or $10. He thought that if I gave too much the man would think I had lots of money and might cause me more problems in the future.

$10 to spring KLaiR from the laundry prison, done and done! However, this would likely segue into another problem. Once KLaiR was out on bail, my only other option would be to park her back on the street, just down from the laundry prison. If she was out on the street and the uncle wanted more money he could vandalize or kidnap KLaiR while I was sleeping inside the hotel at night.

With KLaiR held behind the gates of the home, I entered into some heavy negotiation with the help of the girl who offered the space, Javier and Caesar. The friend was extremely against the idea of handing over any funds to the uncle. With that, Javier and Caesar made some phone calls to friends and eventually found KLaiR another place to rest in the yard of a hostel that belonged to Javier's friend. At least if we could get her out, then she would have a new home.

The day carried on while I wandered the tiny town hoping for a solution that would appease everyone. Eventually, Javier called me and said to come back to the hotel, they had the phone number of the homeowner. By now it was dark and my hopes of oceanside exploration were gone, but was hopefully getting closer to KLaiR's release.

We called the homeowner, an older man who only spoke Spanish. Javier explained the situation to him and then put me on the phone with his son, a young-sounding man who spoke impeccable English. The son was extremely relaxed about the whole situation and laughed when I told him what had happened. I'm glad he was laughing, I certainly wasn't. Apparently, the guy with the keys to KLaiR's release was also his uncle. He said that sometimes his uncle can get some crazy ideas after he'd had a drink or two and I owed them nothing for parking KLaiR at the house. He said he would call the uncle and give him some task that would require him to leave the house. Once he left I could go and get the bike, but I may want to leave a little bottle of local rum behind as a special treat for the boozy uncle.

In 10-minutes the man called back and said I could go get KLaiR. I ran across the road to a small store, bought a bottle with the word "CIHUATAN" on it, and made my way to KLaiR like she was my only present on Christmas day. At this point, there was only one other lady at the house. She smiled when I passed her the bottle and explained who it was for. I thanked her for letting me in, wiped a thick layer of dust from KLaiR's seat and we made our escape from under the linens and into the street. From here on, I resolved to ask all kinds of questions before parking KLaiR for an extended time period. Though this would not be the end of my Central America parking dramas as I would later find out in Costa Rica.

My next misunderstanding that week had me crouched between a truck-mounted machine gun and the police.

* * *

If you were to read the same outdated Lonely Planet guide about Juayua that I did, there were only two activities listed. The most popular was a day at the beautiful cascading waterfalls where you could escape the heat by swimming at the base of the falls or soaking in the natural pools here. To get to the falls, you could either hire a Tuk Tuk taxi or enjoy a 30-minute walk from the village. It was a popular stop for both locals and tourists, but it was said that those walking were often robbed on the empty country road that led to the falls. I felt you could be robbed walking on any country road when it came down to it, and after living in this peaceful village for the last several weeks I decided to walk. Just to be cautious, however, I left all my money and electronics behind.

Some tourists had told me you could request a police escort from the local and extremely bored authorities. I even met a couple of girls who had received a ride from them. As a male, I thought they'd probably laugh at me and opted to go at it alone. With nothing more than a bottle of water and a Pupusa, I set off from the hotel.

It was a Sunday and the road was busy with small motorbikes and cars taking their families to visit the magnificent falls after church. The road was dusty from the traffic, but I never saw anyone walking other than me. Obviously, I knew more than the locals and continued along my way. About halfway into my dusty hike, a police truck came down the road behind me. It was an old white pickup truck with a double cab and open box. The front had four men, one at each window all dressed in full police combat gear. In the bed of the truck were two more men dressed in black police gear. While one man watched out the back of the truck, the other man stood holding onto a large machine gun that was bolted to the bed of the truck. It looked like these boys were headed to the capital for their first coup. Not exactly unusual for El Salvador.

As far as I could tell, I was the only pale, white tourist headed to the falls that day and when the police spotted me walking alone in my shorts and sandals they promptly stopped and asked me some questions. When I explained I was just headed to the falls, they demanded I get in the truck. Staring back at six large men in police combat gear while one of them looked back at me from behind his machine gun, I knew there would be no negotiation here. I hopped in the truck, ducked under the machine gun, and made a place for myself on the edge of the truck box.

There was no conversation in the back of that truck; it was all business, and today's business was dropping my tourist ass off at the falls to play. Five minutes later, I, along with the armored police escort arrived at the entrance to the falls. As we pulled in I immediately became the focal point of a parking lot full of families fresh from the house of God. I knew they did not arrive here via police escort, more likely in an over-stuffed Tuk Tuk. The whole ordeal was completely ridiculous and to avoid looking like an ass, I instead smiled and waved at everyone like I was a one-man royal procession. As the truck parked in front of the gates, I thanked the police for my safe transport from behind a shit-eating grin and sauntered off for a swim.

I'm not sure if I was disappointed I had to actually walk back, or slightly nervous that this road may have really been dangerous. Either way, the machine gun truck wasn't awaiting my royal return.

As for tiny Juayua and equally as small El Salvador, I feel like an entire lifetime of trying to learn about coffee could not have measured up to the hands-on, and extremely in-depth course that was bestowed upon me by Javier and Lechuza Cafe. The experience was incredible and unmatched by any other "work experience" I've ever been a part of. I've since become a hint of a coffee snob, or so others have mentioned. I can honestly say the weeks with Javier changed my entire outlook on what I once considered a cup of hot mud.

(Dropping the beans off at the mill, then catching a ride home with the farmers)

(Photos and political posters from El Salvador's turbulent past)

Honduras
Kiss The Cook

"In rural areas, approximately 1 out of 5 Hondurans live in extreme poverty, or on less than US$1.90 per day."
- Worldbank.org

When packing for a solo excursion the good thing is you can pack whatever the hell you want and there is no travel companion to dictate what you can or can't stuff in your luggage. Your friends still might heckle you for some of the more questionable choices, but if you want to take it you can take it.

Before I left on this little road trip I was living with my friend Andrew. As the trip grew nearer, more and more items for the adventure kept arriving for me in his mailbox. One day a GPS case would arrive, another day a 16-tooth sprocket, the next a new 21" tire for the bike and a led light for my tent and on, and on and on the items trickled in.

On this particular day, a box showed up with my name on it and Andrew gave it to me with a little smirk on his face as he could see what was in the box. It was a cordless hair trimmer.

It wasn't a little nose trimmer or a men's electric razor. It was the full-size trimmer one might use to cut hair in a barbershop. I told him very nonchalantly that I was packing it in my kit for the motorcycle trip. With a short burst of laughter, he said; *You're taking camping gear, motorcycle parts, and of course, a full-size cordless hair trimmer!?*

I'm not built like a Russian Bear, but I've got what you might consider an average amount of male body hair. I'd been to plenty of hot countries and preferred to have as much man-scaping done as possible to deal with the heat. Having grown up in frigid North America I remember arriving in the deserts of Nevada for the Burning Man Festival when I was 24. It was 10-days of relentless heat that was typically well over 40oC during the day.

To combat the extreme heat I'd shaved every bit of body hair from head to toe. I even ran the electric razor across my legs. I looked like a competitive swimmer, less the triangle physique. After this event, I never went to a hot country without a body-wide buzz cut. The shaver also helped to even out my fleeting hairline. Andrew laughed for days.

Along with this shaver and dozens of other things, I packed and probably didn't need, were travel guidebooks. I had two of these thick, heavy books in my luggage. It was 2017 and I was trading my valuable motorcycle space for two travel books that weighed more than my laptop. Later when discussing route plans with a backpacker I pulled out my book to show him a map. The backpacker pulled out his iPad and showed me the same map from a guidebook he had illegally downloaded. I felt like a low-tech ass.

The books did come in handy a few times as kickstand support in the sand and were read during the endless nights alone in my tent. The night before I was going to leave El Salvador for Nicaragua I was reading up on upcoming Honduras and Nicaragua. What I should have done is read the "Top 10 To Do" section and looked at the maps. Instead, I flipped to the part about Honduras' history, a very bad choice before bed.

That night, alone in the darkness, I read about how Guatemala, El Salvador, and Honduras were known to have some of the highest murder rates anywhere on earth. The amount of drug trafficking and conflict between rival gangs was to blame for the deaths. Groups like the Mara Salvatrucha or Barrio 18 were blamed for most of the violence. By 2012 Honduras was experiencing a deadly 20-murders per day. Even though these numbers were now declining, the killings were still happening.

I planned to bypass the capital of Tegucigalpa where most of the problems in Honduras were and explore as much of the calmer south as I could. To achieve this, I'd ridden into northern El Salvador and was planning to cross just above the once heavily militarized town of Perquin. I was spending the night in a part hotel, part campground, part luxury cabins, part petting zoo, spread across a large mass of land in a pine forest. The grounds were so expansive I actually couldn't find where the pool, showers, and toilet were located.

For directions, I went to the lobby of the hotel and asked a worker how to get to the toilet & showers. Instead of directions, they sent a driver to come and pick me up. The driver along with the cook who'd just finished his shift drove me the 3-minutes to the showers. I thanked them then proceeded to use the bathroom and shower.

Today was wash your boxers in the shower day, as it often is when you only have three changes of clothes. Once I and the undies were finally clean I emerged 25-minutes later feeling fresh as a spring flower, I was surprised to see both men still waiting for me. I suppose if they were getting paid for this waste of time then lucky them. I got back in the car and the two men drove me another 2-minutes back to my camp spot. Wow, what service I thought.

The driver said goodbye but the cook hung around to chat. The cook who knew some very basic English asked a number of questions about my trip, but not the usual questions about how far and how long. Instead, the cooks' questions were more focused on why I was traveling alone and if I got scared or lonely along the way. He even explained how much he loved camping but never usually got the chance to do so. After 20-minutes of being peppered with questions from the cook, it was becoming more and more clear why he was still stewing at my campsite.

Finally, he proposed his final question. He re-worded it several different ways to make it very clear that I understood what he was asking. He asked if he could spend the night in the tent with me so that I wouldn't be so lonely! This badass biker image I thought I'd conjured up to fend off danger was maybe less badass than I'd imagined. Perhaps the electric shaver was keeping my appearance a little too polished. Needless to say, the little chef went home and enjoyed dessert alone that night.

Instead of cuddling with the cook, I curled up with my guidebook and read all about the murder rates in Honduras. As I was planning my route, the German guy who'd ridden around the world for 5-years messaged me completely out of the blue. He warned me that the route I was planning through Honduras the next day was under heavy construction and I was in for a much longer ride than I was hoping for. Between the stories of murder and the route warning I chickened out and drove back south through El Salvador to cross into Honduras at the El Amatillo border, a route that would have me missing almost the entire country.

My time crunch concern also rested on the fact that Angie was flying in during her spring break to spend two weeks with me in Nicaragua. Angie and I had already broken things off after our summer love affair, then again after the fluke encounter in Las Vegas. Then said goodbye a final, final, final time after our unlikely meetup in Cabo San Lucas Mexico. It was like ripping off a band aid each time, but there was zero possibility we'd see each other again or so I told myself three times before this.

We'd talked off and on for the last few months and now there was a plan to meet up in Nicaragua. No flukes, no magical timing where the stars of the world had somehow landed me in her path again. This time Angie had spent her hard-earned money to buy a plane ticket and take time off work to meet up with the dirty biker and his moto-girlfriend. She had never mentioned anything about being an orphan with no friends, but if I was her parents or friends there would have been a very slim chance I would have thought this to be a good idea.

On my side, I was now planning the route of my trip around meeting her. This was more of an investment for the two of us, both financially and emotionally. Meeting up with anyone from home wasn't anywhere on my traveling radar before I left. Whether Angie really wanted to see Nicaragua or me I wasn't sure, but the fact she was flying in to do so was going to change the dynamic of our relationship a little.

I requested she bring me two things from Canada. First off I needed two new tent poles as mine had snapped several times and despite being lashed back together with layers of Gorilla Tape, they were now beyond repair. My tent-trauma became incredibly evident when I pitched the tent in a campground one afternoon and the tent next to me was almost identical to mine. The difference was, theirs was a perfectly rounded tent shape like you see on the sales page. Mine however looked more like a blue triangle one breath from death. I laughed every time I looked at the triangle tent next to the proper tent and would mutter *"whose tent is that?"* when people walked by.

The other thing I needed was dental floss. I had run out of floss in El Salvador and was having a hard time finding any. One day I finally tracked some down and it was $7USD for the floss. At $7USD, once I converted that to Canadian it equaled nearly all of my $12/day travel budget. I opted to use business cards and blades of grass to clean my K9s until a less expensive version could be muled in with Angie.

To this day I have no idea what she was thinking, flying into Central America when she realized that buying dental floss locally was out of my budget and seeing photos of the busted blue tent on my Facebook page knowing she would need to spend at least a few nights in it. Either way, good to her word and my sheer delight, the girl, the replacement poles, and the floss would eventually arrive.

Managua
Bribery 101

"When asked for a bribe in a foreign country, it's best to act stupid and speak English. Basically what you were doing before you were asked for the bribe."

- Kix Marshall

I had a running rule that I would avoid major cities at all costs. I felt that if you were to find problems anywhere, it would be in cities. This rule was quickly ignored near the start of the trip when I arrived in the largest frigging city in the Americas, Mexico City, lost and in the dark. This time Angie wasn't going to be flying into a village and I reluctantly needed to drive to the capital of Nicaragua, Managua, to meet her. The upside is I could trade in a sweaty night in the triangle tent and a baby wipes bath for a cheap hotel with a fan and a shower. Angie would be flying in close to midnight, so I dropped off my goods at the hotel, put my electric shaver to good use, and picked up some little gifts of Nicaraguan chocolate and sugary local drinks for her to enjoy after a full day of plane rides.

    I arrived at the airport just after midnight and met Angie at the arrival gate. She was sporting a day pack, a large green backpack, and a spare helmet of mine she had since the Las Vegas trip. The bike wasn't really designed to carry big backpacks, but I had so much shit tied to KLaiR already, what was one more person and a couple of bags going to change? I put the big backpack on top of my rear Pelican case and used some tie straps to lash it all down before we set off for the little hotel in the dark.

It was now well after midnight, extremely dark and we were in a big city with a bad reputation on Angie's first night. We were two obvious foreigners on a motorbike that looked like an ATM machine on two wheels. I wanted to get back quickly and safely without alluding to Angie that I felt like this was a bad idea. It was less than 10-minutes from the airport to the hotel, but somehow I got lost, again. I'd turned left into a dead-end road twice and was getting a little nervous as we backtracked out of each neighborhood. I knew the hotel was down one of these streets, but I was nervously forgetting which one.

By the third wrong turn, I had made a u-turn to come back and was met by a red traffic light. Just then a man stepped into the street and was waving his arms frantically for us to stop. Fuck no, I wasn't stopping for anything, not the man or the red light, and sped right past both.

Angie yelled up at me through the helmet and asked why I didn't stop and see what the guy wanted. I casually yelled back at her that the man likely had a gun. I don't think that was the answer she was expecting or hoping for. Again I took the next left and this time it was the correct turn. Someone from the hotel heard us pull up and came down to open the gate so I could park inside. As we got off the bike Angie looked back and her backpack was gone. Shit! How did a large backpack disappear from right behind us?

Had someone stolen it? Was that guy a distraction while someone cut the straps and took the bag off the back? Fuck now what? Angie got off the bike looking like she was going to puke and my mind was dreading the possibilities of what had happened to her bag with all her gear, passport, and credit cards. She had only been in Nicaragua for 30-minutes and already I had convinced her everyone had a gun and all her worldly possessions had been stolen.

As we both jumped off the bike not knowing if we should ride around and look for it or what to do, Angie noticed her bag was lying on the ground behind the tyre. Holy shit, there it was a little beat up from dragging on the ground! In my nervous haste to leave the airport, I must have done a shit job of tying it onto the bike and it had come loose. Luckily I had run the tie straps under one of the handles on the side of her bag and the hook on the tie strap had caught the handle as the strap was coming out. Holding on by that little hook to the back of the bike the bag dragged along like a little backpack trailer all the way to the hotel. Wow, I couldn't believe it. If we had stopped even once, the tension from the hook would have come loose and let go of the bag. Everything was still there, even the dental floss!

Looking back, was that guy trying to flag us down in the middle of the night to rob two foreigners who were lost? Or did he see the bag dragging behind the bike and came out to tell us to stop and get it before it fell off? I'll never know for sure, but I clearly was still of the mindset that the people I would meet in the city were dangerous or bad. I would need to change my perception of the city folks if I was going to feel comfortable while we were here.

Relieved, relaxed, excited, and tired we headed up to the 1-star hotel room where we were greeted by a fan blowing hot air around. Here we could get reacquainted and Angie could enjoy the chocolates and sugary drinks I'd bought her. Due to the hot and humid conditions, Angie was going to need to change out of her smelly travel attire and into some comfortable sleeping attire. It was at this point I had for the first time in my life seen the body of a female I was legally allowed to touch that had been chiseled out to reveal an 8-pack centered around a tiny frame and toned muscles all smoothed out with an air-brushed tan.

I could feel my throat swell a little, I'm sure she could hear me gulp back saliva while trying to remain calm and act cool. How in the hell was there a half-naked brunette shimmering in the dim light of this $12/night room accented by dirty biker shit everywhere? I had no idea how this was really happening and just tried to keep her talking as a distraction from realizing the situation she'd fallen into.

It wasn't like I was in terribly bad shape; I had run a marathon not long before departure, but I was in a steady routine of eating cookies as my second breakfast, snacking on white bread with bologna, and indulging in a daily chocolate milk or three to keep my energy levels up in the heat. To my surprise, she passed up on the pre-bed chocolates and sugary drink, so I sampled a few on her behalf.

The next morning we were treated to a free breakfast that was included with the $12 room. I was fairly happy to hear FREE anything, especially food. The breakfast buffet included; tea, instant Nescafe coffee, slices of white bread, a toaster, and your choice of some kind of nameless sugary jam spread or a low-grade chocolate spread. I promptly placed two pieces of bread in the toaster while Angie poured us some hot water.

The toast popped and I put one slice on a plate for me and one on a plate for her, then put two more slices in the toaster. I then slathered on a thick layer of the chocolate spread topped by the sugary fruit mixture. Angie was fidgeting with her dry toast a little; it looked like she had never seen toast before. Maybe she was gluten-free? I wasn't sure. I took a big bite of the white toast, smothered with various forms of sugar, and with my mouth half full, I asked her if she wanted the jam or the chocolate? She kind of hesitated and grabbed a teabag. Then it hit me, she likely spent months chiseling away at this 8-pack and probably hadn't eaten a square of white bread or a drop of un-calculated sugar in months. This meal was probably going to send her system into caloric shock.

So I asked her like any inquisitive child would, *when's the last time you had sugar?* Trying to act like she rarely concerned herself with diet, she said. *Ummm, I dunno, probably yesterday.* She was clearly trying to pretend that this low-grade biker life was exactly what she was expecting based on my description of motorcycle adventure. I decided to drop the subject, find her some fresh fruit and vouched to eat the chocolates I had gotten her alone!

We organized our day and got KLaiR ready. This time I tied on the backpack with extreme precision and angled my mirrors so I could see the bag from both sides, then we set off for the coast. The very first stop was just a few minutes in as we pulled in for fuel at a gas station positioned just off the edge of the main roadway out of the city. We pulled in, filled up, and headed back out onto the highway. Instantly we were flagged down by the police. I had only just gotten fuel and wasn't going faster than 20km/h while merging out into traffic, I knew something seemed off. I pulled over and yelled back at Angie to relax as dealing with this cop may take some time.

The first thing out of the policeman's mouth was the phrase *"3000-Cordoba"*. He was asking for money, the equivalent of around $100USD. I decided to act like I had no idea what he was saying and just started rambling on in English as I figured he only spoke Spanish. Considering I'd just driven the length of North America, Mexico, Belize, Guatemala, El Salvador, and a slice of Honduras, this was the first time I'd been pulled over and asked for a bribe. This also lined up perfectly with Angie's first day in Nicaragua. Fuck!

For about 5-minutes the cop kept asking for money in Spanish and I would reply in English, *"Why?"* Then he switched tactics and asked for my license. I acted like I didn't know what he meant. He then pulled out various licenses he had taken from people that were in his jacket. I looked at them closely, smiled, and read the names of the people out loud as though he was showing me family photos. I thought this was pretty funny, he did not. I find that when asked for a bribe in a foreign country, it's best to act stupid and speak English. Basically what you were doing before you were asked for the bribe.

By about minute eight I could see his frustration building. Though I was prepared for moments like this and had pre-made some fake driver's licenses, I certainly wasn't going to pull out my wallet to get him one unless I absolutely had to. We were now about 10-minutes into our little debate in the beating sun with this guy continually asking me for a license, me continually talking a bunch of shit that made no sense in English, and Angie likely wondering what the hell she'd gotten herself into. Just then the cop started to get a little aggressive.

The cop then unzipped the tank bag on my bike and started rooting through it like a honey badger digging for dinner. To my delight, all I had in the tank bag were some brochures of sites from El Salvador, a Tupperware container for snacks, a metal spoon, and a bunch of fuel receipts. While he was rooting through my things Angie said to me that there was another cop across the road who was now laughing hysterically at our current situation. I turned and looked across the road. Sure enough, this other cop was laughing at the spectacle of his partner harassing me and us not giving in to his demands. I got the impression that this bribing of foreigners for money thing usually went much easier for the cop.

Once all three of us had noticed the other cop laughing, the guy harassing us shoved the useless papers back into my bag and told us to leave. I smiled at his friend across the road and without hesitation hit the starter and whizzed off down the road! I yelled back to Angie, "Welcome to Nicaragua!"

(The irony of setting up my broken tent properly attached)
(How it looked when Angie's bag was next to a working replica)

Nicaragua
Body Boxes & Toothpaste Rations

"Flor explained that if the men and boys ever returned home, it was in a box, delivered by other soldiers."

- Aunt Flor. The story of growing up in Nicaragua

After listening to one of the most horrific stories of struggle I'd ever heard, Aunt Flor got up, walked us to the back of their simple home, and showed us where the hole in the backyard used to be. It was the hole her family hid in to avoid being captured by the Nicaraguan military.

It's one thing to read about the brutalities of history, it's another to hear about them right from the mouth of someone who has lived through the unfathomable while sitting in their yard in what was once a bloody war zone.

Brace yourself...

A friend of mine in Canada was from Nicaragua and whenever I talked to her it seemed she had family spread all across the Americas. She had suggested we meet with an Aunt of hers who was living in Canada but happened to be in Nicaragua right now. I always loved to meet the locals and jumped at the opportunity to meet a friend's relative who happened to be Nicaraguan and spoke English.

We were given some extremely vague directions to the house of her aunt in a small city in Northern Nicaragua. The directions described the town, what the street looked like, and some other notable landmarks nearby. The kind of directions you might get if you were visiting a village with one street. Nothing you could punch into Google Maps, not that I had a local phone plan or anything convenient like that.

We rolled into town a touch glossy-eyed from a tour at the local Flor de Cana distillery, the country's prominent rum manufacturer. The two of us were in our shorts and t-shirts with helmets on, straddling a large motorcycle with so much luggage that we looked like an 80's wood panel station wagon loaded down for a family summer vacation. Our obvious looks stood out even more in this non-touristy town.

The directions said the house was located on a road with the house on one side and a car dealership on the other. We finally found the dealership, which was so big there were ten houses across from it. So like any random foreigner does in the city of a country known for its crime you start by banging on the door of the first house and make your way down the street asking each door if you are at the right house.

The first house had an 8-foot steel fence with coiling barbed wire around it. The style you'd see at a prison, only with a nice house tucked behind all that security. The doorbell was on the house, not on the gate, a bit of a design flaw. Unable to ring the bell I started to bang on the gate and yell to see if anyone responded. Needless to say, no one came excitedly running to the door, though the neighborhood sure started to notice us.

After a few minutes of this bang and yell technique, we moved on to the next house where I asked a teenager there if the Aunt we were looking for lived with him or if he knew of her. No, she did not live here, and no he did not know her, however, he did speak English and let us use his wifi to make some WhatsApp calls. After a few calls the aunt, Aunt Flor, came out from behind another gate four doors down to greet us, what luck!

Like long-lost cousins, we were invited in and Aunt Flor suggested we pitch our tent in the yard as the house was already full with her and another visiting Aunt. The house was a typical size for this part of the planet. A single-level layout, a couple of bedrooms, and a kitchen. There was another room at the front of the house that was rented out to a security team who worked for the car dealership at night. If nothing else we were probably safe here.

This was now Angie's second yard-camping experience in Central America. Quickly we set up and were made to feel right at home by the Aunts. However, we might have thrown off the security guys when they came back to see a couple of North Americans living in the driveway.

Aunt Flor, Angie, and I sat down on some plastic chairs and got to chatting as the sun began to set. The other Aunt came out to meet us, but couldn't shake our hands as she had these big cloth wraps around all of her limbs with what looked like iodine staining them. She explained she had come back to Nicaragua from Canada to visit her aging mother and get some treatments done on her aching bones by a well-known doctor who uses only natural herbs to heal anything from aches and pains to broken bones.

The testimonials about this Doctor and his ability to heal aging or broken bones were said to be so unbelievable that she had to try it on her own aches & pains to see if the results were real. The treatment was still in the early stages though she felt as if it was going well and she said she was feeling better.

After a quick round of small talk about how we all came to know one another through their niece and my friend, Aunt Flor quickly drifted into the history of Nicaragua and the family's battles to survive before she eventually migrated to Canada.

The War

Flor explained that during the 70's and 80's Nicaragua was in the midst of a Nicaraguan revolution where the FSLN rebels (Sandinista National Liberation Front) violently began to oust the Somoza dictatorship and eventually take power. The FSLN would then lead the country from 1979-1990 as a dictatorship and the Contras would fight back against this self-imposed dictatorship from 1981-1990. During the 80's Nicaragua was a bloody mess of governments and guerillas. This is where Flors' story of survival started.

Flor said that no one was safe from either side of the struggle. If the government felt they needed your bike or car or cows or home, they would come to you and tell you that the government needed these items and they would take them from you. Such is life under a dictatorship. The same dictatorship was reflected on both sides when it came to finding soldiers for the battle. If the government wanted your husband or son to help fight on their side of the war, they would come to your door and rip them from their families and force them to fight. She said when either side recruited members from your family, you were likely to never see that family member again.

Flor explained that if the men and boys ever returned home, it was in a box, delivered by other soldiers. When the box arrived it would have your son or husband's name on the outside, but you were not permitted to open it to identify the body. The bodies were usually dismembered or missing parts and even though these opposing parties were happy to take your family away to be slaughtered, they didn't want you to see the destruction they had created.

Flor said she remembered hearing screams in the streets as mothers would have their sons taken away only to hear those same mothers screaming in the streets when their sons arrived home later in body boxes.

To avoid having Flor's brother taken away by either side, the family decided to dig a hole in the backyard big enough to fit the family inside then disguise the hole with partially constructed wood and trees so it looked like an old shack in the backyard that was used for storage.

Flor recounted the days the family would spend in the hole in the backyard to avoid capture. They would hear soldiers banging at the house door to recruit family members and even as small children they all had to remain rock still and completely silent in the hole as long as it took. Sometimes they would spend the entire day underground so as not to give up their cover.

With the male labor force either hiding or at war, this also meant supplies were dwindling. The dictatorship government had taken control of most of the food in the country and it would be hard to find sources to feed your family and get supplies. At night one brave young sister would need to sneak out into the darkness to go scavenging for food for the family. The other aunt now sitting across from us would sneak out as a young child and go looking for fruits or try to contact people that might have food. This was daily life, this is how the family was living and the world the children were growing up in.

I pictured a family stuffed in their own backyard, starving, with scared children who were not allowed to make a sound while they helplessly sent a daughter out searching for family food as it was less dangerous than sending a son who might be scooped up and slaughtered. Tears had begun to steadily run from my eyes onto my cheeks as we listened to every word Aunt Flor said.

The lowest moment of her life.

I thought that living in the backyard was going to be the low point of this unimaginable story. However, things soon sunk even lower. By now the dictating FSLN was rationing the country's dwindling supplies to the people while they tried to control everything in the nation. Rations were being handed over to the country's citizens like they were caged animals. Flor said that her or her sister would need to wait with mass crowds of ladies at parks where soldiers would throw items like chicken or other meats into the crowds. A soldier would have something like five hundred portions of chicken for two thousand people and simply toss a chicken breast or leg out into the starving mass and they would need to fight over it like lions in the hopes of taking some to their families. A shocking contrast to the times I enjoyed going to the grocery store as a kid with my parents to choose from thousands of items and leave with a shopping cart full of goods.

Flor's family along with others were given promissory notes to exchange for toiletry items like toothpaste and soap. Items were rationed based on how big your family was. For example; a tube of toothpaste was given to each family of six to last them a month. One day Flor was to pick up the family's toothpaste for the month. As far as the government knew her family was a family of three girls with no boys. Based on this knowledge the distributor of goods took the full tube of toothpaste and right in front of her they cut the toothpaste tube in half. Keeping one half and handing Flor the other half for her family's monthly ration.

Flor said this was the lowest moment of her life. She felt less than a dog, only given half a tube of toothpaste to return to her family with. From here things would get even worse before they got better.

Later in the years when she was older and had her own family, she recounted needing to catch a bus to a neighboring town with her now son. Flor explained that usually, one bus would show up each day for hundreds of people who were hoping to catch it. On one of these daily attempts to catch an impossibly full bus, she needed to get to a neighboring town to meet her family. Again the bus would fill and there was no room for Flor and her son but she had spotted a friend on the bus. Instead of trying to board, Flor passed her young son up through the window and asked the friend to please take her son to her family in the next town. Wow, I could not imagine the heartache of watching your child go on without you.

Relying on your neighbors.

The neighboring countries of Costa Rica, Honduras & El Salvador were the closest places of escape for anyone looking for refuge from the relentless war. For a period of time Flor and her family along with thousands of others had escaped into peaceful Costa Rica. She was amazed by the kindness and warm welcome of the Costa Ricans. The Costa Ricans took the Nicas' in like family, gave them clothes, and fed them while in their country.

Eventually returning to Nicaragua things in the country had become even more desperate and the family decided to liquidate some of their property at a huge discount and use the money to escape to El Salvador for a better life. While in El Salvador many people had been talking about the possibilities to migrate to welcoming Canada though it would be difficult with little funds. The family had heard through the Church that it may be possible to find help with Canadians from the same denomination if they could somehow get themselves onto Canadian soil.

At first attempt, the entire family including twelve children had purchased plane tickets from El Salvador to Toronto with some of the funds from the land sale. They had escaped Nicaragua again and made their way to El Salvador's capital. When they arrived at the San Salvador airport the authorities would not let them on the plane as no one in the family had any type of documents, passports, birth certificates, or anything to identify who they were. They had merely escaped with the clothes on their backs and certainly no vital documents. The family argued with the officials as though their lives depended on it and they did. In the end, the officials would not budge and the family had lost the chance of escape, the plane tickets, and the money. It was looking more bleak as each day passed.

Undeterred and revisiting the same plan, the family then purchased another round of plane tickets to Canada with the last of their money and arrived at the San Salvador airport at a later date. Like all great miracles, these new officials sympathized with their desperation and let the entire family board the plane without documents, but warned them they would not be allowed into Canada on arrival and likely be put on the next plane back to El Salvador.

During this time, the Seventh Day Adventist Church in El Salvador had been in contact about the situation and had then contacted the same denominational church in Toronto to let them know about the possible arrival of the fleeing family. Upon arrival in Canada and after several hours of questioning Flors' family including my then very young friend, eleven other small children and several adults were released into Canadian winter and the loving arms of Canadians who knew nothing more of them than their incredible story.

Life in a new world.

By this point, neither I nor Angie had said a single word in over an hour and the two spots on my shirt under my face seemed to be getting increasingly wetter.

A short time later Flor along with her son who had not been part of the original migration would use the same system to enter Canada. Upon arrival in Toronto, they were separated into rooms and questioned about their previous lives and how they came to be in Canada with no proof of who they were.

With no documentation, Flor could not prove who she was let alone that this was even her son. To test the truthfulness of the story, the Canadian RCMP asked the small boy to tell them about the lady's face he was traveling with. At the time Flor had a very obvious birthmark on her face and they wanted to see if the boy could remember it. They asked him to describe her face to see if it was in fact her son. The boy said to the officer that his mother was easy to describe, as she was the most beautiful woman in the world and everyone could see that.

The RCMP laughed, and probably cried too, then pressed for a few more details. The son eventually described the birthmark in detail and the RCMP reunited them where they too would be greeted by harsh Canadian winter, the original family, and families from the church.

Aunt Flor went on to describe some of the challenges of life in Canada. She said that learning the language, finding work and everyone slowly etching out their own lives was very difficult at first. It had probably been close to an hour and a half by this point and I still had said nothing and didn't even know where to begin. Picturing my friend whom I had known for many years and the prosperous Canadian life she was now living in contrast to where she might be today or the life she would have lived during the war, I was beyond speechless.

Angie seemed at a loss for words too and I think Flor was taken a little aback while we all paused for a few silent moments of reflection before Flor continued on with the story. Once she continued Aunt Flor skipped ahead to explain some interesting moments when living in Canada. She remembered their first bus ride in Toronto where a line of roughly twenty people had been waiting for the bus on a city street. Her now seven-year-old son was beside her and when he saw the bus approaching he looked at the line and began to yell frantically to the people on the bus to open the window while he put his arms up and yelled: "Mommy I'm ready put me up". Until this point getting on a bus through a window was the only way he knew how to board. The three of us burst into laughter and another round of tears.

Life is a miracle.

Flor wound things down explaining she was so happy and proud to be Canadian she was sure she was living a miracle. She wanted to share this feeling with others and over the years had helped several other Nicaraguans with paperwork and money who had wanted to immigrate to Canada.

Having never missed a day of work in 32 years, her lifelong dream and retirement goal was to drive across all of Canada to know the rest of the beauty the country has to offer.

The day after Angie and I got to talking about Flor's story, Angie said she was completely stunned with each part of the story and felt her heart aching more and more as it went on. Sitting in silence, tears slowly fell down her face as she tried to grasp for a moment what that experience would have been like. It impacted her, and made her feel something she's not sure she'd ever felt before. It made her recognize how incredibly fortunate she is, and how much she takes for granted on a daily basis. Appreciating her life at such a different level after hearing all that. Such an unexpected sharing of a family's tragedy, strength, bravery, and ultimately, their incredible vulnerability.

As for my friend, it turns out after living in Canada for thirty years she had only just heard versions of this story and other stories about her past a week before we did. We also found out that at one time, an uncle of hers who had been a pilot for the Contra got word that he was going to be killed one night by the opposing dictatorship so he stole one of their helicopters, put his family in it, and escaped to El Salvador with all of their lives.

In another part of the country, her Dad owned a farm near the Honduran border and both the Contras and the FSLN would use it to cross in and out of the country. While he fed & sheltered both sides her Dad remained neutral to the conflict. Eventually, the Contras said to her father that he was either with or against them, but he refused to pick a side. Some days later a friend came to warn that night the Contras were planning to kill him so the family fled the home. When they returned weeks later the house was riddled with bullet holes. This was just before my friend was born, so had this plan come to fruition her life certainly would not have.

(The aunts with Angie & I) (Where the hole used to be that the family would hide in)

Canada
The Backstory

"No matter where you go, there you are"
– Confucius

I've been accused by more than a few people of "running away" or "avoiding my problems" when I've taken off around the world to explore for months or years at a time. Whether the escape was to avoid dealing with an x-girlfriend, wanting to get away from the mundane life I'd fallen into, or the need to disappear into cities where no one knows my face, name, or history. I don't always know the reason or need a reason. I just need to go. To get lost. To get found.

When I was about 13, my parents were in the 7th year of a 25-year divorce. It was long, it was ugly, and I don't think they ever fully resolved or finalized everything after years of handing over all their earnings to various lawyers. It was your standard, everyone loses, divorce. At this point, I think my father had finally had about enough and said *fuck it*. I've rarely heard the guy swear in my life, but if his mind could do the talking, I'm sure the words FUCK IT! would have come screaming out the top of his hairless head.

He'd been self-employed for a large part of his life, he'd built the house we'd lived in, he'd been married, he had all his kids under one roof and slowly he and my mother had lost it all. I don't know the exact moment or the exact day but I suddenly remember him living in a large canvas tent in an equestrian campground at the end of a long dusty road on the edge of the Albertan wilderness, far from anything. Him, his two horses, a fishing rod, and nature. I remember being there for Easter one year. I was probably on a break from school, my other siblings were older and not as interested in coming out to this cold campground away from their social life. I ended up spending the entire spring break in the frosty wilderness.

The 14x16-foot white canvas tent, held up by slender pine trees thatched together then tied off to the surrounding trees to keep the shelter stable. On the inside were a set of bunk beds he'd made from 2"x4" lumber and sheets of plywood, a layer of old carpet across the ground to keep us from walking directly on snow, an old folding table for doing dishes, and a small wood stove to keep the space warm. There was even a string of Christmas lights on the exterior he'd hook to the truck battery for the holidays or when people would visit. The whole scene would have been reality t.v. gold, "Life Off The Grid". Or in the case of my reality, my father's new tent home in the woods.

It was spring and still very much winter in Canada. There were piles of snow on the ground, the nearby river was frozen and temperatures dipped below -20oC when the sun went down. Most of this wild mountain man living all seemed pretty standard at the time, but if there was one activity that I'll never forget, one activity that outlined my ability to handle any amount of brash living or lack of comfort in life; it was the shower.

Showering in temperatures that never rose above freezing took willpower and cunning innovation. To shower, first my father had shoveled most of the horse shit out of the back of the two-horse trailer that was parked near the tent. Next, he had taken plastic sheets and lined the windows of the horse trailer to keep the wind out. Then, my old man would melt snow over the wood stove and heat it before pouring it into a 20-liter plastic jug with a hose on the end attached to a nozzle with holes in it. The water jug with the hose was then hung inside the horse trailer at a level that made it just awkward enough to duck my head under to shower. Next, I'd strip down to nothing but underwear and a towel, then dash across the snow into the lightly shit-scented trailer that was hovering somewhere between -10oC and -20oC. Finally, I needed to purge the last strip of my clothing and open the water spout to be hit with the steaming hot water.

At first, I would go from a light shiver to a gasping hit of contrastingly hot water fresh from the stove. This would then transition into a nice warm feeling as my skin adjusted to the hot water rushing over me. Then, of course, as sections of my freshly dampened skin were exposed to the cold I would instantly freeze on those points and need to cover them with hot water again. And so the cycle would repeat as I tried to rub soap all over my body while watching the water continually deplete from the jug knowing that when it was empty, it was empty. I best be washed and ready to bolt back to the tent before the ticking clock that was my limited resources ran dry.

At the time I never thought much about it. I needed a shower and this was how we showered. We rode horses through the snow, cooked over the fire inside the tent, and played cribbage to the light of a lantern. I'm not sure if this is how any other kid spent their spring holidays. My mother was probably cringing as I told her about the days in the bush while she smiled and said "ohh, how fun".

This would kick-start a 6-year time period where my Dad first lived in this equestrian campground on the edge of a national park, then ended up working for a guiding and outfitting company taking tourists on horseback trips and hunters into the wilds of the remote Albertan wilderness. For the next few summers, I would head to this guide and outfitting camp and help my father to take tourists into the rocky mountains on horseback. On occasion, I'd catch a ride with this or that person from my town an hour or more to as close as I could get to his camp then hitchhike the rest of the way. I don't think I ever told my parents the hitchhiking part, I don't think they ever asked. Eventually, I'd turn 16, get a driver's license, a truck, find out what girls were, and you'd never see me in this part of the world again.

As moments of this PanAmerican trip unravel and I'm now riding a steel horse across the wilds of the world, showering under waterfalls in Bolivia, pitching my tent in cornfields in Peru, cooking fish over driftwood on the beaches of Mexico, and rarely thinking twice about what I'm sure was the most questionable of questionable accommodation at times. I'd pictured this moment. A 12-year old boy, living in a tent in the snow and showering in freezing temperatures inside an shit-scented old horse trailer. I don't think a person could magically wake up in their 30's and be excited about this life if you hadn't already lived versions of it.

Costa Rica
Assault Weapons & Soup Pots

"A well regulated Militia, being necessary to the security of a free State, the right of the people to keep and bear Arms, shall not be infringed."
- United States Of America Second Amendment. Adopted in 1791 & still shaping a country's beliefs over 200 years later.

In Costa Rica, I'd come across Philippe and Art. Philippe was a Swiss rider who had left on his DR650 and ridden it from Switzerland across part of Europe, shipped into Toronto then journeyed south. His companion at the time was Art, a Belarus-born man who'd grown up in the USA and was riding a KLR650 just like mine, only in red.

I'd stopped at a grocery store and on the way out of the shop I came across this pair of ramshackle bikers that looked just like me. Considering I'd ridden this far, I hadn't met a single long-term biker headed in my direction. I seemed to keep running into families from France drinking wine and eating butter-rich dinners. Compared to camping in the bush and drinking beer with the bikers I wasn't exactly disappointed meeting the well-fed families. To finally see my own kind, I was kind of excited. At last, people who understood me and my dirty-biker ways.

I had a brief chat with the two bikers and said I would wait in the parking lot for them. Considering I'd gone to bed a few nights earlier with a 6-foot boa constrictor lurking under my bike, sleeping next to these guys seemed pretty harmless. When they returned, our scruffy trio headed to the outskirts of town where we all spent the night camped on a hillside overlooking the lush jungles of Costa Rica. At home, you would never meet someone in a parking lot and then go and spend the night with them. On the road, I always feel like my guard is down and I'm 100% more open with people.

In the morning the three of us started to compare motorcycle kit. The conversation started when I spotted this little box attached to Philippe's DR650 tyre spokes. It looked like it would make riding difficult so I walked over and flicked it to see what it was. I jumped when a siren came to life, alerting Philippe I'd touched his bike. It was a little spoke alarm meant to deter thieves. If your motorcycle moved this loud alarm would come to life. I'd never used a motorcycle alarm before and thought they were only for fancy Harleys or expensive bikes that never got dirty. A far cry from my beat-up old dual sport whose value was strictly gauged by rider affection.

Philippe showed me some of his other gear and explained that his bike had no name. He didn't have a name for his bike as he didn't want to get too attached to a piece of metal that he might have to ditch one day. I wasn't too worried about naming mine KLaiR, as I had a pretty good track record of not getting attached to anything. Philippe also had a handy chain oiler that would extend the life of the chain. I didn't have one of these oilers nor had I ever used one. He then showed off his soft luggage that closed with simple leather straps that he said had never been broken into. These seemed more user-friendly than the large pelican cases with two locks on each that I had. Philippe then pulled out various electronics and camera gear that looked like they were worth more than his bike. In the future, whenever I saw Philippe's hands not attached to his handlebars, they were attached to his camera. Maybe under this scrappy bike exterior, there was considerably more value than a shimmering Harley. Overall I felt like he had a pretty standard setup based on what I'd seen other adventure riders using and a tad more trust in people than I had.

Mid-conversation Art came over to explain his setup on the red KLR650. Now Art's setup was a little different. He had added a few extra features that had never crossed my mind either. The first was a secret kill switch he had installed in the event someone tried to steal his entire bike while he was on it, he could quickly immobilize it with the flick of a switch. I thought this was clever but even after seeing it, I wasn't sure I would need it.

Art then reached down along the frame of the bike to a long black thing a bit skinnier than the metal tube that makes up the frame of the bike. In one fluid motion, Art pulled out this short stick and gave it a quick whip away from him. To my surprise, the stick became a long black baton about 3-feet long. What in the fuck, what you would need a baton for? Art explained that in the event he had any problems with people giving him trouble, he could quickly whip out the baton and beat away the attackers.

I wasn't sure what to show these guys now. I'd never considered an alarm or a baton. I had no safety gear at all. One of the most impractical items I was carrying was a large 3-quart non-stick cooking pot with a glass lid. It took up ⅓ of one luggage box and probably weighed 5-pounds or more. I could have purchased a foldable one quart camping pot that would have weighed under a pound. When I was packing though, I was thinking about how I was going to cook dinner for groups of new friends with only a small pot to work with!

What a different way to prepare for a trip. I had the hair trimmer for grooming and this over-sized pot. I was thinking of meeting strangers and making them soup and Art was thinking how he'd beat away attackers. Maybe I was underprepared for part of this adventure and over-prepared for another element of it. Maybe it was because he grew up in war-torn Belarus and a country where everyone thought they deserved to carry a handgun and I grew up in a small town where firemen rescuing cats from trees was more likely to make the front page of the news.

The next day the three of us would end up in the warm welcoming waters of some of Costa Rica's most beautiful natural hot springs. These hot springs run just downstream from the Tabacon Resort Spa and a number of other fancy hotels that line the edge of the water, selling premium rooms with stunning scenery. The free hot springs attract budget travelers, backpackers, and, well, dirty bikers like us. The problem is that the fancy hotels don't want you parking in their premium space near the hotel and frightening off timid vacationers so they employ security to keep drivers from parking in their lots. On a motorbike, we had a small advantage in that we could sneak into small spaces and park. The boys had parked up the hill a bit, on a shoulder of the road along with some cars from the hotel. I had found a little spot near the end of the street closer to the hot springs. To park here I needed to park inside the yellow line on the asphalt or face some sort of parking penalty. This was a far cry from virtually no road rules from Mexico to Nicaragua.

I rolled up and parked my bike just on the edge of the yellow line, by just on the edge I mean my front tyre was just touching the yellow line. For the security guard who was paid to keep people like me from parking anywhere nearby, he wasn't going to let this black rubber tyre kissing the yellow line count as parking inside the line. After him telling me to leave I decided to make a compromise. I'd slide the front wheel back just a hair and off the yellow line and he could let me stay. Now, KLaiR was officially inside the allowable parking area behind the yellow line. I was feeling quite proud of how I'd navigated my bike between the ditch, the other cars, and the yellow line. I thought we were getting somewhere, Mr. Security didn't agree.

Now in his defense, he probably spends his whole day arguing with cheap ass travelers about parking and if for any reason a tour bus or taxi can't access the parking lot he probably loses his job. In my defense I was in fact following the rules of parking, no matter how closely I was treading between following and breaking those rules.

At this point, things were still pretty relaxed and I was trying to negotiate with Mr. Security to let me leave the bike here. Just then Art showed up to step in and began to argue with the guy about where we could and could not park in English. Between the sudden attack on Mr. Security, his lack of English, our lack of understanding Spanish, and a three vs one scenario, things instantly got out of hand.

I was quickly pushed out of the conversation when Art decided to take over for me. Suddenly Art and Mr. Security began yelling at each other. Whatever way this was headed I didn't want myself or KLaiR to be the center of attention. After a few minutes of arguing and Art out-yelling Mr. Security, we finally left KLaiR parked where she was while the three of us went to visit the hot springs. The departing words from Mr. Security were that he was calling *La Policia*.

My whole life was on that bike and for the first time, I had now considered that maybe I should have some type of security system to protect the bike and my goods. Our time at the hot springs didn't last long as I was worried about KLaiR and all of my possessions. Here we were in the safest country in Central America, surrounded by tourists and security and I was now concerned about my bike and belongings.

Within 20-minutes I called it quits at the hot springs and returned to KLaiR. Sure enough, the Police were there talking to Mr. Security. The cops rolled their eyes and asked me to move the bike before driving away. I was getting a sense of why I was packing a soup pot and Art was packing a baton. But what did I know, I didn't grow up in Belarus or the USA. Maybe this dude spent his whole life defending his shit with a baton, whereas I'd spent most of mine making people dinner.

(Soaking in the hot springs with Philippe)

(Greeted in the night by a 6ft Boa Constrictor)

Story Break
Why You Can't Escape Yourself

"The world is what you make it. Make it work or make it up, but don't make it out to be the world you fear."

- Kix Marshall

As the trip rolled on, I met plenty of people who'd left various lives behind to pursue freedom on the open road. I began to observe them and their actions to try and form my own idea of who they used to be in the life they'd left behind. I'd met the family from small-town New Brunswick in eastern Canada who were driving to Panama and back in an RV with their two young kids. They were the type of family you'd see in an RV commercial. Everyone is smiling ear to ear, clean-cut, wearing new beach attire, and enjoying a wholesome adventure together. The parents were French and could speak impeccable English. I'd often hang out with them and the other French families and while the conversation was going on around me, the parents Mathieu or Rachel would translate the entire conversation for me in real time. I was pretty sure they were the textbook family at home too. They showed me how their local newspaper was following their journey for the whole town to enjoy. #wholesome

As my friends in the travel community began to outnumber my friends in real life, I started to notice how people evolved online in reflection to who they likely were at home. One biker started a travel forum separate from the usual travel forums that I was part of. This new group was strictly for bikers. Later this same guy started a group for people who needed auto and motorbike parts "muled" from different locations around the world. Here travelers would volunteer to bring items for other travelers as they made their way across the planet. It was an incredible connection of people helping people and I ended up using the service when a man from the USA brought KLaiR some discounted parts from America into highly taxed Argentina. Later I learned this guy had started and run companies in South Africa where he was from. No matter where this guy was, he was an entrepreneur looking to solve problems.

There were also the people who fed off the drama and I knew that if they were now bringing this drama to these online groups, it surely was nothing new for them. Here is one such, online post copied exactly as it was written/spelled to a forum of over 20,000 travelers who share information on how to help each other:

"So in the last two days my financial situation has gone from good to horrible. People post about loosing a phone or wallet or papers, all are horrible. However I am in the midst of what I thinking is identity theft while I am I'm Colombia. Never an easy thing to deal with. I DO have insurance in Canada to help me in this situations. However, even the simple task of calling CC companies back home is proving to be s monumental task

My CC companies where able to respond online but only to advise me I needed to call from a vaiblable phone number. The people who sell minutes on the road do not work

On top of that I have not been able to call out of country. It is super complicated when using a phone

I finally surrendered too buying Skype minutes. My CC do nit work so I went to Pay Pal. Guess what folks. The account is frozen.

I've been doing a lot of research online and I'm not alone. In fact very few people think of a simple call back home to someone not on their friends list

It is a real big world wide issue. It can be a nightmare

As I research it more there is more I c could have done to assure contact with companies in case of issues.

Just posting so people can research about making a " simple" call

I'm at a point where I may need to ride 8 hours to my embassy for help.

Fortunately I have a small amount of USD that I can exchange while I hope for issues to work out"

This post is ridiculous, the man doesn't ask for help or make any real point. He simply notes how horrendous his personal situation is to the eyes of 20,000ppl and how it's a "worldwide issue". Well unless you count the "just posting... simple call", qualifier that he adds at the end.

So what, everyone has problems, it's awful this is your current state, but ask for help or solve your problem. Why post your problems to drown others in your pool of drama?

At another point further south when Angie had joined me for Christmas we were in the city of Valparaiso Chile for New Years'. This city had a Guinness Book Of World Records fireworks display and we wanted to see what all the hype was about.

Before we arrived I found a couple of mentions online that certain parts of the city were known for tyre slashing. Here, thieves would slash your tyre at a traffic light then follow you until you notice the problem. Once you stop to investigate the flat tyre, the thieves will rob you. We had to ride through these sections of the city and I noted to Angie to watch for anyone and everyone that might be crossing the street when traffic slowed. I also positioned myself at the lights so I could more easily turn or drive over a curb if I had to make a run for it.

The two of us didn't encounter any issues during the day, but when we came back at night for the fireworks, this area had a completely different vibe from its relaxed daytime atmosphere. What were originally open business doors inviting in clients during the day, were now steel doors covering the business from top to bottom and covered in graffiti. Shoppers had been replaced by questionable looking people lurking the streets, and the whole vibe felt unwelcoming at best. At this hour we just rolled through stop signs and red lights as I felt it was better than stopping. Who cares, if the police pull us over, all the better.

A week later I read in our online travel forum of some travelers who were CAMPING IN THEIR RV in those same areas I wouldn't even stop at. One night, camped in a parking lot, they were sleeping in the RV while someone was trying to break into it. They said that they woke up and fought the intruder out of the RV. Congratulations, you were able to counter-attack a potentially dangerous situation. I was sympathizing with them a little, but then they did probably the dumbest thing I'd ever read.

Instead of moving, they continued to camp in the parking lot and never moved the RV! Later that night someone else broke into their vehicle! How they were sleeping at this point I have no idea. This intruder stole items right out of their RV with them in it! Maybe they were drunk, maybe they were highly medicated, maybe they were the dumbest fucking people on the planet, I have no idea, but my sympathy ended here.

They had posted on the exact same travel forums about being robbed that I had found the information about tyre slashing! This is what I felt like they were really saying; *Dear travelers, we are too fucking stupid to read further down the page about the information on this city and somehow missed all the signs that camping in a parking lot in a big city in what has a glaring graffiti and homeless problem. Instead of camping in the campground 15-minutes up the road or a hotel, we are going to put a neon-sign on our roof illuminated with the words "Rob Our Dumb Asses".*

Three months later I saw another post from them. They had been robbed again! At this point, these people were considering ending their multi-country road trip and were reaching out to the travel community for help. They were telling the online community and posting in these travel forums about how awful and how dangerous Chile was. From here they would obviously go home and tell everyone their dramatic stories and "spread the word." The worst part was they had the evidence to back it up and there was no one to defend the other side of the coin.

What these people failed to mention is the complete lack of respect they paid to areas that are known as no-go zones and that they had failed to research or pick up on any signs of their surroundings. Who in the fuck parks their RV in a bad part of a city, has it broken into, and then goes back to sleep? I was trying to balance my reply to their post between full-on telling them how stupid they were and just telling them how positive my experience was. These are the people that ruin a country's image for the entire world.

Later down the dusty trail, I was camping in March in El Calafate Argentina to go and see the Perito Moreno Glacier. This incredible piece of frozen beauty crumbles in gigantic echoing chunks of ice into the waters below. The scene is breathtaking and unbelievably magical.

I was in this shitty little campground where they had several camping spots divided by a few trees. It was located at the end of a short road lined with houses on both sides. Every house seemed to have a dog, as most do in the Americas, and most of these dogs roamed free. On the way in, about eight of these dogs came running towards the bike. The bike sounds like a loud growling dog and usually attracts barking attention. Ok, no big deal, I just slowly drive past them while they bark at what is the growling dog inside my engine.

Later that night a cute little Dutch couple camping here wants to walk to town for dinner. They get to the campground exit knowing they will be met by these dogs. The couple is acting very frightened and when the dogs come they back away from the dogs and eventually run back to the camping spot, packing up all of their shit, closing their rooftop tent, and driving the 2-minutes to town. I'm like WTF?

I went to leave 25-minutes later. I don't want to get attacked by dogs either, but I'd rather walk to town than drive for 2-minutes. I walk up to the dogs, they all start barking aggressively and growling so I start to walk faster right towards them. The loudest one tries to sneak behind me so I turn around and walk towards him aggressively. He backs off and slowly the rest do and just like that, I walk right by. Sure it could have gone horribly wrong, but it didn't and it probably won't next time. I'm not the fucking dog whisperer, I was actually bit once in Colombia. But I think if you look at a situation and try to plan the outcome rather than look for the problem it will likely work out better.

Later I saw that these people wrote a review about the campground and noted that if you stay here you need to risk getting attacked by a pack of dogs. Thanks for ruining the reputation of their business because you are a dumb ass.

The world is what you make it, so make it work or make it up, but don't make it out to be the world you fear.

Panama
From Police Detention To Police Escort

McDonald's, Burger King, Subway, Kentucky Fried Chicken, Popeye's Chicken, Carl's Jr., Taco Bell, Dominos, Wingstop, Little Caesars, Pizza Hut, Nathan's Hotdogs, Dunkin' Donuts, Starbucks, Smashburger, Coffee Bean & Tea Leaf, Dairy Queen.
- List of American fast food franchises in Panama

Panama wasn't exactly on my list of must-see places along the road. I knew of Panama's ties to American history and how the US had completed the Panama Canal, but that was about the extent of my knowledge. The more I read about Panama the more it sounded very Americanized. Now that I had ridden through the calamity of El Salvador and Nicaragua followed up by the natural beauty of Costa Rica, skyscrapers and KFC weren't really discoveries I was hoping to make. Nonetheless, I would be passing through.

Like every other border crossing, I'd done a reasonable amount of reading up online before crossing so I knew what to expect, the approximate fees, and what to avoid doing so I wouldn't have problems with the local customs. From Costa Rica into Panama, it all sounded pretty straightforward. I set the GPS to take me from my camp spot to the border post and set off.

Now you would think with a GPS, Google Maps, maps.me, and various signs posted on roadways that getting lost wouldn't happen all that often. Somehow despite all of this, I seemed to get lost nearly every day. Sometimes I'd take a wrong turn here and there, sometimes I'd miss a landmark, and sometimes I'd miss entire towns. I took a little comfort when I met a man from Bulgaria traveling from the US to Argentina with his wife and two young girls in a 1-ton Ford with a camper on the back and I asked him what he used for directions to travel with?

The guy looked at me like it was my first day on the road and explained that he had a GPS, used Google Maps, had downloaded Maps.Me and occasionally found some use with the local road signs. So I asked him, "Do you ever get lost?" Again he looked at me like it was my first day on the road and said; "Yeah, every single day!"

I spent the previous night camped on the beach in Pavones, Costa Rica next to what is meant to be the "world's longest warm water left breaking wave", you can ride it for over a mile! It's a bit tricky to get there and despite its reputation, the extreme southern location keeps away the heavy tourism felt elsewhere in Costa Rica. All the hype of this world wonder may have been lost on me & my non-surfing, landlubbing lifestyle. All I noticed was the hippy tent colony that was taking up prime real estate on the beach and the salty ocean waves out front.

Instead of sleeping in the colony of long beards and hula hoops that seemed a little under-thrilled with my helmet and boots attire, I opted to stay a little more out of town and ran into some chatty Brazilians on a rushed drive up to Alaska for the summer. I love meeting up with people who are on multi-continent summer road trips.

In the morning I had my usual oatmeal and nuts, then organized some snacks and drinks. Border crossings can be a little demanding on one's time and stress levels, so it's best to be prepared with food and drink for the day. Just crossing into Costa Rica I'd bumped into a lady from Las Vegas, whose busty physique suggested she may have been in the entertainment world in Vegas. Her van was covered in dust and looked like it had been there awhile. She said her paperwork for her child was not clear enough to enter into Costa Rica and she had already stamped out of Nicaragua so she could not return. This was day 3 of her new life at the border, trapped in no man's land. It's often good to be prepared.

Once I finally set off in the morning I opted to take the scenic route. This was my preferred route, usually winding through small towns using the less-traveled gravel roads that took me through the real heart of a country. As usual, the GPS and I were fighting over routing options. The GPS usually suggested the main routes that I wanted to avoid. I decided she could win the turn through the farming community, however, once we got through I wasn't going to backtrack and take the highway as she suggested, but turn back onto the gravel to ride through the towns.

In the end, I took several side streets through the little town of Canoas Abajo and eventually came out of an alley near the main highway. It appeared like I had passed everything and was nearly at the border. It all seemed a little faster than I thought, but if this was the last bit of highway before the border then great. I cut across the grass from the alley through a little ditch to the highway and headed towards Panama. Well shit, if that little five-foot grass shortcut didn't put me on the fast track to illegal immigration.

Some fifteen or twenty kilometers later, making great time I might add, I was flagged down at a random military checkpoint. Upon request, I handed over all documents I had related to Costa Rica, but the military guard kept asking for more. Unable to produce any more paperwork they asked where I was headed? Panama I said. They asked where I was? Then I asked where I was??

It was here I realized they had "Panama" stitched on these cute camouflage jumpsuits they were wearing and my broken Spanish, charming smile and elaborate hand gestures suddenly jumped into action to explain on my two inch phone map what had happened.

The man told me to wait a minute, then came back with a female officer. Despite her being about half my size I got the impression she could easily kick my ass. She asked me a series of questions while I tried to explain that I had missed the border. This was all in my shitty Spanish and I wasn't really getting my point across.

Unlike the ragged police in places like Nicaragua, the Military Police in Panama look more like badass Navy Seals that you might see in America. Not to be fucked with!

My crap Spanish followed with over-enthusiasm usually worked for getting drinks after the bar closed or asking adorable locals to teach me some funny Spanish words. These tricks were not so effective with the military police.

The bike was parked and I was asked to step away from it. The problem was the ground was flat here and KLaiR was so heavy that she could only be parked on a downhill slope. On the flat ground, she would sink too low to put the kickstand down properly and fall over. Now I was looking more and more suspicious while I was trying to explain why I could not get off the bike. Finally, they said I could push her someplace to park, but not start her.

Once I found enough of a slope to park, they said to wait while they called the boss. Now no one was smiling in my direction. It looks like I'll need to work on my "I'm a dumb tourist" cuteness a little…

The lady came back and her questions shifted from where I was going to if I had any drugs, how much drugs I had, when was the last time I used drugs, and if I'd ever had any problems with the police before? Shit! The last place I wanted to be was in a Panamanian prison!

They wanted to search my luggage. Sure, no problem. I knew I had a knife in there for cooking, but otherwise, I was riding clean. I opened the rear box on KLaiR and she looked surprised at all the shit I had. The first question was about my tent, luckily I knew the word for this and explained it was a "Carpa para camping." Next, she searched through my toothbrush and some food, then pulled out my electric hair trimmer. I started to giggle.

This was not the time to be giggling, but I could hear Andrew ringing in my ears about why in the hell of all the things I'd be packing on a trip across the planet I'd bring a fucking electric hair trimmer!

I made the motions of shaving my face, smiled and she placed the hair trimmer back in the bike.

Shortly the boss rolled up with a couple of his crony sidekicks in a little yellow and white immigration truck with his air conditioning on high, hair freshly combed, wearing an out-of-place white collared shirt with a few too many buttons undone. He looked more like a military accountant than a guy who uses a machete to shave like I was expecting. To my delight, he's all smiles and shakes my hand while I attempt to explain the problem again in Spanish. He doesn't care or more likely doesn't understand and asks if the other officer can search my stuff again.

She pretended to look around some more, but found no drugs or guns and this illegal crossing quickly turned into a personal escort back to the border. Following the little yellow and white truck, we made our way right through all the traffic and to the front of the line. I got a few strange looks from the Costa Rica officials about why the hell I'm doing everything backward, but they rushed me through customs with the help of my escort from the boss and suddenly I'm legally out of Costa and back into Panama in record time.

I have no idea where these occasional horseshoes that randomly fall out of my ass come from, but I try not to ask.

Goodbye Costa Rica, Hello Panama!

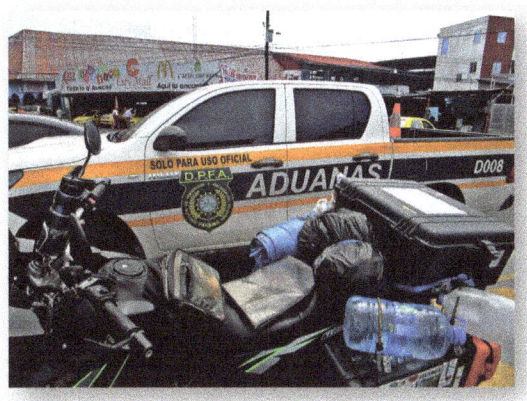

(My escort back to Costa Rica)

Panama
The Dump Truck Of Death

"In 1928 Richard Halliburton swam the length of the Panama Canal, paying a toll of $0.36. The lowest ever recorded."
- *The most exciting thing I learned by visiting the Panama canal.*

Crossing into Colombia was going to be the biggest logistical challenge of my entire journey. The road runs between 40-50,000kms from Alaska to Argentina depending on the route you ride. The only break in the road lies between Panama and Colombia. This section of cartel-controlled swampy jungle, dense forest, and mountainous terrain about 100-kilometers long is known as *The Darian Gap*. It's here that Colombia's Chocó Department and Panama's Darién Province meet in an untamable section of the PanAm.

The Darian Gap is shrouded in folklore. The most practical reasons this section isn't paved are that governments on both sides of the continents don't want an easily accessible route to move cocaine from South America into North America. As a result, narco groups control most of what would otherwise be an uninhabited jungle and have etched out various routes to smuggle people and drugs from one side of the world to the other.

Not entirely impassable, various people have passed through the gap. I met a German guy in Mexico whose friends were egging him on to tell me the story about how he crossed "The Gap" with a backpack back in the 70's. I got the impression that he'd told this story after several pints of beer in the back of many a seedy bar across the planet. On that sunny Mexican day at an old mission in the Baja, all he said was that it was possible, but things had certainly changed in 40+ years.

A few months after I'd passed into Colombia a group of X-U.S. Marines had plotted a trip through The Gap with none other than KLR motorcycles on route from Alaska to Argentina. The expedition was dubbed *"Where The Road Ends"*, and later became a 1-hour documentary.

As I had no formal military training, no team, no sponsorship, and was quite frankly scared shitless to attempt the crossing alone. There were a few more practical options open to me.

- **Option 1:** Strap KLaiR to a wooden crate and fly her from Panama City to Bogota for around $1000 USD. DHL could handle this service.

- **Option 2:** Take one of a few various sea vessels that sailed through the San Blas Islands enjoying a 5-day excursion while snorkeling and sleeping on a sailing ship. The most popular and reputable being the Stahratte, a 110-year old schooner manned by an eccentric German. Around $1200 USD.

- **Option 3**: Find a few other travelers who were willing to share a sea can and float the lot across the ocean to Colombia. In this scenario, we'd cram two SUV's in the front and KLaiR in the back of the can. Then I'd hop on a plane and meet KLaiR in Cartagena 10-days later. Cost $450 for KLaiR, $100 for the flight. This was the cheapest, yet least exciting option, but with my $12/day budget, this is what we went with.

To share the sea can, I'd teamed up with a pair of young guys from Germany in an old Land Rover and a couple from Australia and Europe in a smaller SUV. We split the cost of the shipment 3-ways. Next, I just needed to arrange a flight from Panama City and into Cartagena.

I had met back up with the Swiss rider Philippe in Panama City as he was preparing to ship his bike via the San Blas Islands around the same time as me and shared a room with him. Though I had been instructed to camp close to the shipping port roughly an hour from the city, I chose to stay in the city so I could have all my stuff packed rather than trying to pack it up in the morning after a night of camping. In my mind this seemed like the faster option. I'd just wake up an hour earlier and ride to the shipping port.

I was given specific instructions about what road to take out of the city and that all three of us that were sharing the container needed to arrive at the port by 9 am or we would risk, literally, missing the boat. If we weren't on time we would lose our money and shipping opportunity.

That morning, right from the start, everything started going sideways. Even though I'd left the hotel early, I'd instantly ended up on the wrong road. I was on a toll road and met the unmanned toll gates that required a prepaid swipe card to pass through. I was trapped at the toll gate with cement barriers on both sides while traffic piled up behind me waiting to swipe and go. After what felt like an eternity of me pushing the little red help button on the toll gate someone finally answered in scratchy Spanish and I couldn't understand a thing they said. It felt like I'd showed up at the gates of heaven hoping to bluff my way in while hundreds of God-loving Christians lined up watching me smolder before bursting into flames.

One by one, I had to get the cars behind me to each back up so I could turn KLaiR around and ride the wrong way out of the toll lane to find another route. I'd just made all these people late for work and wouldn't be leaving Panama making any new friends.

Eventually, I found a route that turned off this road and instantly took it. I was hoping my GPS would sort out the new route and get us to the meeting point without issue. Again, this didn't go exactly as I'd imagined it. Instead of the two-lane super speedy toll road I was meant to be on, I was now on a single-lane free road with a mix of clunky old transport trucks and dilapidated cars moving like three-legged turtles where the hare found an occasional opportunity to pass.

At this point it hit me with a depleting thud. I knew I was going to be late and couldn't find a way off of this secondary road and back to the main roadway. I was now beginning to drive like the Mexicans and began passing people with any opportunity I could find. I started riding the asses of other cars like a porn star working on the money shot. If they didn't speed up, I'd look for any opportunity to pass. I was the porn star, the other car was the ass and KLaiR was the condom. If anything went wrong that might break the condom, I'd be dead.

After a series of risky passing maneuvers, I eventually found myself behind a big, road-blocking dump truck that choked along like it was his last ride to the dump. The truck looked like it had been rusting by the sea for the last 30-years. The tires were as smooth as the pavement and the lights were rattling out from the rusty-holes in which they came. I was looking to pass him before I'd miss the boat and piss everyone off.

Oncoming traffic was relentless so I opted to try out a move I'd learned in Guatemala. In Guatemala and other Central American countries most of the little bikes rode on the shoulder as they were often slower, yet more nimble. Here they could either be passed by faster traffic or pass on the shoulder when traffic got too slow. As long as no one from the road moved onto the shoulder, then everything went fine.

Dumpy the dump truck was now getting slower and slower and I decided to forget everything I'd ever learned about safe driving in North America and go for the Guatemalan shoulder-pass. As Dumpy slowed even more, I couldn't see around him, so I moved into the shoulder to make my move. At this point, we were both barely going 30km/h and I figured this would be an easy maneuver. Now in that little 3-foot shoulder-space between the main lane and the ditch I gave KLaiR some gas and went for the pass. Just then the truck braked and made a right turn onto a side road. Ohh Fuck, it's over!

I hit the brakes, nailed the side of the dump truck, and laid down KLaiR like a coffin. She skidded down the shoulder just as the dump truck driver slammed on the air brakes. The rumbling truck stopped in an instant. If nothing else worked on this truck, I was glad the brakes were still operational.

KLaiR had fallen just behind his dual-set of rear tyres where the bike-crushing rubber was just kissing her frame. I couldn't believe it. KLaiR was just inches from becoming a heap of twisted metal and spending her remaining days oxidizing to a rusty demise in a Panamanian scrap yard.

I stood up and went over to check on KLaiR. The man from the truck came running out and instead of being mad he was quite concerned about me and asked how I was. He said it was impossible for him to see me. Luckily this was all unfolding right next to a bus stop and now I had a crowd of onlookers watching the scene of a lawless foreigner and hardworking local unfold.

The one bit of defense I had on my side was that this man had no working signal lights or tail lights. This would have meant something in North America, however, I knew this was nothing unusual for the locals and I would be owning all the blame for this scenario. I took it all right on the chin and apologized to the man for trying to pass on the inside. Occasionally I know when to just eat shit and move on.

The driver came back and helped me pick up KLaiR. The only thing that had happened to her aside from some new scratches was that I'd lost my water bottle and the GPS that had both been mounted to the handlebars. This would officially mark my first ever motorcycle accident. Luckily, I was wearing full riding gear to help cut down on what needed to be packed for shipping as opposed to the shorts and flip-flops I wore riding through most of Central America. The driver told me to be careful, wished me luck, and we both set off on our way.

Having just had a near-death experience I was a touch rattled. I knew I was going to be late, I knew I was going to lose my money for the transport, and I knew that there was going to be a small group of people really pissed off at me. Since I had no local phone plan for Panama I couldn't even send a message to explain what was going on or why I was going to be late.

At that moment I decided that my life was not worth the rush and even if it all went wrong I'd at least show up alive rather than not at all. From here I settled into the same pace as the locals and never attempted to pass another car. Eventually, I'd arrive at the meeting point at precisely 9:07 am. The entire group was elated. Their engines fired up when they saw me. I yelled out to the group. *"I know you don't care, but I got in an accident with a large dump truck and almost died, but I made it."* They all smiled like I was talking a bunch of shit for sleeping in and we took off to the shipping dock.

Goodbye Panama, thank you for not killing me!

(Loading KLaiR backwards into the sea can) (Our crew for the shared container)

(A Panama City photo shoot with Philippe Berini. *Photo credit Moto Phil)

Colombia
HaMerotz LaMillion

During the height of its operations, the Medellin Cartel brought in more than US$70 million per day (roughly $26 billion in a year). Smuggling 15 tons of cocaine per day, worth more than half a billion dollars, into the United States, the cartel spent over US$1,000 per week purchasing rubber bands to wrap the stacks of cash, storing most of it in their warehouses.
- Wikipedia

But that was then, this is now...

Landing in Cartagena is like being dropped off at a wedding at 2 am. Instantly you are the guest of honor and everyone needs to drink and dance with you.

Walking the streets, music floods out from behind colorfully painted wooden doors that line the centuries-old rocky roads. A left turn takes you down a narrow road crowded with Cumbia dancers in peacock-inspired attire all for the delight of tourists. A right turn takes you past small variety shops where raspy music plays over worn-out speakers. Out front are rickety tables where middle-aged men drink cold Aguila beer and watch elderly couples slowly salsa dancing next to inquisitive children trying to replicate their grandparents' steps. There's a buzz about everyone; they all seem wildly happy and genuinely excited to see you and all the other tourists that stroll through the streets.

There are women selling souvenirs, children selling cold drinks, and men selling discount trinkets on little platters. At first, this seems harmless, then as you get in a little closer, the men quickly shift from housewares to party favors and follow you for a few steps offering pure Colombian cocaine. The contrasting sales technique is a bit off-putting, but without demand from tourists, there would be no supply. This is the last time I'm offered cocaine on the streets in Colombia during the following months I spent there.

The city is a mix of old fortified castle walls and centuries-old buildings along with modern office buildings and condominiums. It's easy to sip the ice-cold beer in the stifling heat, mesmerized by the music and dancing while letting your thoughts slip away to a life here decades ago. It's a magical feeling of blissful escape.

I'd been in Cartagena for about two days, and while wandering the streets, today felt a bit different around town than the first day. There were some small swimming pools set up near the walled city. I saw a bunch of random people with large video cameras standing suspiciously about the streets. Groups of people seemed to be hanging around in random places for no apparent reason. These people didn't look like the locals, or like tourists. It felt more like the president was at the beach today and large men in black suits with sunglasses were trying to blend in on the sand behind him. Something wasn't quite right.

At this moment I'm walking down the side of a busy street and a couple starts to yell at me in English. They had been yelling at a few people who walked right past them, like you would if random people started yelling at you in a foreign language. It's always best to avoid the crazies.

This moment was one of a handful of times speaking English paid off for me more than fumbling my way through Spanish. The yelling couple asked me in English if I could help them? I had no reference of what they needed, but being the stand-up guy that I am or maybe because I had nothing else going on today, I said yes!

I crossed the road, met the couple, and asked what they needed. They were both in their thirties, quite attractive, wearing backpacks and athletic gear and frantically trying to explain to me what they needed.

They explained that to help, I just needed to use the phone of this lady who was set up on the street to call anyone in Colombia and have a one-minute conversation.

I hadn't even noticed this row of people at what looked like stands that sold phone minutes all standing by with phones on the table. You can buy phone minutes almost anywhere, but they usually don't supply a test phone along with it. This seemed a bit odd. Either way, I said no problem and that I was happy to do it.

Then it dawned on me, who am I going to call, and why am I doing this?

Not one for details, I now noticed a guy with a huge camera over his shoulder filming us, then another couple not far from us also flagging down people, then I noticed the Amazing Race trademark yellow and black clue in their hand. I laughed and said "What, you are on the Amazing Race?"

The guy said yes, and I instantly launched into a rant about how many times I had applied to be on The Amazing Race and how it had been a dream of mine, and how I'd shot three video applications to be on the show. Naturally, they didn't care about my sob story, they had been picked, I had not, they just needed someone to start dialing and it looked like I might know how to use a phone.

I thought I'd just ring my hostel as they could speak Spanish and English. Unfortunately, I didn't seem to have a receipt or a copy of anything from the hostel that might have their phone number on it. I tried to look up the number on my phone. Ironically I was standing in front of several booths selling phone minutes and I hadn't yet bought Colombian phone minutes or data. Now we had a problem. I scanned my phone for Colombia contacts we could call. I hadn't made any Colombian friends yet and didn't know anyone. Shit, was I going to fail at my only Amazing Race challenge? The clock was ticking and the camera was in my face wondering what my next move was going to be. As time ticked by, the couple were getting anxious for me to help them complete this task so they could move on.

After what seemed like an embarrassing lifetime, we flagged down a local on the streets and asked him if we could have the phone number of one of his friends and just call them to talk. Could you imagine if a tourist stopped you on the street and frantically asked for the phone number of one of your friends so they could call them? It likely would not go over well. Yet, in typical, friendly Colombian fashion he gives us his girlfriend's phone number. I pick up the phone on the table and call her. My Spanish is extremely basic and I proceed to recite the most basic and random questions all plucked from conversations I've had in Spanish leading up to this.

Me (In Spanish)
- "Hello, I'm Kix."
- "Do you have a boyfriend?"
- "Is your boyfriend's name Juan?"
- "I know Juan, he is very handsome."
- "Does he have a motorcycle?"
- "How many cylinders is his motorcycle?"
- "How old is Juan?"
- "How old are you?"
- "Do you live in Cartagena?"
- "Do you like beer?"
- "I like beer."

I'm split between nervously fucking up my questions and bursting out laughing from how ridiculously alarming this phone call from a gringo with bad Spanish likely is. I'm sure she's thinking we'd kidnapped Juan and are now calling to verify his identity for the ransom money. I had no idea what she was asking me back and am finding it painstakingly difficult to ask a full minute of questions. The judges finally have mercy on me and let me go on to the next challenge.

I told Juan he better explain to his bewildered girlfriend it was for a television show and pointed to the cameras.

Next, the couple explains they are from Israel and the judge will play me two recorded messages in Hebrew that I must repeat out loud and they will try to figure out what I am saying before they are given the next clue and continue on. Seriously what the fuck is going on? It's one thing to moderately ramble out a few butchered Spanish phrases after having eight months or so to practice them. Hebrew though, really, do I look like a curly-haired Rabbi?

The judges play me the two messages ten times each while I repeat out loud what I think I heard on the recording. I picture a dog being given a series of commands from their master then going back to the rest of the pack and trying to explain what he heard in English so the rest of the hounds can be ready for the upcoming game of fetch.

The look of confusion on the faces of this attractive couple who I'm assuming had been selected for a television show based more on their looks as opposed to the ones who are selected for being nine-time cancer survivors, Siamese twins, or the inter-racial vegan gay couple who were both adopted from a religious cult.

After my ten translations, I'm sure they are further behind than ahead, but time was up. I snapped a quick selfie with the duo, then we exchanged a sweaty hug and I bitched some more about how I'd never been picked to be on the show. Then, as fast as it happened, it was all over and left me to lick my 5-minutes of fame wounds.

I have no confirmation of what series this was on, though I suspect it was HaMerotz LaMillion. The Israeli version of The Amazing Race. Perhaps I'll send my next submission their way.

(The couple I "helped")   (The infamous Amazing Race clue box)

Colombia
Streeeeeeeeetching

"Together, we see a world where people unite and take action to create lasting change — across the globe, in our communities, and in ourselves."

- Rotary.org

Before departure, I'd been a member of the local Rotary club, an international brotherhood of do-gooders who'd originally come together to end Polio. Since this primary goal, Rotary has expanded into helping a swath of local and international causes. I'd pushed my departure date back in Canada to October 29th, about as close as you can get to risking a trip-stopping winter snowstorm for Rotary. There was a black-tie fundraising dinner and auction being put on by my local Rotary Club, District 5360, on October 28th and I had promised I'd help with the event.

To keep from living in the shadows of my own inabilities along the way, I'd set myself little challenges. Things like eating with the locals or staying with the locals were usually on that list to help me understand the culture as well as practice the language.

This time I'd set the goal that once I landed in South America I'd find a group and give a presentation about my trip entirely in Spanish. A month or so earlier I'd sent an email to various Rotary groups in Colombia noting that I wanted to give them a presentation about my journey. One of the few to respond was from a group in Cartagena and their welcoming president, Jaime (pronounced; Hi-Me). He said he would love to have me, and we agreed on a day, four days after my arrival in Colombia.

I prepared like I'd never prepared before. I wanted the presentation to be simple, but full of photos to help supplement my crap Spanish. I put together a slideshow with lots of bullet points next to the photos to help cheat my way through. I practiced my opening, a full explanation of the trip thus far, and tried to anticipate any questions.

I rehearsed day and night leading up to the event. The day before I was set to speak I asked a Colombian lady staying at my hostel who could speak English to listen to me give the presentation. I would read it off a piece of paper and see if she could understand me. After giving her my all, she noted it wasn't perfect, but she understood the main idea of what I was talking about. Ok, 6 out of 10. Hopefully, it's a patient crowd.

I had anticipated having KLaiR back from the shipping container by this point so I could ride her there as well as get some fresh clothes from my luggage. However, there had been some delays and all of my gear was still with her, locked inside the sea can at the port. I'd been sweating it out in the Colombian heat with the same black pants and a blue shirt on for four days. I had nothing more than one change of clothes, a bandana, and a toothbrush. To add to the look, today I had been running around the shipping port in 40oC weather trying to spring KLaiR from the sea can only to be told to come back the next day for her final release.

I'd been sweating so much that huge salty white sweat stains had built up on my black pants, my personal hygiene had hit a new low. With no time to launder them, no chance of getting my clothes from the bike, and no room in the $12/day budget for new clothes, I resolved to give the presentation with an "authentic travelers look".

I showed up to meet the group of esteemed locals and give a presentation about myself and life on the road. I hadn't shaved in over a week, I was wearing my shower-washed bandana, a shirt I'd been wearing every day since I landed, and sporting black pants with salty white sweat stains seeping through them. If anything, this truly reflected how most of my days looked on the road.

I was so nervous about getting all my points accurate in Spanish and fretting over how much of a dirty biker I looked like, I wasn't sure I'd be able to face a live audience. My Rotary club in Canada was around 80-members and the average lunch had at least 50-60 people in attendance, so I was prepared for a full room. The upside was that I'm typically more comfortable talking to large groups than small ones. Put me on a stage in front of 500-people and I'll tell you anything you want to know. Sit me down at an intimate table over lunch, I'll likely dodge every personal question that comes my way.

I arrived early, met the president Jaime in the lobby of this beautiful condominium overlooking the Caribbean Sea and we rode the elevator to the top floor where the meeting room and pool were located.

Jaime spoke flawless English and I asked him if he would help translate a few points if I got lost. He said sure, but didn't look too concerned. Roughly 10-minutes went by as a few people trickled into the room. Each person said hello and Jaime introduced me while the conversation carried on around me in English. Another 10-minutes or so went by and a couple more people arrived, this time with beer, sporting American accents. One man gave me a beer as we talked about my trip while I tried to side-step the questions that would be answered in the presentation. Finally, Jaime said the meeting would start and with about 8-people in attendance and half of them enjoying a casual beer or three, Jaime went over the current Rotary events.

Everything was going on in English, barely a word of Spanish was spoken. Finally, Jaime explained to the group why I was there, and with a beer in hand to an audience of eight, wearing some of the dirtiest clothes I'd worn the entire trip, I got up. To this intimate group of eight, I explained how I'd planned to do this whole event in Spanish, but was now entirely relaxed as everyone spoke English. However, I was determined to give the opening part of the presentation in Spanish just to prove I did it.

The group laughed, the American expats who made up half of the audience said they barely understood Spanish but would listen. Then I laughed, took a swig of the beer, and gave my Spanish spiel. I gave my opener in Spanish just like I had practiced, and Jaime smiled when I screwed up some of the keywords, but knew what I meant. Then I switched to English and explained that I felt things would be more authentic if I showed up looking like I did on most days during the trip, wearing dirty clothes and having not shaved. Then my entire presentation promptly came unraveled as the group turned things into a 30-minute question and answer period and handed me another beer to keep me talking.

All of the preparation in the world can not force an audience into something when they want something else!

Mission accomplished, and I had made a few new friends and found myself at a local house party of mostly Americans the following week wearing shorts, a clean shirt, and freshly shaved.

(The "presentation")   (Jaime showing me the view over Cartagena)

Colombia
Problems In The Mirror Are Closer Than They Appear

> "Life's short, break the rules…"
> - Mark Twain

It was D-day and I had to face some harsh realities. I likely wasn't going to be able to finish the trip. Despite all the scrounging, camping in the bush for free, eating from dirt-cheap food stands, hustling through expensive countries like Costa Rica, taking it slow through cheap countries like Mexico, and having out-of-budget items like dental floss smuggled in from Canada, I was running out of funds.

When I planned this trip originally with the idea of television sponsorship and a film crew following me around, I made a budget of $200,000. As this dream of a rockstar road trip had dwindled from stardom to starvation, I was assuming closer to $20,000 for a budget. Now, with an actual departure budget below the poverty line at around $12/day, it was getting incredibly difficult to put fuel in KLaiR as well as myself day after day.

In Central America $12/day was possible and I knew it would also be possible through parts of South America like Peru and Bolivia. Though once I got down to Chile this poverty line lifestyle would die a fast death. Not just day-to-day living. If KLaiR needed even one out-of-pocket repair, I'd starve trying to keep her alive.

I would either need to ride like hell to reach the bottom of South America and skip nearly every site off the beaten path while hoping for zero breakdowns, or tuck my tail between my legs and spend the last of my money and fly back to Canada to work for the summer.

If I had no ego this would be an easy choice. Sadly my ego often controlled my rational thinking and made it painfully impossible to make choices that might seem easy to make from the outside looking in.

I made a sheepish phone call to Brett, a guy I'd done business with for many years. The same guy I'd worked for the year before my departure. The same guy who paid me while I turned right back around and paid down a line of credit I used to pay off a hefty invoice I had with his company. I asked him if he'd give me a summer job? I could tell he was a bit confused as to why the hell I'd be leaving this life to return to Canada. Either way, he said he'd be happy to help me out for the summer. I then promptly spent the rest of my money on a plane ticket home and a scuba diving trip.

I felt like a failure. I felt like I couldn't accomplish my initial goal of reaching the end of South America before riding around the world. I felt like I was still relying on the crutch of Canada to run back to when things got hard. Either way, I swallowed my pride on the basis that if I didn't go back and work now, the pain of possibly not getting to Ushuaia would be worse than the pain of dying a slow, broke, death.

This however presented a new problem.

Typically an owner of a foreign vehicle is only allowed 90-days to temporarily import their vehicle into any country, not a universal rule, but it applies to most countries on the PanAm route. If you go over the 90-days the vehicle is either confiscated by the government and becomes their property or is considered imported property and you are meant to pay taxes on the imported goods along with filing a stack of paperwork. The taxes are often atrocious, sometimes reaching 100% or more of the vehicle's value.

I had made several requests with the Colombian government to extend my temporary import papers for KlaiR but they were all denied. I was feeling desperate to continue the trip, but not lose KLaiR to the government while doing so. I had even gone so far as to fake death certificates and cited a funeral as my reason for return as I heard this was an option for visa extensions. The government didn't care about the funeral and again denied my claim. When this fell through I rode for two days up the coast to another immigration office and tried for the extension there. I was now getting more and more desperate for a solution.

When a four day road trip and a funeral had not worked I had decided to store KLaiR in Colombia. This was more of a band aid than a solution, but would buy me some time to think about what to do. When I returned I hoped I could later smuggle her out of the country when the time came. This also meant sneaking around Colombia with an illegally imported bike from one side of the country to the other. Trying to avoid the endless police checks in Colombia was like trying to avoid a hangover after a New Years party. The party eventually ends and the consequences catch up with you.

If I was caught with expired documents at the police checks I would either face a fine, have KLaiR confiscated by the government, or possibly end up in prison. It would be tough to plead my case as I had applied for an extension in two different cities and been denied in both. It's not that I'm a criminal, it's just that the rules are so hard to follow that upstanding citizens like myself are often forced to bend these rules just to enjoy the beauty of each country and give it the attention it deserves.

I returned to Canada, told everyone some excuse about how great it was to be home for the summer, and agonizingly counted each day until my return.

Shortly before departure from Colombia, I'd called Angie in the hopes of rekindling this impractical international relationship that would spark in one country, then fade, then flare up again in another part of the planet before being snuffed out again.

I was so sure she was going to be excited to see me that I'd booked my flight back to Edmonton where she was living. She was as shocked as I was that I was returning to Canada for the summer, however, the little spark we had was again faded and she had booked herself an extended summer vacation to Europe.

Who was I kidding, I knew this "thing" we had was not sustainable and clearly, so did she. In all fairness, I had not requested that she come to South America at any point nor had I given any reason that I might be back in Canada within the next year or more.

Back in Canada, I worked, kept a close eye on the calendar along with my bank account, and managed to cross paths with Angie a few times before returning to my real girlfriend KLaiR. The summer was fun, but it was merely a stepping stone back to the bike trip

Eventually, I landed back in Colombia with some parts for KLaiR, a new camera, some money, and a new outlook on the trip. To make this all possible I'd stored KLaiR with some new Colombian friends on a little acreage not far from Cartagena. When I returned I was shocked to see her covered in debris and the tarp I had covered her with shredded, having barely survived the relentless rainy season. With all the excess humidity and all my gear stuck inside my Pelican cases and under a tarp, everything had molded. Moldy green boots, speckled pants, fuzzy helmet, even the air filter was covered in a thick mold. Imagine slipping your head into a big wheel of blue cheese before riding off into the beating sun!

I knew the risks of riding illegally through the country and had carefully been plotting out my trip to ride mostly backroads and remote village routes to avoid the police checkpoints. This was going fairly well and it had been a couple of months without hitting a single police checkpoint. Eventually though, I needed to pass through the city of Bucaramanga and here things suddenly came unraveled.

Every part of this scene was going wrong. I had no desire to be anywhere near a city, but needed to cross through Bucaramanga, I had no other option. The sun was setting and I needed to find a place to stay or camp before it finally got dark. I had hardly slept the night before as the pouring rains that were bashing at the exterior of the tent had kept me up all night. I hadn't eaten since breakfast as I was rushing most of the day to get to, then through this city. It was getting alarmingly darker, I was officially out of water and the heat of the day had exhausted & dehydrated me. Hungry, thirsty, and irritated, I was now navigating the madness of city traffic trying to avoid being run over.

Dealing with city traffic is one of my least favorite scenarios. The two Pelican cases on KLaiRs hips result in her having a huge ass. Where small, local bikes can easily dart in and out of traffic getting to places faster, I'm typically reduced to the same speed and obstacles as a car. I was getting a little fed up with the endless traffic jams and I was now trying to weave KlaiR and her huge ass in and out of crammed cars while trying to avoid crashing into anyone.

Colombians have this incredible motorbike culture and their love of motorbikes lends to them being true masters on two wheels. To watch them delicately wind in and out of traffic and between lights was inspiring, but well out of my skill set. As the cars got closer and closer to each other and the traffic began to build along with my hunger, dehydration, and frustration, I was looking to get out of this edgy madness as soon as possible. I spotted a small opening in the thick traffic and decided to go for it.

I hit the throttle and just narrowly avoided two cars, but I was free, I made it! Well, free for a minute anyways. I soon met the next red light. As the light turned green I took off, but shortly after a car came up beside me and very angrily started yelling at me and pointing at his car. I had no idea what was going on, the guy probably just liked Canadians. I waved and continued on hoping to avoid having to stop and take some selfies with the guy.

At the next set of lights, he pulled up beside me and began to yell again. I didn't know what was happening so I turned off of the main road to find a place to park and to talk to him. It was here that I noticed he was pointing to his rearview mirror hanging like a broken arm from his door and pointing to KLaiR. Ohh shit, maybe I didn't make it so effortlessly through those last set of cars. I put the kickstand down and got off.

Normally this little incident would not have been such a concern to me. I'd probably work out a deal with the guy for some light car repair then be on my way. However, at this particular time, I had the minor backend problem of KLaiR being here illegally weighing on my mind.

This broken mirror was reflecting a "Problems in the mirror may be closer than they appear '' situation into what could be my imprisonment in Colombia. If this guy called the police or the police happened to drive by and see the accident it could be game over. As I stopped the bike, instantly the attention of the locals were drawn to us like kids to a clown. Only I was the clown and no one was laughing. An accident with the obvious foreign bike and a pale white gringo along with one of the locals seemed more captivating than anything else going on around us at that moment.

In my best Spanish I apologized profusely and assured the man I could fix it. I was more than nervous. I was pissing my pants nervous. I was dreading prison time in Colombia nervous. I was going to have my girlfriend taken away from me nervous.

The guy was driving an old family sedan. The type of car you drive when you have no money and just need a car that can taxi around a six-person family. He had what looked like his elderly mother in the front seat, maybe his wife in the back, and a small child next to the potential mother. Great, the rich-looking westerner had just wrecked the family car in front of the whole family. When the driver stepped out of the front seat he was a chubby 250-pounds and easily dwarfed me. I knew there would be no escape if I couldn't solve this little issue fast.

I looked at the mirror and tried to make out how it may have originally looked, then tried to gently set it back in place. Somehow my YouTube mechanic skills were not shining through. I then tried to reassure the man and told him I had some tools. Sweating, starving, tired, and concerned I might be going to jail over a mirror, I quickly got my tools and tried to unscrew the rest of the mirror. The small crowd of onlookers grew and the 250-pound man and his family all watched me fumble nervously with the mirror.

15-minutes of my clumsy mirror repair service went by in what felt like hours and I was sure grandma, who was seeing right through my facade, had called the police. By now the man realized I didn't know what I was doing and called my mechanical bluff. He put his large baseball glove-sized hand on my tiny shoulder and pushed me out of the way like I was a small child. He then grabbed the broken arm looking mirror, lined it up with the hole it had fallen out of, and rammed it back into place with his giant hands. Holy shit, it held! He then adjusted the mirror and just like that everything was back to normal.

I took a deep breath, felt like an idiot, and then contemplated my options. There was a bar right across the road, so I asked him if he wanted me to buy him some beer. He said no. I asked him if he wanted some money for his trouble. He looked insulted. He took my little biker hand in his big baseball mitt, shook it, and asked me if I needed anything? I said no. He told me to ride safely and wished me luck. Just like that, all the concerns of bribes and jail disappeared.

This was a far cry from the Colombian criminals you see on t.v. that I was originally assuming I'd be running into everywhere. He did fit the description of nearly every welcoming and friendly Colombian I'd meet during my months in the country though. I feel appalled that I've been across half the planet quite intensely and still buy into preconceived notions about a culture before I get there. Colombians aren't the deadly criminals the world thinks they are. One man was, many, many years ago, and he left a nearly irreversible stain on the country's image that is so shockingly different from who the people really are. Do they think Canadians live in igloos and use the same two letters in every sentence? Fuck, I hope not, eh.

(Colombia's backroads) Photo by Philippe Berini / Moto Phil

Colombia
Coffee's Poster Child, Juan Valdez or Kix Marshall?

"The Prophet Joseph Smith received the Word of Wisdom as a revelation from God in 1833… In the Word of Wisdom, the Lord commands Latter-day Saints to abstain from harmful substances… (Mormons) are also taught not to drink "hot drinks," meaning coffee…"

- uk.churchofjesuschrist.org

Juan Valdez is the face of Colombia coffee. He is the man that represents all of the hardworking coffee farmers of Colombia. Though he's actually a fictional character dreamt up by the National Federation of Coffee Growers of Colombia. Juan is a bit like the Ronald McDonald of the coffee world. OK, maybe Ronald doesn't represent all of the hardworking restauranteurs of America, but you get the idea. That and he has a great name.

Was I about to become the new face of the Colombian coffee world? What better choice than a man who'd only just learned how coffee was grown a few months ago. Instead of an old farmer with a donkey, maybe a dirty biker with a motorbike was what the country needed, and I was about to get my shot at the title.

Some days I'll find myself getting fuel and fielding a variety of questions with the attendant in Spanish and carrying on like a local. These days I think to myself, wow, I've finally got this. I'm speaking like the locals. Then I'm quickly given a reminder that my comprehension might be half-imagined and I'm just enjoying the bliss of what I think is going on in the conversation. Today was one of these moments.

I found myself in Filandia, a small farming community with a big heart smack dab in the womb of the coffee family in the mother of coffee countries. On this particular Wednesday afternoon, I'd just come from a day of repairs at the local furniture refinishing store where they had fixed a broken zipper on my bike and ran a bunch of screws, staples, and finally glue into my boots to reattach the soles.

The boots that were previously looking like an open mouth talking as I walked, did not come from the repair shop as pretty as I was hoping. Based on the shop's crafty furniture work and expert attention to detail, I was expecting a bit more than a series of screws run through the soles, however, they were still quite functional. I paid my repair bill based on their shop rate of one bottle of Aguardiente, a local liquor flavored with aniseed, and was off.

With my fresh look of screwed and glued boots, I headed into the town square to strut my stuff and find a local coffee shop. I knew that based on the area alone I could walk blindly into any coffee establishment within a hundred miles and have an extremely good chance to land on a premium cup of the locally grown harvest that had been coddled to perfection from bean to brew.

The small coffee shop I found was beautiful. The exterior depicted a series of workers and horses at a local coffee Finca painted on the outside walls to reflect the area. The inside was a mix of old-world culture and hand-crafted furniture with modern espresso machines. Now that I've been converted to a coffee connoisseur, I like to enjoy the actual flavor and get to know the bean a little so I ordered an Americano then quickly changed my mind to an Espresso. OK, maybe I still don't know what I'm doing.

Apparently, there was no changing your mind and I ended up with a well-balanced Americano with the little bubbles and glistening bean oil whirling around the top. Sure enough, it was the kind of flavor you secretly wish for each time you're let down at a North American franchise. Flavorful, full of body, and with as much anticipation as a first date kiss.

Being the only oddly dressed out-of-place gringo in the shop that day, I would be a natural selection for a premium opinion on the coffee of the region. And, with overwhelming enthusiasm, I was invited back to the shop later that day.

When I was leaving the owner had rushed out onto the street and asked me to come back that evening. He first thanked me profusely for coming in then we had a brief chat in a mix of his poor English and my poor Spanish. This is where he invited me back at 7 pm to enjoy a movie about coffee from the region that they were showing, or so I thought…

With exactly zero other plans booked for the night, I arrived just before seven to a completely empty store and ordered another espresso, just what one needs at 7 pm. By 7:20 pm I am feeling a bit awkward as I have not seen another soul, including the owner who had made it very clear he would like me here for 7 pm. Silly me forgot that Colombia time is not equivalent to say German time. Whereas Germans will either be early or on time, Colombians are more likely to be 30-60 minutes late for everything.

At 7:25 pm, the owner rushed in and said hello before quickly tending to some things behind the bar. Following him, a family of five came in and sat down, then a few single onlookers. Shortly after a man with a large box that looked like my Pelican cases arrived along with a lady with some more boxes. Then the duo left and came back with some lighting equipment, some cords, and a few more boxes. I figured for such a small crowd they were going all out to show this little movie.

Eventually, the owner came over and put one hand on my shoulder and the other on my neck to assure he had my full attention. He again over-enthusiastically thanked me for coming and then got me a beer. He explained a few things about when we would start and asked if I was comfortable. By now I had started to notice some cameras being set up and the lighting equipment being tested. Then, before I even had a sip out of my first beer, another beer was brought to me. My suspicions about this screening were growing.

The guy with the camera finally got it all set up and came over to chat me up in English.

"Hello, how are you? My name is Pedro, are you comfortable and do you know what it is that we are doing here?"

"Umm, well, I thought we were watching a movie about coffee. However, now I think we are making a movie about coffee. Yes?"

"Yes, sort of. We are making a commercial about coffee from this region as we feel it is some of the best in the world and we would like to capture on camera how you feel about the coffee."

"Great, you could not have picked a better person to give their opinion of Colombian coffee and I'm happy to help!"

Holy shit, I was going to be in a Colombian commercial about coffee!

A year ago I would not have known the difference between a cup of tobacco spit and a cup of premium, organically grown, hand-roasted beans from Filandia Colombia. Yet after my intensive stint working on an organic coffee farm in El Salvador earlier that year where Javier taught me everything from planting for flavor influence and altitude, to roasting, brewing, and even helping to run coffee tours. Then crisscrossing country to country in the Americas getting my lips on every premium brew I could find and soaking up everything I could about the soil and the process, I would now fancy myself a well-opinionated authority for all things coffee. Well at least this felt true when I was drinking a roadside coffee with Stanley and KLaiR and I was happy to share this opinion on camera. However, in the company of highly trained coffee cuppers, I was just a shit-talking gringo who believed his own story, but no one knew that here.

From the time I walked through the door to when the shoot finally wrapped up I was fed seven beers and two more espressos. For about twenty minutes we did several takes where they would ask me how I felt about the cup of coffee and what drinking the coffee meant to me. I think I nailed it with something about it feeling like I was tasting the culture and they seemed delighted with my answers that included the word "magic" all while I smiled ear-to-ear like a kid in front of a cake on his birthday.

The film crew also interviewed the barista. He looked the part, but he didn't fare so well on camera. When the director yelled "action" the barista started stuttering up a storm, frothing at the mouth and drawing blanks for all of his twenty minutes. In the final video, he was left out entirely. I'm sure if they had fed him the seven beers along with the three espressos they fed me, he might have done a better job.

The coffee was fantastic and the aroma alone would leave the average barista drooling with delight instead of nervousness. The owner took a bag of roasted beans off the shelf and squeezed it under my nose. He allowed just a single sacred breath to escape the valve on the coffee bag. The warm aroma of caramelized brown sugar-scented, thick bakery-like air would encompass my senses, the bag was then placed in my hands as a parting gift.

I'm sure if Juan Valdez was around he would have been appalled by the use of some newbie coffee gringo in a Colombian coffee commercial. However, he was just as big a fraud as I was.

To watch the commercial you can search YouTube for:

CAFÉ FILANDIA'S - DOCUMENTAL FAMILIAS or use this link https://youtu.be/V0WufTGbVgs.

Or check out the little behind the scenes video I made by searching; Kix Marshall the most respected man in coffee, or was that Juan Valdez?

Or use the link https://youtu.be/UdPRWyyaauo .

Unfortunately the quality of the website http://cafefilandia.com/ its design and video quality are subpar in comparison to the coffee. Overall it was an amazing experience.

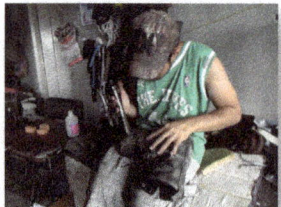  

(Screw & staple boot repair all paid for with Aguardiente. Why leather Harley boots? Because I could hike in them and they were on sale for $99!)

(The set of the coffee commercial and the exterior of the colorful coffee shop)

Venezuela
Oil Corruption & Salon Sacrifices

- *Venezuela has the most oil reserves of any country on the planet, with 299,953,000,000 proven barrels in 2016.*
- *In the 1950's, Venezuela was the world's 4th wealthiest nation per capita.*
- *In the 60's-70's Venezuelan workers "enjoyed the highest wages in Latin America".*
- *The oil collapse of the 80's brought inflation as high as 84%.*
- *1996 saw the highest inflation rate, hitting 100%.*
- *In 2013 the Bolivar Fuerte had devalued to the point locals could not buy toilet paper, milk or flour.*
- *By July of 2018, prices in Venezuela were doubling every 28-days and annual inflation had hit 25,000%*
- *Today, Venezuela still has the highest oil reserves on the planet.*

You can watch people fleeing from their countries on the news a thousand times, but it has no comparison to seeing the devastation unfolding in a heart-crushing reality before your eyes.

The lady I'd met in the hostel in Cartagena who critiqued the Spanish presentation I never really gave had invited me to visit her in Cucuta. Cucuta sits just on the edge of Colombia, bordering Venezuela. Taking any opportunity I could to see the world through the eyes of the locals, I said I would come and visit and so I did.

What had once been an economically prosperous country with rich oil production was now facing the same global oil price collapse as the rest of the planet, including Alberta where I'd come from. For the Venezuelans however, it was crippling.

The country had spiraled out of control under the "leadership" of iron fist ruler and former bus driver, Nicolás Maduro, a man who seemed to be blind to the fact he was leading his country's demise. Since taking power, more than 4-million people have fled Venezuela, nearly 90% of the country now lived in poverty, inflation had spiraled out of control, and the country now had the second-highest homicide rate in the Caribbean. On this day I would catch a glimpse of this demise.

Liliana had graciously allowed me to stay at her home for a few days on the couch while she toured me to local sites and took me to karaoke bars to watch me sweat before a live audience.

Travel tip: no matter what country you are in, everyone at a karaoke bar knows the song Zombie by the Cranberries, everyone!

One day she asked if I wanted to go to the Venezuelan border. I knew I would not be allowed to cross into Venezuela and even if I did get in, the chances of having my motorcycle for long were very slim.

We hired a cab to the border along with her friend who'd gone to karaoke with us the night before. The main difference between our cab and the others is that all other cabs would arrive at the border empty and leave with people and luggage in them. We were the only cab on the Colombian side to arrive with people in it. I wasn't sure why there was only a one-way service. Liliana explained that every day hundreds of people fled over the border from Venezuela into Colombia seeking a better life and no one was trying to return.

Once we finally arrived at the border it was organized chaos. It felt like we were trying to walk against a parade that didn't know where it was going. There was a non-stop stream of people walking across the bridge as the border was closed to all motorized vehicles. On the Venezuelan side old school busses would pull up and let people off, then the people would either walk across or a porter with a dolly or a wheel barrel would load up their possessions and help them get across the bridge for a fee.

The people just kept coming and coming. They didn't look like refugees you might see fleeing war or dressed in clothing that had been reduced to shreds from a lifetime of poverty and starvation. These were people who looked like they had just walked out of the office or left a day at university. Most were wearing business casual attire and carrying name-brand luggage and backpacks. The older men had on dress shoes and button up shirts; the younger men were in Nike sneakers with nice shirts and jackets. Older ladies wore dresses and the girls were usually wearing heels and things like Versace and Louis Vuitton accent pieces. Most of these ladies had long beautiful black hair that shimmered in the sunlight and appeared to be the well-kept focal point of their look.

Some people weren't carrying bags, instead, they had televisions or appliances boxes packed up that were then loaded onto the dolly and carried across the bridge to Colombia. It looked like someone had just gone into a city on a Tuesday at 3 pm, rounded up all the people, and told them to grab their favorite possessions before leaving. It was so strange to see all these people who did not fit the role of a refugee. It felt eerily 70's Pol Pot.

Our group sat in silence as the events unfolded one by one. I didn't want to ask too many questions, I didn't want to know the answers. I got up and went into a little shop to buy a cold drink. Just in front of me, a lady around sixty years of age asked to use the washroom. The man pointed to a sign that said *BANO 3000 PESOS*, meaning the price to use the bathroom was 3000 Pesos or a little under $1. The lady opened a bag and reluctantly pulled out a Looney Tunes amount of bills, and handed them to the man to count. Venezuela's currency was depleting at such a rapid rate that just to use the bathroom in Colombia meant you needed a bag full of Venezuelan pesos. I could feel the woman's distress as she had just been confronted with her first exchange rate tragedy in this new country.

As I walked outside I saw a line of five taxi cabs all nervously waiting to meet a guy who was dumping 2-liter pop bottles of fuel into the cabs gas tanks before handing over some Colombian pesos and driving away. As one taxi would pull away, another would swoop into line. The fuel guy would look around quickly and proceed to dump the fuel from the Coke bottles into the taxi tank and on and on the process went. No one ever stuck around to get more than 2 or 3 pop bottles full before scurrying off.

I went and asked the taxi guy what was going on with the impromptu fuel station. He explained the fuel was smuggled from Venezuela where it was virtually free, and sold here for a fraction of the price that you would pay at the pumps. I was somewhat pleased to see that at least someone had found a way to make a profit out of the situation in the least shady way possible.

The final currency exchange I saw crushed me. It was legal, no one was being forced into anything, you had a choice here, but it wasn't much of a choice. It was an exchange made by the young ladies that had come walking across the bridge trying to hold their heads up while sporting their designer heels, Vuitton bags, and wearing their favorite outfits from home. Those same girls with the long black shimmering hair that looked like it had been the focal point of their morning routine for years. These same girls were about to make a similar decision to the one Sala's father had to make back in El Salvador, the equivalent to killing off something to feed something else.

The ladies would walk to the immigration booth, have their passports stamped, walk over to the currency exchange guys, ask a couple of questions, then continue on to meet their families before making their way closer to the city. It all seemed pretty standard.

We would see these ladies again a few minutes up the road as we got back to the city. From the hurried pace of getting across the bridge and into the immigration line then into the country where they would reunite with their family. Then they would get into these one way cabs and stop at a row of makeshift businesses.

Here, things quickly transitioned from rushing about into a slow, forced saunter. The kind of walk you do when you're told to go to the principal's office when you are in trouble. The walk you do when it's time to leave the theme park at the end of the day. It looked like their designer shoes had suddenly filled with cement. These young, beautiful girls with long shimmering hair were now standing in front of a series of doors with the word "Peluquería" written above the entrance. These appeared to be makeshift hair salons. It was here that you could sell your hair and this beautiful lifelong achievement was then re-sold and turned into wigs.

Beautiful girls with the type of hair you would see on the front of Revlon boxes, shimmering black and lying flat down their backs would reluctantly walk in these peluqueria doors and exit heads down, crying, with pixie cuts to their ear line. No one walked out smiling, no one walked out happy, no one walked out excited to show off their new look. It was nothing like the hair salon commercials you see on t.v.; it was nothing like any hair salon I'd ever been to.

I don't know what they were paid, but I'm certain it was less than they ever thought this life's achievement was worth and more than they had earned in a long time.

There is no emotional connection to seeing the scenario of people who are forced to flee their country on television where it's easy to turn the volume down or simply switch the channel. In person it's awful, it's devastating, it's completely disconnected from reality. When you see a lady that reminds you of your mother handing over a portion of her life savings just to use the bathroom and then watch her daughter that reminds you of your sister handing over her hair to feed her family, it's a sickening feeling that reminds me that there is something not right in the world.

That night I sat and thought of where I was from in relation to where these people were from. Oil was also the backbone of the economy in my hometown. It created a lot of jobs and brought unimaginable amounts of wealth to blue-collared people. The basic standard of living in my part of the world was higher than nearly any other country I'd been to in my life. Not so different from that of many Venezuelans not too many years earlier. Could it all be taken away that easily? Could a few years of depleted oil prices and a couple of terms of bad governing reduce us to rubble? I wondered how my friends might react if this was them, if their wives had to cut off their hair to feed their families. I wondered if they appreciated their houses, their jobs, their one-click online shopping. I wondered if I did…?

(Roadside take out near the sugarcane fields)   (Colombia, a country of color)

Colombia
Emerald Tears

95% of Colombia's cacao exports are considered "Fine Flavor" by the International Cacao Organization. Cacao, the raw ingredient in chocolate, is also an important part of the country's bid to cut coca (the main ingredient in cocaine) production and end its internal conflict.

- Colombia.co

It was two GPS points, that's all I had to go on. I was given the point where I was to turn onto a road that wasn't noted on any of my three mapping applications or my GPS. The second set of coordinates was for the chocolate farm I was searching for, hidden deep in the mountains of Colombia's Emerald zone.

As part of my back roads route from Medellin and around Bogotá, I was still heavily focused on avoiding the police checkpoints with my illegally imported motorcycle. This did provide a few hidden benefits though, and I was about to be given an unplanned opportunity to learn a bit more about the starting point for the four-thousand-year-old tradition of chocolate making. Or at least this was the story I was telling myself to justify that I was an adventurer and not a criminal.

I drove past the first GPS point not even noticing a road. I stopped, turned back around, found the road, and made a right-hand turn down a gravel track into Colombia's Emerald Mountain Range. I wasn't sure if following this road alone up into the mountains was a good or bad idea. No one in the world knew where I was or where I was headed. I took a deep breath and followed a series of routes on my GPS that looked like floating pink lines on an otherwise blank screen that was chasing a little flag indicating the finish point.

En route, I missed a few turning points, turned around in the yard of some bewildered farmers, drove the wrong way to a dead-end road a number of times, and eventually found the closed gates of the Cocoa farm I was searching for. Damnit, all this effort and the gates were closed and no one was around.

Naturally, I decided that instead of turning around, I'd let myself in. I think this is called breaking and entering in North America, but Colombians aren't North Americans and I assumed they wouldn't mind me coming over unannounced. I made my way up a short hill to a house perched on the edge of a mountain. I looked around and couldn't find anyone at home. So I poked around the property a bit yelling out for anyone and then used their open-aired bathroom behind the house. The bathroom was decorated in stunning modern design and only had walls on two sides so you were staring out into the woods when showering. Incredible!

About 45-minutes into my non-breaking and entering and making myself at home, a pleasant worker stopped by and greeted me. She explained in Spanish that the boss wasn't home, but to make myself comfortable and set up my tent on this purpose-built platform that overlooked the stunningly lush mountain range in the valley below.

Just to review, I had ridden down a road that wasn't identifiable on any maps. Had found a farm I'd only ever heard of second hand. Let myself into a property through a closed gate. Used the facilities. Set up my camp, and still had not met, talked to, or gotten any type of invite from the guy who owned the place. I arrived once after hours at a campground down a gravel road with an open gate in a camper van, during camping season in America where I was greeted by the attendant wearing an oversized muscle shirt toting a handgun who not so politely asked me to leave without using the bathroom. You tell me where the scariest countries in the world are?

Don Alejandro was the sort of guy you would want to do business with. He was a mix of charm that would attract a loyal following of friendships, the right amount of encouragement peppering that always seemed like it could lead up to the sale of something, and enough knowledge to make you trust he knew what he was talking about.

When he arrived home after dark with his wife later that night, he greeted me like we were old friends. Don Alejandro seemed delighted my bike was out front and my tent was out back. He then promptly extended me an invitation to breakfast in the morning. After breakfast, we walked down to the property entrance for a seat in the second kitchen. This kitchen was set in a wood shack with smoke billowing from a wood-burning stove where water was boiling to make us a cup of coffee from the neighbors' beans.

While we sat there Alejandro explained to me what was staring before us. There under a red shade tarp sat one of the first strains of government-appointed TCS13 and TCS19 cacao plants.

Alejandro looks at me and asks *"Do you know why those plants are under a red shade tarp and not a black shade tarp?"* I thought for about half a second; *"Was red on sale that day?"*.

He laughs *"No, I'm really into NASA and I once watched a program where the NASA team was explaining colors and sunlight. The scientist noted that black would merely reduce the sunlight, where purple and red would filter UV rays. Purple was not an option, so I bought red"*.

This scientific reasoning would set the stage for every decision he would explain to me about his business for the three days while I was treated to personal tours of the property and area.

Don Alejandro, as he liked to be called. Don, meaning leader or boss, and Alejandro being his actual name, considers himself to be a "medium-big" farmer. He was sitting on roughly eighteen-thousand cacao trees and in this area, the average was closer to three-thousand trees on a farm. He has Hershey's-size plans for his operation, everything from chocolate-making classes on the property to international chocolate bar distribution. To achieve this he had strategically chosen the Occidente de Boyacá region near the Penas Blancas range of Colombia, right in the heart of the emerald zone.

The location we were at came with a number of promising benefits. Firstly the area had a magical history he would soon recount to me, as well as the land's premium growing capabilities. Once the beans were grown and manufactured into chocolate, his ultimate goal, he could then affix the area's story to his bars of chocolate gold and start selling.

Draped across the backside of his property sits a majestic mountain peak dripping with lush green tropical beauty that has been slowly carved by the small river below into what was the sculpted and stunning scenery before us. The legend of how this beauty came to be is recounted to me as follows.

Ares, the river god, created the region for the indigenous people to enjoy for eternity so long as there was no treason against the land. One historical day a doctor came to the area in search of the coveted flower for eternal youth that grew here. Fura, a local woman, had helped him find, then harvest the flower, and with this fateful move, treason had found her.

As a punishment, Ares turned Furas' husband Tena into stone and he became the smaller rocky mountain peak to our left. Then Ares turned Fura to stone and she became the stunning jagged cliff covered in the lush jungle to our right. Here Fura would have to sit and stare at Tena for eternity, just out of reach.

Throughout the region and especially at the base of Fura and Tena many precious emeralds have been found. It's said that these emeralds are the tears that have fallen from Furas' rocky face over thousands of years. Just across the river is now home to the cacao plants for Alejandro's, soon to be "Emerald Chocolate Bars."

* * *

On this day Alejandro was dawning a fashionable mismatched outfit of pastels and khakis chosen to help filter the sun's UV rays from his skin. He in his well-selected attire and me and my biker pants and dashing bandana that was usually washed in a river, were treated to a guided tour of the Finca where the rising King Of Cacao would explain every inch of his operation to me.

Don Alejandro explained it all, right from the beginning, right from how he originally purchased the property. He had to negotiate with nine children and their mother who had inherited the property from their deceased father. The property had been in the family for over one hundred and seventy years and did not have any sort of modern-day title.

Then he explained each and every government-regulated plant and why it had been planted on that part of the farm based on sun or soil and where that little cacao's life had originated as either a graphed plant or in a scientific lab. As you might have guessed I was grappling a little to keep up with the intricate details.

Alejandro had started planting in the front section of the property closest to the view of Tena and Fura with a strain of TCS01 and TCS06 plants that were coming into full bloom. However, he had more hopes for the new strain sitting under the red shade tarp, the TCS13 and TCS19's that had been bred for an overall bigger yield and more restraint to disease. The goal was for a 100% organic product. It meant the plant and its abilities to grow naturally and resist disease were of great importance. To date, they had needed to graph twelve-hundred-and-eighty plants by hand in the hopes of achieving a premium product.

To maintain such a pedigree he had to meet a large number of standards laid out by the B.B.A, *Buenas Prácticas Agrícolas*, a Colombian standard certified alongside the F.D.A. in Europe and the United States. This way he would be able to sell his product directly to foreign markets, skipping the dreaded middle man.

As an added treat to my personal visit, he had invited me to meet a friend of his up the road a little deeper into the mountains. This man mined for Emeralds in the mountainside with a small group of pick and axe-wielding mountain men for some twenty-five years.

On the drive up we passed a series of smaller cacao farms that had been sponsored by the BBA with financial support from countries like Canada, I swelled with pride. The idea was to help the farmers with equipment such as sheltered drying areas and education on how to be more productive with their land. Alejandro explained to me that his green-jewel-hunting friend had been mulling over the idea of building a small pool in the hillside for years and had actually spent some time shoveling out the ground rather than the mountain.

As our old rickety Land Rover rattled up over the last mountain crest, Alejandro looked over at me and explained that I should not be concerned by the people we were going to meet. He said that the owners of the mine were, umm…, "Questionable people", but I was with him and the actual workers there would not be a problem for us.

Just then both of us caught a glimpse of the work camp at the same time. I wasn't sure what I was seeing was real; this must be some mirage brought on by the spell of the area's eclectic presence. Here in the backside of absolutely fucking nowhere, as the rocky road came to an abrupt end in the face of a mountain was a sight that looked as out of place as the pale white gringo in the passenger seat of this ramshackle truck did here.

Right here, right before us both, right at the end of the mountain road, a fucking pool! Not just a pool, a pool long enough to swim laps, made from hand-laid tile with a small waterfall built from the rocks of the Emerald mountain range. All fed by a clear mountain river spring, next to a small wooden bar, fully stocked! I mean this would rival a posh infinity pool at any 5-star resort, and here it was where the track met the mountain and came to an abrupt end at an illegal mining camp. Where in the hell was I?

We were awkwardly greeted by a small team of men who clearly didn't see too many visitors. This group would define the term, *rough around the edges*. Here they were etching out a living and a lifestyle gently laying rocks on the edge of this nearly-completed pool to enjoy a slice of heaven mixed with I'm sure a lot of hell.

We borrowed some headlamps and Don Alejandro toured me inside the mining cave through a small opening into the side of the mountain just big enough to fit a worker with some simple tools. The interior was thatched together from lumber harvested from the hillside and murky, ankle-deep water flowed from deep inside the mountain, eroding the ground as we walked on it. As we tramped our way into the mountainside both of us could feel this was not a place you'd want to spend much time. We stopped and Alejandro broke off a bit of the fragile earth inside. As he rubbed away at the stone under the water, sure enough bits of sparkling green emerald began to reveal themselves. Holy shit, the legend was true. Centuries of Furas' tears were buried here.

Even though what we found was more like flecks than stone, Alejandro suggested we leave any of the emerald bits behind so as not to cause any problems. With a sigh of relief, we turned around and scurried our way back to the sunlight and fresh air we'd left behind.

If cacao was waiting on a new King, my rubber boot wearing guide who would be sat in his neighbors' spring-fed pool overlooking a breathtaking tropical valley, at the middle of two GPS points, N05.69826 W074.05265, up the road from the middle of nowhere and wearing an emerald encrusted chocolate crown, Don Alejandro of Finca San Louis would be that man.

Want to take a chocolate making class, learn more about the working of a cacao farm, take a tour of an emerald mine or maybe spend a few subtropical nights sipping wine in the spring-fed pool? These are the final details I parted with.

Alejandro of Finca San Louis

-Email: Itoro30@hotmail.com

(Don Alejandro & his prized cocoa plants) (The pool at the end of the road)

(Entrance to mining cave, with prayer stop) (Inside the mine)

Colombia
Desert Rains & KLaiR Strains

"I've heard that while the Beemer can probobly manage 100k, the KLR might be on it's last legg with as little as 30,000 miles on it."

- Horizonsunlimited.com

(posted exactly as it was written and spelled by wildwade.)

A deep snort screamed from his nostrils like a fire-breathing dragon as he reared back on two legs as though he was preparing to drive his front hoofs right through my skull. It was at this moment I was ripped from a deep relaxing sleep under the stars and thrown into attack-defense mode. I instinctually threw my arms in front of my face in the hopes that this might be able to stop him from crushing me from above. It was my first night in the desert, a place I thought to be lifeless.

To get me to this moment I had been looking for an escape from the mountains of Colombia. The mountains in this part of the world are beautiful, but after spending several nights freezing in the damp highlands shivering myself to sleep in the tent, I was looking for some dry, dusty warmth. KLaiR, Stanley, and I had spent the previous night camping in a mango orchard behind a fuel station and after an oatmeal breakfast with fresh mangos, we headed to the Tatacoa Desert. A 300-square kilometer arid landscape, located in the Huila Department of the country that is curiously flanked by lush, green vegetation on all sides. If you had to give directions from anywhere in the world, you might say Tatacoa is located between Cali and Bogota.

The route to get here is a motorcyclist's road-riding dream. As Tatacoa isn't really on the route to anywhere specific, the roads are nearly vacant and those on the road putt along as if every day were Sunday. The ride is blessed with winding pavement that takes you over bridged rivers flowing with clean mountain-fed water before the pavement suddenly plunges deep into the mountainside through tunnels completely void of light. Once our trio arrived in the heart of the Tatacoa, KLaiRs tyres went from gripping asphalt roads to spinning up a dusty red track from the red powdery sands dotted with tall cacti resembling those from Mexico's Baja so many months earlier.

There are only a few different tracks that pass through this region so I opt for what I believe is the road less traveled and search out a camp for the night in the setting sun. KLaiR, Stanley, and I pass several ranches tucked down one-lane roads and I decide to veer off the track and cut across the open desert to set up camp in a small section of brush hidden in a valley. It was quiet, hidden from the road, and wonderfully tranquil.

While our trio sat after dinner to watch the orange sunset behind the red hills it became apparent our hiding spot wasn't so hidden. In the dim light, a rancher herding his cattle home for the night spotted our oddly placed green tent and black motorcycle amongst the brown brittle brush and red sands. As soon as he spotted us, he stopped the horse mid-stride, looked at us like a group of suspicious cattle rustlers on his property, and quickly sorted out the fastest route to our camp. Ohh shit I thought, maybe this is his dried-up riverbed and maybe these are his brittle bushes.

The man could have been the poster child for a Colombian wild west movie. He came prancing into camp on a small horse that was vibrating with the energy of an Arabian show pony and dripping with a sweaty thick froth from the dry heat. The man sat in this old, worn leather saddle that could have fetched thousands of dollars at an antique auction. He wore a slightly flattened Colombian-style cowboy hat with a red handkerchief tied around his neck to catch the sweat before running into his thin, white cowboy shirt unbuttoned halfway down his tanned chest, smoking a cigarette John Wayne style. I was feeling oddly intimidated by this man who was clearly more at home here than I was. The idea of asking for a photo kept racing through my mind. I knew I'd never see such an authentic western setting in Colombia again, but I just couldn't spit out the words while he was staring down at me from the vibrating steed.

He greeted me with an intense curiosity and started to pepper me with questions I could not understand. He had a thicker accent than the other Colombians I was used to speaking with and continued to fire at me with different questions. I felt like he was more curious about me than suspicious. I'm sure looking back at my pale skin under a baseball cap, next to a large motorbike and small green house were just as odd to him as he was to me. One of the questions he repeated five times, each time faster and louder. I explained I did not understand and he just kept repeating the question again and again. Finally, I answered, *"si, un poco"* (yes, a little) and he regained the look of curiosity, wished me goodnight, and turned the anxious horse around before riding off into the last glimmer of sunset. It was all so surreal, and then it was over.

I watched the sun finally set, waited for the first of the night stars to appear, then retreated into my tent as the little black flies began their nightly attack and feed routine on my skin. When the days are intensely hot and the sun sets shortly after 6 pm, I'll often be sound asleep by 8 pm. This was one of those early nights. I'd left the rain cover off the top of the tent to allow a breeze to pass through, hoping to avoid waking up and looking like the horse in my self-made pool of frothy sweat.

That's when it happened.

The snort, the rearing up on two legs, me lurching to life trying to figure out what was happening, putting my hands up to block my face, and rolling from side to side inside the tent hoping to avoid having my skull crushed.

Then, in an instant, he came down right on the spot he was standing, spun around, and took off running in the direction he'd come. Seeing the big round rump and short tail, I realized It was a donkey!

If you've never had the chance to wake up underneath a donkey whose hoofs are reared up above your head, it is an entirely different experience than seeing them face to face. I got up out of the tent to relieve myself with a pee. It was nearly daylight, but close to 2 am. The desert stars had come to life and illuminated the entire night's sky. It was incredible! I stood and watched the twinkling lights dance as shooting star after shooting star exploded in the sky. It felt like a fireworks show put on by the heavens. Moments ago I was nearly trampled by a donkey in the night, and now here I was trying to focus on peeing with one hand and focus my phone camera on shooting stars with the other hand. If that crazy donkey had never stumbled onto me, I would have missed it all.

I eventually retired back to the tent to watch a few more falling stars through the topless tent before falling back asleep. Then I was interrupted a short time later when history quickly repeated itself. It seems the donkey had a goldfish memory and came stumbling right into my tent again, snorting and standing just as he had earlier. Again, I sprang to life covering my face from a potential trample.

I was back up at 6 am making breakfast and packing my camp, and holy shit, if a little old man on a little old donkey didn't come down this same trail. I thought I had set up in no man's land, however, it seems I set up right on the backroads superhighway of the Tatacoa Desert. My tent was right in the middle of a trail for all things donkey. He too looked a little surprised, so I greeted him with a pleasant *"Hola"* while he quickly slipped around me.

I spent the rest of the day hiding from the heat in one of the area pools that tourists frequent as they pass through the area, a small, freshwater oasis set in the hoodoos for all to enjoy. For a part of the world that likely spends most of its days well above 30oC, it was a great escape to be swimming and splashing around here.

That night I went searching for someplace that would hopefully be a little more hidden than the night before. Hoping to capitalize on the previous night's breeze and starry view, I set up the tent without the rain fly again. However, this time I would again be awoken in the middle of the night, but for entirely different reasons.

Around 5 am I woke to wet drops hitting my face. What the hell? It was raining. It was raining in the fucking desert! I quickly got up, ran outside in my underwear, and screwed-together boots to put the fly over the tent before dashing back inside and falling back asleep. This was short-lived and woke up a short time later to a sudden crash outside.

I always parked KLaiR so if she fell, she would fall away from the tent and not on my head while I was sleeping. I'm not sure who told me to do this, but it saved my life on a couple of occasions. It had rained so much that the rock I'd put under her kickstand had begun to sink in the wet sand and suddenly she fell over. To my delight, she had fallen down a hill, into some prickly shrubs with a full load on, even the spare tyre was still tied on top of my luggage.

I got back out of bed, put my boots back on, a jacket, and headed outside. By this time it was pouring and I was sliding around the muddy sands trying to get to KLaiR. She was lying there tyres-up, with fuel flowing out over the fairing while the heavens poured down on us. I tried to lift her and couldn't. I tried to sink my feet into the sand and pull her up, but I just kept sliding in what was now sticky red mud. It was impossible, but I had to get her up before all the fuel ran out. With crash bars, luggage, gear, tools, fuel, and on and on, she weighed close to 700-pounds. The icing on my muddy cake was this spare tyre I was currently carrying around. I looked like Alfalfa trying to fight Butterbean in a mud-match.

I switched tactics and began emptying her exposed Pelican case, removing all the contents. I removed the spare tyre and pulled her up the hill a little. After taking off as much weight as I could, utilizing some heavy grunting, and enjoying some lower back trauma I finally got KLaiR up. However, my moment of triumph was quickly deflated. Once up on two wheels, I realized I had no way of keeping her up. The ground was too soft for the kickstand, I had no keys to try and ride her and there was no place to lean her. Fuck!

Peering around through the rain and into the darkness, I then spotted a small stick near the base of the prickly shrubs, but it was just out of reach. I slid around to the downslope and positioned myself as far as I could from KLaiR without her falling over. I just barely had my fingertips pushing her up as I stretched my muddy feet back to try and grip the stick. It felt like some high-risk yoga move where if you failed you'd end up with two broken legs. Lucky, I had no pants on allowing me the maximum amount of stretch. Finally, I managed to work the stick to the bike with my muddy screw-boot, slide it under KLaiR's kickstand, and headed for cover in the tent, a sopping muddy mess.

A short time later the day had begun. The sun had brought the light of day and the heat had forced me out of the tent to pack up and hit the road. By 8 am I was ready to roll, but the world was not ready for us. My camp was only 100-feet from the main road, but this route was no longer powdery sand, it was sticky mud. With a lot of throttle and some crafty clutch work, I was eventually able to get us out of the disaster camp and onto the road.

Once I got to the road I was surprised to see there were no other tracks. Usually, there would be deliveries or farmers or tourists or something passing by on this busier section of road. I would soon realize why. The road was a sticky-clay disaster that was nearly impossible to use, especially on a heavy motorbike with road tyres. However, I was nearly out of water and food and needed to make my escape from the desert.

This plan of escape turned out to be a terrible idea. I spent the next six hours trying to pass the 13-kilometers of peanut butter-like roads to the closest town. I hit the gas, I fluttered the clutch, I slipped, I slid. I dropped and picked up heavy-ass KLaiR over ten times. The more I fought with the peanut butter roads the more I sweat and the more I realized my water rations were falling faster then my energy reserves.

Sometime around drop #11, it all became too much. I no longer had the strength to brace my muddy boots in the soupy sands and try to lift KLaiR up and back on two wheels. While she sat lodged in the muck, I crouched down behind a leafless bush hoping for a break from the sun. It was just then I heard my first engine of the day. A man and his girlfriend on a tiny 125cc motorbike came sliding around the corner. They stopped and looked at me like the cowboy had from a couple of nights earlier. They looked at me, then looked at a KLaiR with wide eyes like we'd fallen from another planet.

His bike was light and easy to maneuver so long as he could keep his momentum going. If the bike began to slide he would gently put a foot out to regain direction as he kept sliding along effortlessly down the peanut butter roads. I was having a moment of skinny bike envy. The couple stopped and offered to help, they were both so clean, just a bit of mud on the sole of the guy's shoes. The girlfriend just stared at my sweaty, muddy existence. Her eyes popped open and her mouth dropped while she kept the video on her phone recording me and my mess like it was a crime scene.

I said hello and the man said hello back, but the girl didn't know what to do, she just stared. The boyfriend smacked her on the arm to break her concentration and suggested she say hello back. I don't think they saw a lot of sweaty gringos who crashed their overloaded outer space bikes on this road.

A few days earlier I'd stopped and fixed a flat tyre for a guy. To his surprise, I had a patch kit, tools, and air pump. I was feeling like this move of good karma had quickly come back to me and I looked up to thank the karma gods for sending someone to help my sorry ass.

The boyfriend reluctantly sunk his clean shoes into the mud and helped me lift KLaiR up to get her going again. Then as I slowly rode away he kept an eye on me in his rearview mirror for a kilometer or so on this straight section until I suddenly stopped again. I knew he was watching because he suddenly stopped when I suddenly stopped. KLaiR had lost power and died going up a hill. Everything on the dash was black and I knew it would be a while to fix her and I didn't want to be a further bother to this couple. I waved him on and he waved back as they effortlessly continued down the road.

After giving KLaiR some open-heart surgery in the beating sun, I fixed the electronics issue and got back on the road. This moment of bliss was soon interrupted again another couple of kilometers down the road. This time the clutch had stopped working. Again I stopped, consulted the last dribbles of my now very hot water supply then got to work fixing the clutch cable. While digging around for tools I found a stray orange that had been hiding for who knows how long. In my starved, dehydrated state, I devoured the rotting orange, clinging to every hint of natural sugars for a little helpful boost of energy before tackling the last few kilometers of improving roads.

By the late afternoon I rolled into a small town on the outskirts of the desert to the amused looks of the locals. KLaiR was a mucky disaster and as she limped down the road, clumps of drying clay would spin and fall from her frame. I found a shop, purchased three drinks, several pastries, and banged off my boots street side to a small crowd of onlookers who walked by in comfortable-looking shorts and sandals.

Back on paved roads I finally had a chance to get moving and put KLaiR in second gear for the first time that day, but something was wrong. Every time I went to give her some throttle she couldn't get up to speed. I felt like she had lost all her energy and would only slowly get up to speed with plenty of patience; it was impossible to go up hills or pass anyone. I stopped in the next town, rented a room at a bed & breakfast with wifi and spent the night contacting KLR forums about my issue. The general consensus was that after spending the day riding the shit out of the clutch, it had worn her clutch plates bald and she needed repair.

The closest dealership I could find was back in Cali, and so we backtracked nearly 400-kilometers with a top speed of around 60kmph to find some parts. It was Cali that opened my eyes to the obsession of Colombia's motorbike culture when I was invited into the legendary local shop *Taller Asturias* to fix the bike. To see the excitement of moto-junkies who were ecstatic about my adventure was the morale boost I needed right now. The motorbike shop I had landed at had photos of the owner Jorge and his motorbike adventuring from all over South America. I was back with my people.

Here I met a number of interesting locals. The first was a man in his 60's who wanted so badly to talk to me, like a kid who'd finally seen his cartoon hero in real life. I could tell he used to know English very well but hadn't used it in a while. As he rediscovered his English, we chatted and he explained that he had once made a business deal with some Canadians. He was the first Colombian to import white Charolais cattle into Colombia and he had purchased 100-head of the beasts from a farm in a place called Calgary Canada! Hahaha, Calgary Canada I thought, just one hour from where I had left a year and a half ago. The guy explained they had taken the cows in Canadian winter and had them trucked to Florida in the southern USA where they were then put on a huge cargo plane and flown into Colombia. What they hadn't accounted for was the incredible change in temperatures the cattle were going to go through. Once these large cows arrived in Colombia with their thick winter coats on, they had to continually spray the cattle with cold water to keep them cool and one by one they shaved off their fur to help them adjust. The man said it was an incredible amount of work, but eventually, it all paid off and he'd made quite a lot of money in the end.

The next guy I met would play a pivotal role in the future of my trip. He pulled up to the shop on a KLR and we got to chatting. It turned out John was a KLR fanatic. Not a fan, but a fanatic. He and his wife each had a KLR's and he had kitted out his all in orange, with every accessory imaginable. When he couldn't add any more farkels, he began to make KLR parts and sell them. He even had a kennel fitted to the back of the bike for his dog. He loved hearing about my adventure and explained his dream was to eventually ride his KLR from Colombia to Alaska with his wife & dog in a couple of years.

Like most enterprising Colombians not only did he make KLR parts, he also managed a company that made a product similar to Slime, that green goo you put in tyres to stop leaks. I ended up buying some KLR parts he'd made while enjoying a tour of his shop one day. We exchanged information and I told him if he had any questions about the road to Alaska, to let me know.

After a few days in the shop with various motorbike mechanics hovering over my shoulder explaining what I was doing right or wrong, KLaiR was eventually put back together and back on the road. Unable to find my parts in Colombia on short notice, the owner had a friend from Venezuela put the parts on a bus and have them shipped across the border and down to us in record time. The owner showed me the price of the parts in Colombia, then proceeded to charge me the exact cost plus shipping for my parts, no markup. He then refused any payment for the use of his shop, tools, or the team's mechanical knowledge and sent me on my way with a handshake and the parting words *"Suerte, suerte, mucho suerte"*.

(Fixing the battery issue)   (KLaiR overloaded and stuck in the desert)

Ecuador
Criminal Or Adventurer?

"I'm not afraid to go to jail. I'm afraid to be incarcerated."
- Martha Stewart

This was it, border crossing day. I'd spent months and miles sneaking around the backroads of Colombia, passing through the most remote of villages, via the most unconventional roads possible just to evade police checkpoints to get here. The plan was to eventually arrive at this more remote border post with the hopes of smuggling KLaiR out of Colombia and into Ecuador. It was my only shot to get out of one country and into the other without having the bike impounded, having to pay some hefty fines, or possibly landing in a Colombian prison. It was all feeling very Pablo Escobar. In this scenario, KLaiR was the cocaine and I was Pablo.

It had all gone fairly well and I'd managed to use every backroad I could find. As a result, I had only one encounter, and this was with the military. It was in this small mountain village on the way to nowhere and when they flagged me down and asked for my passport; I thought it was over. I knew I would be something of interest to them on this otherwise untraveled trail, and instead of handing over any paperwork or my passport I just kept talking. From the moment I stopped to the moment they asked for my documents and about the bike, I did not shut up. I used every Spanish word I could think of to describe the country and how great the people were. I was suddenly going on like Spanish was my mother tongue. Funny how things come to you when you absolutely need them to.

After five or ten minutes of me enthusiastically commenting on how wonderful everyone was and how great Colombia is, I eventually rounded up the men and had them pose with me for a few group photos while the youngest guy in the group took our picture. The whole time I just kept on talking, showing them the photos on my camera then packing it up and putting my helmet back on. Then I got back on KLaiR, handed out a round of handshakes like I was running for local office, and rode off waving. I never stopped until I was well out of town and further down the road. Not once did a piece of paper or photo i.d. make its way into the conversation.

Was all of this effort going to be worth it? I was betting the rest of the trip through South America on this one escape route into Ecuador and was sweating up a nervous storm thinking about what might happen if I got caught.

The final night before crossing the border I found a Love Motel to spend the night in. On the edge of this tiny border town of bright lights and cheap markets was a pink home with a large water fountain at the entrance and in the back was an equally bright pink row of rooms. It looked like the Pink Panthers' personal residence.

I was greeted by a small child about seven who asked me a few questions about what I was looking for and how long I planned to stay. Her role as the greeter of the pink sex house felt a little *City Of God*, but she was very professional and I professionally addressed her questions stating I only needed a room for one person and planned to spend the entire night, not just a few hours. After listening to my response she let out a little grin, her persona switched from front of house receptionist to a seven-year-old girl and she ran off to get her dad as a messy ponytail bounced along behind her.

Her dad soon arrived and was caught between confusion and suspicion about my being alone and not expecting to meet anyone. Then the topic quickly switched to my motorbike and travels. While he questioned me about the trip we walked down to a large pink gate that enclosed the car park and the room hidden behind it. Inside the room was a queen-sized bed, some towels, a television, and air conditioning. At first glance, it looked like a standard hotel. Then a few oddities began to appear. The most obvious being a 24" x 36" poster on the wall covered with 20+ sex positions depicted in photos. Then I realized the mints on the pillows were not mints, they were condoms. Then I noticed a little door that could open from the outside and drinks or whatever could be passed inside without barging into the room. How romantic I thought.

The guy was so thrilled with my presence as a hotel guest with this crazy motorbike who had arrived with an entirely different agenda than the usual guests. He said I could stay for the whole night for the 3-hour price and invited me up for dinner later. Sure enough, I found myself at the dining room table a few hours later with the seven-year-old greeter, her mum, and her grandparents.

It was during family dinner that I was again shocked to learn that my assumption about places was not always what they seemed. I asked the family why they wanted to own a brothel and if it was a good business? At this point, the son who'd checked me in was making dinner, and the dad, probably in his 70's, was watching tv in the living room, while the mum was setting the table. In one heartbeat each stopped what they were doing, turned, and looked at me like I'd just cursed the family name.

The parents looked at the son as if to say, explain to this man what he just asked. He finished up dinner then sat down to explain the situation to me. He said that a love motel was a place for lovers to come, not a road-side stop for hookers and truckers. In many countries in Latin America families often lived together for most of their lives, partially for the love of the family, but more realistically for economic reasons.

The idea of trying to enjoy an intimate evening with your wife while your parents were in the next room or possibly even the next bed was a touch unrealistic. Instead, you might arrange a date with your lover and spend an hour or three at a Love Motel to take care of the details that might not be as welcome in a room with your parents.

Now, it's not all sunshine and lollipops. There is of course a fair number of brothels too, and having a wife as well as a mistress was nothing unusual in Latin America. Having seen these well-advertised and questionable-looking hotels since Mexico, it had taken me to Colombia to find out what was really inside. Wifi, showers, AC, and room service all for the hourly rate. Hot damn I had been missing out on some well-serviced sleeping options at discount rates. Again I had to remind myself to stop judging books by their cover.

After dinner, the guy took me on a private tour of the town on the back of his motorbike explaining the hundreds of shops and how they made money exporting goods like clothes, food, and housewares back and forth across the border with Ecuador. The tour felt a bit more like a parade at times as he would honk at everyone he knew and wave excitedly noting the grubby gringo on the backseat.

A night of sexy sleeping for one and family supper with the locals, it was the type of farewell that only Colombia could provide. Next, I was off to face my final challenge of the country. I just needed to get across the border and into Ecuador. One final meeting with border officials and I'd be through. The nervousness was countered by my excitement to see the Amazon. This route would take me directly into the Amazon Rainforest of Ecuador, a dream I could have never imagined coming true.

I'd read from others who'd used this border (that will remain nameless) that all the paperwork here happened in one building. Here they would stamp you out of Colombia and into Ecuador under one efficient roof. Not the usual running around from official to official and line up to line up getting stamps, photocopies, and slips of paper like back in Central America.

Due to the low amount of traffic at this border, officials relied on a checkout, check-in honor system for vehicles. I knew I would not be honoring one half of this arrangement. Doing so would risk the whole fines, prison, bike impoundment scenario I was dreading. The problem with this plan was that KLaiR could never come back to Colombia with me or any other traveler if I chose to sell her down the line. I was a bit concerned if I wanted to ride back to Canada, but I knew I would never in my life dream of selling off my girlfriend.

I arrived at the border post and to my surprise, it was virtually deserted; in contrast to a border like say that of Mexico and Guatemala. A road traveler was often greeted by a swarm of 10-15 "helpers" who rushed you wanting to aid with the daunting paperwork and translations for a fee. On top of this, there were usually busloads of people crossing, hawkers selling food and drink, those begging for money, the possibility of theft, and sometimes corrupt officials presenting "stamping fees" invented for their own personal gain.

At this border, it was just me and a few border officials inside an air-conditioned building along with one Ecuadorian couple crossing in their car, otherwise nothing. This was my first vacant border post in ten countries. As the only obvious tourist there I was worried that everyone working would be expecting me to come and see them. No distractions or other people asking questions. Just little old me wanting to get my paperwork done. Usually, this scenario of undivided official attention would be a blessing. My dreams of a quiet border were answered but at entirely the wrong moment.

I pulled up, parked KLaiR behind some trees in the parking lot, and went inside. Here I talked to an official who stamped my passport out of Colombia, then directed me to where I do the bike paperwork. I asked him where to go after the bike paperwork and he directed me to the stamp guy to get me into Ecuador. I walked confidently past the "check out of Colombia" office like it didn't exist and avoided honoring the honor system. Instead, I walked into the office of the guy who did the bike paperwork to get me into Ecuador.

As this guy was stamping me in, he noted that I needed to get the bike stamped out still. *Ahh, Si Senor.* I acted confused like I'd forgotten that step and said I'd do it after. I knew to get into the country I only needed my bike documents and passport stamped, no proof of leaving the country with the bike. I walked out, nervously confident, knowing that if this failed I was fucked.

I took a deep breath, remembered to keep my Spanish to a minimum, and proceeded for the bike stamps to get me into Ecuador. In under a minute the paperwork was complete. This guy looked at my documents and he too noticed that I didn't have the stamp to check KLaiR out of Colombia. The words *"Fuck-Fuck-Fuck!"*, were screaming inside my head. He pointed one door over and said that was the door to complete that part of the process. Fucking hell! I was just one door from complete or criminal.

I smiled, said *Si*. Then asked where the bathroom was. *Donde es el baño?* I knew the bathroom was in the opposite direction of the Colombian (SOAT) stamp office. I left his office staring at my documents as though I was looking for something and walked towards the bathroom. Instead of walking into the bathroom, I turned and walked right out the front door like Billy's final exit in the movie Midnight Express.

No stopping, no running, no putting the paperwork away, just a confident and direct line to KLaiR. Some guy in the parking lot was standing beside KLaiR waiting to ask me some questions while he was on his smoke break. I just smiled, put on my helmet, hit the starter button, and dropped KLaiR into first gear as I steadily made our way to Ecuador.

Driving this impossibly long strip of fresh pavement I noted a number of video cameras that watch everyone as they leave Colombia and enter Ecuador. Otherwise, nothing. No stops, no officials checking paperwork, no one chasing me down. That was it, nothing. Not one person came for me. Two painfully long minutes later and we were officially in Ecuador!

I drove until I hit the first town then made a few turns down dusty side roads looking to see if anyone was following me. Nope, nothing. We were home free. Welcome to Ecuador!

(Activity options in the Love Motel room)   (BBQ, Colombia style)

Ecuador
Life & Death In The Amazon

*"**Integrity:** Ethics and integrity are the foundation of our brand and the guiding principles for all we do." - Halliburton.com - Company Mission Vision Values Statement*

*"**Global Stewardship:** Developing a unique approach to sustainability and committing to social and environmental responsibility."*
SLB.com (Schlumberger) - Companies Guiding Principles

The good news was I was in Ecuador, the bad news was it was Sunday and virtually everything was closed. I tried to find a place to get American dollars, the currency of Ecuador, and a sim card to access the internet from my phone. I found a small shop selling candies and cigarettes so I stopped for a sim card, cookies, and chocolate milk. The guy couldn't understand a word of my Spanish and wouldn't help me with the sim card. After the cookies and milk, I ended up at another hole-in-the-wall shop and got the sim card. I couldn't get the card to work and surprisingly the owner took it back, put a little bit of tape on it, and sent me on my way. I would not be sharing my triumphant success with the world of social media today.

Ecuador has gone through several currencies in its history like the Peso and most recently the Sucre. In 1950 the Sucre had a rate of about 15 - 1 against the US dollar. By 1960 it was 18 - 1, by 1970 25 - 1. By 1983 the Sucre had slipped to 42 - 1. Then by 1990 had fallen even further to 800 - 1 and by 1995 was spiraling out of control where $1USD would buy nearly 3000 Sucre. It was an economic disaster.

During the calamity of the turn of the century, most Americans were worried about the Mayan calendar ending the world and computers erasing all records of their savings. In Ecuador, the reality was their currency was literally being erased, no computer necessary. On the morning of January 7th, 2000 you could buy 25,000 Sucre for $1USD. Along with the crashing currency, the state of the country was crumbling too. For Ecuador, the Mayan myth was coming to life.

Two days later on January 9th, 2000, President Jamil Mahuad announced that Ecuador would adopt the USD as the country's currency and the locals exploded into a furious rioting rage. To counter this loss of control a left-wing coup overthrew Mahuad on the premise of his dollar adoption and Gustavo Noboa took over power of the country. Three months later, in a bizarre state of events, Noboa, whose anti-dollar revolution that had brought him to power then adopted the dollar himself and life rallied on. Unlike Panama who also uses USD as the currency but instead calls it a Balboa, Ecuador has relented to roll with the USD as its currency and by its real name.

Aside from cookies and sim cards I was happy to see that you could also buy fuel on Sundays. My $12/day budget was elated to discover that at a time when gasoline in Canada was about $1.10/L CAD ($0.85USD) here it was $0.50/L! This was the cheapest fuel I'd seen this whole trip. I filled up using some USD I had stashed in the bike and opted to drive as far as I could towards the rainforest and find food on Monday.

I was so close to the Amazon rainforest I couldn't believe it. My whole life I'd been feeding off National Geographic stories and wanting to see the magic of the Amazon with my own eyes. My mind was racing with the excitement of passing through where rare and incredible wildlife are still evolving, seeing the clear rivers that endlessly wandered through history, the natural medicines being discovered, indigenous people who'd never seen the western world. I felt like a kid in a giant candy store on the brink of a sugar-rush explosion. The build-up to this moment was 3-decades in the making. Now I was within a 30-minute drive from entering this monumental rainforest that stretches across Colombia, Ecuador, Brazil, Venezuela, Peru, and Bolivia, responsible for providing oxygen and life to a massive part of the planet.

As I rode down the quiet paved road towards the edge of the jungle, I could sense a large grin expanding across my face. I could feel the warm feeling of excitement building as my heart flooded my body with blood and my endorphins began to light up. Then, like hundreds of times before, I got distracted by what was going on around me and missed the turn entirely. Once I realized the error, like hundreds of times before, I looped around and made my way back to the gravel road that would lead me into my first Amazon experience.

It felt like I had come home after being gone for years with the anticipation of meeting my beautiful lover who would be waiting for me with a fluttering heart of excitement and welcoming open arms. We would embrace and kiss passionately in the excitement of the moment and rekindle our long-lost love in endless happiness.

Instead of this envisioned moment of loving bliss, it felt more like I had opened the door only to find her bent over a kitchen table being fucked by another man.

I was almost sick as I rounded the corner. The grin dropped, the warmth cooled, the excitement was crushed, the moment with the lover had turned to betrayal, and the kid at the candy store suddenly felt a cavity coming on. I felt a part of my 3-decades long dream die in an instant.

A large blue and white truck hauling industrial equipment came thundering out from behind a chain-link fence with black diesel fumes spewing out into the clean air, smothering the view of the road in front of me while red dust came kicking out from its eighteen or so tyres. I'd seen these identical trucks hundreds of times before, but seeing them here was entirely different. It was an oilfield truck from the company Schlumberger and right across the road, equally as glaring, was a large Halliburton sign.

Coming from oil-rich Alberta Canada I knew exactly what these trucks were doing here. They were set-up to extract oil from the heart of the Amazon. It was not the National Geographic painted picture of a harmonious natural existence I'd dreamed of my entire life. It was the gates of hell, greeted by big oil who were making their way through the Amazon with chainsaws and bulldozers, not cameras and conservation.

An hour earlier I was impressed with how cheap the fuel was in the country, then when I was faced with the reality of knowing where it came from, I was devastated. The first 5-minutes of my rainforest experience were following a flat deck oil truck hauling destructive, earth-killing equipment down a dusty road. It was clear that I lived in a world of personal conflict and brushing topics under the rug as they suited or didn't suit me. I'd never worked directly in the oil industry, but in one form or another, all of the abundant wealth where I'd come from was obtained from oil. I was a part of the problem and all at once I finally realized it.

The truck rumbled on as I stopped to take a few photos of my scruffy jungle surroundings. In this part of the world, right on the equator, there are around 12-hours of daylight and 12-hours of darkness. I knew I'd need to find a place to camp in the next couple of hours as it was getting close to 6 pm and the world wasn't about to stop spinning for me.

I ended up on the river's edge down a lonely road and decided to take out my rod for some river fishing while waiting for it to get a little darker before setting up my tent. Behind me was a wooden building that appeared to have been a small restaurant at one point, a bit strange as there was only one house here, just up the hill behind a small fence. They both seemed as out of place as did this road that led to nowhere.

It looked like no one was around at either building and hadn't been for quite a while. After 30-minutes of fishing and not catching dinner, I opted to put up the tent before dark. Suddenly I heard a vehicle coming down the road. Damnit, I never like to be in a situation where I know there is only one way out and I'm the only one around. I just pretend like I come here all the time and continued to fish. Coming down the road were a few small motorbikes and what looked like a small family all dressed like they might spend more time in the jungle than the city. They pulled up to the river's edge and longingly peered up and down the river like they were looking for something then proceeded to wait.

Then they noticed me, my bike, and how I was fishing with a rod and reel. They all looked confused, a look I was used to. I smiled, waved, and continued to fish. One of the kids walked upstream, jumped into the river with a big splash, and floated down a short distance before hopping out where the family was waiting. Then out of what felt like thin air, a long barge ferry with four large outboard motors came roaring upstream. The barge had a one ton Ford work truck on the deck and room for probably 4-5 more. The ferry and its row of speed boat engines pushed up on the gravel edge of the shore. The truck drove off onto the mainland and the motorbikes and family got on, then they all roared off up the river.

I'll never know the full story, but the assumption I made in my head was that the oil company needed the land in the rainforest to get the oil. I'm guessing they made a deal with the locals that lived there that they could use the oil company ferry to get back and forth across the river to where they lived, no questions asked, as they needed to, and the oil company could operate without issue inside the forest. I had no idea, but that's how I felt the story went based on the contrast between the passengers on the boat vs the workers.

As everyone left and the sun started to set, I decided to finish putting my sleeping bag in the tent. One quick zip of the tent door and I heard another vehicle coming down the road, so much for the remote jungle isolation I was expecting. I was worried someone had heard I was there from this group and was coming to check on me. With my tent now fully erect, there would be no hiding the fact that I was aiming to sleep here.

The truck pulled up near the entrance to the home and an older lady in the passenger seat looked at me with the usual outer space look while the dog in the back barked in my direction to see what my reaction would be. I just smiled, waved, and continued on with what I was doing. The truck made a quick turn and the driver went straight up the hill towards the house.

A few minutes later the lady and the dog came down to see me. The lady asked what I was doing, so I explained in my best Spanish what I was up to. We chatted for a bit and she explained this road had been built by the oil company and workers used it to go into the bush at this point and work. She had owned the little restaurant across the road. Things had now changed as it was 2016 and global oil prices had dropped drastically. She said that the oil companies' worked considerably less than they used to and she had to close the restaurant because hardly any workers came into the forest to extract the oil. Even with the restaurant closed she decided to continue to live on the hill down this dead-end road. I knew that just like where I was from these workers were focused on feeding their families, but I couldn't help but think they must know they were extracting part of their heritage along with the oil.

I think by this point she realized I wasn't a threat and told me it would be safer if I came and camped inside the fence on their property at the top of the hill. Wow, this had certainly turned out different than I was expecting. I took the tent down and rode KLaiR up the hill and inside the gate. The lady showed me to a large room beside the house she used to rent out. I could put my tent inside the room to keep the bugs and rain out while I slept.

The little home had a series of rooms for rent behind it and a strip of cement bathrooms with showers efficiently lined up in a row of about ten. In a matter of moments, I went from camping in the bush to hotel accommodations in the jungle! A short time later she came back to check on me and to explain how the block of bathrooms and showers operated.

By this point, I was cooking soup in my pot over the small Dragonfly camping stove inside the room. The lady had never seen anything like my little MSR stove and was completely entranced. She had me show her how this little cooker worked and I was now just as excited as she was to walk through how it operated. She then left and quickly returned with another man who was here, possibly her husband, and had me show him how the stove operated. They both wanted to understand how it all came apart to how it made a flame from the gasoline in the canister. To add to the excitement I don't think he'd seen a tent like this before. The man then had me explain the tent and how it held together along with my inflatable sleeping mat. I was feeling very foreign at this point, but quite happy to explain the workings of my mobile living quarters to their interest.

That night it rained in biblical proportions and I was again amazed how I had ended up under this tin roof and not being washed downriver. In the morning I thanked my gracious hosts for the interesting bug, and tropical storm-free night and gave them some Canada pins I had stashed in the bike before continuing into the jungle.

As the day wound on, I tried to explore any side roads I could find towards the river. The main road was nice, but all I could see was thick jungle on either side. A few stops for river fishing and odd looks from locals living in small villages dotted with wooden huts built on tall stilts and I was again looking for a place to stay before the sun went down at 6 pm.

I found a place marker on my travel app where someone had parked in the yard of a local family a couple of years earlier. It was a long shot, but I wanted to see if I could camp in the yard of these people too. Eventually, I found this industrial-looking building not far off the road.

The yard was massive, probably two acres, and the building you could see from the road was a dull yellow with two separate buildings that were quite large. It looked like a two-story storage bay about 100-feet long. I wasn't sure if it was a home or an office or some kind of working area. Either way, when I came rumbling down the driveway I was greeted by a couple of small children and one kid who was maybe 12 or 13.

I asked if they lived here and explained in my best Spanish what I was up to and where I'd come from. I then asked if their mum or dad was home? Just then the mum appeared and I repeated my introduction and asked if I could spend the night in my tent in the yard. A few clarity questions were exchanged about wanting to sleep outside and they explained that the heavy rains might be too much for sleeping outside at night.

The mum then led me to a door at the bottom of the building closest to where we were standing. She opened the door and spread all across the tiled floor were ears of maize with the husk peeled back. The maize was in this room to dry. They likely didn't have a fridge for keeping things cool, but they did have a whole room for drying. The plan was that they would clear out all of this maize just so I could pitch my tent inside out of the rain.

I tried to explain I would be fine in the tent outside, but they said it was no problem and in an instant, the kids began to clear out the maize while the mum left to fetch a broom. Shortly the room was cleared out and they brought in a little table. Just like that, I'd rolled up to the home of strangers in the jungle, asked a couple of questions, and they rearranged their lives for my convenience, it was incredible!

The kids focused on me like I was a new family pet. The 12 or 13-year-old suggested I put the bike behind the house so it couldn't be seen from the road. I moved it around back and the boy eagerly started to run his hands across KLaiR as he inspected all of my gear, GPS, water bottle holder, and the various items that were strapped onto her. I don't think he'd seen a motorcycle used quite like this before. As we talked, more kids started to come walking down the driveway. They'd come from school and spotted me at the house. I could see their conversation fading a little as their attention shifted towards me.

The younger kids at the house proudly introduced me like I was a known friend of theirs and explained I was spending the night. With the ice broken, the questions began flooding in. I explained that my Spanish wasn't the best and if they could please speak slowly it would help. They said their Spanish wasn't the best either as they spoke a regional language and they learned Spanish as a second language. I wasn't getting much Spanish sympathy here.

After the interrogation, they felt like I was ready for a tour of the property and took me down to the river and showed me where they went swimming. To get here we followed a grassy path with purposed-placed rocks to keep the path from washing away with the rains. The path followed down through the trees to the river. Eventually, we got to the water's edge and I asked if I could fish here. They said of course, people fished here all the time. I said I'd had some fishing stuff and I'd go get it. All four kids wanted to come back to the house with me to get it.

When we got back to the bike I pulled out my little telescopic fishing rod and hooks. Again I don't think they'd ever seen a fishing setup like this and were all very curious how this little rod and flashing hooks were going to work. I think everyone was expecting big results from my high-tech gear.

We walked back to the river and all four kids watched attentively as I slowly extended the rod from just over a foot to a full length of about six feet. I then put a spinner hook on the end and began to cast into the fast-moving, murky water. After about the 20th cast and no results, the crowd was not very impressed. The oldest kid told me I needed chicken skin or chunks of meat on my hook or I'd never catch anything. They also said the water was very high this time of year and wasn't great for swimming or fishing. I caught nothing.

The sun of the day was fading and we headed back to the house. I retreated into my maize room and started sorting out my stove to make dinner. I wondered if I could use one of these maize corn things in the other room as part of my dinner. Just as I lit the MSR stove there was a little knock at the door. The old wooden door to the maize room creaked open and an older man, small and slender, with rugged regional features where his dark skin had been weathered from the sun, smiled at me and said "Hello, welcome" in English. It was the father of this family and this was his maize room I was staying in.

In Spanish, the father asked what I was up to and I explained I was about to cook dinner. He looked surprised and said no, we are making dinner and you can come and eat with us. So off went my little cooker and inside the house we strolled. It was here that I came to learn about the full extent of this family and the property.

To get inside the house you walk up a large cement staircase roughly 30-feet wide and 25 or 30 steps to the top. The steps lead to the main doors of this worn cement building. Entering you're met by a landing area that feels like the greeting room to a large corporate office. Only instead of a desk and receptionist, this office had a large kitchen and industrial stove behind a long counter that led into another room. The kitchen was outfitted with a 6-burner stove that runs on propane, the type used by catering companies or at large events. The room was dim with only a bit of natural light coming in from outside. Cooking was the mum from earlier and a couple of teenage girls along with some of the smaller children. I smiled and said hello to the curious faces I hadn't met yet before then, dad led me into the next room.

This room was huge, probably 70-feet long and 30-feet across, with cement walls painted in a peeling whitewash with one photo clinging to otherwise empty walls. The space had one light hanging from a single wire some 15-feet up, dimly flickering and dwarfed by the large room it was trying to illuminate. Awkwardly off to one side was a series of mismatched tables and chairs that made up a long seating area. I felt like we were eating dinner in a gymnasium furnished on a university student's budget.

There were a few more children in this room, plus one young man probably 19 or 20. He smiled and said hello in Spanish. Then the mum began to bring in the food and quickly behind her, children began to pour into the room in a steady stream. I wasn't sure if they were having a party on my behalf or if I'd shown up for some event. In total there were twelve people plus me for dinner in the gym.

The dad spoke some very basic English, but more than enough that I could chat with him and explain my trip and answer questions about North America, of which he had plenty. He sat at one end directly across from me while the rest of the guests filled up the other sections of the table. Aside from us talking lightly, the room of thirteen was eerily quiet. Everyone just stared at me talking to the dad. When I'd look over at the group to see why it was so quiet they'd all instantly glance away like they were looking at something on the empty walls. That move you do when someone has a booger hanging from their nose that you can't stop staring at and you want them to notice and do something about it but you don't want to say anything.

Dinner was then served and to break the silence I asked them what they wanted to know about me? The room then settled into little conversations amongst themselves about what they wanted to ask, then there was a pause while an older kid asked a question, then the little conversations would start again based on my response. Something like *"How fast does your motorbike drive?"* Or *"Where are you going in Ecuador?"*

Dinner was a mix of scrambled eggs, ground maize toasted in a pan with oil and onion, some fried plantains, a few nuts, and some vegetables I'd never seen before. No meat. I asked if this many people were always here for dinner. The dad laughed along with the whole table and said yes, these were all his children. What, all 10-kids are yours? They could sense my shock. I explained I came from a family of 4-kids and that was quite big where I was from. I asked if we could go around the table and have everyone say their name again along with their age. From six to nineteen, one by one, they recited their name and age, and one by one like studying for a high school exam, I instantly forgot everything they said.

As the conversations trickled in I learned that this used to be an oil camp that housed workers who were searching for oil in the area. Wow, I thought, how perfect for this family. There were something like 16 rooms here, a block of showers, a block of toilets, a big kitchen, formerly an office, and this huge dining area. The family had acquired it when the oil company had moved out years ago when the work dried up. I used this information as my positive focal point about the oil companies. It was by far the biggest "house" I'd seen anywhere around here. I got the feeling this family might be a big deal in this area.

The more we talked the more I learned and it turned out the dad was the principal of the school just up the road. How perfect I thought, to have your work and home so close together. The dad had learned a bit of English growing up, but for the most part, everyone spoke a regional language first, then learned Spanish in school. The kids were also taught a bit of English but it was by teachers who'd learned it second hand and the dad said it was very hard to get a native English speaker to come out and live in the jungle to teach the locals. He said they once had a German lady who spoke English and lived with them for a year while she was learning about natural medicines in the jungle. She spoke to the kids in English but that was lost on them now. Just then I could see a thought spark in his mind.

The dad asked how long I was staying? I said I wasn't sure but probably just the night. He suggested I stay a couple of days and come to the school with him to teach English. Well, here I was in the home of the local principal having dinner that his family prepared and staying in his corn room. I'd never taught English before, actually, I'd hardly taught anything before. I had no idea what to do, but I was in no position to say no.

The next day at 5 am I could hear the house come to life, I got up and began the day with everyone else. After a quick breakfast that looked similar to dinner, we all walked to school at 6:30 am. The kids were going to learn, and well, I was going to teach. Here I was in my only pair of pants with my only clean shirt, looking to pull off some miracle to a group of jungle kids who may or may not have ever heard English from a native speaker or even seen an English speaker before. I wished myself luck and off we went.

Upon arrival, Dad/principal excitedly began to parade me around the school like I was a freshly awarded prize. I wish I was as excited as he was. We started by barging into the classroom of the youngest children, 6 & 7-year-olds, who were playing games with their teacher. As the door burst open and I was presented, the principal announced that the class would be interrupted while I, a native English speaker from America, would rehearse the alphabet and play games with the children in English. I was sweating more than I was during the bike smuggling day all while the teacher looked at us with that, *you're a bunch of assholes, I just got these kids settled down look*, and relented to the principal's wishes as he walked out the door leaving me to teach.

Feeling completely out of my element and having no idea what to do, I introduced myself in Spanish and then began to show the kids letters on the board and recite the alphabet to them in English. After my English pronunciation, I had the kids repeat what I said. This trick was going pretty well I thought as it was holding the children's attention. Maybe I was a good teacher. After going through the alphabet once, the teacher decided I was fine to look after the kids and left the room too. Shit!

No principal, no teacher, and me in a room full of children who were just playing games three minutes earlier. Having only one trick up my sleeve I decided to start over with the alphabet. Then I spotted a list of numbers on the wall and shifted the teaching over to reciting the numbers one through twenty in English. The kids' excitement began to fade. I wasn't jumping overboard just yet, but I could feel this ship sinking.

This whole charade lasted for 20-minutes or so until one kid after another began to focus more on playing and less on the strange guy talking a bunch of repetitive nonsense at the front of the room. Finally, the chaos reached a breaking point as all attention spans were off of me and back on the games. Just then, the teacher strolled back into the room followed by my principal savior. He thanked the kids and had them thank me in English, then the gringo parade continued on into the next room.

This scenario of barging into room after room to interrupt math, science, reading, games or whatever continued throughout the morning. My excited guide continued to open each door, producing a pale white "American" who only spoke English to a group of students who mainly spoke their native language in the hopes of them learning something before I was taken to the next class 20-30 minutes later. Starting from the youngest class we would eventually reach the oldest students, a group of teenagers who were certainly less excited about hearing the alphabet in English than 7-year-olds were.

When we reached the second last door it was getting close to noon and temperatures in the jungle were heating up. Between my endless nervousness and the general heat of the day I knew my only clean shirt was now soaked with unappealing sweat. I was getting into a bit of a routine with the younger kids and started to ask each one of them a basic question in Spanish then have them answer in English, with a bit of help.

I was now with the 10-12-year-olds and I asked each student what their name was and how many brothers and sisters they had. Then they would say something like, my name is James, and I have one brother and one sister. Except it went nothing like this.

First, no one was ever named James and I could rarely pronounce their names correctly. Next, when the first child went, she casually explained she had 7-brothers and 5-sisters. Thinking I misunderstood her Spanish reply, I asked again to clarify how many brothers and sisters she had. Again she said 7-brothers and 5-sisters. I thought she was joking, but either way, I smiled and said ok then moved on to the next student.

The next student was little Timmy (it was never Timmy) and I asked him what his name was and how many brothers and sisters he had? Timmy said he had 9-brothers and 2-sisters. Again my mouth dropped and I thought these kids were messing with me. Either way, I said his reply in English and he repeated what I said.

Now by the 5th kid, I was getting the impression that these kids were in fact telling the truth and not just bullshitting the American substitute teacher. I don't think there was one kid in the room who had less than double-digit family members. This is where it hit me that it was such a surprise to the family when at dinner the night before what I thought was a party, was just a family dinner. Everyone who lived around this little village had 8, 12, 14, or more children. It was like 1940's Canada. The more kids you had the more help there was around the farm. Wow, we were from two completely different points in world history.

After my local sex-ed lesson I was taken to the final room. The door opened and right in the middle of a math lesson, I was presented to the oldest students in the school. A group of about 12 students, roughly 14-16-years-old. One of the girls in the class was from the house where I was staying. I looked at her and smiled and said hello. She looked mortified like maybe I shouldn't have pointed her out of the crowd. This game of what's your name and how many siblings do you have wasn't going to go far with teenagers. Again the teacher looked relieved for a break and after my introduction, she promptly left the room.

In my best/worst Spanish I explained who I was and what I was doing here then asked them if they had any questions? If they did, I would try to answer in Spanish and English and then have them ask me the question again in English. As you can imagine, putting a group of teenagers on the spot to point out their weaknesses was a terrible idea.

There was complete silence. No one wanted to ask me anything. Here in my only pair of pants and sweaty t-shirt staring at a group of unamused teenagers I hit a wall. Ok I thought, I'll ask you a question and you can answer it in Spanish and then again in English. I started to ask the room a few questions. I figured geography would be a good place to start.

"Do you know where Colombia is?", no one responded.

I started to pick people out. I asked the guy in the front if he knew where Colombia was. He said *"Si."*. OK, now repeat my question in English. This agonizing task of trying to pull information from teenagers in two languages they didn't enjoy speaking was going nowhere fast. I was feeling like an imposter who was wasting their time and they had no idea what to do with me. Finally, after what felt like an awkward eternity, the school bell rang. We were all saved by the bell, and class was over.

It was just after 12 pm and school was done for the day. I started to walk home alone. The teenage girl from class didn't want to walk with me. Luckily one of the little kids found me and walked the rest of the way home with me. She explained that class started early when it was still cool and ended before the tropical heat of the day set in unless there was an afterschool activity like sports, the reason they had arrived home later the day before. The heat of the day had never been a problem where I grew up. School started at 8:15 am and finished at 3:27 pm and you only got to miss a day when it was colder than -40oC, which happened more often than you might imagine.

My first day of teaching English ended in an exhausting and sticky state. I think my brain was drained much more than it had been for any task previous to this. In Mexico I could barely ask for the right meat in a taco, now I was stumbling around as an under-trained English teacher on the back of street Spanish. Despite what felt like a complete blunder I was slightly impressed that I held my own in two languages for part of the day.

I ended up staying for five days with my adoptive jungle family learning the life of the locals. On the second last day, in a strange turn of fishing events, I finally caught something. I had been fishing just before sundown when all of the bugs and birds came out to hunt in a flurry of kill or be killed. There had been plenty of bats swarming by to catch bugs as they do every evening at this time. Mid-cast there was suddenly a huge pull on the line. Finally, I had caught something, I was so excited to finally reel a fish out of the water and take it to the family. It wasn't a fish at all I'd caught a fucking bat! He'd flown right into my line and was flailing around with one wing. Trying to avoid being bitten by this little vampire, myself and one of the kids managed to reel him in and get him loose from the line. Everyone was shockingly-amused with my catch of the day.

If I had one missed opportunity during this stay it was my lack of photographic timing. One evening I went with the family to harvest fruits and nuts in the forest. The mum had a big woven basket made from the thick fibers of the tree bark under her arms and one of the older kids had one over his shoulder. As we cut through what looked like dense vegetation I was taken to the beginning of what turned out to be over 90-acres of fruits and vegetables the family was growing inside the jungle, fields of maize, rice, bananas, nuts, and other fruits. It was incredible what was hidden here in plain sight.

This evening we were harvesting some cocoa, white beans, and a few tomatoes that had grown. I now understood why the meals had been vegetarian; they didn't raise animals and there wasn't much hunting in the area so they ate what they could grow. As the mist settled in around us and we forged for the bounty hidden inside the jungle, it made for an incredible Nat. Geo. worthy photo of the natives harvesting in the forest with their self-made baskets. The type of image I had dreamed about inside the Amazon. A stunning moment I'll forever have captured in my mind but I can only share with the world in words.

I parted ways with the family hoping that they had learned even a hint as much from me as I did from them. Before leaving the father gave me his cell phone number and asked that if I could find anyone who would be willing to come to the jungle and teach English he would be forever grateful. I did test that number on a few occasions, but to no avail, it never worked.

(Class photo with some of the students) (No fish, but one bat!)

(An evening outside with half the family)

Ecuador
Motorcycling To The Highest Point From Center Earth

The following story was published in the March 7th 2018 online edition of Adventuremotorcycle.com & posted as it was written.

Luckily, even in blinding weather, my GPS could watch the route and I could watch the GPS. Particularly useful at this moment as I could make out nothing on the road, I felt more like a navigating pilot in foggy air than a biker on the road. Then, just before my main highway route turned to the final bit of two-lane track towards the national park entrance, I could make out a faint swirling of red lights. Out of the fog, like an action movie set, abruptly sat several parked cars on the highway, then a smattering of police and ambulances. I crept to the front of the line to investigate the turmoil before veering off. It seemed I was not the only one having trouble seeing, as a large bus from the volcano road had not seen another large bus coming from the main road and b*ammm!*, out of the fog one t-boned the other. I snapped a quick photo, checked the road for ice, then sent a quick request to the heavens for safe passage before continuing up the road.

Some miles later I still couldn't make out anything outside of what was right in front of my wheel, the GPS finally insisted I turn left. However, I saw no sign of a road and continued on, eventually stopping to consult another mapping application. Sure enough, I had somehow missed what would normally have been a very obvious gravel entrance marked with a large sign "Bienvenidos/Welcome Chimborazo."

I had only been wearing my rain jacket and not the rain pants. As a result, by the time I rolled in, my gloves and pants were soaked to the skin, not what one wants when the temperature is hovering just above freezing. I felt it was too cold to stop and had skipped the entrance sign-in area hoping to find a faster route to a hot drink. Instead, I was greeted by one of the park rangers who shivered the words in Spanish for me to please come back and sign in and that I not go any further with the motorcycle, as motorcycles were not allowed to drive to the base of the summit. Apparently, they felt it was unsafe to try and ride a motorcycle up a snow-covered peak across an icy route. I would need to explain to them I was from Canada and this was how we normally got around!

All formalities aside I found the hot chocolate seller and let him give me a quick chocolate fix. While searching for the hot chocolate I noticed the only shot I had for putting my tent out of the wind or snow was either half covered at the entrance to the bathrooms or entirely covered at the entrance to the museum. Being entirely covered was looking better than the bathrooms so I asked the indigenous woman selling caps and mitts at the museum entrance if I could camp there. She seemed to like the idea but suggested I ask the park ranger. After a brief chat, no one seemed to think it was out of place that a gringo on a motorbike wanted a night at the museum. So, I set up in the museum entrance right in front in the ambiance of a giant photo of the volcano and an alpaca hanging on the wall.

I hoped I might find some other tourists headed to the base of the summit and hitch a ride, however, the park would be closing shortly and no more vehicles were allowed in. This was all starting to look like a bit of a letdown as it was so foggy I couldn't see my feet, let alone the ice-capped peak, and I wouldn't be allowed to go any further with the bike for a closer look. Then slowly, one by one, the last of the vehicles trickled out of the park, a man selling cheese and the lady selling mitts packed up, a new night guard rolled in, and I was alone in the foggy silence freezing and a bit miffed.

Like all great ideas I've had, just before being asked to leave someplace or having the police called, it dawned on me that I might have a little heart to heart with the new night watchmen and see if we can get around this "no motorcycles" rule. As I marched up to his door, I could hear him chuckle at the television and thought that if nothing else his mood would be right.

I knocked and was greeted with a pleasant "Buenas noches." I replied with some Spanish pleasantries and then got straight to business. First confirming that it was only the two of us on the mountain right now, he confirmed I was correct. Then followed by asking for a small favor, that favor being that I could take my motorcycle up to the top and no one would know. He looked at me, smiled, then all he asked was how long I was going to be? It was 5:30 p.m. and would be dark in thirty minutes when I would likely be more of a going concern. I explained I would be no more than twenty to thirty minutes, he nodded and waved me in the direction of the top.

Chimborazo, Ecuador, is actually the *tallest* peak on earth. Being on the equator, it's measured from the earth's core as opposed to sea level, which is how they justify Everest being the highest. The peak sits at 20,548 feet. The highest point one can drive is 15,912 feet. Too excited to consider the side effects for myself or the bike at such a height, I put the heated grips on high, dropped into first gear, and up we went.

The track up was lined with skittish alpacas who added nicely to the danger by bolting in front of me as the engine rumbled closer. Aside from a visibility of about ten feet, the road was surprisingly easy at first. Then, as I rounded the last part of the route, I found the snow and ice that were the reason behind the "No Motorcycles" posting. I knew going up was going to be easier than going down, so I resolved to just deal with that later. Slowly, I reached the base of the summit, and the view from there was no better than the view from below, still completely encased in clouds.

While looking around, the weather suddenly began to change, and as if the volcano knew that I'd put in the effort to see her, she put her best effort into being seen. A little wind picked up and like the parting of the Red Sea, clouds quickly swept to each side opening up a beautiful snow-capped volcano kissed by the sunset. I'm not sure if it was the lack of oxygen, a shot of adrenalin, or sheer luck, but I was suddenly bouncing about like a sugary six-year-old snapping photos from all angles. Then, like the waters rising back up, in just a few minutes it was all over, and the volcano was again shielded by a blanket of clouds.

I soon realized that running around in fifty-pounds of biker gear at 15,000-feet had made me quite dizzy and that I'd best settle before heading back down. Having taken longer to ascend than I had anticipated, I'd be navigating a light snowfall with even less visibility in the dark for the route back. With my alpaca friends thankfully sticking to the roadside this time, I reached the bottom, started my little pocket stove at the museum, and served up a classic biker pasta dinner in front of the alpaca picture.

Finishing up the day with the stove pushing out some heat in the port of my tent, I was bundled up in every piece of clothing I could fit on. After a sleepless night of thin air, altitude sickness, and chattering teeth, I was all too happy to get up and packing by 5:30 a.m. and heading back down to warmer weather.

One of the rarest photos on earth? For me it sure is. A KLR 650 at 15,000-feet sitting at the base of the Chimborazo Volcano, I'm happy to share it with the world.

As I worked my way through the rest of Ecuador the clock was ticking. I was meant to meet Angie for Christmas in Lima Peru over 2000-kilometers from here in less than a month. Before that I was still scheduled for a week of volunteering to teach kids how to make pizza in the city of Banos further south. I eventually made it to teach the pizza class for a week and used some other skills I'd learned to make chocolate from a pound of cocoa beans given to me by the jungle family. After a fast few weeks, I quickly kissed Ecuador goodbye before entering the captivating country of Peru.

(Edited image heading from Adventuremotorcycle.com)

(The snowy ride to the top) (A brief glimpse of Chimborazo)

Peru

The Girl

Fun Fact- Peru has over 4,000 varieties of potatoes. Offering every shape and color imaginable, including blue, red, purple, and pink potatoes. May 30th is national potato day in Peru.

KLaiR dropped like a three-legged table and began to skid out of control around the bend of one of the countless hair-raising turns it took to cross the infamous Andes mountains in Peru. As the bike hit the pavement Angie became ejected from the backseat and landed right in the middle of what could be oncoming traffic. As she slid across the pavement, I was still holding onto the handlebars in shock that I was now riding KLaiR sideways into the mountains on her crash bars and not on two tyres.

As KLaiR started to spin on her side my pants and jacket gripped the pavement as I came to a wretched halt in the other lane of traffic. The whole world suddenly slowed to a frame-by-frame movement like I was watching a 50's cartoon come to life when each page it was drawn on turned. By now sparks were spitting off one of the locks from the rear luggage box as well as her crash bars. Those electrified crash bars were just like a seatbelt, I never knew I really needed them until they were in full use.

Millisecond by millisecond KLaiR would continue to spin wildly out of control as I lay on the pavement watching her inch closer and closer to the face of the mountain. I could feel every emotion of the adventure, every visualized road trip dream, and every upcoming country goal come to an end. Had I just killed both of my girlfriends?

* * *

The build-up to Machu Picchu was fourteen months in the making and during this time I had all but forgotten what a deadline was. For the first time since Nicaragua, I had somewhere to be with a date attached to it and the obstacles of the road kept showing up at some of the most inconvenient moments.

That muddy night in Colombia about a month earlier where I'd stripped KLaiRs' clutch plates off in the mud had set me back a couple of weeks. This had resulted in spending my birthday alone in a roadside hotel, arriving late for the volunteering stint teaching kids how to make pizzas, and put a lot more pressure on my timeline to arrive in Lima Peru to meet Angie for Christmas in a few weeks.

I had canceled a few Ecuador stops and hustled down the long northern length of Peru to make it to Lima just in time for Christmas along with some other misfit travelers. Christmas dinner was a potluck event with about ten overlanding travelers, the most memorable person being the event organizer. A lady in her 40's from the US who proceeded to get so drunk on Christmas day, and many other days, had been readying herself over cocktails before coming to the dinner party she was putting on. Finally, she came out of her camper for Christmas dinner to a humble group of politely sat dinner guests wearing nothing more than a shirt and panties. She had completely forgotten to put her pants on.

With our table of eager Christmas dinner-goers along with the lady's boyfriend waiting for the final guest at the dinner table. We each watched in shocked silence as she made her way to the table with a drink in her hand. She got about 4-steps from our festive dinner table, caught a look from her boyfriend, then suddenly realized she wasn't wearing pants! Without skipping a beat she turned around in her shirt & panties, stumbled right back into the camper and returned moments later with her Christmas attire complete. Not one person made a single comment about the pants-less error, but the elephant in the room was bigger than any elephant you'd see in your life.

The next day and right on cue, Angie arrived in Lima on boxing day and we made our way back to the Christmas hostel I had been staying at before setting out towards Machu a couple of days later.

Now there wasn't exactly a plan and I wasn't accustomed to making plans much further ahead than a few days. I knew we had a couple of weeks to see as much of Peru as possible and find our way to Machu Picchu a thousand kilometers east of here. In my head, I was thinking that since the infamous Dakar Race was in Peru that we would have this once in a lifetime opportunity to catch part of the race, then make our way to Machu before skipping over to Cusco where Angie could catch a flight to Lima and then back to Canada.

This would allow us to casually make our way cross country and finish up in Cusco where I could get a new rear tyre for KLaiR before pressing on further South. I knew that the rear tyre had about 1000kms left on it and maybe less with two people on the bike. Without any outside consultation, this sounded like a flawless plan that couldn't possibly go wrong. Especially on a two-week timeline.

What I hadn't considered is that for the girl on a two-week vacation the idea of spending a third of that time chasing the Dakar in the hopes of catching a glimpse of bikes and cars ripping by in the sand wasn't all that enticing. Neither was losing a day of adventure just to catch a flight from Cusco and another day waiting in Lima to catch the next flight back to Canada. After hearing her concerns I knew my Dakar/plane ride/tyre plan would need some adjusting. I tried to find a new tyre on short notice, but most everything was closed for Christmas. Instead, we headed down the coast towards Pisco and I figured a plan and a tyre would present themselves as we drove.

Peru is likely one of the most culturally rich countries on the planet. Its ancient Inca history dating back hundreds of years is still being lived out by the Quechua and other natives that live in the country to this day. People can still be found living in earth homes, wearing vibrant, traditional dress, and speaking their native tongues. This combined with a continually evolving cuisine derived from historic staples like quinoa and over 1000 varieties of potatoes make it an excellent country to eat your way through. Peru even boasts some of the top restaurants in the world, with one restaurant in the world's top ten and three in the world's top fifty restaurants, incredible! To add to this you can still hike the trail into world-famous locations like Machu and camp right next to centuries-old locations like the intriguing Nazca lines, even if they did pave right through parts of them. Peru is a world of endless discovery.

Within just a few days we managed to camp on the ocean's edge in a national park watching the sea come to life, spend a night peering over the Nazca lines, drink Pisco sours in its namesake town, and even met a couple of the Dakar Rally teams en route to the race. Surprisingly the Dakar teams were equally as excited to meet a motorbiking duo who were making their way across the country on one of the slowest motorbikes known to man as we were to meet them on their way to race one of the most important overland races on the planet at break-neck speeds.

Some locals along the way had asked how long I'd be planning to stay in Peru. Until the end of March, I answered. They laughed and said I would be here for the entire rainy season. What, wasn't this summer? I misunderstood what "summer" in Peru meant, actually there were a lot of things I misunderstood about Peru.

Over a platter of Piscos, we devised an updated plan and opted to take one route up over the Andes to Machu and a different route back in order to catch as many different sites as possible. In all Peru has 37 peaks, some over 18,000-feet, and at one point or another, you are going to have to deal with them. If you've never taken yourself and a bike to such heights I might note that it's difficult on both the motorbike and the rider.

The bike needs some constant teething to deal with the lack of oxygen, as I would soon find out, so did we. As we crisscrossed little passes and camped along the way Angie and I were adjusting nicely to the altitude and never got sick. I think we just got lucky as I had first come down with altitude sickness the night on Chimborazo where I'd snuck KLaiR to the peak and later after Angie had left, in a little village way up in the Andes where the hotel manager had come to my rescue with coca tea and hot water bottles.

Altitude sickness is an awful mix of what feels like a dry, cramped brain where someone is kicking their way through your skull from the inside out. Some preventative measures were to adjust to the heights by going up higher than you planned to stay, then come back down and spend the night before continuing up again. It's also recommended that a person stays extremely hydrated and if you start to feel the effects, drink coca tea made from the energizing leaf that makes the base ingredient for cocaine, a popular plant in this part of the world. You could also take Doctor prescribed medication, but I usually trust the local cure over chemical compounds wherever possible.

Wearing every piece of clothing we owned, hopped up on coca leaves, and wrapped in decaying rain gear, we aimed to pass one of the summits taking us over the Andes towards Machu. Somewhere around the 15,000-foot mark of the pass, we hit a full-on blizzard. We were two-up, overloaded with gear, and blinded by the elements. Several hours went by as ice continued to build over the windshield as well as our visors.

Though the road was smooth I'd occasionally feel Angie's helmet bump into the back of mine, I wasn't sure what she was doing but I couldn't stop to talk to her and was intently focused on trying to see even a hint of the road to keep us on it. Occasionally we'd come up behind large trucks and it was only once we were within a few meters of them that I could make out the occasional glowing red ember of their tail lights. On literal blind faith, I'd pull out into the other lane to pass these crawling behemoths as we too inched our way to the top.

At one point I couldn't take it anymore; I was past fatigued. I'm sure Angie was having the time of her vacation life and could have endured several more hours shivering in the wet snow, but my frozen body had become exhausted from the cold and intense concentration of trying to navigate our team. We arrived at a tiny mountain village, right at the top of the mountain. I couldn't believe anyone lived up here.

Like two scared cubs without their mum to guide them along, we came bursting into a small shop looking for shelter, warmth, and the possibility of something to eat. I will never forget the faces of the locals whose front door we came barreling through, sopping wet, teeth chattering, and unable to speak their local dialect. It was the front entrance of someone's house that doubled as a place to sell items like gum and crackers. With no other food for sale or a bathroom to use, they directed us across the road to another small storefront home.

Again we were greeted with surprised looks and again my Spanish was useless towards their Quechua language. The only food was cookies, candies, and dry quinoa. I bought a handful of cookies and began to shove them in my mouth washed down by the country's infamously sugary Inca Cola. Angie said she wasn't hungry, but it had been hours in the cold since we'd eaten anything and I knew a side-effect of the altitude and coca was lack of appetite. Against her wishes, she ate some dry crackers and drank the liquid sugar.

There was no heating inside these tiny spaces made of wood and earth, but out of the elements we began to warm slightly and Angie needed to use the bathroom. If there is one look I will never forget in all my life, it was the look on her face after returning from "the bathroom".

A small boy about six or seven was given the job of taking this strange lady out back to the toilet. Upon their return, the child had been expecting a tip for his duties, but I don't think Angie was overly impressed by the whole scenario. We fished around for some coins to give the boy, then Angie took me on a tour of "the bathroom".

A short walk down a wet path behind the small home was an area maybe 200-feet x 200-feet closed in by rocks to fence in farm animals. Here in the yard was a tiny earth hut made from dirt with a grassy roof and no door. Inside was a small hole in the ground with the dribbles, drips, and spillover from years of use as the family's toilet. To add to the bathroom challenge Angie was wearing layer upon layer of clothing all wrapped up in fisherman-style yellow rain gear that latched closed like a bib. To pee, she'd need to strip down in the frigid temperatures trying to avoid dropping the clothes in the spills and splatters of the toilet while the small boy waited just outside the opening. I was getting the impression that what I felt an adventure looked like and what she perceived as a two-week Christmas vacation in Peru were turning out to be slightly different.

After a bit of questioning back in the cracker sales center, I realized that the reason Angie's helmet kept bumping mine is that she had been passing out from the lack of oxygen at this altitude, and when she would fall asleep her helmet would hit mine. At sea level there is roughly 21% oxygen in the air we breathe, here at 15,000-feet it's closer to 11%, nearly half the amount we were accustomed to breathing. Ohh shit, I was killing the poor girl! With the extremity of the situation not getting any better, we opted to press on to lower ground in search of warmer weather and more oxygen to spend what was New Year's eve.

(The icy view while crossing the Andes)   ("Off to the market" *Angie's photo)

Peru
Smashu Picchu

Fun Fact: The train from Cusco to Machu Picchu is about 4-hours. To hike the Inca Trail takes 3-4 days. To drive from Canada is roughly 13,000kms, or nearly the same distance as Vancouver, BC to Halifax, NS and back.

Having dropped back down through the clouds and out of the blizzard we were finally back in dry and warmer weather a few thousand feet lower than we were hours earlier. The general mood of our team had improved and we had settled on a plan to make it to a village just a few hours further on. I'd read you could spend the night in a room here next to a natural hot spring that came bubbling up from the center of the earth, the description alone was enough to lure our chilled bones to the location. How nice I thought, we could ring in New Years' soaking in hot pools with a few drinks and really start to enjoy Peru after the craziness of the blizzard mountain pass. As you can imagine, this plan came unwound nearly as fast as it came together.

As we snaked our way down the mountain, Angie, KLaiR, Stanley and I leaned in lightly to make a wide turn that would take us around one of the endless mountain curves that greeted us on this road. The rains had just started to sprinkle, but it was nothing like the snowy blizzard from earlier that day.

We now had all of my usual gear, camping supplies, extra fuel, pelican cases, and so on. To add to this we had Angie, plus Angie's suitcase strapped to the rear box with a ratchet strap. KLaiR had a brand new tyre on the front and a balding rear that was wearing faster and faster under the heavy load we were carrying. Even though we'd done hundreds of corners like this before at my average cruising speed of turtle, this one went drastically different.

These infamous roads that crisscross the Andes through Peru are incredible on a motorbike as the relentless twists, turns, climbs and descents keep the rider lazer-focused and cause your heart to pound as you lean in for corner after corner. As I leaned into this particular corner, KLaiR dropped like a three-legged table covered in fine China. She hit the ground with an alarming steel-on-pavement smash and began to skid out of control. Instantly Angie hit the road and the pavement ripped at her clothes ejecting her from the backseat. She came to a sliding stop right in the middle of the oncoming traffic lane. With Angie laying on the road I was still holding onto the handlebars in shock that I was now actually riding KLaiR sideways into the mountain on her crash bars and not on two tyres down the roadway.

As KLaiR started to spin, my pants and jacket finally gripped the pavement and I too came to a wretched halt in the oncoming lane of traffic. The whole world suddenly slowed to a frame-by-frame movement like I was watching a 50's cartoon come to life one image at a time.

By now sparks were spewing from the crash bars and one of the luggage locks looked like an electric waterfall lighting up the road. Millisecond by millisecond KLaiR would continue to spin wildly out of control as I lay on the pavement watching her inch closer and closer to the wall of the mountain. I could feel every emotion of the adventure, every visualized road trip dream, every upcoming country goal, and everything that was now my world, my identity, and my life coming to an end. Had I just killed both of my girlfriends?

KLaiR hit the cement ditch like a lifeless crash test dummy, landing tyres up, sideways in the ditch with fuel leaking across her fairing and into the ditch below. I stood up and checked myself over, surprisingly I was entirely intact, not one of my body parts appeared to be out of place. Then I looked over at Angie who was also picking herself up off the road. She too appeared to be in one piece so I asked her if she was ok and in a sort of blank shock we stared at each other then locked in for a huge hug. I think we were both surprised that each other was relatively unharmed. We then realized we were standing in the middle of the road on a blind corner and quickly moved to the shoulder near KLaiR.

Staring at KLaiR, tyres up in the ditch I was absolutely devastated. I knew this trip was over, all wiped away by one miscalculation. What had been an incredible sigh of relief that Angie and I were basically unscathed, was now stripped away by this empty feeling that KLaiR was a heap of potentially explosive metal, tyres up in a cement ditch. If there was one photo I wished I had captured on this entire trip it would have been this image of KLaiR at her most helpless moment. However, photos were nowhere near the top of the current priority list.

Just then a small car came around the corner and spotted our situation. A couple roughly the same age as us had stopped and entirely unphased like they had seen this situation plenty of times before, asked if we'd like some help. Together the four of us reached down to pull KLaiR from the ditch. As we rolled her over I needed to put my hand on the clutch to release the rear tyre and get her moving as she was still in gear.

Once KLaiR was back on two wheels the couple bid us good luck and drove away as if two rescue angels had just popped in and popped out on their way back to heaven. I then cautiously walked around KLaiR to investigate the damages. The lock had been ripped off in the electric waterfall, the GPS and water bottle had come loose and fell off, the one side was scratched heavily, but otherwise, I could see no major damage. Even Angie's bag, though a bit dirty, was still strapped exactly in place on the rear Pelican case. If nothing else my strapping skills were much better then they were in Nicaragua.

Feeling a bit more optimistic I cautiously turned the key and hit the starter button. A few little chugs to sort out the fuel that had been going the wrong way and she fired right back up. We were back, a motorcycle miracle! Well almost back. Once I was sitting on the bike I realized the handlebars were heavily twisted and I'd need to ride with my left hand hanging down below the center of the bars and my right hand twisted up. I felt like I was riding a cartoon bull with his horns drawn on his head in an S shape. This made for some extremely tricky riding, but nonetheless, we were still riding!

Looking at us and the bike I realized the crash bars and Pelican case on the side had provided a buffer zone where our legs were given enough room to stay off the road and not be crushed under the weight of the bike. This setup had acted just like a seatbelt, that I never knew I needed until they were in full use.

I can't say that God is my go-to guy for anything, but along the trip, KLaiR had been blessed with a safe journey by so many different people with various religious backgrounds using everything from flowers to ribbons, to holy water and hugs, I was thankful that whoever was watching our ass that day had done an incredible job. If we had fallen the other way, KLaiR would have gone rocketing over the cliff face to an explosive death some 15,000-feet below. Had there been anyone on the road at that moment we could have easily been run over and killed.

To think we had basically walked away from the crash and someone had shown up to help us pull KLaiR from the ditch getting us back on the road virtually unharmed was nothing short of a miracle! However, the day still wasn't over and we still had to make it to the hot springs.

I don't know how many hours had passed by the time we had reached the hot springs village, but it was pitch black and raining heavily. I asked in town how to get to the springs and was directed to a one-lane track that led up the side of another mountain. The road was made of dirt and had turned to a slippery mess of mud. I was well past exhausted both mentally and physically and I'm sure Angie was too. With one handlebar bent down, one bent up, and spinning our way through the mud on a balding tyre we finally reached the hot springs, but the tiny parking area was packed. I had Angie wait in the rain to watch the bike with all our gear and to keep the bike from falling over in the mud. I was so relieved to be here, I couldn't wait to find a room and hop in the hot springs to relax while eating some local cuisine and drinking a refreshing beer. If we deserved a break from any day, this was the day.

I walked over to a small booth that acted as the entryway to the hot springs and hotel. I was so happy to be here I hardly noticed the pouring rain and the fact my mouth was shivering so much my Spanish was likely inaudible. I yelled to the lady in the booth so she could hear me over the rain. I explained that I would like a room, any room would do. The lady explained that it was New Years' and there were no more rooms. I said I don't care about the price, I just wanted a room. She said that the price was only about $15, but no matter the price there was no room for us. I argued hard and explained we would sleep anywhere, we just needed a room. In a bizarre reenactment of Christmas events, even though we'd likely been saved by Jesus during this holiday season, there was no room at the INN for Kix and

Angie. Deflated, I went back to explain the news to Motorbike Mary while we mounted our broken steel donkey to ride off in the storm.

My eyes welled up, I was sure I was going to break down and cry. I was so tired, so hungry, so exhausted from the blizzard, the altitude, and the crash. I had used my final bits of energy to navigate up the muddy mountain to the hot springs. With shaking hands, endless braking and constantly putting out my feet to stabilize us through the mud, we made our way back down the muddy track into the village and found another room.

Instead of warm hot springs with cold beer and a starry view, New Years' was spent in a small restaurant with no heat where we dined on chicken foot soup and french fries to the blank stares of the locals who were incredibly curious about our presence here. Afterward, we headed back to our room, where we were treated to a cold shower, and drank flavored Pisco out of National Lampoon's-style moose antler shooter glasses Angie had brought. It was so cold we made our New Years' cheers under the blankets. The time was 12:03 am and I resolved to wake up with the events from the year before well behind us.

The rest of this Peruvian route was a spectacular combination of incredible sights and amazing people. Taking the road less traveled towards Machu Picchu we were treated to endless waterfalls, wild Alpacas, tiny earth homes, and endless hidden gems. I wondered if the local farmers etching out a life of farming potatoes in the open landscape had any idea that people the world over sought the chance to view the magic of this hidden Inca city tucked deep in the Andes just over the hill from their farms.

We eventually arrived in the town of Santa Teresa, the closest you can drive on the way to Machu before walking or catching a ride to Hidroeléctrica where it's a further two hour hike to Aguas Calientes, the jump off point to Machu Picchu. To see Machu is incredible, to be treated to the rewarding ride into this hidden wonder is half the prize, a prize awarded to few.

Eventually, it was decided that we would skip Cusco entirely and wind our way back via another route to Lima. This meant Angie was able to enjoy more of her time in Peru and less of her time in airports. The catch was that I was unable to source another tyre for KLaiR before returning to Lima. With the extra road we had to cover, rocky conditions, and added weight I continually fretted over the state of the rear tyre. I refused to point out the dilapidated state of the rubber to Angie until we were back in Lima and she was headed back to the airport. I figured only one of us needed to lose sleep over the thinning tread. By the time we landed back in Lima the seams of the rubber had split and we were riding on the exposed woven bias material of the tyre and rubber tube. I was starting to actively thank whomever it was that seemed to continually look out for our journey.

(The drive to Machu *Angie's photo)   (A tyre that rolls on luck)

Peru
From Life To Lunch

"What nicer thing can you do for somebody than make them breakfast?" Anthony Bourdain

(Written on a "November note")

Have all the taboo topics been covered? Religion always seems to bring out the argumentative or violent side in people. Abortion is a fun way to end a blind date. Politics are perfect for cleaning up your Facebook friends list in a hurry. What else is left that hasn't pissed off enough people?

You are in luck, I found one… Cooking the family pet!

Welcome to a tutorial I like to call "From Life To Lunch". We go step by step on how to cook cuy, better known in North America as the guinea pig.

Step one: Make friends with a local family.

I always wanted my first edible guinea pig experience to be memorable and while traveling through Peru I ran across many roadside stalls selling these little pigs right off the spit. Maybe it was my high-standard for street meat, but the mini-pig on a spit just didn't appeal to me.

As fate would have it, I ended up in the small village of Villa Rica near the jungles of Peru and found myself as an added member of a local family for a month. I had asked Ruban, the dad of the family, where I could get KLaiR welded as she again had some broken bones. He said he could do the job and took me to his parent's house to work on her. After the welding job he invited me in for lunch with his parents and young son.

The usual staples of rice and yucca were on the table along with some regional vegetables. Yet the protein I could not identify. Everyone had a little leg or a little back, and Ruban's son of about three years old had this little limb half hanging out of his mouth. I finally asked what the dish was? As casually as I'd explain to someone at my house that we are having chicken for dinner, Rubans Mum said "Cuy". Instantly my face split into an exaggerated smile, and I started to giggle. The family looked confused. I said I hadn't eaten much cuy. They all looked at me like I'd just said I don't breathe much air.

As the meal went on I knew an opportunity like this would never present itself this intimately again, and the forever aspiring chef in me proposed to Grandma; *"Enséñame a cocinar cuy." "Teach me to cook cuy".*

Grandma seemed to think this might be an interesting experience for the both of us and with that, I would find myself in her kitchen at 10 am the next morning.

Step Two: Turn off mental controversies.

Upon my arrival, Grandma took me to where the cuy lived in little pens behind her house. She wanted to make sure I understood how life to lunch really worked. She explained that the cuy grows quickly and are typically full-grown in three months. She reached down into the pen of about 12 cuy's and picked up a nice chubby brown and white one who'd been gnawing casually on a husk of corn.

With this fuzzy bundle of meat hanging from her hands, Grandma notes that cuy have a lot of babies. Then she holds this little guy up and grabs a bit of his skin pointing out that there is not much fat on the cuy, that they are mostly meat, thus having less cholesterol. She then pointed to the corn and other vegetables in the cage and explained their vegetarian diet and said that cuy eat a clean diet making them a healthy option for human consumption.

Grandma was selling me hard on the benefits of these fuzzy pigs, yet there was a mental battle going on inside my head. As a kid, I had hamsters as a pet and was now faced with harvesting a super-sized lunch version of them. The thought of killing and eating my childhood pet was almost unbearable. I was getting fidgety and reluctant to help with the selection process from the wooden pen they called home. I could feel Grandma's eyes roll back in her head as I took a step back when she put the brown and white one back and began the selection process of who would be our lunch. I did not want to be the decider of fates for this meal.

Finally, Grandma made the decision and a boy was chosen who fit the bill of being about three months old and just the right size. Grandma says that usually, they eat the "macho's" or males first, so the females can continue to produce more offspring. Our little male friend was squirming as Grandma placed him in a big burlap coffee sack and we headed to the kitchen to prepare lunch.

Growing up in the sheltered Canadian lifestyle, I was typically protected from the processing of animals aside from some chickens we'd raised and harvested when I was quite young. By the time I saw meat that was ready to eat, it was sitting on a grocery store shelf shrink-wrapped in plastic with a price per pound on the label and paid for with my credit card. The whole idea of taking a life to feed a life was a huge mental challenge and I was now faced with being part of the steps it took to make my lunch.

Step Three: Brace yourself.

From here the process escalated quickly. It was an hour of rapid non-stop hand movements from a spirited lady who clearly does not spend much time sitting still. She was crafty, talented, and swift. With a quick swipe of the neck from her sharp knife, the blood rushed from the cuys' body and right out of my face as well. This was the turning point.

I recall when I went sky-diving at sixteen, it was solo, not tandem, and I was so hungover I could hardly see. Yet jumping out of a perfectly good plane while my Mother sat crying at home seemed like a good idea. The whole lead-up to jumping out of the plane was quite relaxed. Right up until the plane door opened. It was that moment when the wind came rushing in and the barrier of safety had been removed that I was scared shitless. This was the exact feeling in reverse. I had so much angst built up to this moment but as soon it was over for the cuy, I suddenly felt calm, as though we were prepping up a roast chicken for Sunday brunch that I'd bought from the store.

Step Four: Get your hands dirty.

The blood was drained into a bowl and saved for the dogs. While this was going on water had been boiling on the stove. Now that it was hot the cuy was dipped in the water to loosen the hair.

After a quick dip, the cuy was taken to the sink where the hair was removed by hand before a knife was used to scrape off the remaining hairs, then a final roll of the corpse across open flames to singe off any microfibers the knife could not get. The pig was now nothing but a light pink skin with little limbs.

Back on the stove was another pot of water mixed with local herbs, spices, and some cut-up lemons. While we waited for this to boil, Grandma cleaned and quartered the tiny sections of meat, all the while reiterating to me the health benefits and again noting the cuys' lack of cholesterol.

Next, the cuy was boiled in the herb and lemon water for roughly 10-minutes. The cuy was then removed from the water and laid to rest while a separate pot of oil was heated. Like all great South American meals, this too would be finished in a hot boiling broth of "healthy" oil. Once the oil was at 375oF, each little micro limb was dusted in flour then placed into the oil bath. When the wet meat met the hot oil the whole process dramatically snapped and spit to life. I think all the non-cholesterol benefits were being erased by the oil.

From here, Grandma side-stepped over to another pot where some yucca was boiling then slipped to a separate kitchen to whip up a quick salad. Next, the salad was run through a quick Clorox and water cleanse to kill any bacteria. I have worked in dozens of commercial restaurants and could see this was clearly not Grandma's first day in the kitchen.

In what seemed like one swift motion, the cuy was lifted out from the pot of hot oil, then into the oil pot slid some sliced plantain. Like an elegantly choreographed move, she sashayed over to retrieve the boiling yucca and quickly disappeared to shake off the greens and get our salad ready. Next, out of the oil with the plantain, off with the gas burner, a quick wipe of all the counters and stove, some speedy disinfecting of the cuy sink with the leftover Clorox & water, and we headed to the main house with lunch for me and the rest of my Peruvian family. It all seemed so smooth and effortlessly brought together, it felt more like a dance class than a culinary class.

Step Five: Insert Guinea pig in mouth without awkwardly giggling.

I could hardly keep from smirking as Grandma, Grandpa, son, grandson and a niece all sat down with me for lunch in their house. They asked what the grin was about? In my mid-grade Spanish, I explained that I had never in my life prepared then eaten this dish that they had been eating weekly since they had teeth.

I said that if someone in Canada had walked in on our family eating cuy, they would call the police and I would be in prison. They looked at me as though I'd just used a page from their favorite Bible to wipe cuy oil off of my face. I could feel the intense inquisitiveness. Those moments when you witness cultural differences politely unfold. Both sides knew the other wouldn't understand, and no questions or explanations were exchanged.

With a six-year-old gnawing on a little leg and Grandpa going for the micro-rib, they tried to explain to me the benefits of each piece to help aid my decision-making process. It all just looked like a kids' meal from KFC to me. I went for the leg.

Aside from the mental aspect, it was tasty, light, and just as enjoyable as any Sunday family chicken I'd had in my own country. Maybe don't try this at home, people. However, if you find yourself in Peru, don't miss such a cultural opportunity.

(Grandma sharpening the knives)

(Carefully inspecting the pot of herbs, spices & cuy)

(Family lunch that day, smiles all around)

Peru
Mental Shifts

"It is in your moments of decision that your destiny is shaped."
- Tony Robbins

If you were to follow our little adventure on social media you were usually treated to a steady stream of adventure photos, river fishing, pulling KLaiR out of the mud, meals by the campfire, and a host of positive stimuli to make it look like I had the most fantastic life on planet earth. In short, I was posting the same filtered bullshit that everyone posts. To the outsider, every day in my life was a full and amazing adventure.

I was definitely living out a dream of mine, but it wasn't all a bubblegum & rainbows adventure full of blissful happiness, even though I was putting in the effort to be as positive as I could. The relentless amount of alone time can start to drag down even the most upbeat of individuals. Most days I was regularly talking to Stanley on the handlebars as we toured around and was continually congratulating KLaiR after each little adventure we accomplished together. Limited social interaction with humans was taking its toll.

Some days I would wake up in the morning, look around at my ramshackle tent life that was always hidden in one bush or another, think about my lack of funds, two pairs of pants and four shirts, zero real-life friends, and how I was all alone, then instantly think about how much of a loser I was. This loser feeling would then cycle through my head for hours and sometimes drone on for days until I would finally catch myself in this negative cycle and try to drown out the negativity with extreme positivity. It felt like I was in zombie-loser-mode and when left unmonitored, would spiral out of control. One day I might feel like a social media success story living off likes and the next day I drift right back into feeling like the lonesome loser. It felt so bizarre to me to constantly deal with the mental extremes of a life alone.

For hours and days and weeks alone inside my quiet helmet, I would mentally cycle through my life. I would relive each positive and negative challenge from the past in great detail. Some days I would think through all of the wonderful girlfriends I'd had and the amazing things we had done together then relive how each of those relationships had ended in some disastrous event brought on by me and what I should have done differently.

Other days I'd relive the years of my childhood and my parents' relentless divorce along with all of the challenges that came with it, but how it had made me incredibly independent. Other days I'd cycle through my life as a teenager, a time where I would go as far out of my way as possible to act, dress, and be as different as I could from anyone else just to prove I was my own person. I relived the moments of previous travels, ruined businesses, being bullied, bullying others, things I'd stolen, things that had been stolen from me, times I'd lied or been lied to, of going broke, moments I'd been proud of myself & doubted myself, and of all of my failures at one point or another in life.

There was a moment when I was about 4-years-old. My family was in our 1980's car driving slowly down the lane of our countryside home. I was in the backseat with my sister. Our family dog had come running out to greet us and my father had accidentally driven over part of her. My sister, several years older than me, came unglued and began to scream frantically at the sight of our family dog half run over by the car. My father called the vet who came to our home to euthanize the family pet. It was an awful experience for everyone involved. I don't think I'd thought about this moment since that week and at that age should have completely forgotten about it. Now here I was, recycling each and every one of the highs and extreme lows of my life. Moments I thought were completely erased, and I now relieved each of them quietly inside my helmet in vivid mental detail as the miles rolled.

 In life, if you think there are emotional scars left by loved ones you have forgotten, bite-sized memories from your childhood that altered your perception of the world, or bitter breakups you have long since swept under the rug. A couple of years alone in thought will give you the chance to touch on each of these moments again and again and again and again. Then, one by one, you are given the opportunity to confront them in painstakingly slow and incredibly vivid detail inside a helmet. There is no escape from these moments and memories, only a lifetime of self-imposed distraction that will one day catch up with you like a cancer of thought that you either fight head-on or allow to smother your mind until you are an empty shell of avoided emotion. It was difficult to recount these compiled and compressed situations that had been building for 36-years. I could not imagine doing this for the first time alone in a home, reaching my deathbed in my final years like so many I'm sure are faced with. The amount of catastrophic failures in my own life combined with things I wish I'd done or never done with an additional two lifetimes under my belt feels crippling.

To counter some of the negativity that would spring up I had downloaded a series of podcasts and YouTube videos that were ripe with positive stimulus. There were little reminders about how important it was to work towards your goals, how no challenge was easy, or how I should just be thankful to be me. I began listening to these every morning when I was preparing breakfast to avoid starting the day in what often felt like "loser mode". When I left from Canada I had set a reminder on my phone to go off each day at 8:30 pm that would tell me to write down three things to be thankful for.

Each night alone in the tent or a hotel room, I'd come up with three things that I was thankful for. If I missed a night I'd go back and fill in that day with those three things. On most days I was looking forward to finding something new to be thankful for and never missed a day without three thankful moments for the entire trip.

It was here in Peru I'd come across the Netflix special, *I'm Not Your Guru, a* Tony Robbins production where they film one of his major events "A Date With Destiny" showing a behind the scenes look at what it's like to face your personal challenges head on.

I'd watched this film once or twice when I had internet access in a hotel room. Then I finally downloaded it so I could watch chunks of it as I traveled. Then I started to watch it once a week. By the time I'd met this Peruvian family in Villa Rica I started to watch *I'm Not Your Guru* every single day in the tiny house where I was living behind their lakeside home.

Looking for some refuge from the relentless rains and cool high-altitude temperatures I'd been riding in for weeks, I came down to the warmth of the jungle. Here in the jungle I had found the home of this local family and asked if I could camp on their property. They explained that even here the rains were still too heavy for camping outside. Instead, they cleaned out a tiny cement shelter behind their home that was full of garbage and animal shit for me to pitch my tent in. The room was about 20-feet by 15-feet with a small bathroom, made entirely of cement. It appeared that no one had lived here for a very long time.

At this point, I think I was ready for some family time and the Peruvians, Ruban, Karina, and Karina's sister Jenny came along at just the right moment. What was meant to be a one night sleep in their yard turned into a month of family fun where I was welcomed into the family like a brother.

In the little lakeside cement hut I'd set up *I'm Not Your Guru* on my tablet on the kitchen table. Each day I'd start my day with a family breakfast then come back and do some exercises until the 2-hour Guru program was over. By the 30th day here, I could recite nearly every moment that was about to take place in the video. There was the Belgian guy with red shoes who had tried to commit suicide. There was the Brazilian lady who'd grown up in a sex-based religion that had ruined her family and had wanted to commit suicide. There was the American couple whom the husband had transformed himself into a lion-roaring, crowd-crushing, dominant male from the cowardly sheep he had been, only to have his wife shove a baseball bat up his ass and crush his impending transformation. There was the young girl with the food eating issues who was really just masking her father-pleasing side. Then there was Tony, the well-known larger than life "Guru" who talked about growing up with a mother who'd kick his ass and pour soap down his throat trying to control him.

Every time I watched it, I knew exactly what was going to happen next and I still wanted to see it. I was looking to take more than just the positive energy from the program, I was looking to take some of these lessons and apply them to my day to day life. There were even some practicable lessons that I ended up using in the 20x15-foot cement Hilton I was living in.

The cement Hilton had been transformed from the shit and garbage shack into a full living quarters by now. There was a wooden door on the front that had warped and worn over the years and if you pulled too hard to shut it, the door would come loose from its nails and fall right off. The inside was a faded shade of green and there was a window etched out from brickwork next to my single bed that had been stolen from one of the kids' rooms. I had a little desk, a wooden table with two chairs in the event I might ever have company for dinner. Then there was a partially divided room with no door that housed the sink, a toilet that required a bucket of water to flush it, and a shower made from cinder blocks with no curtain and no shower head. Compared to the tent, it was 5-star accommodation.

When I'd first seen this room it was filled with broken glass, scrap wood, and smattered with bird and mouse shit from the animals who'd called it home for years before my arrival. But now, it was my cement Hilton.

The biggest challenge I had with the room was the shower. The pressure was immense and without a shower head, a relentless stream of icy water pillaged right from the soul of the earth that came down like a projectile 3" waterfall. I'd showered in plenty of waterfalls and rivers leading up to this but was it hard to get excited about having my ass kicked each day by an intense stream of ice water. However, like millions before me, I'd found the solution in Tony Robbins.

At one point in *I'm Not Your Guru,* the film crew goes to Tony's house for some insight into how Tony's days look. They showcase clips of his pool, they film him working out, they show him meditating. He talks about his life and his wife, and they show touching moments of this little dog who likely lives better than 90% of the world's human population. It's exactly what you'd think a day in the life of Tony Robbins looks like.

There is one scene that completely changed my outlook on my current situation. One simple step in the life of T. Robbins. To the side of his house is a small plunge pool. It's a square in the ground about 4-feet x 4-feet with a small ladder on the side to exit the pool from. The deep plunge pool is filled with water hovering around freezing and the idea is that once you plunge into the frigid water, that all of your senses come screaming to life rather than sauntering to life like the average person does each day.

Tony comes towards the plunge pool wearing nothing but a pair of swimming trunks exposing his massive Paul Bunyan tree trunk legs and Babe The Ox-like chest. He's talking the whole time explaining the benefits of the pool and how it helps him. Just before entering the water he shudders a little and says "*57 degrees baby*" then plunges below the depths of the water before emerging revitalized shortly after.

I'd seen this part of the program 60+ times by now, but suddenly it had a new meaning. I stopped the show right there and went and turned on my headless shower. The frigid water came spewing out from the pipe in the wall and directly onto the floor like a pipe had just burst. I took off my shorts, looked at the water, and began to chant *plunge pool, plunge pool, plunge pool, plunge pool, plunge pool.* Then I jumped excitedly into the oncoming assault of glacier water.

I suddenly felt alive, revitalized, energized, invigorated by the shower. This didn't translate into showering any longer, however, it now gave me an entirely new outlook on this part of my day. For the rest of my time in the cement Hilton, I would start each day chanting to myself *plunge pool, plunge pool, plunge pool,* as I gasped for breath and tried to wash the soap off of my clammy skin. I'd step out of that shower and into the day with a whole new outlook.

It's incredible how every rainy or snowy day, flat tyre, cold sleepless night, life-threatening motorcycle crash, lonely-loser moment, and on and on could suddenly change from dread to inspiration if I looked at it from the angle of an icy attack or as a stream of revitalizing energy.

Each day after the plunge-pool I'd go to town to use the internet to write articles and try to get one magazine or online publication or another to publish a story I'd written and hopefully pay me. One day Ruban had asked me what I did each day and I explained I was writing stories about the trip and trying to sell them. He looked shocked. Ruban said I thought you were a millionaire? I almost pissed my pants laughing.

Ruban said that whenever he saw a foreigner they were always spending money and not working, usually in an expensive traveling car or on an expensive motorbike like my KLR650. From what he'd seen about America on television and from foreigners in real life he thought we were all millionaires just spending money and having fun. I laughed and explained that it was true these people were usually not working here, but we were usually looking for ways to try and make money while traveling or we had used money we saved from working at home.

Typically our strong currencies used in places like Peru that were much cheaper than America or Europe meant we were able to travel and have fun here for much less than at home. I told him about my $12/day budget versus what it would cost to live each day in Canada and how $12 would rarely buy you lunch. Ruban couldn't believe it. This whole time while I was living in the cement Hilton because the rent was about $6/day, he thought I was just enjoying the millionaire lifestyle!

What an incredible opportunity it was to spend a month with this family on the edge of the Peruvian jungle. The family took me to meet their native relatives that lived a modern jungle life, taught me about the local food and culture, allowed me to be part of their family, and even nursed me back to health one day when I'd poisoned myself while experimenting with some local fruits and vegetables I'd never seen before. At one point it even dawned on me I hadn't spoken a word of English in nearly a month. I think we both learned a lot from each other and they made me very aware that I needed more family time. The day I left they filled bags full of local coffee they grew, smoked meats they had made, little gifts from their home, and chocolates they knew I liked. The goodbye was considerably more dramatic than when I had left my own family back in Canada. It was a mess of hugs, tears, and well-wishes that came at a much-needed point of the trip. These people are now the Peruvian family I never knew I had.

(The tilapia spear fisherman)　(Ruban smoking pork with lemon wood in a barrel)

(Pizza class always went over well)　(Saying goodbye to my Peruvian family)

Peru
What Lies In The Rainbow Mountains?

"Until you truly let go, until you truly form humility, can you find empathy and in that empathy you find contact and in that contact you find out who you truly are, and who the people are around you."

- Jimmy Nelson (One Of The World's Top Photographers)

I couldn't get enough of Peru and its endless bounty of breathtaking sites. Just riding around the Andes with KLaiR and Stanley watching the weather change in a heartbeat from sun to slush. Riding past blue-green waterfalls that have been carving their way through rock since the dawn of history, and witnessing historical monuments that have stood the test of time for centuries. It was captivating to the point of distraction.

I did develop a bit of a gripe with travelers who took some of the most sacred images of the country and doctor them up to make them out to be something of a bombshell blonde with bleached hair, fake tits, and rubber lips.

The Rainbow Mountains, a.k.a. Vinicunca, a.k.a. Montaña de Colores, are a captivating setting located in the south of Peru. These mountains sit around 17,000-feet and look like someone opened a box of crayons and let the sun melt them down either side of the landscape, sort of…

To get here, you can spend the night in Cusco, hop on a bus in the morning and take the 2-3 hour ride to the base of the mountains then rent a horse with a guide to take you round trip to the top of the mountains. Then, snap a couple selfies and head back down before getting the "look what I did" t-shirt. Or you can do what the dirty bikers do and camp at night beside the river in a nearby maize field. Only to find out that what you thought was a sneaky spot is actually right next to where the workers from the fields walk past as the sun is setting. Now instead of a sneaky cornfield camper, you're more like the guy who set up camp in the middle of Walmart wondering why you're getting all these strange looks.

Next on my list of misunderstandings was to stop at the "Welcome To The Rainbow Mountains" sign just before the final ascent to the parking lot at the base camp of said Crayola mountains. The road from this point is a series of hairpin turns on a one-lane gravel road with a couple of questionable creek crossings. I thought this sign would make a nice photo opportunity and a good place to pee before heading to the top and meeting a bunch of tourists where I'd likely need to pay to pee and get bombarded with pony rental pushers.

About 50-feet from the sign, dressed in full indigenous wear that included layers and layers of intricately woven skirts and sweaters that I'm sure were made from heavy felt, topped off with a sort of colorful Vietnamese Rice hat. I find a hefty Peruvian woman selling something like Tupperware. It looked like she had her makeshift shop set up here while she waited for the bus to take her to the top of the road where the tourists were.

I drove past the colorful Tupperware saleslady, gave her a little wave, and headed for the selfie-sign. Midway through my pee I hear a rustle of goods behind me and look over my shoulder, penis in hand, to see that Tupperware lady has closed up shop, packed up all her wares, and is standing next to KLaiR.

I quickly finish up, turn around and say *Hola!* The lady replies, *no Español*. She doesn't speak Spanish, and it's more likely that she speaks one of the native dialects like Quechua. Then she points at KLaiR, points to the top of the mountain, and smiles. Shit, she thinks I stopped to give her a ride to the top of the mountain!

KLaiR is obviously overloaded, plus I'm carrying extra fuel, around 10-liters of water tied on top of the side cases, and various bags of food tied in beside these. This lady easily outweighs me by 40-pounds, plus her 30-40 pounds of felt clothing, plus this mess of Tupperware all wrapped in a blanket that is bigger than the green backpack Angie had tied on the back when she was with me. I instantly start to laugh at the impossible hilarity and misunderstanding of the situation.

In my mind, there is likely a truck or a bus coming at some point that would be much more suited for the task at hand. To top it off, the idea of adding any more calamity to this already death-defying route is likely a bad one. I'm sure in her mind this is the biggest motorcycle she's ever seen and feels that it is more than capable of moving her and her business to the prime selling spots at the top. Either way, trying to explain my point in any language is impossible and I resolve to move some of the groceries off the backseat to make room for the 200+ pounds of my new friend and her wares.

I hop on KLaiR and brace my feet firmly to support our incoming guest and I am laughing so hard inside my helmet I can hardly focus on the task. This is the true selfie gold and I snap a quick headshot of our duo, wishing I had a selfie stick to capture everything. With my balls now being pushed into my throat from the fuel tank, I pull in the clutch and drop into first as our two-wheeled circus attempts the summit. If anything, our timing was impeccable as most of the busses had made their way up the mountain already and we only passed by one truck making its way back down.

When myself, Tupperware Lady, Stanley, and KLaiR with her wide ass of luggage and various amounts of mine and my new friend's shit strapped on everywhere came barreling into the parking lot of locals and tourists, I could feel the mic drop. One by one conversations slowed, eyes rolled in our direction and people stopped what they were doing to watch what I'm sure looked like a train wreck about to happen. I wish I had a copy of someone else's photo of that moment. Already these mountains had superseded expectations.

With my feet firmly planted on the ground again, off came our new friend along with her plastics business, and she gave a quick smile before setting off to get selling. I wondered just how many plastic bowl sets she offloaded that day?

These mountains were originally sacred ground for the locals, but after a few doctored Instagram photos made their way 'round the internet and money from tours and trinkets came pouring in, as you can imagine, things have changed. I opted to forgo the horse ride and hike to the 17,000-foot peak myself. Wearing boots, biker jacket, biker pants, and carrying a backpack full of shit I was hoping to avoid getting stolen. I spent most of the morning panting my way to the top nearly as much as the swayback horses I'd see with 200-pound gringos strapped to their backs trudging their way to the top. Poor KLaiR, this is likely how she felt just an hour earlier.

I hit two blizzards on the way up and a lucky sunny patch at the top when I finally arrived. The upside to making your own schedule is that most of the tourists had made their way back down as I was going up and I had the top to myself for a brief time.

Back to the rubber lips and fake tits let down, the Rainbow Mountains aren't exactly what the internet makes them out to be. They are incredibly magical to see in person and I've never seen anything like them in my life. The colors come from a variety of minerals inside the rocks that wash down over the mountain. The reality is that they are minerals and are not made from melted Crayons. The world wants you to believe that whatever they saw was the most beautiful and most amazing thing in the world and what they've seen was better than anything you've seen. These people are lifeless fakes and so are their doctored photos. Such is life on social media it's not like I haven't been part of the problem.

The colors are amazingly wonderful, but they are dull, just like any powdery mineral you may have seen. Picture a piece of chalk that's melted into your sidewalk after the rains. The colors are not Tickle Me Pink, Robins Egg Blue, and Shamrock Green. They are delightfully dull and naturally naturalistic. Why are we trying to make nature out to be something it's not? Invent bullshit in your own world but please leave nature out of it.

A few weeks later there was some discussion on my travel forums about whether a trip to the Rainbow Mountains was worth it? A few people chimed in yes, a few chimed in no, and such is the result when you ask peoples' opinions. Then one guy put up one of these fake tits and rubber lips bubblegum-colored photos of the mountains he had taken as a means to supplement his argument of how you absolutely must go. So I put up one of my undoctored photos and noted that it was amazing but his photos were well-crafted lies. The guy came back with some of his original photos, explaining that yes he had provided those images with a bit of plastic surgery before unveiling them to the world.

Peru is more than you could ever imagine, but not always what is invented out of the imagination of others.

(What's one more person & her entire business on the back of the bike!)

(The farmers inspecting my suspicious camp spot on their way home)

Bolivia
Black Markets & Bribes

Tips For Travel: "Take An Interest In The Culture &
Don't Be An Asshole."

- Kix Marshall

The first time I traveled somewhere that required a passport I was 17 and was on a family trip to Mexico. My sister had her two young sons with her, one of them was very blonde with very blue eyes. As we strolled around the markets a number of the ladies selling goods would leave their booths and come walking over to touch my nephew on the shoulder or feel his nearly transparent hair and give him a little motherly affection. To us, this seemed a bit threatening as though they might try to take him and we would keep a tighter grip on the kids. No one in Canada would stop what they were doing to come over and touch your kids and feel their hair unless they knew them or they were dressed up for an event that made them look differently.

Later in life, I would learn that Mexicans LOVE children and family as a whole. This love for children coupled with seeing a little kid who has shimmering blonde hair and blue eyes, unlike the dark features they saw every day was too much for the ladies to resist. They had to go and give my nephew some love, even if it was just touching his hair and telling him he was cute. We were new to international travel and had much to learn.

If you are an overlander who has been crisscrossing the planet by road, you should know better than to assume the worst in people. The chances are extremely high that you've been assisted by people in every culture along your route and know already to give them the benefit of the doubt. Knowing some of a country's rules and customs is a great benefit to you and them.

Bolivia as a whole is a marvelous country to visit, though as a local Bolivian you do face some hardships. Bolivians have the lowest GDP per capita among the Latin countries of South America. A study from 1996 to 2019 found that the average income during that period was roughly $330USD/month. As I drove through the country it's easy to see the locals aren't swimming in economic abundance. Their cars and bikes are held together from the scraps of other old cars and bikes and meals are often simple meats and root vegetables that cost less than a few dollars. You can see the weathered hands and faces of those who spend their working hours doing manual labor outdoors, and driving by rural housing it's easy to spot the shared or lacking sanitation systems outside the homes. It's not all bad, but there are certainly some challenges. To help combat the global rise of fuel prices that are out of reach of the average Bolivian, the government has subsidized fuel for the locals.

When the fuel in the US was around $0.85/ liter USD I was buying it for closer to $0.55-$0.65 USD in Bolivia. Bolivia being bordered by countries with much more economic abundance like Chile and Brazil, the government has implemented a two-tiered system for fuel prices. Locals pay the advertised lower rate and anyone with foreign license plates pays an increased price that's more reflective of the global market. This way tanker trucks aren't coming over to Bolivia, filling up, and going back to Brazil loaded with government-subsidized fuel. Well, that's the idea anyway.

The two-tiered system causes some problems and as a whole, it's flawed. At the fuel station, the attendant who is likely being paid next to nothing has a few issues to deal with when it comes to foreign license plates. First, they need to deal with a confused foreigner who likely doesn't understand the language clearly and needs to explain to us that we are going to be paying more than the advertised price, and that it's not a scam, it's actually a government promoted program!

To the foreigner, this feels like you are being blatantly ripped off. If you sat down for dinner and ordered the $10 steak and the $3 beer and when your bill came it was $25, you'd likely be a tad angry. If the foreigner at the pump agrees to this price increase because they need fuel, the attendant then needs to stop what they are doing and fill out a series of government forms documenting the foreigners personal and car information and then charge the higher rate all while the line is growing longer for the locals. In short, a foreign plate at the pumps is a huge pain in the ass for everyone.

Naturally, no one wants to be on either side of this problem, and generally another scenario unfolds. What typically happens is you park your vehicle out of sight of the fuel attendant and its government-appointed video cameras. You then grab a fuel can or empty pop bottle (these are easy to find) and get in line on foot. You then fill the pop bottle at the local rate with no license plates on camera and take it back to your vehicle for filling. On a motorbike this is only a trip or four if you have a couple of bottles, in a large SUV you'll be filling empty Coke bottles all afternoon.

The second and most likely scenario is that you bargain for a price with the fuel attendant. This only works if the cameras aren't working. and usually the cameras aren't working as this is Bolivia. This negotiated price is usually around 10% over the Bolivian price, but much lower than you'd normally pay. The fuel attendant then pockets the 10% profit for their risk and negotiating skills and rings through the purchase at Bolivian price. In this scenario the attendant is happy with the 10% tip, you are happy with the discount, and you are both fucking the government. It's a beautifully flawed system.

The third scenario typically takes place near busy and patrolled border crossings or in cities where cameras are actually working. In this scenario, a traveler with foreign license plates gets in line with the locals to get fuel. When they arrive at the pump the attendant knows how much of a pain it is to fill out the paperwork, how you are going to bitch about the price, and how it's going to make the locals wait longer as your foreign ass needs undivided special attention. To save everyone the headache, they simply refuse to sell you fuel.

Plenty of times before you showed up, they've had some other asshole in a brand new Chilean Land Rover, kitted out campervan, or BMW motorbike who's been traveling the world for a year or three pull up and had to listen to them bitch about paying for fuel at the foreign rate while the attendant likely walked to work and has never been on an international holiday.

It's this third scenario where we meet a man we'll call "Robert S.". Robert was traveling the world in one of these flashy overlanding vehicles and found himself in Bolivia for the first time trying to get fuel in the city of La Paz. Even though Robert is aware of the two-tiered fuel situation he chooses to blame the locals for his problems. Robert, in his frustration, decided to post these frustrations to an extremely active traveling forum with around 20,000 members. I am one of those members.

Robert S. to 20,000 travelers: *"How do you guys deal with the gas stations in Bolivia? We are having a very hard time getting gas here. Only 1 out of 5 gas stations is selling us gas because of the subsidizing for Bolivians. In our eyes this is pure racism and makes us not want to come back here."*

Upon reading Roberts' post, I and a large number of other travelers had a keyboard meltdown on Robert and his low-blow racism comment that he cited as the reason behind his problem.

Here was my response to Robert S; *"Racism! Cause you can't get government-subsidized fuel! Hahahha, as a traveler you might want to understand cultures better before you pull the racist card!*

This wins for the most absurd post I've seen on this page!

Just pay the foreign rate and get used to the racist fuel!

Can't get gas and it because you're white? Ohhhh the racism!

Hahaha haha! Enjoy Bolivia, the most economically depressed country in this part of South America & you have fuel problems!

Racism, ohhh man I look forward to your next post!"

Naturally, it didn't end here and after a harsh rebuttal from plenty of others on the forum, Robert made the realization that blaming the locals for his problems was maybe not the right choice. I have a low tolerance for racism and an even lower tolerance for using it as an excuse as to why your privileged life is having some troubles.

Over the several months I spent in Bolivia I was part of all three fuel scenarios as well as the bonus one, buying black market fuel. Fuel and the often lack of it became part of my daily to do list.

Bolivia
Blindsided By The Police

Born into a subsistence farming family. Leader of the Cocaleros (farmer of coca leaves). Championed indigenous rights, environmentalism, economic growth, and reduced poverty.

First indigenous and 65th president of Bolivia. Evo Morales

Does leadership trickle from the top down?

If Lake Titicaca were in high school, you know she'd have heard every name slander under the sun. Titi and Caca, did no one consider the English translation and endless poking of fun that might result from such a name?

At around 12,000-feet, Lake Titicaca is the "highest navigable lake in the world", a lake split between Peru and Bolivia. To cross from one side to the next you have three options; either take the popular western route that funnels the brunt of the traffic from one country to another, take the boat (not an option with a vehicle), or take the rarely used eastern route that's more of a pain in the ass to get to. I heard that by taking the western route there would be a very good chance I was going to be singled out as a foreigner and need to deal with corrupt police on the Peruvian side and again deal with more corruption on the Bolivian side.

Each day endless amounts of tourists and cargo shipments pass from one direction to the next on the west side. This made it easy pickings for the police who may want to invent fines for anything from a "road tax", to incorrectly blinking signal lights. I think I'd heard it all in terms of fines and crooked police leading up to this crossing, not something I was interested in dealing with.

I planned to instead go the long way around to the eastern side of the lake crossing near the village of Puerto Acosta in the hopes of avoiding these corrupt police I'd continually heard about at the border. That and the road less traveled always sounded better to me.

In the majority of other countries on the PanAm, if you overstay the terms of your vehicle's temporary import by only a few days, the officials typically fine you a minimal amount then send you on your way. In Peru, they confiscate your vehicle and make it the property of the state. Having used 88-days of my 90-day visa, the time to depart was drawing near and I wanted to exit safely with KLaiR.

My final night in Peru I camped on the eastern side of the lake in a eucalyptus forest on an empty section of the road, near the water, and enjoyed an aromatic evening by the eucalyptus-fueled campfire. This was probably the best I'd ever smelled after a night by a campfire.

In the morning I stopped in the final town on this route before departing Peru. This day coincided with the first day back to school for the local children and the town was in full parade mode. To celebrate this occasion all of the children walked the town streets playing instruments, dancing to music, and presenting themselves for the whole community to see.

Even school teachers and notable members of the community were part of the action. I had stopped to get a drink at a local shop and take some pictures of the event. While I was enjoying the show and imagining how terribly low the attendance would have been in my town growing up if they tried to parade us around before cramming us back into classrooms, a man came excitedly walking towards me.

The man, appearing to be in his late 50's, was dressed in what looked like his best Sunday attire. Not a new outfit, but the way he wore the clothes gave the impression today's top and bottoms were saved for a special occasion.

He came over to me, introduced himself as the Mayor of the community, and delightfully shook my hand like it was election day. I got the impression many tourists didn't come this way. In contrast to the Mayor, I was wearing the same dirty biker clothes I'd worn every day for a year and a half now, and likely smelled of strong campfire and earthy eucalyptus tones.

He asked what I was doing here and I tried to explain my trip briefly. I always find that if I explained to locals that I drove from North America they couldn't comprehend it. However, if I mentioned the neighboring country they were always amazed by the distance traveled. I explained I was riding from Ecuador to Bolivia. He was impressed and asked if I'd like to spend the day there in the village with him. I politely declined, explaining I needed to continue on. He shook my hand again, I took some more photos of the school parade, drank my final Inca Kola, and continued to the border.

Further down the road, I arrived at a small border post with a long steel pipe acting as the stopping point to cross the road. The pipe was held shut by a rusting chain and old lock. To the right of the gate was a small house-like building and just on the other side of the gate was a smaller shelter that looked more like a posting where someone might wait and check vehicles as they pass through. Though it didn't look like many vehicles passed through or like anyone was at either side of this gate.

I went to the house closest to me. The door was locked so I walked around looking for another way in and I found nothing. I knocked on the door, still nothing. Then I yelled a little "Hola". Finally, a man dressed in military clothing popped his head out from the small posting on the other side of the steel-pipe-fence across the road. We looked equally surprised to see each other.

I yelled over to him to see if he could help me. He yelled back that I needed to go inside the building I'd just yelled into. I began to physically show him that the door wouldn't open. He got out from behind the small posting and came under the gate and over towards me.

This guy dressed in military clothes looked at me and looked at the bike and asked the usual questions about where I was from and what I was up to? Again I got the impression not many people came this way. Military guy then went over to the same door I'd been knocking on and tried the handle. It was still locked. He then explained we'd need to wake up the sleeping border official.

Military guy then began to bang on the door like he was going to bust it down and started to yell the guy's name we were looking for. Sure enough from out of the little house came a slightly disheveled man who was putting himself together as the door opened. Half asleep the man greeted me and the military guy. He looked surprised to see me and the bike and invited me in. The man asked a few questions, stamped my paperwork, then came out and unlocked the gate to let me through. This was the kind of lazy border excitement I preferred. One border down, one to go.

Leaving from this post I then needed to navigate my way towards Bolivia. The pavement had stopped and the road was a gravel track that led along the lake past a tiny village. It was later explained to me that the people who lived here were not really citizens of Peru or Bolivia and instead etched out an existence in the small strip between the two countries.

I have never been to North Korea, but this desolate section of twisty track along the lake and past this nameless village gave me an impression of what I thought it might feel like to cross the demilitarized zone from South to North Korea. It felt empty, eerie, and a bit unwelcoming. I was passed by one truck whose driver never made eye contact with me when I had stopped to take some photos. Otherwise, despite the housing and buildings, I never saw another person anywhere.

With only two trails to choose from, I naturally chose the wrong one and looped back around through a forest and 20-minutes later was right next to the Peruvian border I'd just left. Knowing this would look extremely suspicious, I cut through the bush and back to the trail leading back towards Bolivia.

Eventually, I would find my way into Bolivia. Having come the back way out of Peru I was nearly out of fuel and decided to head to the center of this Bolivian village to find some. I knew that the fuel here was extremely cheap. In Peru, it was closer to $1USD/liter and right now it is around $0.65/liter in Bolivia. I was also told this cheap fuel was meant to be inferior compared to the rest of the Americas. I'd heard claims of octane levels below the 80's. Either way, I need fuel and the carburetor on KLaiR could burn nearly anything.

As I pulled into the town square an eruption of hushed voices began to exchange with the workers in the street and the shop owners. I could hear the words "Gringo, Gringo, Gringo, Gringo" bounce back and forth between everyone. Again I could sense not too many of us came through town.

A gringo translates directly to a foreigner. In Mexico, this was usually a derogatory term, but in South America it just meant foreigner.

To break the ice on my sudden out-of-place presence in town I started to walk towards the workers, then positioned myself between them and began to dramatically look around and ask everyone where the gringo was? I told them to be careful because gringos were crazy. Some laughed, some knew I was indeed the crazy gringo. Either way that ended the gringo whispers pretty fast.

I needed fuel and asked them where to buy it. Everyone pointed at a little storefront across the street. So I headed that way to solve my fuel problem.

Inside was a man who said he had fuel and it would be $1USD/liter, this was outrageously higher than the $0.65 you could get it for at the pumps. He told me that what he was doing was a black market sale and because of this he would need to make money to cover the risk. He also knew he was the only fuel option for quite some distance.

I'm pretty good at negotiation, but the man was fully aware he had the upper hand and could charge $2/liter and I'd still pay it. In the end, I handed over the equivalent of $1/liter for 5 liters of fuel in Bolivianos (Bolivias currency), and out he came with a hose and 5-liter jug to fill me up. I laughed, snapped a few photos of this black market fuel station, and headed to the next border post.

I arrived at the border at 12 pm. There was a little office on one side where I would need to fill out all of the papers for the motorcycle. This guy said he was just leaving for lunch and would be back in two hours. I said I was probably the only guy who was coming across that day, could he just do up my papers quickly and set me free. Unlike areas that deal with tourists all the time, I think my comeback caught him off guard and he reluctantly stayed.

Everything was in order but he would need a photocopy of the paperwork we just did and directed me back to town to get it done. I knew if I left he would be gone on his two-hour break as soon as I was out of sight. I asked if I could just use his photocopy/printer. He said no it was only for his official use. I explained that I knew he would not be waiting for me to get back, all I needed was one copy and I would happily pay him for it. He accepted my payment, one copy was made and he sent me across the road to get my passport stamped to be on my way.

When I got to the stamp building across the road the door was locked, so I took the same action as the military guy on the Peru side and began to bang on the door and start yelling "Hola, Hola!". The guy who just did my bike papers came rushing out to see what was going on. I don't think this aggressive approach was the ideal scenario on the Bolivia side. He came over and looked inside then looked at his watch. It was now 12:15 pm. He said the stamp guy had gone for lunch and was typically gone for 2-3 hours. There was nothing I could do.

I went back to the village, found some lunch in the local park, and took a little siesta on the park bench. At 2 pm I came back to the border and the photocopy guy from earlier was at his office but the stamp guy was still not around. Knowing that 3-hours was much too long of a lunch break for me to wrap my head around, I had the photocopy guy telephone the stamp guy for me. No answer.

Finally a local came by who was headed to the next village. Photocopy guy stopped him and asked him to knock on the door of the home of stamp guy to tell him someone needed his stamping services. Another 30-minutes passed and finally, the stamp guy showed up looking not too happy about his premature return to the office. My first question was to ask why he took a 3-hour lunch each day? I don't think this was the welcome he was looking for.

Once inside his little building, I saw photos, stickers and handwritten notes from probably 20-30 other tourist gringos. I asked him why he had all of this stuff. He said those were his friends and that they were all the other people that had used this border in the past! There was no way that the other border crossing would have this arrangement, likely hundreds of people cross there each day, but here the crossings could be measured in stickers and photos. I asked him how many people in total used this border post each week. He said I was the first this week and there was usually only one. Then he asked me where my stickers were for his wall? Sadly I had none.

He asked me how many days I wanted in Bolivia, I said 90. He said that was not possible, I was only allowed 30. I said Canadians are allowed

90-days then began to ramble off all the European countries that were also allowed 90-days. He said no way, not possible. I said yes way. I knew the rules. He then directed me to a poster on the wall explaining the allowable time for each country. Upon investigation, he saw that Canadians were allowed 90-days. He looked impressed with my knowledge of the border. He then stamped me for 90-days and sent me on my way.

After 5 or 6 hours, two borders, once getting lost, waking up border officials, negotiating for gas, negotiating for photocopies, one nap, and making friends with the Mayor as well as some locals who were alarmed by gringos, I was officially in Bolivia! But my progress was quickly halted.

15-minutes into the country my police fears would come to realization. Thinking that I'd gone all this way and went through all this extra effort just to avoid dealing with the corrupt police in Bolivia, I would ride right into a police checkpoint.

I'd done dozens of police checkpoints and always stuck to the same routine. I kept my GoPro camera mounted on my helmet to give the impression I was recording the event. Not that I could do anything with the footage, but this trick usually worked. I would then only speak quickly in English in the hopes the officers would soon grow tired of not being able to talk to me and just send me on my way. This usually worked if the camera didn't.

Here, the officer flagged me down and I reluctantly pulled over. I was a touch nervous, but had plenty of police practice and knew I could hold my ground. The man in his late 40's, was dressed in official police attire that looked nicer than the other men's clothing he was with, he appeared to be of higher rank than them. He greeted me and asked me in Spanish where I was headed?

In English I responded with; Hello, How Are You?

In English he replied back; Hello, I am fine thank you. You speak English?

Damnit, my plan was coming unraveled.

The other men went blank and I got the impression they only spoke Spanish. Why hadn't it just been them who pulled me over!

The officer continued in English and asked me some questions about where I had come from and where I was headed? He then asked me what country I was from. I explained I was from Canada.

He looked shocked and asked if I'd ridden this motorcycle from Canada? I got the sense his geography was better than most I'd met. We continued to chat about my trip a bit.

The officer then explained that his dream in life was to take his family to Canada and raise his children there. He knew the education was better and that the kids' lives would have much more opportunity for success in Canada. He had even applied for a visa to come but had initially been denied. Seeing what he thought must have been a rare opportunity for help from a citizen of his dream country, he asked me for some advice on how to get into the country. I passed along some positive tips that we did in fact welcome foreigners from all over the world with open arms, but I personally didn't know how to go about applying.

He wanted to know why if I was from such a great country would I leave it to come to Bolivia? I was wondering why he chose Canada and not The American Dream I assumed the world south of us was always seeking. I explained I just enjoyed seeing how other people lived and wanted to learn about the cultures of others. He was surprised but seemed excited I was here.

He then told me to be very careful as I would be very recognizable as a foreigner. He said that overall Bolivians were very nice, but the economic situation of the locals might make me a target for theft or robbery. I'd heard this plenty of times before in other countries and pretended to take his advice to heart.

He then came over and with a big smile on his face, he wrapped his arms around me in a giant bear hug and said welcome to Bolivia! I took a couple of photos of the two of us and thanked him profusely.

All this mental preparation, all these tactics to avoid the police, all of the drama I'd heard about crossing into Bolivia, and the first person I met was a police officer who speaks English, has a life-long dream to move to Canada and greeted me with a giant hug! Wow, if anyone was surprised and taken aback, it was the Canadian gringo.

Welcome To Bolivia!

Unfortunately I had my camera stolen in a busy market and lost a lot of Peru & Bolivia photos, including my welcome hug with the policeman.

(One day I followed a dirt road I couldn't find on a map. Along the way this family with baskets of yucca appeared from the bush. A couple days later the road ended. The day after that a barge appeared and we took it through the jungle. You never know where you're going to end up)

(A night of experimenting with ants, turns out they weren't the lemongrass ants I was looking for)

Bolivia
Motorcycle Maintenance?

"Why glue it, when you can J-B Weld it."
- J-B Weld Motto.

Before I'd left on this adventure I was fretting over what I'd do if things went mechanically wrong. My motorcycle mechanics were limited, though I'd fixed a lifetime of shitty cars, restaurant equipment, and household appliances to know how to bolt one thing to another long enough to make something work. I would learn that preventative maintenance was considerably easier than fixing something after it broke.

The shims of the KLR are set in place and depending on thickness, will determine the life of the valve. These tiny steel circles about the size of an American quarter, let fuel into the cylinders and allow exhaust out. If the shims are not the right thickness the motorcycle will sputter and choke until they are adjusted. Or so was my understanding.

The engine was the one part of the motorcycle I knew the least about. Somehow of all the possible maintenance that needed to be done, the adjustment of these shims was the one thing I was worried about and never wanted to attempt on my own. It was suggested to me to check the shims at around the 30,000-kilometer mark.

Before crossing into South America I'd asked around on some KLR forums about how to do this job successfully and a British man living in Panama had invited me over to show me how to do the work. Lucky for me, the world is full of people willing to offer up help.

I arrived (after getting lost for an hour), at this man's house in the suburbs of Panama City and we spent the day talking motorbikes while he helped me strip KLaiR down to the bare engine and put her back together. He seemed satisfied with their setting, invited me to spend the night with his family, and with 42,573kms on the dial I was on the way again the next morning.

Down the road another 20,000kms, I was feeling a bit concerned about my shim situation again. Having kept some detailed notes about people who may be able to help me along the way I reached out to a guy in Bolivia. Actually, he'd reached out to me first.

In the first weeks of my ride through the Baja in Mexico, this guy from Bolivia had casually suggested that once I made it to Bolivia I could look him up if I needed anything. Well, 2-years later here I was, in need of some help in Bolivia. I sent him a message. He was on the southern side of Bolivia in the small town of El Torno, not far from Santa Cruz. Bolivia didn't look too big on the map and he was getting ready to take off the following week so I decided to ride directly to his place for some help before venturing back north to explore Bolivia then come south again.

A few days later I arrived at a small orchard in the backside of tiny El Torno. I knew this guy owned a motorcycle tour company, Bolivia Motorcycle Tours. So I was expecting a business, some signs, that sort of thing. When I couldn't find it, I started asking the neighbors where it was. No one knew what I was talking about. Maybe I'd been led astray?

After a few minutes of walking the dusty street a friendly guy in his 30's with an American accent greeted me, then yelled something in regional Spanish to the neighbor I'd been talking to and opened the long wooden gate into his property for me while introducing himself as Chris.

Nice guy, but I could sense he wanted to get a feel for me before he trusted some random guy who came barreling across the country looking for help around his property. I think the introduction went something like this.

Chris: *So you drove this bike from Canada hey?*

Me: *Yeah, the whole way. It's been quite the ride.*

Chris: *Great, well let's get to work and see if she's running ok.*

There wasn't your usual 5-10 minutes of bullshitting or getting to know each other. He knew I needed some help and got right down to business. Once Chris started to get a closer look at the motorcycle he quickly relaxed into a state of humor. The humor was inspired by my complete lack of motorcycle maintenance.

In the front yard of this orchard tucked behind some fruit trees was a large rust-colored sea can. Just as I was asking Chris about his business, where his sign I'd seen online was, how long he'd been here and why the neighbors didn't know who he was, he began to open the sea can.

A series of locks and chains came off the doors, then some pulling followed by some screeching sounds and the doors to the sea can lurched open like a giant treasure chest we'd just discovered. Inside, treasure there was. There were two rows of 1st generation KLR motorbikes, parts, tools, workbenches, fuel cans, and motorcycle gear. Wow, this was his whole business right here!

He explained that he didn't want to draw much attention to his motorcycle business so he kept it well hidden and out of sight from the neighbors and family friends. Having a dozen or so large and small motorcycles parked in your driveway in rural Bolivia wasn't what you wanted the town talking about.

Chris hauled a quad and a couple of bikes out of the can to make room for KLaiR and in a matter of minutes, he started taking her apart. It was like having my own personal pit crew.

Chris is your standard blue-collar guy who works hard and works hard with his hands. I looked at my dainty fingers that had hardly done a labor job in their life and then looked at Chris' hands that had clearly seen thousands of hours wrenching on motorbikes and other projects. They looked like tiny tree trunks that had been smashed with a hatchet; this was my guy. If I could trust anyone's hands on KLaiRs body, it was a guy in rural Bolivia with a sea can full of KLR's who didn't mess around with his time.

The process of taking KLaiR apart lasted for about 2-minutes before Chris dropped a tool and reached down to pick it up. It was in that moment that I saw his all-business face quickly crack into a gut-busting laugh. He looked up at me from down beside KLaiR and said between laughs. *"When… is the last time… you changed… THESE SPROCKETS?!"*

Chris was caught between a look of impressed, disappointed, and bemusement.

I looked at the sprocket without thinking much about it, and thought for a second. *Well, actually, let me think about it. I'd put a new chain and sprockets on before I'd left Canada and, well, that was the last time.*

Christ burst into a slightly more shallow, gut-busting laugh, then said back to me with utter amazement. *You rode on this chain and these sprockets since Canada!*

Again I wasn't too sure if he was impressed or disappointed and tried to maintain a neutral look about me.

Chris stopped working on KLaiR, walked over to a spare sprocket he had, and brought it over for me to look at. He then held these well-defined spikey knobs from his sprocket next to the lumpy circle that was keeping KLaiR on the road and pointed out what these parts should look like. There was no contest. It had been about 35,000kms of rough roads on my current setup and now KLaiR was rolling down the road on steel nubs and a steady supply of luck.

Chris said he wasn't sure if we could find sprockets and a chain for the KLR around here, but I wasn't going to make it much further without one. We shifted back to working on her engine and he said he would help me try to solve some of my other issues later.

The day continued on inside the heat of the ventless sea can and one by one Chris took KLaiR right down to the open-engine explaining to me why this or that needed adjustment and how to do it. To the eyes of the foolhardy moto-traveler, he was a motorcycle genius.

Eventually, we got to the shims and 3 of 4 were good. Chris had a small supply of replacement shims, however, at one point in the future he would need them to maintain his own fleet that kept his business running and his family fed. Here in Bolivia these shims were hard to replace. Knowing I couldn't source my own anytime soon, he parted with one of his valued shim supplies and bolted KLaiR back together.

As KLaiR regained her original composure, Chris checked each and every bolt that was clinging to life on her fragile frame. Again I'm not sure if he was impressed or surprised by the mix & match selection of bolts, zip ties, and J-B Weld I had used to affix parts and replace things that had rattled away on the road. Chris proceeded to tighten brakes, adjusted levers, change out screws, and showed me where my subframe bolt was about one full twist of the nut from falling off. If it had fallen off, it would cause the bike to buckle and collapse in the middle. I was thankful for a lot of people I'd met on this trip, but Chris from Bolivia Motorcycle Tours and his sea can full of KLR's was topping the list. If the sub-frame bolt had come out on the highway or the brakes had given way coming down the Andes or the sprocket had made its last turn crossing a river, that might have been the end of our motorcycle adventure. This man quite literally saved my life.

By now I knew that Chris' wife and two young sons would be coming home from school shortly and the idea of a random dirty biker looking for help at their house was maybe not the "Welcome Home!" he wanted to offer them. Either way, he knew the luck on my current setup was dwindling fast and he suggested I spend the night at his place so he could help me look for parts in the morning.

Like meeting a radio announcer for the first time in person that you'd listened to for years, both Chris and his family were not what I was picturing in my head. At first, I had assumed that Chris was Bolivian. Then once I met him and realized he was an American I was now picturing your classic case of an American man in a developing nation who'd found some beautiful young girl that was looking for a sugar daddy to support her. Why a guy who lives in a tent and operates on a cycle of two changes of clothes is ever making assumptions about other people is still beyond me.

Once the family came barreling through the gates at the house I was totally shocked. Though beautiful, Chris' wife Rebecca was anything but a sugar-daddy-seeking Bolivian. Rebecca was Bolivian, but a blonde Bolivian who spoke like an American. As for the kids, two rambunctious blondies with all kinds of questions for the guy with the broken motorcycle in their sea can didn't waste any time getting down to business either.

We all had a little chat, Chris then directed me to the washing machine for my motorcycle gear and two changes of clothes, and Rebecca started making dinner. The kids got out their motorcycle gear and small motorcycles to take a rip around the motorcycle track they'd developed around their little orchard. These kids rode like little Evel Knievel's. Matias, the older brother, took off in a whizz of two-stroke fumes, and Marcos, a couple years younger and unable to touch both feet to the ground while sitting on the seat, took off after him. I tried to keep up for a couple of laps on one of their small Hondas. Not a chance, I might as well have been on a unicycle.

If there is one line I'll never forget that came out of the mouth of this proud father while we both stood there watching his kids rip up the property, it's this. I looked over at Chris and casually muttered the phrase, "Wow, your boys can really ride." He didn't even hesitate and said back to me; "Yup, they're going to be the first Bolivians to win the Dakar." Shit, I could get the sense he was going to make this idea a reality.

In the end, I spent 3-days with the family. They took me to a birthday party at a Church and introduced me to the community. They fed me, the kids told me about school and their lives between living in the USA and Bolivia, and Chris took me all over Santa Cruz looking for KLR parts.

A few days later I'd leave with some questionable sprockets that we needed to weld washers onto so they would fit my bike, but we were unable to find a proper chain. I was back on the road north with 60,200kms on the dial and a new friend in the books.

(The sprocket I was using next to a new one) (Making friends along the way)

Bolivia
Monumental Moments Never Talked About

"If a tree falls in a forest and no one is around to hear it, does it make a sound?"

- No confirmed origin. Though Bruce Cockburn may get a little credit.

Suddenly like a ghost from the woods emerged a short man with dark skin, a small belly, in roughly his late 40's and dripping with water. He appeared wearing nothing more than a pair of tattered, grandpa-style, white Brief underwear that were nearly see through and carrying a Nokia cell phone from the 90's as he came slogging his way through the swamp. He looked at us like we had come to rescue him and yelled something to me in a language I wasn't familiar with. I smiled and stared blankly back at him with my eyes bulging from my face.

* * *

Along this epic adventure, I'd posted photos online of me catching piranhas in the Amazon, riding through life-ending mudslides, partying at weddings of people I'd only just met, picking and eating what I thought was lemongrass ants from the ground in Bolivia, volunteering in remote Andean villages, making chocolate in Nicaragua, crushing coffee in El Salvador, and generally keeping my tiny world up to date about my adventures.

Then, one evening I was giving a presentation about this adventure to a packed bar in the city I used to live in and I told this story. During that presentation, it dawned on me that despite this being my personal biggest accomplishment and being the biggest mental game-changer of the entire trip, I had never written a word about it, or posted a single photo of the day.

I've talked and shared stories about the most mundane of topics over and over again from life on the road. Somehow, this story that was so dear to me had never been made public.

Here it is. Here's the day that changed my entire mental outlook. Well, aside from never being able to erase the image of the man in white Brief underwear dripping in water, holding nothing more than an old cell phone from my mind.

So, where was I and why was I here? To find the exact location I spent hours searching through my unstolen photos, social media posts, and thousands of iOverlander camping spots trying to retrace my steps. The problem with enjoying these moments with a machine and monkey along with never sharing the story publicly, means the details can fade away. In general, I was in the mountains of Bolivia, sort of. I had come this way hoping to explore some of the lesser-traveled parts of Bolivia, and at this time of year, I had found them.

I'd started this adventure when I left Chris' place in central Bolivia and headed back north to the Death Road before making my way to Trinidad in the north-central region, eventually landing back at Chris' again. I knew it wouldn't be a total cake-walk, but it wasn't like I was blazing a new trail either. It was a gravel road connecting some small villages in the Bolivian countryside. The weather was hot enough to ride in a t-shirt at all hours, but by midday, it was usually sweltering and I'd need to keep KLaiR moving to catch a breeze and stay out of the dust.

The day before I'd run into swampy underwear man, I had been blessed with my 3rd flat tyre in 24-hours. If you believe in omens, this would have been the sign to turn around and head back to where you came from. At this moment I was on the second of those three flat tyres, and to add insult to injury it was midday on the side of a dusty mountain road with no shelter or shade.

I'd pulled the wobbly bike over to the edge of the road and began to unpack my tools and repair kit just like I had less than 100-kilometers earlier. Halfway through this sweaty project, an old truck with an elderly man and woman came slowly rumbling around the corner. Since I was the only person I'd seen that day on the road, I was sure they were going to pull over for a little chat and maybe to see if I needed help. Without even so much as a tap of the brakes, they rolled by and looked straight ahead as though I never existed!

I was shocked. Was I somewhere I wasn't supposed to be? Were they somewhere they weren't supposed to be? What if I actually needed help? Who knows, but I kept plugging along on my tyre repair as they looked on without stopping. The culprit turned out to be half of a small nail sticking out from the rubber in the wall of the tyre. I must not have noticed this when I was doing the tube repair the last time and it had caused yet another flat. I was happy I'd discovered the steel assassin.

Later that evening I found a quiet spot near a creek to set up my camp for the night. While making dinner I looked over and sure as shit, the same tyre was flat again. Now what! It was too dark to deal with it and I hoped there would be no need to make a hasty escape in the night. I resolved to fix it in the morning.

After breakfast I took the tyre off the bike, took the tube out, and gave it a thorough inspection. I found the problem, again, here was the other half of the nail. It had broken into two and I had taken the one side out, but the other side continued to roll around between my tyre and my tube just waiting to wreak havoc again and again!

Finally, with all rubber in good repair and three patches holding my tube together we were back on the road. As I mapped out the day I saw that there was one final village on the way where I could stop for supplies before making my way to the river crossing that I knew lay ahead for me.

At the store, I purchased some bread, my go-to chocolate milk & cookies, and tried to scrounge up some fuel before heading on. I had about 100kms left in my tank, but I wasn't convinced that would take me all the way to the next village after the river. After asking around no one had any fuel to sell or if they did they weren't willing to part with it in this remote area, so I pressed on.

It might have been an hour, it might have been two hours. I find that when I'm unsure about where I am going or even a little nervous, time feels like it doubles in length and things take much longer to reach than they really do. Later, if I take that same route confidently knowing where I am going, the time to get there is always considerably less.

What was a respectable (for Bolivia standards) gravel road, was slowly getting worse and worse. The road was full of bumps and holes and the further I went the worse it got. My pace started to slow as I navigated around wash-outs where heavy rains had made creeks across the road that were now dry, leaving behind huge ruts. With a lack of travelers on this road, the grasses on the roadside had begun to eat away at the road.

Not having seen anyone since the chocolate milk village an hour or two back and with no fuel in sight, I was happy to be alone in the hills, but a bit nervous. If anything were to happen where I needed help there was no chance of getting it and likely no one coming this way to find us. With KLaiR and Stanley at my side, I pushed the "what if's" out of my mind as our trio pressed on.

Eventually, we came to a point where I could see the river through the trees as the road came to a fork. To the right was a gravel path that looked like a large grader had pushed earth and stones out of the way to open up the road. Maybe it was once washed away and they had to open it back up again with a large machine. To the left was a little road that carried on downhill towards the river. I opted to go left to the river.

To my surprise, near the bottom of the road was a nice-looking cabin with a barbed wire fence all around it. Great I thought, people live here. As I got closer it looked like no one was home, so I decided to first investigate the river and hoped that someone would eventually arrive home and greet me. I was still a little nervous about where I was but was sure something good would come out of it.

Less than 100-meters around the corner everything came to an end. KLaiR's overloaded weight was wearing on me going downhill, I had been pushing hard against the handgrips trying to keep us balanced. Whether it was my fatigue, jittery nerves, or a combination of both, I came around the last bend only to find the road was partially washed out. I tried to veer to the inside track to avoid the missing part of the road. It was nothing spectacular, no major negotiating, and I probably could have coasted by easily, but I didn't want to risk anything.

However, I suddenly lost control of KLaiR and dropped her on the road. She went down and started to slide towards the side of the road that was washed out. Fuck, what if she goes over. Even if she did remain intact, there was no chance of me dragging her out from the trees below.

KLaiR skidded to a halt before going over the edge. I was shaking. I pulled my camera out of my pocket and snapped a quick photo then walked over and pulled and heaved until I could get her back up on two wheels and put the kickstand down to park her. I decided to walk the rest of the road until I found the end of it. For one, I needed a break from the pushback against the handlebars, and second, I didn't think I'd be able to turn her around if the road narrowed anymore and I couldn't go ahead.

A short walk quickly answered my question. The road leveled off and hit a flat spot. This section had become part of a swampy pond that had been created from the rainy season that we were nearing the end of.

The water was murky and the road wound around the corner so I couldn't see the end of it. There was no way I was going to be able to get to the river on this road. At least not at this time of year. I walked back up to KLaiR and decided to investigate the cabin and the other road for an alternate route. It was sometime after lunch and I needed another cookie break anyway.

The cabin was empty. Whoever built it had done so to a much higher standard than the usual slapped-together shacks around this part of Bolivia. The home was nicely built of wood, there was a deck, a porch, and bathrooms. There were even stables for presumably horses or cows. I don't think I'd ever seen a barbed wire fence with more than one wire on it in and this one had three. Either way, no one was home and hadn't been for a long time. I peed off the front of the porch, took my well-deserved cookie break on their deck, and snooped around to see if there was anywhere to sleep on the property if it came to that.

Back on the trail, KLaiR, Stanley, and I went to investigate the other road. Hopefully, it would take us back to the river and there would be a path where we could cross. When we finally reached the end of the road I couldn't believe what I saw.

There was a massive bridge at the end of this road that hung 40 or 50-feet in the air. It looked like it was well-built of cement with pillars up out of the water to support it. It was your standard modern bridge, designed for large trucks or any other vehicle to pass over. The modern design looked as out of place as the cabin did in the desolate area where I was. There was just one problem… exactly half of the bridge had been washed away.

Either the design wasn't that great and it had crumbled against the waters or when the rivers raged here they swelled up 40+ feet and had washed it away. All that was left was a couple of pillars holding up a large chunk of cement in the middle. Unless I could launch KLaiR from the bank up and over about 50-feet, there was no way I could use it. From where I was the road had also washed away and there was a drop some 20-feet to the gravel bed below. Maybe for Evel Knievel and his stunting Harley Davidson, but not for heavy ass KLaiR and I.

Peering down into the base of the riverbed below, it looked more like four or five rivers all met here before joining forces and becoming one big river at the height of the rainy season. Today these rivers were dissipating and had separated leaving behind large tracts of gravel each divided by the remaining rivers that ran through here. Getting down to investigate these various rivers and plotting out a plan to cross wasn't looking easy.

Looking at my options, I couldn't go down the steep embankment the 20 or more feet to the bottom, and back the other direction the road was washed out by the murky swamp. I sat, had another cookie, and thought about what to do.

Finally, I decided to head back towards the washed-out section I'd come from and look for some other options. Maybe there was a path through the trees I hadn't seen, maybe there was a secret road near the abandoned cabin in the woods. Maybe I would need to go back to the village and beg for fuel to try and go back where I'd come from several days earlier. There were always options; I just didn't always like them.

I went back to the edge of the washout, parked KLaiR, and started to look for a solution. It was getting later in the day and I knew I'd be limited on time to figure it out before the sun went down. About 10-minutes into my looking around I heard the thundering sounds of an old motorbike with no exhaust pipe up in the hills. With each turn in the road, I could hear the road rocket rumbling closer. Perfect I thought, a local who knew the area well and knew how to get across. Lucky me.

Eventually, the man appeared. He was wearing old blue jeans with a dusty faded red shirt on. No helmet, no safety equipment, and sandals. His bike looked like it was built by the same people that had built Frankenstein, then driven through a landmine. Small, maybe 110cc, the seat was either torn or half-eaten, no mirrors, chain clinging on for life with bits of wire holding this and that to the bike. After the maintenance lessons from Chris, I now knew what to look for! I thought, if he can get across on that, I should be fine.

The man came zipping around the corner looking a bit surprised to see me. He then took one look at the washed-out road, looked at me again, and immediately turned around. He didn't even pause for a second look at me or the road.

I knew this was my only chance to get some local advice so I yelled at him in Spanish to stop. He stopped and I began to ask him if he was going to cross or where to cross. He asked me to slow my speech. I realized that Spanish wasn't his first language as he spoke some regional language I knew nothing about.

In my basic Spanish, I asked him about the road and where to go, if there was another route, and how far the next town was. In his basic Spanish response, he explained this was the only road and it was very far to the next town if I got across. He said he would return in 3-weeks to try and cross it again. I could sense he didn't want to chat as he got ready to leave again.

Suddenly like a ghost from the woods emerged a short man with dark skin, a small belly, in roughly his late 40's and dripping with water. He appeared wearing nothing more than a pair of tattered, grandpa-style, white brief underwear that were nearly see through and carrying a Nokia cell phone from the 90's as he came slogging his way through the swamp. He looked at us like we had come to rescue him and yelled something to me in a language I wasn't familiar with. I smiled and stared blankly back at him with my eyes bulging from my face.

The guy I had been talking to replied to him and they got to chatting. I had no idea what they were saying, but based on the dramatic actions of underwear man and the visual state of him, I got the idea.

He'd been on the other side of the river in a truck and was looking for a way to cross. I'm guessing to save his clothes from getting wet, he'd taken them all off and took his cell phone to call for help or maybe call back to the truck once he reached the higher side of the mountain where we were.

The top two moments on this entire trip when I wished I had taken a photo and never did were when KLaiR was tyres up in the ditch when I had crashed her into the side of the Andes mountains on the way to Machu Picchu. The second was of underwear man standing there dripping in his nearly see through white briefs on this side of a swamp holding nothing more than an old Nokia Cell phone. Some moments will be forever cherished as just memories.

The two of them talked for 2-3 minutes in their regional tongue while I sat atop KLaiR between them and tried to make out what was going on. Then, just like they had both appeared, the conversation stopped and the man on the one-breath-from-death motorcycle fired up the rumbling beast and took off back up the hill while underwear man turned back to slog his way through the swamp. Neither looked at me, neither said goodbye to me. They just disappeared to where they had come from. It was all very surreal and the timing of these events was almost unimaginable.

If I wasn't willing to recognize the omens of three flat tyres, would I take note of the incredible timing of the one-breath-from-death bike and the underwear man who weren't going to brave this crossing? The most unbelievable things happen in the most unbelievable moments.

As I sat there trying to make some sense of this encounter and what I wanted to choose to believe I'd heard from the conversation where I didn't actually understand so much as one word, something dawned on me. Underwear man had walked through the swamp I was concerned about riding through. That meant there was a bottom shallow enough to at least walk through. Actually, I don't think it had gone much above his knees as he was walking away. Maybe there was a way to the river. Either way, I knew it would be dark in a couple of hours and I didn't want to risk getting stuck this late in the day. I'd camp and think about what to do for the night.

Looking around the cabin I didn't feel comfortable being exposed to the road in case anyone came back that night and I didn't want to risk being found if the owner showed up and didn't want me there. I rode back up to where the bridge was washed out to search for a spot to camp.

I found a little nook hidden from the road and to my delight I could randomly send and receive WhatsApp messages as the phone service flickered on and off. Night fell, I made dinner, and worked on a couple of articles about "Top 10-Wedding Venus In Sussex" for the content company I was working for online. The internet service was just good enough to tether to my tablet so I could send the articles into the company if the signal held for long enough. When the phone vibrated with an incoming WhatsApp message I knew my article had likely been sent too. Camping, adventure, and working from anywhere was my ideal life-scenario coming to realization.

I made the standard biker pasta dinner I'd made hundreds of times before and ate it in the early moonlight next to a small fire I'd built from bits of scavenged wood. Four or five bites of pasta and I suddenly heard the sound of an engine in low gear back in the trees across the river. Then I saw two headlights dimly shining through the trees. I'd never seen underwear man again and thought that maybe this was him. Maybe he'd made his way back to the truck he'd come from. I watched as the vehicle's lights bounce their way through the darkness across the rocky part of the dry river bed.

In the moonlight, the truck looked like a white Toyota Tacoma raised up a few inches with the bed modified to carry passengers with bench seating and a tarp cover. This was a pretty standard taxi in South America but likely lifted a bit to travel this region. In the complete silence of night, I could clearly hear the whining of a truck in low gear given plenty of gas so it didn't get stuck in the rocks and sand.

As the truck drove closer to the river I could see it quickly turn to angle itself into the water going upstream as opposed to coming into the water sideways and risk flipping over. The lights sunk under the water as it nosed in, then popped back out as the truck leveled out in the riverbed. There was no hesitation to his method. The driver pointed the truck straight ahead and drove upstream until I could see the water recede against the side of the truck. When the water level appeared to be safe enough to handle at an angle, the truck turned and ground its way up the embankment to dry land. This process would repeat itself three or four more times as the truck made its way across each of the rivers that passed here. Clearly, this wasn't the driver's first rodeo.

During one of the crossings, I wasn't convinced they would make it. Just like the first crossing the lights had gone under the water as the truck dropped into the riverbed before leveling out and coming up above the waterline. This time though, the water got deeper before it got shallow. The water came up over the tyres, then over the lights, and up over the hood. The truck had a snorkel, but shit, it wasn't built for swimming and I wasn't sure they'd get much further if the water continued like this.

I could see the illuminated river from the truck lights and I knew they must have water in their cab. Would this old Bolivian Toyota grinding upstream in the dark of night with the man at the wheel wearing nothing more than a pair of wet white Briefs holding an old Nokia cell phone above the waterline make it? The truck pushed on, and for what seemed like a breathless eternity pushed back against the relentless river. If they so much as hit a large rock or log in the riverbed, it would be all over.

Suddenly the water began to recede and the lights rose from the flooding waters. The driver had found a high point in the river bed and cranked the wheels to drive the truck up and out of the water. Wow, I could feel myself cheering them on!

The truck then disappeared up the dry riverbed and I couldn't see the lights any longer. Ten to fifteen minutes would pass before I would eventually hear the truck on the road on this side of the river. I saw the lights making their way up towards me on the road and as they came towards the vacant section I was camped on, they made a quick right turn following the rutted gravel towards the village I had come from.

I was suddenly alive with excitement. This truck had made it across the river, it was possible. KLaiR couldn't take the same route they took, but it was passable. If they could do it, we could do it. Or so I was hoping.

(Flat #3. Patched with an old tube)   (Lucky I didn't drop her a few feet sooner!)

Bolivia
Teaching KLaiR To Swim

"I'm strong to the finish 'cause I eats me spinach."
- *Popeye*

I awoke around 8 am, this time making the typical oatmeal breakfast I'd had nearly every day for two years, and methodically began to pack my camera, phone, tablet, and all other electronics in various Ziploc and plastic bags. I kept my GoPro camera out in the hopes of documenting some of the excitement. I then tried to place every item I could inside my plastic Pelican Case Panniers. Technically Pelican cases are fully waterproof, but I had drilled holes in the boxes to mount them to the bike and this would allow water to creep inside. Hopefully, it won't come to that.

I was back at the washed-out road where fate had placed me between the one-breath-from-death biker and underwear man. I parked KLaiR and proceeded to slowly walk in my boots and biker pants across the murky washed-out road. It was muddy but no deeper than my knees. I walked both sides of the path to find out where the deeper tyre tracks were and where the higher middle point was. The left side was a bit more shallow and I wouldn't risk hitting the trees on that side. I mounted KLaiR and we entered the water, easy-peasy I thought as we slid through the water effortlessly. I repeated this process several more times as we worked our way down the road and through the washout. Eventually, we ended up at the dry section of the riverbed. One section down, four or five to go. This section was a false confidence builder, a bit like having a few beers before going to a party.

I tried to follow various tracks on the dry riverbed hoping that one of them would lead me to the right place to cross the water. Some tracks faded away to nothing, others circled back to where I was. Finally, I just made my own trail and slowly rode my way to the first of the river crossings.

Once I was finally on the edge of the water it was considerably more intimidating than it looked from four or five hundred feet away where I was camped the night before. This party might require a few confidence-building shooters to go with my proverbial beers. The water was flowing more like a waterfall than a river and was probably fifty or sixty feet from one side to the other. I'd only ever crossed a river once before on a motorbike, like actually once before. That crossing was in the Amazon region of Ecuador months earlier and it was nothing like this. I believe the expression for this moment was, *Trial By Fire*.

I slowly rode up and down the edge of the river looking for the tracks of the Toyota from last night. I never found them. I lowered my standards and started to look for any recent tracks where anyone might have crossed, ever. I didn't see anything. My courage was dwindling faster than it had appeared. I parked KLaiR and decided to take underwear man's approach to river crossing, only I'd do it fully clothed.

For forty-five minutes to an hour, I walked up and down the river with my biker boots and pants on searching for a spot where I felt it would be shallow enough to navigate KLaiR across. I then found bits of garbage on the shore (sadly, this was easy to do in most countries along the journey) I found old torn-up oil jugs in red and blue and yellow. When I found a shallow point on my side of the river I'd mark it with these bright pieces of garbage. Then, I'd walk back and forth across the river hoping to navigate a line where I could successfully drive across to the other side then mark it with more of the brightly colored garbage.

On one foot-crossing attempt the water got up towards my chest and I made a quick retreat, making a mental note not to go that way! Eventually, I found what I felt was the right path and decided I would attempt to ride KLaiR across here.

My luggage setup was ridiculously heavy and unbelievably un-aerodynamic. Why I never resolved to take the boxes off and walk them across before coming back for the bike I'll never know. Maybe I felt they were too heavy to carry. Maybe I thought it would take too long. Maybe I never thought about it because I was too distracted with the idea of shitting my pants over the daunting task ahead.

I took off my helmet and set it on the other side of the river. The GoPro camera was attached to the top and I wanted to record the, hopefully uneventful, events.

The plan was to ride KLaiR into the river like the truck the night before, pointing her slightly upstream and slowly working my way across to the other side. The angle couldn't be too straight or the river would push me over and I'd lose KLaiR or end up being trapped underneath her. It also couldn't be directly upriver or I'd never hit my mark on the other side and get up out of the water. Holy shit I was scared.

I rode KLaiR right to the edge of the river, just touching the water with her front tyre. Then, like the flip of a coin, I changed my mind. I stopped, put down the kickstand, and hopped off. I decided I'd walk her across instead. I figured if I stayed upstream, at least if the river knocked us over or I lost control she would go down but I would end up on top of her, opposed to being pinned underneath.

I pulled in the clutch, dropped KLaiR into first gear, wished Stanley luck, and inched down into the rushing waters. I knew I'd need to keep a respectable twist on the throttle so that if the exhaust pipe went under the water that the propulsion of the exhaust would force the liquid out. I also knew I would need to keep her steadily going forward without stalling. If I went too fast and lost control it was over. If I stalled her it was over. If I tripped on a rock or hit a tree, it was over. Fuck she was overloaded, fuck I was scared.

Onwards we went. The water rushed, my heart rate increased and I kept her revving as I fluttered the clutch trying to regulate her speed along with my steps. I kept tripping on the rocks below the water and banging my leg into the Pelican case on her side. Doing this on dry ground would have been a pain in the ass, in my current situation it felt more like a kick in the balls.

We inched, we tripped, we struggled, we stumbled, water crept up the side of the Pelican cases and sweat rolled off of me under the Bolivian sun and dripped down in the waters that filled my boots. I'd continually check KLaiR and the RPMs, then focused back on my garbage targets on the other side to make sure we were on track. I knew if this failed not one person in the world would have any idea where I was. I also knew the chances of meeting up with anyone who might be able to rescue me today were unlikely. I was so focused on the water, the garbage target, and KLaiR's progress that a war could have been raging around us and I wouldn't have noticed it. I just needed to win the battle I was in, and all would be fine.

It could have been 5-minutes, it could have been 45-minutes, I have no idea how much time had passed. Then suddenly KLaiR's front tyre began to lift from the water and the garbage target was near. I made it! Hold shit, I actually made it!

The celebration was short-lived. I'd need to repeat this process four more times. I parked KLaiR, dug a cookie from my luggage, and began to walk the next river placing garbage on opposing shores to mark a path once I discovered it. It was only on the final river crossing where I'd eventually lose control of KLaiR trying to navigate the crossing.

Walk the river, mark the crossing with garbage, inch KLaiR across, and repeat. By now it was late afternoon. The day's events had taken hours and I was glad I didn't attempt this the night before. It was the final river to cross before I was home free. I walked the track, marked it with garbage, and set up the GoPro on my helmet to catch the action.

This final crossing was shorter from bank to bank, only fifty to sixty feet across. But the bank on either side was steeper and I would need to direct KLaiR downhill into the water, then turn her into the oncoming waters, then somehow get her up the bank and out the other side. Despite the cookie-power I was living off of, I was growing tired. About halfway across this final river crossing, I heard the familiar sound of a low-geared Toyota in the bush. It was coming from the direction I was headed so I knew it was a different one than the one that had crossed the night before. Here I was with KLaiR halfway across the river, shaking with fatigue, mentally and physically exhausted, negotiating steep embankments with all this gear strapped to her back and suddenly this truck appears and stops about two hundred feet away and out pops a family of five to watch me.

I stand out enough as it is, but to find me here in this situation I'm sure would have been equally as surprising as if I'd seen a Bolivian family pop out of the woods where I was camping in Canada. They all got out to enjoy the show, I was hoping not to give them.

I got to the other side of the river and began to get KLaiRs front tyre up and out of the water. The bank was slick with mud. Just then as the tyre lifted and my boots hit the slippery edge, I lost her. KLaiR went toppling over and I was sure this was going to sink her. As she hit the water's edge the Pelican case caught the embankment and propped her out of the water. It was a mini-miracle. If I'd taken the luggage off, her engine would be filling up with river water right now.

In the most non-textbook, unorthodox way possible, I got on the other side of her and reached under the seat to lift her up. Using strictly my back, arms, and final blast of cookie-power, I heaved her up in a sputtering burst of breathless rage. If there had been a chiropractor watching they would have berated me like a schoolboy who'd broken the most basic of rules. The family watched as my impressive river crossing skills came unwound.

Once she was up, I quickly jumped on the seat, and in one fluid stroke, pulled in the clutch, hit the starter as she cranked over and fired up. Like a drunken stuntman on a rental bike, I cracked the throttle and opened her wide up. First gear sprung into action and we came flying up over the final embankment in a spewing mess of rock and mud to the wide-eyes of the Bolivian family watching from beside their truck.

We'd made it. It took the entire day to walk the swampy road and navigate the river crossings that followed, but we'd made it. We'd actually fucking made it! It was at that moment that I suddenly felt that I could accomplish anything. Solutions would present themselves, big tasks would need to be broken into small chunks to achieve them, and sometimes the most major of life's accomplishments would find you on the edge of a riverbank in a foreign country with only wide-eyed locals watching and not a single person cheering you on. But the feeling of accomplishment was incredible and I knew I'd never be able to share the feeling of that moment with anyone. Just a steel motorcycle named KLaiR and a plastic monkey named Stanley. I wasn't sure I'd be able to explain these moments to real people and ever have it make sense. I felt like sometimes steel and plastic friends were the only friends I could relate to.

The family came over to see this big crazy motorcycle I was on and invited me to come fruit picking with them. Right there, hidden in plain sight on the river's edge was an orchard! From where we were standing all I could see was a wall of trees just like the trees that surrounded the entire area. The family took me along with them and we walked right through the trees and there it was, a house on a giant orchard, completely invisible when you looked right at it from the road. Maybe that was their cabin across the river?

In season the place was full of various fruits, but it seemed we were a touch too early. The worker walked us around and I picked a few oranges to eat, but there weren't enough fruits ready for harvest. I thanked the family and headed back to KLaiR.

Our trio headed up the road to find the next village and continue on. Less than two minutes into the ride she began to sputter. We were out of fuel! I was sure I did the math and had enough to get us at least 100-kilometers. What I hadn't factored in was all of the heavy revs to get her across the rivers. I'd burnt up all the fuel. If this same thing had happened crossing the river it would have been just as fatal as a clutch stall. On the other side of the coin, had I found fuel in the last village and filled her up, I would have been dealing with another 30-40 pounds of weight. What an endless night and day of highs and lows.

I quickly reached down and flipped the fuel over to the reserve tank. This would buy us another 35-40 kilometers, but not to the next village that I discovered on the GPS. A short time later and running on fumes I looked back to see that I'd lost my sleeping pad that had been tied to the back. Jesus, does it never end? I had to think about what to do. If I had to go back all the way to the river I would only have enough fuel to get me to where I was currently parked. So nowhere. If I pressed on, I would be sleeping on hard ground until I could find a replacement. I decided to go back no more than 5-kilometers to look for the mat.

Slowly, I rode back, about 4-kilometers down the road. There it was, sprawled across the gravel, my sleeping pad. Having been wet from the river it was now covered in a light mud from the dust. I grabbed the bag and turned around. Shortly I'd come to another fork in the road with several houses. My fumes were thinning and I was worried my luck was too. I went to a house to ask for fuel and was met by two excited men who asked me some questions about the river then happily handed over a few liters of fuel that I was happy to pay double the going rate for. Perception changes things in a heartbeat and with a freshly purchased pack of cookies and some fuel, off we went. Onto the next adventure.

(The final river crossing)

(Dropped her at the last minute)

(The family of onlookers)

Bolivia
Jungle People

North Yungas or "Death Road" saw roughly 300-deaths per year until an alternate route came under construction in the mid-1990's.

- Fact

If a drunken spider were to dip his feet in ink and stumble across a map of Bolivia, you'd get an idea of what my route looked like. This same drunken spider could account for most of my South America riding. After my direct route south to Bolivia Motorcycle Tours near Santa Cruz from La Paz, I then rode back North towards La Paz taking side routes and backroads. Then up and over to "The World's Most Dangerous Road" then west towards Brazil then back southwest towards Bolivia Motorcycle Tours a couple of months later. You'd wonder what the hell I was doing and if I was lost, and often I was.

I wanted to ride "The World's Most Dangerous Road" just to say I did it. I got lucky, it was absolutely pouring rain that day. This meant little rivers had formed and begun running down the road I was trying to ride up. What were likely trickles of water down the side of the mountain had now become waterfalls pouring down over me at points. To add to my luck I was treated to a cloudy view of the surrounding mountains.

I chose to go from the bottom up, and driving this way first thing in the morning with virtually no other traffic on the road meant that the drive was considerably less dramatic than the name might lead you to believe. Navigating collapsed mountain roads that were half washed away in places like Colombia and Guatemala were certainly scarier, but imagining what it might have been like sitting on a bus back when this was the main route, now that would have a person praying to any God that would listen.

On the ride you round this blind corner and that hairpin turn, taking note of the headstones and car parts that mark where various people plummeted to their deaths. It's at these points where one can envision what it must have been like when the bus you were on that was going uphill suddenly came nose to nose with an overloaded dump truck who'd lost his brakes going downhill and your driver had to decide if he was going to swing his two rear tyres over the edge or try to plow the dump truck into the mountain. Faaaaaaaaaaaak....

These days there's a freshly paved twin roadway that takes travelers around this once deadly section and to ride the road you need to go out of your way and pay a fee to do so. The majority of road traffic is from thrill-seeking peddle bikers winding from top to bottom looking to get the "I'm So Crazy" t-shirt to show their friends.

After checking World's Most Dangerous Road off my to-do list, I was hoping to find the World's Most Untraveled Roads, and headed towards the Amazon. These red clay roads lead up towards Brazil and hold some of the country's most pristine wilderness. My plan was to ride up towards the town of Yucumo, then ride the road to Rurrenabaque and continue on up towards the Brazil border before routing back towards the small city of Trinidad. The only catch to this plan was that a large section of the road ends before turning into rivers and swamps. At the right time of year, various local boats can ferry you across the rivers from one patch of dry land to another. The closer I got the more I learned that this was not that time of year and the water was still much too high to make it passable. Instead, I hung a right on the red clay and headed towards San Borja, a road that would take me to Trinidad.

In the heat of the day, the ride was mostly calm dusty roads and cattle farmers moving their livestock from one pasture to another. However, sure as shit, right here about 50-kilometers from nowhere and a week or so since I'd seen anyone who might vaguely resemble a tourist I spotted another "large" motorcycle coming my way. As I slowed, they slowed. As I stopped, they stopped. I had a quick glance at the bike and its rider as they glanced back at me. This bike looked similarly out of place as I did.

Here on the dusty red clay road was a DR650 with off-road tyres and about 1/3 as much luggage as me was another bike looking for some adventure. In contrast, I was riding on 50/50 tyres that felt more like 80/20 tyres and my load of luggage. This guy had Arizona license plates, wow I thought, an American way out here.

 We got to talking and this DR650 guy was headed to Brazil. I knew with my balding tyres and the watery route I wanted to take back that I couldn't make that route happen, but he seemed set up well for the adventure. As we exchanged some quick information about the roads I discovered he wasn't American at all. In fact, the man I came to know as Steve's Travels was from Edmonton Alberta, 2-hours north of where my adventure had begun a couple of years earlier. We had a brief chat, wished each other luck, and parted ways.

Two hours into my dusty ride and the heavens opened up letting the rains pour down on KLaiR and I. It was a mess. The road instantly went from red dust to slick red peanut butter. After the Colombia clutch disaster in the desert mud, I decided to get KLaiR off the road and set up my tent to wait out the storm. The road became so bad so fast, we came to a sticky stop. The 50/50 tyres had no traction and slid around like we were riding across a fire on melting rubber. Then, she fell right into the red muck. The handlebar was stuck in about 3" of red clay and the wide Pelican case stuck to the ground like glue. I tried everything to get her up. I pulled and lifted, and pushed, but nothing, I just couldn't budge KLaiR from the clay.

Finally, after a rainy and sweaty 30-minutes, I was able to drag her by pulling on one tyre at a time over to a small dip in the road that would provide a gap between the Pelican case and the ground, a bit of an air pocket. Soaked and covered in the sticky clay I heaved and pulled and finally got her back up on two wheels. I just needed to get her off the road. Soon the rains began to settle and the sweltering sun was back, but it was too late, the road was too much of a mess for my set up. I resolved to walk beside KLaiR and try to push and drive her to a nearby lane that led to someone's house. Three feet into this amazing plan and KLaiRs legs came out from under her and she dropped again.

As my head continued to bake in the heat like a hardboiled egg inside my black helmet there was nothing I could do. No matter what I tried I just couldn't lift KLaiR from the mud this time. Twisted across the road, she lay there like a beached whale in the sun, hoping for help to get her going again.

Forty-five minutes passed while I sat there hoping the roads would dry before I got heat stroke and ended up dying next to her. Then, in the distance, I spotted a large cattle truck grinding its way in low gear towards me. I knew I was blocking the road, but I could do nothing to move. Finally, the truck came within about twenty feet of me and stopped. A man with no shirt on and no shoes on got out, stood on the step of his large cattle liner looking down at me, and yelled, asking what the problem was? I explained I was stuck and couldn't move. I could physically see disappointment come over his face and wash down over his slouching shoulders, he knew what was going to happen next. He climbed back in his cab.

The man proceeded to put on his clean shoes, roll up his pants, put on a shirt, and come to my assistance. Like a monkey wading through water to get to the food on the other side, he reluctantly made his way towards me through the sticky muck.

I asked him how he was and where he was going? *"Fine, that way"* was his response. He was less than impressed to be hauling a stuck gringo on a large moto from the mud. With each of us on one side we heaved KLaiR up off the ground and I walked her to the edge of the road where the ground was drier. I thanked the man profusely as he waded his way back through the red mud to the truck and slowly rumbled on by.

How great I thought, we were back on two wheels and the roads were starting to dry. I sipped some hot water from my water bottle, ate a cookie from my cookie stash and decided to press on to the next village before the rains came again. That thought passed with a blink of an eye and suddenly the clouds rolled in and the skies opened up again. Fuck! It was pouring again. About two hundred feet ahead was another side road with some bushes. I thought if I could just get to that spot I could put the tent under the bushes and set up a camp for shelter.

KLaiR and I slowly followed the edge of the road until we made it to the bushes. Finally, we were off the main route and would be out of the way of any potential traffic. As I investigated the bushes I realized they were swimming in water and I wasn't putting my tent there. I was feeling like a kitten who'd lost his mother in a storm and didn't know what to do. It was pouring and I had zero shelter. I could put my rubber rain suit on but I was more likely to broil in the humid heat and I was already wet and muddy.

Right across the road was a little farm but it had a gate blocking the entrance and looked like no one was home. And so, I just stood there next to KLaiR in the pouring rain and took it all in. Eventually, the rains would again pass and I heard the sound of motorbikes from the farm across the road. Two men rode up to the gate and went to open it and ride out on their little 125cc bikes that could navigate the mud easier. I yelled to them and walked across the road to ask if I might spend the night at their farm?

Both of the men were extremely friendly and said they were just taking off but I was more than welcome to spend the night in the yard under a wooden roof with no sides that looked like it was used to keep animal feed dry. How nice, I went from stranded in the rain to a night's accommodation under a wooden roof at the neighbors. I got on KLaiR and rode her across to the farm. Once I was inside the yard and my new friends were closing the gate, the one man looked at me and said in Spanish; *"Actually this isn't my place, it's my brother-in-law's and he'll be home later. Not to worry though, just tell him I let you in and he'll be happy you're here."*

Fuck, I was on a roller coaster of emotions. I went from worried about being stranded to excited about having a place to stay to being concerned if I was allowed to be on this property at all. Was this really the owner's brother-in-law? Maybe they were robbing the place and I was now their scapegoat, blame the rich American! With no time to consider alternatives the two men wished me good luck and slid off down the road on their nimble bikes.

So here I was. Miles from nowhere, no one knew where I was, I had no phone service, I was literally stuck, and now I was on someone's property I'd never met who didn't know I was here and I was to set up camp hoping to explain my situation in Spanish, if they spoke Spanish. Nothing about this scenario felt relaxing.

An hour passed and I still hadn't set up my tent or seen anyone come down the road. It was getting close to sunset and I finally gave in and started to set up the tent. As I threw the tarp over the top I suddenly saw what looked like a herd of Saavedreño Creole cattle, known to this part of Bolivia, making their way down the road. First five or six, then ten, then twenty, then more of these dirty white beasts came grunting down the road.

Making up the rear I spotted two massive bulls tethered together by their yokes and tied to the long wooden pole that divided them. They were pulling a wooden cart with a man at the reins, a lady next to him on the wooden seat, and two small children perched between them excitedly trying to get a look at me. It was like some low-budget wild west movie born from the backroads of Bolivia. This view coming down the road felt unreal, I couldn't blink. The lush green jungle grass was making up the edge of the road against the red clay ground. In the back was the fiery orange sun setting on the blue sky and coming towards me the herd of white cattle pushed from behind by this larger than life team of bulls pulling a family in a wooden cart. The scene was wildly surreal.

I wanted a photo of this scene so badly but I knew they were looking at me suspiciously and if anyone was the spectacle here it was me and not them. I resolved to keep my camera in my pocket.

The mum ran ahead of the group and past the cattle, opening the gates to the land, before running ahead and blocking the road, driving the cattle into the pasture followed by the two bulls pulling the rest of the family. I ran over to quickly explain my presence there and about the brother-in-law who let me in and asked if they needed any help. The man was too busy dealing with his cattle to chat and pointed to a couple of cattle that had walked by the gate and told me to get ahead of them. The son who looked 7 or 8 years old took the reins of the bulls who easily weighed more than a car.

With me running ahead to hopefully stop these fleeting beasts who could easily run me over like a speed bump, the Bolivian cowboy pulled out a long whip he'd grabbed from the cart and let it loose. It cracked like thunder and the cattle stopped. It was incredible, they looked like trained elephants. With the cows stopped, I began to walk towards them as they reluctantly turned around. The man then made his way past the cattle and beside me cracking his whip of thunder. The wife came out from her position at the gate to block the road they'd come from and the cattle turned into the pasture with the others. The man then noted there was still one more stray cow and grabbed a horse from the pasture. He wrapped a rope around its neck, threw a leg over the back, and set off down the road bareback with his whip. Where in the fuck was I and what had just happened?

I tried to make small talk with the lady about why I was there. She just smiled, didn't say a word, and kept an eye on the team of bulls her son was wrangling. A short time later as the skies were turning to a stormy black again, the man and his whip of thunder came cracking down the road with the stray cow in front of him. I ran to my position blocking the road as we guided the last one home.

The Bolivian cowboy came to let the boy free of his duties with the bulls and I followed him around asking about everything I could to keep the conversation going. He released the bulls from the cart but left them tethered by the yolk. He said they were brothers and would spend their lives together working as a team. At this stage of life, they were left together 24-hours a day to get used to eating, sleeping, and working as a team.

He asked where I was from? To make things easier I explained I was from Brazil and had ridden my motorcycle from there. I knew trying to explain Canada and all the countries in between was going to be no simple task. He seemed impressed with my journey. The conversation ended and the family made their way home, some 200-feet from me. As they walked away he said goodnight and that was that. Not your Holiday Inn greeting with complimentary mints and front desk ass-kissing, but more of your wild west cattle rustler welcome. I had a place to stay under the roof and felt like I'd pitched in a little at the ranch.

The night was a bit noisy, I felt like small birds kept landing on my tent and walking around before taking off again. When I awoke in the morning I realized there was mouse shit scattered all over the top of the tent. There had been mice walking around above me all night. Luckily I slept with my boots inside! In the morning the boy came by to ask a thousand questions and explain that the dog in the yard was his pet and the pig was his dinner. He was without question a farm kid. I briefly saw the mother and thanked her, but never saw the man again.

* * *

The route to adventure always seemed to be on whatever road I was on, and I was more than happy to be on it. With dry 34oC days, the roads were back to dust again the following day as KLaiR, Stanley, and I continued on, spending the day dodging potholes left behind from those who'd driven in the mud.

We made it near the town of San Borja, it was a Sunday and I was absolutely melting in the heat. A black helmet felt like the look I was going for when I left, but a white one or wrapping this one in tinfoil might have been the better choice. I was sure my brain was cooking in the intense humidity and my damp feet inside my leather boots were swelling like a corpse left in the summer sun. It was nearly unbearable.

I crossed a bridge and made a quick u-turn that took me down under it to the river below. I parked KLaiR in the shade and like my clothes were on fire I began to peel off everything I was wearing, right down to my underwear leaving a heap of sweaty clothes draped over the seat. I ran down to the river and dove in. It was sheer bliss! As the boiled egg that was my brain began to cool, I popped out of the water only to take notice of the thirty or so other families and couples that were enjoying a day at the river. Again, I got that all eyes on me alien look and simply smiled while enjoying the water in nothing more than my underwear. I decided this was as far as I wanted to ride today and was going to set up my tent when the sun went down later and the people thinned out.

Not long after my spa day started a raft made from lashed together logs and people in make-shift shelters came floating down the river. One can never assume too much, however, they appeared to be indigenous people whom I was assuming came from deep inside this Amazon region. I'd watched enough National Geographic to get a sense of who might be of indigenous background living in civilization and who likely still lived in the jungles of the world. I could not stop looking at them as my curiosity rose. I sensed the feeling was mutual. Everyone else on the shoreline seemed pretty keen on watching them too and I came to the conclusion that these 40-foot long make-shift rafts were not an everyday sight around here.

The two rafts came to shore and started to unload the kids on board then unload bunches of plantains and the makeshift shelters lashed to the rafts. My curiosity was getting the better of me, I wanted to ask them so many questions. My years of watching Nat. Geo. had finally found me. I wasn't sure that they spoke Spanish or if they wanted to talk to me. Finally, after about half an hour the group began to unlash the wood they were hauling and bring it to shore. I decided to help them in the hopes of learning a bit about who they were.

I asked in Spanish if they wanted help and one lady explained to the men my request. They didn't seem overly interested and simply nodded. I jumped in the river and began lifting these incredibly heavy hardwood logs onto the shore. In all, there were around 20-people in the group, from around 2-years-old up to somewhere in their late forties. I began to pepper each person I got close to with little questions in Spanish. I asked what the wood was for? How far they floated from? If they were all family? Or any mundane question I could think of. This casual interrogation yielded the interest of one boy about nine years old who knew Spanish and could not stop looking at me or the bike. Finally, I might be making a friend here.

I then asked the lady who translated for the group what language they spoke, as she was the only one replying to me other than the boy. She explained the group spoke an indigenous language that started with an "A" sound I'd never heard of and some also spoke Spanish. Only getting responses from the lady and the boy I was feeling very awkward about the whole situation, but my curiosity continued.

By this time some thirty or so people had gathered at the top of the bridge to watch what we were up to. I'm not entirely sure if they were watching the spectacle of these people who arrived on rafts or of the pale white biker lifting wood for them. It was pretty funny to see the growing crowd staring down at us like some circus act.

Forty-five minutes passed and another raft of lashed together logs from the jungle came floating downstream just like this group had. As they came to shore, this group just sat to watch me and the group work. I was getting a bit miffed that no one wanted to be my friend aside from the kid. I began to get the impression they were suspicious of my motives to help and I'm sure they had every right to be. Here I was a random pale-white guy on a strange bike from a strange land, offering to lift logs for free while asking all kinds of questions about them. I'm sure if they showed up out of nowhere at my family BBQ and started chopping wood for the fire and asking why we were all here, it might be seen as a little odd too.

I now felt obligated to show that I was only there to help and wanted nothing in return. I felt like I was the first "westerner" interaction that the super-nice nine-year-old had ever had, and despite some previous possible mishaps his elders might have had with someone like me, I really wanted that kid to feel like outsiders could be trusted. Who knows, maybe I invented a huge dialogue in my head about some fantasy encounter with jungle people and it was just some prison camp on day leave, I'll never know for sure.

As time ticked on I was starting to get even more pissed as more of the family was now taking a break to watch me work and would not talk to me in any language. I decided to call this social experiment quits.

Once I was finished the kid came to talk to me again near the bike. I explained to him that I was from far, far away. I told him that when he is older he should travel around his country and maybe to other countries to meet people that were different from him as there were nice people everywhere in the world. I thanked him for asking me some questions about myself and for him to enjoy his day with his family.

The group ended up setting up camp on the beach where I had wanted to, so I resolved to move back about 500-feet off the shore and towards the bush. Before I left, a few of them thanked me for my help in Spanish. As I set up my camp in the distance I could see them keeping an eye on me as they worked long into the night. I'm not sure what they were feeling about me, but for some reason, I could not help but to shake the idea that I wanted to leave the best impression possible as a foreigner.

My plan to make new friends from the jungle may have backfired or perhaps my motivation for helping wasn't fully sincere. It made for an interesting experience either way and likely gave a wide number of people something to talk about. If you're going to take the route less traveled, you are eventually going to meet the people less traveled across.

Mental Shifts
You Never Forget The First $7 You Made Online

"Cynics don't want results; they want an excuse to not take action."
- Ramit Sethi

After falling flat on my face and needing to return to Canada to make some money in the hopes of reaching Ushuaia without going broke, I decided I was going to cut the Canadian umbilical cord for good. I made a deal with myself that I would find a means to fund my travels through South America and ship our traveling trio to Africa and continue across the world without ever needing to abandon the road again.

Now, anyone I met who was on the road for more than a year suddenly found themselves in my cross-hairs of economic support questioning. *"How are you doing this?", "Where does your money come from?", "What special skill do you have that I can learn?"*. Social encounters with other travelers had now become an interrogation about funds, skills, and lifestyle. Everyone became a target.

There was the German guy who'd been motorcycling around the world for 5+ years and he worked part time for a company in Germany doing tech work. There was the Danish guy who'd been driving around the world for 10+ years and he worked part time as an accountant for a European company. These were dead ends, as I had zero tech skills and as you might have noticed by how many times I ran out of money, math wasn't exactly my strong point.

I then started to ask around on online forums and question more and more people about what others did to make an income while traveling. The more I dug, the more I found. I discovered a guy who made YouTube cartoons and had millions of subscribers, the advertisements paid for his travels. There was one couple who owned racehorses, they made profits breeding. There was another guy that owned a small U.S.-based I.T. company who hired workers from his home country of Bosnia and made his cash on the discount labor. Tech, I.T., horses, YouTube (I have 11 subscribers), these all sounded like impossible accomplishments and I had exactly zero of these skills. I felt like the more I looked the less I knew.

Then one day on a travel forum I saw someone post that they worked as a content writer and their employer had lots of work if anyone was looking. This sparked my attention.

I'd written a couple of articles for a widely popular motorcycle magazine that had been proofread and heavily edited by friends before submission and had been accepted for publication. Armed with this hint of false confidence I asked for their employers' contact information.

I knew that people enjoyed my stories, however, I was also very clear that my grammar and spelling were horrendous (maybe you still feel that way!). Either way, I applied for the job and submitted my two previously accepted stories by major publications as relevant experience hoping this might sway some attention. I knew that with a little help on the editing side of things I could probably figure it out. The company liked my article and said they would pay me $7USD for every 800-word article I wrote.

Here I was in Bolivia where things were extremely inexpensive, $7/day was my average daily budget. I figured if I could write one article per day this would stretch my budget to last into the more expensive countries south of here. I was mentally torn. Getting paid $7 for something that would likely take me several hours to complete, compared to what I might get paid to do even the most trivial job in Canada for a few hours felt like I was working for slave wages. On the other hand, I would be getting paid for a job that there was no chance anyone would hire me for in Canada without a long list of credentials and some work experience. I had to remind myself that the real goal here was to generate some type of online income to fund my travel goals.

I decided that the goal of funding my travels was more important than what I might be able to earn if I was elsewhere in the world not traveling. I wrote and submitted two articles. The company came back to me with a few grammar tips and paid me $14. I was officially making money online!

Years earlier I'd watched an interview with the famous musician Dave Grohl. He noted that making music was such a bizarre experience where you, the writer, share some of your most personal and intimate stories with complete strangers. Then you wait for them to judge it, then give you their feedback about your experience. I felt the same about writing as it was an incredibly uncomfortable experience. I needed someone externally to judge my stories and somehow if they liked them, I then felt confident they were good. I'd suddenly become a teenage girl who'd worn her favorite t-shirt to a party but knew if anyone said they didn't like it, I'd immediately change shirts to appease the crowd.

Almost instantly the stars of the universe started to line up. I was writing $7 articles about mattresses and wedding venues for British companies from on top of my rear Pelican case beside campfires in rural Bolivia. Then I was editing other people's shit articles and making them my own for $5. Within a couple of months, I suddenly found myself writing for an American motorcycle website about things I actually liked and was now being paid $85USD for 1500 word articles. A short time later I landed a gig writing for a large motorcycle rental and travel company out of Vietnam that was owned by a British guy. Now I was making $100USD for 1000-2500 word articles. All I had to do was start asking people how they made a living online and just like that, the solution to my problem started rolling in.

I now had more work than time to do it and much more money coming in than I was used to spending. I hadn't actually spent one dollar of the funds I'd earned in Canada the summer before. Good thing, as I invested all of that in weed and oil stocks and promptly lost it all!

(The Three Amigos. *Somewhere in Bolivia)

Paraguay
Umm, Sort Of...

"← I'm With Stupid"
- Seen next to an arrow on a novelty t-shirt.

A new problem was festering inside my helmet. Even though I had eliminated my need to return to Canada to make money, I had to go back to attend a wedding I was meant to be sitting at the head table for. This was likely the closest I'd ever come to being married, so I thought I best attend. The catch was, I needed to store my motorcycle somewhere in Brazil or Chile for a few months while I was away, a complicated task that would again require bending the rules a little.

In Chile, you're only allowed 90-days to temporarily import the motorcycle and they make a note of your vehicle entry alongside your personal entry into the country in their computer system. When you leave the country so does the bike, otherwise, you're not going anywhere. Brazil is slightly different. In Brazil when you enter the country they give you and the motorbike the same 90-days, however, your 90-days is noted on your passport and logged into one computer system. The motorcycle is kept separate and logged into a completely different computing system. These separate logging systems are where we find our storage loophole.

Technically you could leave the country without the bike and it would go unnoticed. However, if you were away more than 90-days then you would return to expired papers for the bike and face some hefty fines trying to cross a border. I'd planned to spend the summer in Canada and knew I'd be over the 90-day limit. How was I going to leave without risking the loss of KLaiR or having to pay out the ass to the Brazilian government to get her back? Fuck, it was like leaving Colombia all over again.

My previous roommate in Canada was Brazilian and his uncle had a friend that lived in Brazil, but Brazil was a massive country and I needed to store KLaiR as close as I could to the border with Paraguay or Bolivia. Again, like some cosmic lining up of all the stars in the world, a miracle of miracles found me. The friend did not live 2500-kilometers south in Rio, he did not live 4000-kilometers away in Fortaleza on the coast, he did not even live anywhere near the center of the country in Brasilia. He lived in fucking Campo Grande, the closest city to the border of Paraguay! If I could somehow smuggle KLaiR into Brazil through Paraguay I could leave her there while I was away.

I began to research endlessly about where I might be able to cross the border into Brazil undetected and if anyone had tried to do something similar. As it turned out, I wasn't the first person who wanted to slide unnoticed into Brazil and store a motorbike. Others had gotten just across the border and left bikes at campgrounds and shops of locals, but I needed to get a few hundred kilometers into the country, not just across the border.

Brazil is such a massive country with limited federal funding and I learned of a few roads that crossed into Brazil that would be unmanned. I just needed to get into the country and continue undetected until I found a border post where the vehicle and personal border crossing formalities were in separate buildings. Eventually, I devised a route that crossed at Ponta Pora, a city split between the two countries where I would have my best chance of success. I was still in Bolivia, and with only one option available to me, I bought a plane ticket out of Brazil that departed in two weeks. I decided I'd cross Paraguay then into Brazil to get papers for me, but not for KLaiR. Then I would sneak through the country trying to avoid endless police checkpoints where I could then park her at the friends' place in Campo Grande. When I returned several months later I'd reverse the smuggling back to the border then come back into Brazil getting all of my paperwork done legally. It sounded like a flawless plan in my head. Just two international borders, twenty or so police checkpoints, and a couple of thousand kilometers and I'd be home free.

Before departing Bolivia I met up with Chris and again he did a tune up on KLaiR then put me in touch with some friends he had in Paraguay where I could spend a couple of nights during my week-long Paraguay exploration. The following night I stayed at the closest town to the border of Paraguay to get an early start on things the next day. Alone in my hotel room that night, I was triple checking my route on Google Maps with snail-slow wifi while sitting in my underwear sweating in the heat with no fan. I heard some commotion outside the door. Suddenly there was a loud bang on my door. *"La policía, abre la puerta"*, *The police, open the door.*

Yeah right I thought, the police? I trusted no one and wasn't totally convinced it was really the police. I quickly slid my computer, phone, and wallet under the blanket and slid back the curtains. Sure as shit outside my door was the police, about four of them all banging on doors. While still in my underwear, I opened the door and the man in uniform asked to see my passport and asked if that was my motorcycle outside the door. I replied by asking why he needed to see my papers? He was firm and a bit surprised I was the one questioning him. He said this was a popular smuggling route for drugs & people and needed to check the papers of everyone to make sure they were legally in the country.

My passport and bike documents were on the bike so I told the guy I needed to get dressed and grab the papers. He didn't trust me much either, and the door remained open while I readied myself. From inside the Pelican cases, I got him my passport and the papers for KLaiR then he relaxed and walked me back to the room. He asked what I was doing and where I was going? I told him a little about my trip. He then explained that I should never leave any of my documents out of my sight. He said this area was very dangerous and that I should be very careful. He then came in close and lowered his voice. He told me to never accept food or drink from anyone I met as it might be poisoned and I would be robbed. This was the exact opposite of what I'd been doing, as I was routinely accepting little gifts of drinks or lunch from all kinds of people. I thanked him for the much too late information as he walked away. As I looked around I saw various men being questioned and it wasn't looking nearly as good for them as it did for me. I closed my door as the officer continued on to the next room. *"La policía, abre la puerta"*...

Fuck, now I wasn't feeling so enthused about my plan to smuggle KLaiR into Brazil. If this scenario had been in Brazil it would have ended much differently. I would have been spending the night with the police as opposed to alone with shit wifi in my underwear. What was I thinking, was this plan going to work?

The next morning I woke early, had the complimentary breakfast of tea and stale bread, then headed down the road to Paraguay. Like most every other country, the less popular routes across the border are rarely maintained. This route went on for hours with loose gravel that caused KLaiR to pull dramatically to each side as I tried to keep her up on two wheels. After several hours we eventually arrived at what again felt like nowhere-ville, where I was delightfully greeted by two men with machine guns who asked about my journey. They wanted to search my gear for drugs and guns and after a 10-second search of opening one box to look at what was on top, they shook my hand and welcomed me to Paraguay. So far so good.

Mr. Machine gun explained that the guy who does the paperwork was on lunch and should be back in about an hour but I could ride down to a series of trailers where he was taking his break to get him. I decided to check out of Bolivia first and see how long that took before interrupting anyone's lunch break. I walked into the small building and explained to a lady there that I needed to stamp out of Bolivia and into Paraguay. She said no problem, she could stamp me out but the other guy on his lunch break would need to stamp me in. I gave her my paperwork and she flipped through the pages of my passport, finally, she reached the end and asked where my visa was?

I said there was no visa. For Bolivia, I didn't need a special visa as I was Canadian. She said no, my visa for Paraguay? This time I explained that Canadians didn't require visas for anywhere in South America aside from Brazil and I already had that visa. Naturally, I knew more than she did about customs and visas. She said ok, but was pretty sure I needed a visa, and just to be sure, she wasn't going to stamp me out until the other guy came back to stamp me in. I retreated back outside to talk to the friendly machine gun guys.

Now waiting with them was a Brazilian who it turns out had been here at the border for a couple of days trying to cross into Bolivia. He looked skinny and worn from life on the road. He said he'd been hitchhiking across Brazil and planned to hitchhike as far as he could north but was currently stuck here as he didn't have the proper papers to cross into Bolivia. It was nice to see someone who had even worse planning than I did.

Behind him was a trucker who had just arrived looking to cross into Bolivia as well. With the small line growing, Mr. machine gun called the paperwork guy and requested he cut his lunch short. Moments later an official government truck arrived and the man stepped out into the hot sun followed by a waft of cool air conditioning that hovered around him like a little cloud. He said hello, asked who was first and I followed him into the office.

The stamp guy looked over my passport and the first thing he asked was where my visa for Paraguay was? A bit less confident this time, I explained I was Canadian and didn't require a visa. He explained I was Canadian and did require a visa, but that he'd check his computer to be sure.

Paraguay stamp guy turned his screen towards me, clicked some boxes that said Canada etc, and a little window popped up saying visa required. I thought this was a cute little scam they had running to get money from tourists, as this screen looked pretty basic, and so did the little box he checked.

Assured I was being set up, I said ok, how much is the visa? Stamp guy replied with a bunch of questions to which I answered *YES*, though I actually had no idea what he said. The other language in Paraguay was Guarani and had influenced the country's more popular Spanish language to a point where I found it impossible to decipher the words. In situations like this where I don't know what is being said, *YES*, was my default word. Apparently yes wasn't the fitting response for his statement and he looked confused and repeated himself. After a second attempt, he asked if I understood. This time I said no. Stamp guy then pulled out some books showing the visa and explaining the price of $130USD. I was now sure he was full of shit as this was a crazy price to pay for a South American visa. Then he said I needed to ride back to Santa Cruz 3-days from here in Bolivia and apply for the visa there. Then, in a couple of weeks, I'd likely have the visa and could return. I felt the lump in my throat sink into my stomach and knew this wasn't a scam.

Switching tactics I then asked how much it would be to get an on the spot visa. He said it was impossible, there was no such visa. I needed to be illegally in Brazil in less than two weeks and on a plane into Canada. There were exactly zero other options. I needed into Paraguay and I needed in right now. To summarize, I was fucked.

Then stamp guy told me to please leave the office as he waved the trucker behind me ahead.

I refused to leave and persisted that I would require a visa on the spot and to please explain the price. The trucker then pushed ahead of me and gave his papers to the stamp guy. I kept talking and refused to move. Stamp guy said just a moment and he'd call his boss in the capital of Asunción to see if there was anything he could do.

A few moments later he was off the phone and explained that there was nothing that could be done, could I please leave his office. Now the trucker began to position himself in front of me. My protest continued and I refused to move from my seat. The trucker went on requesting his stamps and I continued to explain I needed this visa and I would need it right now. Please tell me the price.

While stamp guy fumbled around in his desk I pulled out my phone, luckily I had some service from my Bolivian phone plan and Googled the visa conundrum. Shit, they were telling the truth. I did need a visa, but the cost was closer to $100USD. Either way, I didn't have one.

I wasn't leaving. I had no other plan or options. Instead, I sat in the seat at his desk and didn't move. I told him I needed to get into the country. He told me to leave. I could see his patience fading quickly. He again told me to leave, but I just sat there like a four-year-old who doesn't want to leave grandma's house without a cookie. He waved the truck driver closer. The truck driver put his documents on the table. Now it was really awkward as I was sitting in this small office between stamp guy's face and truck driver guy's crotch, refusing to move. They awkwardly worked around me for the next ten minutes.

Once they were done I started in again with needing to be let into the country today. The confusing Spanish communication only made things worse and we were getting nowhere. Hitchhiker guy thought I might be making some headway into an immediate border crossing and jumped into our awkward circle to make his protest. Hitchhiker only knew Portuguese and appeared to have some visa problems too. Our awkward circle of faces, crotches, Spanish, English, Portuguese, and Guarani was a minefield of miscommunication. After talking in circles for a few minutes, it seemed like hitchhiker guy wasn't getting out of the country and I wasn't getting in. Hitchhiker guy finally gave up on our explosive circle of miscommunication and went outside for a cigarette.

At this point about an hour had passed since I first sat down in what was now my protest chair. With the office empty, stamp guy then asked me something about money? I did have a stash of around $200 American dollars for emergency situations, about $50 in Paraguay cash, and around $5 in Bolivia cash. I still didn't feel this was quite at an emergency level to use the USD and I couldn't part with the Paraguay money as I needed it to buy fuel. Instead, I told stamp guy I only had Bolivian currency. I didn't disclose how much.

He said he'd make some more calls. He pulled out a little beat up black book with folded papers and scribbled numbers, searched for a number, then called someone. I didn't know what he was saying, but I could understand it was basically an overview of my situation. He got off the phone and explained there would be no helping me. I knew this was the end of the line for my Paraguay plans and getting KLaiR into Brazil to store her while I returned to Canada. Shit, why didn't I ever have a Plan B!

Before departing Canada I had made a pact with myself not to pay any bribes on this trip no matter the situation. Things had changed a bit here and I wasn't being asked for a bribe at all, in this scenario I was suggesting I'd pay one. Just then the hitchhiker came back with some new evidence as to why he should be allowed to cross and the two men worked around me while I maintained my position in the protest chair.

My shit explanations in Spanish, hitchhiker guy's Portuguese protests, stamp guy's short lunch, and my ongoing stronghold in the chair suddenly came to a tipping point. Stamp guy lost patience with both of us and stood up to very firmly tell us to please leave his office. I was crushed. I could feel my eyes well up as I envisioned being out of options and not making it into Brazil. I'd miss my flight, miss the wedding, and let everyone down with my stupid plan to try and illegally smuggle KLaiR into Brazil. I gathered my things from his desk and sulked my way outside with the weight of the world's disappointment pushing down on me.

The machine gun duo came over to wish me well and noticed I was distraught. I explained I would not be allowed in and would need to return to Bolivia. They consoled me with a hand on the shoulder like old friends and wished me well. I put my helmet back on, wiped my snotty nose and started KLaiR. What the fuck was I going to do now?

Just then stamp guy came running out of the office talking on his cell phone yelling at me. He looked like a disheveled Wall Street trader who'd just been given some insider news and was yelling at everyone to sell their position. He told me to come back inside. He'd gotten a call back from his boss who said they would issue me a 48-hour transit visa to cross the country. The man had reluctantly done me a huge favor. I ran back inside. Organizing the paperwork from his computer he explained how lucky I was and that this visa would usually be around $180USD. For such a huge favor I should probably tip him for his efforts. I noticed that the visa price went up every time he talked about it. No problem I thought, I had the Bolivian Bolivianos. I pulled it out and gave it to him. He smiled and put the money in his desk.

I could see his thoughts start to connect and he stopped, opened the drawer, pulled out the 50-Bolivianos, and threw them back at me. He said that was like $5 and this visa was closer to $190, and that I should give him more. I asked if he wanted the 50-Bolivianos, he said no. I said ok, thanked him, put the 50 B's back in my pocket, and walked out the door with my visa.

19-hours of riding over the next two days and I was face to face with my next negotiation, smuggling KLaiR into Brazil.

Brazil
Motorcycle Smuggling Take 3

"If At First You Don't Succeed, Redefine Success."
- Notebook Cover

I never had a reputation for following the rules. For the most part, I hate rules. If anything, I get more pleasure out of breaking the rules than following them. The times in life I was an employer I made it very clear that we had rules and I'd put them in a little binder for everyone to read, then added a verbal clause that I would not be enforcing the rules. I just couldn't do it; the internal conflict was too much. If you worked for me, you were basically your own boss.

I was now faced with more rules, which were outlined by the government of Brazil, a government not exactly known for following their own rules either. I was to enter their country and bypass the rule that says, let us know your motorcycle is coming with you into the country so we don't take it away from you when we catch your sorry smuggling ass. This rule wasn't going to work for me right now, but I would be happy to follow the rule at some point in the future.

I'd beaten the 48-hour deadline to get out of Paraguay and now I needed to get into Brazil undetected and ride a further 300+ kilometers into Brazil where I would be able to stash KLaiR with my new Brazilian friend while I returned to Canada to attend the wedding. I knew that if I couldn't get into Brazil I was going to be extremely fucked, as Paraguay wasn't going to let me back in.

To prepare, I'd packed enough snacks to last me a couple of days in the event something went wrong with my route, and filled up with enough fuel to make the full journey to Campo Grande, further in Brazil. When I arrived at the border city I was amazed to find that there was no official border post at all. It was a city spread across Paraguay and Brazil. Instead of trying to sneak across, I would need to go looking for the border officials. Lucky for me, the office for a personal passport stamp was located in one part of the city and the place for the bike documentation was in another part of the city. I also know this was a bit of false encouragement as there were always police stops checking documents just outside of every border city.

I found the airport where they would stamp my passport and promptly headed to the closest back road I could find. I'd researched various roads and felt like I could get most of the way to my destination on countryside roads and should be able to avoid the police checkpoints on the main roads. If I was wrong, I knew that making a u-turn at a police checkpoint would immediately trigger suspicion and again, I'd be fucked.

Once I started riding through the border city, Brazil looked nothing like any of the other countries I'd been through since North America. People drove new cars and big pickup trucks. The roads were perfectly paved and I was surrounded by large cornfields and cattle farms. I went from being the largest motorcycle that could easily pass anyone on the road, to the slowest moving machine that was in the way of everyone racing down the highway. Everything was larger than life again. It felt like I was riding through the southern United States in sweltering temperatures.

As soon as I spotted a red clay countryside road, I turned and took it. It was a relief to be away from the fast moving traffic and concern of police checks. The red clay roads were smooth and dusty, but I knew that being on the cusp of the rainy season, if the rains began I would be stuck in my tracks just like I was back in Bolivia not so long ago. I started to ride as fast as I could, only stopping to check when the next turn was on this mystery corn maze I was trying to navigate. The GPS continually re-routed me looking for better and faster roads and I needed to continually stop at every possible turn making sure we never landed on any of these faster roads.

I'm not sure if it was the heat or my luck, but the GPS suddenly started to shut off as I rode, then turned on again, before shutting off again. It was just like the night I landed in Mexico City and all of my navigation tools were suddenly against me. I had no local phone reception and couldn't get Google Maps to load properly to navigate. To add to this streak of great luck, I'd forgotten to download Brazil on my MAPS.me application so I could navigate offline. I was relying completely on the cratering GPS. With the GPS screen now blank, I was trying to use the dot marking Campo Grande on a blank Google Map on my phone to navigate what direction to go. With no place to mount the phone on the bike, I was also riding with one hand on the phone and the other on the throttle. This system worked until I needed to shift gears or stop.

In this part of the planet, the sun rises and sets early and it was now late afternoon. I knew I wouldn't make it all the way in one day and I'd need to find a place to stay for the night so I could continue in the morning. I located a fuel station on another app just off the highway that appeared to be in the middle of nowhere. If I could get there, this seemed like a good point to stop for the day. The catch was I needed to ride the highway for a few kilometers to reach it.

I found a road that would exit onto the highway at about the highway's midpoint, as opposed to just before or after a town, where police checkpoints generally are. Now it was officially black outside and trying to navigate with a bright cell phone light shining in my eyes then refocusing on the road in the blackness while riding with one hand, was an accident waiting to happen. I stopped and made some mental notes about where to turn on what road to get to where I needed to enter on the highway.

As you might imagine those mental notes quickly mixed with mental notes about how concerned I was to avoid the police checkpoints and I made a wrong turn that landed me on the main highway about 3-kilometers sooner than I had hoped. I tried to find an exit or turn around point, but there were no immediate roads off of this road and no way to cross over to the other side of the road, dammit! I hoped I'd find that fuel station soon and be able to camp for the night so I could put an end to this mental madness.

My luck ran out faster than my daylight had. As soon as traffic on the highway rounded the next turn the road suddenly lit up with flashing lights under a large canopy set up, right in the middle of the highway. Sure as shit, there was a permanent police checkpoint right here. The road widened to make an extra lane on either side, as traffic slowed the police were pulling over all of the transport trucks and vehicles with out of country plates along with random suspicious vehicles. In this case, I fell into both categories.

After chanting the magic words of serenity "FUCK-FUCK-FUCK!" inside my helmet, I quickly looked for a large transport truck with Brazil license plates. In Mexico, I learned that if I slid in behind large trucks at police stops the police couldn't see me. When we got close, I'd pass the truck on the opposite side of the police and could ride by undetected. I hoped like hell I could pull this off here.

I spotted a truck, but there was only one, and it had Paraguay plates. I knew this truck would be pulled over. It was my only chance to hide. For an agonizing kilometer of slowing traffic, I kept KLaiR just a couple of feet behind the big truck. The closer we got to the police, the more nervous I was and I could feel the traffic watching me wondering why I didn't pass this truck. Our traveling trio and the transport truck were both suddenly under the bright lights of the police checkpoint in the middle of the black night. It felt like a giant interrogation room. Three of the police had two vehicles pulled over and were checking their papers. Two of the other police were standing with machine guns hanging off their shoulders watching traffic to see whom they might pull over next. Then they spotted the front of the big truck I was following and I knew they recognized it was not from Brazil. They waved to the driver to pull over and I could feel the nervous sweat rolling down my face.

The truck shifted down a gear and I was looking for an option to pull beside him. The traffic to my right was nose to tail and I knew if I cut in front of someone it would instantly draw attention to me. I took a deep breath, focused as hard as I could on the idea that I was somehow invisible, and crept KLaiR within kissing distance of the back right tail light of the truck. The truck then veered into the checkpoint lane and I quickly shifted gears to slide into his open spot. Just as I pulled ahead I saw the one policeman out of the side of my visor. He elbowed the other policeman and pointed to my bike. Apparently, I wasn't invisible. I pulled back on KLaiR's throttle, looked up, thanked my lucky stars as we rode on to the fuel station where I camped for the night.

This all seemed fine and well for tonight, but I had a long way to go to get into the city where I was headed and knew I'd need to turn around and hopefully smuggle myself back out of the country in a few months.

The fuel station had wifi and I sorted out my navigation issues that night. In the morning I cut in and out of enough backroads that eventually took me in the back way to Campo Grande. The irony was the last turn before the city took me past a large prison. I felt like this was the universe's little reminder that it was cutting me a break here, but not to screw it up or I might end up behind the razor wire I was riding past.

Eventually, I found the business of Gilberto, my new friend, and was greeted with open arms like a long-lost relative he'd never met. I never told Gilberto the backstory about KLaiR, only that we made it into the country without issue. In friendly Brazilian fashion, he spent the next week touring me around his city and introducing me to local friends and other adventure bikers before storing KLaiR at his home while I returned to Canada.

Brazil
Would You Do It?

"There are three ways to ultimate success: The first way is to be kind. The second way is to be kind. The third way is to be kind."

- Mr. Rogers

The Canadian summer was fun, I held up my wedding duties by abusing the open-bar policy I had appointed myself, and was now back in Brazil. KLaiR and I had successfully snuck back to the border and were now legally in the country. It was here I decided that a dream I thought was never going to be a reality was suddenly possible.

I decided that since I was already in Brazil and the chances of ever having this opportunity again fell somewhere between slim and none, that our trio was going to make a slight 7000-kilometer detour up into the Amazon Rainforest to Manaus and back down towards Chile via another route. It was October and I needed to be in Santiago Chile to meet up with Angie for Christmas. 3-months to make the 7000-kilometer detour and a further 4000-kilometers down to Santiago. What could possibly go wrong in 11,000 kilometers and 3-countries?

* * *

It was dark and I was on road 364 from the town of Bonito making my way the 2500-kilometers up towards Porto Velho. On this particular night, I had planned to stay in a shitty hotel to shower and use the internet to do some work. When I arrived at the place I'd planned to stay, they didn't have safe parking for KLaiR, so I left. Instead, I opted for a busy truck stop just off the highway. A local had told me that Brazil decided to invest their money in roads for transport trucks to move goods instead of railroads for trains. This decision had a knock-on effect on how busy the roads were and how easily you could find a truck stop. On the main roads, you would come across hundreds of large trucks on what were often two-lane roadways. If you found yourself behind a slow-moving truck it was a frustrating position and often incredibly dangerous to try and pass. On the upside, there were always plenty of places to get fuel and places to spend the night at the massive truck stops, though it was never quiet or relaxing.

This particular stop was one of the largest truck stops I'd ever seen. It had fuel bays, showers, convenience stores, a few restaurants, a tyre shop, mechanic shops, and loads of dusty parking. The only place I could hide away from the parking lot to possibly pitch a tent was behind a little machine shop in some trees. It was pitch black and I snuck back in the woods with my bike hoping to pitch a tent with the help from KLaiRs headlight. It wasn't long before I was found lurking around trying to set up camp.

While I was working away, a guy in his late forties came out of the darkness wearing nothing more than a towel from what looks like a tool cleaning shed next to the old mechanic shop. With only the bike's light on so I can see enough to put up the tent, I'm now a deer in the headlights. All he could see of me was the tent and my outline.

If you've never heard people speaking Portuguese it's a very colorful language that sounds like a harmonic song being spoken. I could never tell when the Brazilians were speaking if they were happy, or upset, as the tone of the speech was so musical. The guy in front of me wearing the towel was talking a mile a minute and I didn't understand a word he was saying, I thought he might be telling me to leave. I decided to walk over and say, "No Portuguese" the only words I'm sure he could understand if I spoke them.

The man gets a closer look at me. He sees all of the shit tied to KLaiR and could see how sweaty and dirty I was. I'd been having baby wipe baths for a few days, but by the end of each day, my face was usually covered in dust that would stick to the sweat as it rolled off my forehead. The man then tried to explain quite dramatically about my poor choice of sleeping arrangements. I figure out that he wants me to know that it will probably rain and

I'll get very wet back here. He then walks me to the front of his shop and explains that I should set my tent here on the porch of his shop. The man then points to the various shops and explains where I can find fresh water. Then, he takes me over to the tool cleaning shed and shows me a shower inside. The structure is an old tin building rusting apart, full of old tools on one side and a rusty toilet and leaking shower behind a half tin wall on the other side. It seems that both people and tools are cleaned in this shed.

The man questions me with some slow, simple, Portuguese about my trip, where I started and where I'm going. I try to dramatically explain that I'm going to the Amazon. He tells me a bunch of things about the Amazon where I vaguely pick up that it's better to go in July and August when it's dry and to be careful.

I then leave to go and get the fresh water to help rehydrate myself. The days hover around 33oC and no matter how much I drink I'm beyond parched. I come back, gather my things, and proceed to move them to his front step. As I'm setting up, the man presents me with a piece of paper that looks like a receipt with a handwritten note on it. He points at the restaurant about 100-feet away and explains in great detail something to do with the note. I'm tired, confused, hungry, and can not for the life of me figure out what the note has to do with the restaurant or with me.

After several attempts at explaining the paper to me the man finally changes tactics and decides to walk me over to the lady at the entrance of the restaurant he was pointing at. The lady then takes me over and tries to explain to me again what the paper is all about. The paper has something to do with the buffet and the note has something to do with the guy, but I'm still as confused as when we started this game of clues.

By now, my pale appearance and green eyes along with the calamity of actors trying to explain to me what the paper meant has caught the attention of the fifty or so truckers. All of whom are sitting solo on this large patio eating dinner to the distraction of a large television on the wall. Now I am now the distraction. I could see that this man has no interest in being the center of attention here and if anything, did not want to be noticed by anyone, let alone everyone. Finally, the lady gets the attention of the waiter who takes my hand and walks me past 100-watching eyes to the buffet. The waiter then picks up a plate and shows me how to put food on it. He then walks me to a table and shows me that if I sit down he will bring me a drink and some meat from the large barbeque over by the wall. He then dramatically explains that when I'm done, there will be no cost and that this is what was written on the piece of paper the man gave me.

It finally clicked! This guy had pre-paid for dinner and a drink for me and wanted to do it discreetly. Instead, I have the whole place watching us while I'm being walked through a four-item buffet like I've never eaten out before then taken to my seat like a child. I feel honored and like a complete jackass at exactly the same moment.

Five minutes after sitting down I spot the mechanic shop guy sneaking by to check on me and make sure I'm ok before he disappears back into the darkness. The waiter then comes by and presents me with a huge piece of BBQ'd meat on a skewer. I devour the meat along with some various starches and beans from the 4-item buffet like a ravenous animal. Thirty minutes later I finish up, tip the waiter and head back to the guys' workshop where his car is now gone. I shower in his tool shed, fall asleep on his patio, and wake up about twenty times that night to the sound of truckers' air brakes.

By 5:40 am I hear the man back at his shop and I get up to greet him. In reality, I barely slept. He gives me some more Amazon tips, explains the drive a little, and tells me where to turn for this road and that road like I have any idea what he's really saying or have any hope of remembering it. I pack up my stuff so he can open his shop. He then takes me for a coffee, where he REFUSES to let me pay. I explain via my google translate app that he is extremely helpful and friendly. We take a selfie where he forgets to smile, and I'm back on the road.

As I'm driving down the road in the blistering heat that day I question myself and what I would do in his situation. What if I heard a rustling behind my shop in the darkness and I came out in my towel to see what was going on. Would my first reaction be to invite a random man into my world with whom I can not communicate? Let him in for a shower, direct him to fresh water, buy him dinner, let him spend the night at my place while he knows I am away, and buy him a coffee in the morning without exchanging a single clear word? I feel a bit guilty, I'm not sure the story would be the same...

(My tent, his doorstep)   (Friendly guy, but forgets to smile here)

Brazil

Amazon Rainforest. The Most Amazing & Disappointing Place On The Planet

Between August 2017 and July 2018 About 7,900 km2 (3,050 sq miles) of the Amazon rainforest was destroyed. One of the highest rates on record. It is suggested that at some point the forest will reach a tipping point, where it will no longer be able to produce enough rainfall to sustain itself
- Wikipedia

I pressed further North towards the Amazon region. The roads got worse, the drivers got more aggressive and the heat and humidity intensified. On the way, I detoured into the largest tropical wetland on the planet, the Pantanal. In the dry season, a one way dirt road takes you into the wetland and offers the possibility to see jaguars, capybara, snakes, piranha, howler monkeys, caiman, and endless other wildlife. Like Dora The Explorer I hung my camera from my neck as I rode in first gear looking for wildlife on a sort of Brazilian motorbike safari. Some of the highlights included a boa constrictor over 8-feet long crossing the road, a couple of jaguar cubs, and piranhas so thick in the river the water looked like a bubbling fish soup.

After several sweaty days in the mosquito-infested wetlands, I'm sure I smelled putrid enough to keep the rest of the wildlife away. On my final night here I returned to a little bush camp I'd stayed at a couple of nights earlier. Here I met a couple from France who had shipped into French Guiana with their overlanding truck and were at the start of their South American adventure. They looked at me, had a brief chat in French, then dug out a small pop-up tent and a compressed container that held 4-liters of water I could use to have a shower. Kids on Christmas morning didn't look as excited as I did when they presented me with the gift of a 4-liter shower!

As the journey continued I'd eventually come to the final town heading on my way North that had food and fuel before riding the infamous BR319 road into Manus, deep in Brazil's Amazon. From where I was in Humaita to Manus is roughly 700-kilometers of dirt roads that partially turn into a nearly impassible muddy river during the rainy season that was fast approaching.

If the rains began to pour I'd never get through to Manaus on the BR319 with my current setup. I'd consulted other adventurers who'd ridden this route. Some had done it in the dry season and it was a dusty piece of two-day cake. Some others I'd talked to attempted the road during the start or end of the rainy season and it was more than a week-long nightmare of truck-eating mud that required multiple vehicles working together to make it.

On a full tank, including the reserve fuel, KLaiR could make it close to 340-kilometers if we rode at a smooth steady pace. That would drop considerably if she got stuck or needed to work hard in lower gears. Getting mixed reviews on whether the road was good or bad, I was advised to bring double my fuel load, and double my food and water for a possible week-long journey. To help with the excursion I purchased aggressive off-road tyres in Paraguay during the return border run and had them put on KLaiR to deal with any unruly road conditions. I then scavenged around the town for empty 2-liter pop bottles to fill with fuel. Once I had enough bottles I loaded up KLaiR with 18-liters of spare fuel, 12-liters of water, and several days of food. Not exactly double my fuel load, but I was well over the weight limit for KLaiR's carrying capacity and was trying not to create a new problem while preventing another.

I took a photo of KLaiR's obscene amount of cargo next to a discouraging road sign that read "Manaus 685" (kilometers), and hit the road.

Truckers in the region have been hoping for years that the government will pave this route to make access through the Amazon easier. Indigenous groups are hoping otherwise as it will make it even easier to poach the limited resources of the Amazon, like rare animals and ancient trees. I personally felt that if the government paved the road they would be re-paving it yearly as the floods would wash away the work from the year before, which seemed to be mother nature's only chance at fighting back. As I turned onto this very first section of unmaintained road, the first vehicle I saw was an unmarked logging truck turning off a dirt track in front of me. He was carrying the mid-section of a giant rainforest tree that was spilling out over the end of his flat deck strapped on like a dead carcass headed to market. I could feel a piece of my heart break. I knew what probably took hundreds of years to create, had taken an afternoon to destroy.

The road was dry & dusty, and to my delight, I was making better time than I'd anticipated. Later in the first day, I rode past a small wooden house with two guys sitting under a tree. One guy enthusiastically waved at me, so I slowed down and turned around to meet them. He was a fellow biker who'd stopped for a coffee and to talk to a local farmer. Lucky for me he spoke English and we swapped adventure stories while he helped me to ask questions of the farmer. While I was stopped I went to fill the small water bottle on my handlebars from one of the spare jugs of water I was carrying. To my surprise, one of my 4-liter water jugs sprung a leak and was completely empty. Fuck, already down to one day of water and I just got started. I noticed the Brazilian guy had his pop bottles of spare fuel wrapped in cardboard to prevent this from happening. I decided to wrap my water in some of my clothes and to continually top off my fuel to help reduce my load.

The Brazilian biker and I decided to ride together. This lasted for a couple of hours until he finally stopped and said he was aiming for a small village up the road to camp at and I was too slow to ride with if he was going to make it before sundown! That night I'd camp alone in the jungle.

Eventually, I found a little pullout off the main road that was tucked back in the trees. I thought this was the safest option to keep me out of sight from anyone who might pass by in the night. As the sun was setting I pulled into the spot through a small path in the bush and proceeded to set up my tent.

Minutes later I heard a motorbike coming down the little path towards my camp. Shit! Not only could I not be seen from the road, but I was also being followed and no one would notice me while this guy came to rob me. A large indigenous-looking man who easily outweighed me by 50-pounds pulled through the trees and parked his bike in the bushes just on the other side of my camp. I could see a rifle hanging over his shoulder as he parked. Fuck, I was a little concerned. Not only could he kick my ass he also had a rifle!

Dealing with the situation head-on I decided to walk right over and greet him in shitty Spanish. I used this trick so people knew I couldn't speak Portuguese, but if they knew Spanish then they would at least try to communicate with me that way.

The guy was startled when he saw me and his eyes lit up with surprise. He smiled, shook my hand, and started asking me all kinds of bike and travel questions. Seems he wasn't looking to rob me at all. He was just headed out hunting at dusk and this is where he hid his bike from the road too. Neither of us knew exactly what the other was saying, but we had a nice little 15-minute chat before he set off looking for something called an "Onca".

I wanted to go hunting with this guy so badly but would have probably cost him the possibility of getting anything. He set off into the bush and I finished setting up camp in the dark. I ate the typical biker pasta in a pot and was exhausted, but I didn't want to fall asleep before the man came back. I made a little fire and paced around to keep myself awake waiting for his return. About an hour later I heard two fast gunshots in the distance. It seemed odd as he had only a single round rifle, a bit like a .22. That was it, two shots then no more sound.

Another hour passed, then out of the darkness, the hunter appeared. I was shocked I never heard a sound as he approached, he was just suddenly standing here before me. He was with another man who also had a rifle. I asked how he was so quiet, he pointed at my boots and motioned for me to walk around. Sure enough, as I walked over leaves you could hear -crunch - crunch - crunch. Then he pointed down at his blood-stained bare feet. Then he walked along the same path I just did. He didn't make a sound. Clearly, he was a hunter and I was a going concern.

His friend would explain why I had heard two gunshots back to back. It seemed they had killed this "Onca" thing or seen one while hunting something else. The friend wasn't very social and seemed quietly intimidating, a bit like an undertaker. I'm glad I met them in the order I did.

We had a little chat while the hunter drew pictures in the dirt explaining the area, his hunting trip and what they had killed that had gotten the blood on their hands and feet. Then we took some photos of me holding the gun. I shook the hunters' big baseball mitt-like hand and we parted ways. Without further concern, I bedded down in the jungle for the night.

If you've never slept in the jungle, it's exactly the opposite of what you might assume. Instead of calming silence, at night the jungle comes to life and is anything but quiet. Monkeys scream out, small rodents scavenge for food in the bush, you can hear the echoing calls of animals deep in the distance, even the continual micro-crunches of ants working away through the night, the sounds are endless. Eventually, the sun came up, and much like dinner, I had the standard biker-oatmeal breakfast I'd had hundreds of times before and headed a few more hours up the road to a small village just before the Amazon River that surprisingly had fuel and food.

Waiting in line for the boat to take me and the other passengers across the murky Amazon River to where it meets the jet black Rio Negro that borders Manaus, a man in a pick up truck came along selling Acai juice from a cooler in his truck box. People were going crazy for it. This thick, dark fruit juice that comes from the heart of the Amazon is meant to cure all of life's ailments. I wanted some but felt oddly intimidated by how to consume it or ask for it. I'd only ever seen dried acai berries or a bottled concoction of it as a sweet juice in a bottle. I instead watched people buy up what looked like 1-liter bags and hide them away for later. I never saw anyone drink it.

Before we took off I ran down to the water's edge and excitedly put my hand in the Amazon River. I still couldn't believe I was here. Sadly the edge of the water was a polluted mix of plastic bags and debris, not what I had imagined in my dream. I boarded the boat with KLaiR and we set off across the Amazon River. Wow, I was actually here and I'd arrived on two wheels from Canada.

Having done the bare minimum research before reaching most destinations I was shocked to see that Manaus wasn't a tiny underdeveloped town tucked in the Amazon as I'd assumed. Here was this massive industrial city pumping out cars, motorbikes, and electronics for Brazil and the rest of the world. This same thing happened in reverse when I arrived in Cusco (450,000ppl) a city I'd heard so much about because of its relation to Machu

Picchu. I had assumed it was bigger than Lima (9,000,000ppl) a place I'd heard virtually nothing about.

Being as Manus was the exact opposite of what I was expecting, I didn't exactly love it. I was however treated to another evening at the strippers/brothel by a colorful traveler from Jordan and a local Brazilian guy looking for fun. How I end up at brothels and strip clubs all the time is beyond me, it's like the default activity of large cities. There was some serious disappointment from ladies as not everyone in our trio was here for the full experience.

When I got back to the hotel wifi there was an Instagram message on my phone. That day I had been out riding in the city and a local man had followed me trying to get my attention. Trying to avoid being run over in city traffic I rarely notice much outside what's right around me. This guy had spotted a sticker on my Pelican Case that said KixMarshall.com. When he couldn't stop me he had instead searched me out and sent me a message. I questioned him for 20-minutes over Instagram messenger about what he wanted from me and to be sure he didn't want to kill me. After passing the sniff test, I then agreed to meet him the next day for a personalized tour of the city via Google Translate and a lot of hand gestures. All he wanted was to know why I was in his city and if he could show me around. The Brazilians will stop at nothing to extend their hospitality!

My newly found tour guide had asked me some questions about how the road was to Manaus and where I stayed? I very casually explained to him about the ride, sleeping in the jungle, the two hunters I had met, and this Onca thing they were hunting. My new friend looked at me like I just told him I'd been hunting witches all night. He wanted to clarify that I'd slept in a tent in the jungle and met two men hunting Oncas? I said yes, and what exactly is an Onca?

With a concerned look about him, the man explained that an Onca was a jaguar, that these two men were probably hunting them to sell their fur, and that if an Onca had come across me in the jungle or asleep in my tent I would have likely been killed. He said that if the hunters really did kill an Onca that close to my camp, that they may have very well have saved my life that night. The man was very surprised I slept alone in the jungle in a tent that night, good I didn't tell him of all the other questionable camps along the way. Whether they did kill an Onca or not, I'll never know for sure, but it once again felt like someone, somewhere was always watching out for my naive adventure.

With various tours of Manaus in the daylight and darkness behind me, I knew the rainy season was approaching and I needed to get back on the road if I was to avoid hitting the mud on my way back south. I found a route from the city of Santarém downriver that would take us via a dirt track on the BR230 that would mirror my original route, except this road was meant to be longer and worse. I was told it would take 4-5 days in good weather and closer to 10-days if it rained.

I loaded KLaiR on a questionable-looking slow boat heading down the Amazon River towards the Atlantic Ocean and left town. I nervously left her unattended under a tarp on the bottom deck while I sat swinging in a hammock on the open-aired top deck for a couple of days. I was anything but relaxed in my hammock or leaving my things unattended around the other eighty or so passengers. After two restless days, we landed in the middle of the night at the port of Santarém. I was told we would not be allowed to depart the boat at night as it was too dangerous. Instead, we slept docked and in the morning passengers would be allowed to depart. Well, all the passengers could depart except me as I wouldn't be able to get KLaiR off the deck without help from the workers and they weren't going to help me until they unloaded 500, 50-pound bags of what looked like sugar from the lower deck.

Three hours of impatiently watching sweaty men pile sugar on the dock and the men would devise a plan to get my bike down the four-foot drop from the deck to the dock below. Originally they planned to lower KLaiR down with a couple of guys, just like they did with the little 125cc bikes. I tried to explain that my bike weighs about 5-times that of the little bikes and this was not an option.

After some heavy debate, the workers decided a long plank about 1-foot wide and 15-feet long was the best way to dismount the boat. They would hold half of the plank up until I rode to the point where the bike was near the edge of the boat and the plank would then fall to the ground where I'd ride her down. A bit like having an elephant tip-toe along a wooden teeter-totter and gracefully walk out the other side, except I had no previous circus training. I was scared for my life and the fate of KLaiR falling to the dock of death below. I was basically putting both of our lives in the hands of some carnies who'd come up with a plan to keep me from bothering them. I knew no one would believe this death-defying feat so I set up my GoPro on my helmet on the dock to catch what I was sure would be a crashing failure.

Sweating and nervous, to an audience of about 30-people who were equally as confident this would be a failure as I was, I slowly rode KLaiR down the narrow wooden plank to where the boat ended and the four-foot drop began. Then the workers let go of the plank and it dropped like a rock in the river. I let go of the brake, took a deep breath, gave KlaiR a touch of throttle, and rolled out the other side like a ballerina. I'd survived the dock of death! There was a small round of applause from the crowd who were equally as surprised I made it. The excitement ended as fast as it started.

Just 50-feet away I needed to transition from this dock to another one. This required going up a two-foot-long ramp with a small 8-inch gap between it, then a 3-foot drop to a lower deck before I was finally finished. Little bikes were riding up the plank on the other side then two men would lift the bike down the 2-feet to get to where I was. However, there were now two large trucks unloading goods and loading up the sugar on either side of the little plank. Fuck, is nothing easy! There was no way I could squeeze through the 8-inch gap or make it down the other side without hitting the trucks. I again asked for help from a few workers to get me safely over.

Together we got KLaiR up the ramp, but I was so nervous about dropping the bike and hitting a truck I wouldn't pull in the clutch to let KLaiR go down the other side. Finally one of the workers ripped my hand off the clutch, pulled it in himself, and the bike slid down the plank while a few men cratered her through the other side narrowly avoiding the trucks or falling off the plank. Jesus, it was only 9 am and I was exhausted from the lack of sleep and continual concern of KLaiR crashing off of one dock or another. I bought all the men who helped me some breakfast pastry from a lady selling goods near the dock. They seemed pleased with the exchange and we parted ways. Sadly I checked the GoPro footage later, the memory card was full and caught exactly zero of the action that unfolded.

(Wildlife through the Pantanal)

(Level & with a ramp, loading was easy!)

(Hanging out on an Amazon riverboat)

(The hunters in the jungle)

Gil Serique
Alcoholic, Drama Queen, & Most Hospitable Man On The Planet.

"Aiiiiiiiiieeeeeeeeeeeee!!!"
-Gil Siquire
(The sound made in a deafening pitch loud enough to shake the Amazonian monkeys from the tree tops.)

I'd heard of an eclectic man who lived a short ride from the Amazon River ship I'd just departed in Santarém, an industrial city in the state of Pará, where the Tapajós River and the Amazon River meet. A 45-minute ride from here took me to his lake-side home in the tiny town of Alter Do Chão, a village with one main street, a central square full of bead-selling hippies, on the edge of Tapajós. The waters were said to be the home of mystical pink dolphins that folklore recounted as being able to come to land at night and transform into humans. These human dolphins were known for being incredibly beautiful and had been responsible for charming countless mortals into the waters where they were never seen again. The more I thought about it, every dolphin I'd ever seen anywhere captivated my attention, and here they were pink. The setting of this small village was warm, welcoming, and felt very surreal.

His home on the lake-side was where I was hoping to camp for a night. After finding his number on a travel posting by other overlanders, I sent him a message asking if I could camp at his place. He responded to my request in English. All it said was, "Be Welcome".

I arrived at Alter Do Chao exhausted, beyond exhausted. Despite carrying a small travel hammock I'd received on my birthday in the Baja two years earlier, I had no idea how to actually sleep in it for more than a couple of hours. Everyone on the ship slept sideways in large hammocks and looked perfectly at home. In my tiny travel hammock I could not find a position of comfort. This fighting for sleep, combined with worrying that KLaiR might be robbed dry on the lower deck while I was swaying in the tropical heat two floors up, combined with the mornings' disembarkment events had depleted all of my energy.

When I arrived at Gil's I was greeted by a man named Celso. He was wearing only shorts and a warm smile. Celso was Gil's cousin, a man in his late 40's or early 50's with young boyish looks, a full head of salt and pepper hair, evenly tanned amazon skin that had worn from the sun, and spoke strictly Portuguese.

Celso showed me around the little property and took me to where I could pitch my tent on the patio under the sort of modern treehouse they lived in. I set up my tent, set up my hammock, and immediately fell asleep spilling out over the hammock like a wet noodle. I had passed the point of not knowing how to sleep in the hammock and could have slept in a cage with a lion at this point.

I awoke several hours later. I could feel warm drool on the edge of my mouth and felt my joints crack as my weight shifted. I had clearly not moved one inch during my nap. As I slowly came back to life, I noticed a steady breeze across my torso and face. Celso had set a fan across from me and as the air blew across my sweaty body I could feel the cooling effects. To my right, I noticed a glass filled with fresh juice. The juice turned out to be from the cashew tree nearby; I'd never seen a cashew tree before let alone drank cashew juice. The incredible spot to sleep, the cooling fan, and fresh juice were amazing to wake up to. This unimaginable hospitality set the scene for my entire unexpected stay here. I'd been greeted to next-level hospitality many times on my trip, but this was something else.

Later that day Gil arrived back at his property. Gil is like no one else on the planet. His eclectic character brings an air to the space he's arriving at before he actually gets there, the same kind of feeling you get waiting for a subway train where the winds in the tunnel shift in anticipation before the roar of the train is heard or seen.

Gil could be 21, 47, or 65 years old depending on if you saw him, heard him, or just heard about him without meeting him. He was a bit shorter than me, probably 30-pounds lighter, and had the toned outlines of a man who was obviously quite fit in his youth. Gil greeted me in flawless English with a cocktail in his hand. He asked how I was, told me it would be an honor to have me for dinner, then proceeded to make me a Caipirinha, Brazil's most famous cocktail.

To say Gil is a character is to say God is holy. Gil can hold a one-sided conversation in English and Portuguese while mixing drinks and entertaining a crowd like no one I'd met before him. He was loud, constantly loud. He'd let out a type of rattling scream like that of a crazed sports fan or drunk college girl at the most random of moments. *"Aiiiiiiiiiiiiiiiiiiiiiiiii iiiiiieeeeeeeeeeeeeeeeeeeeeeeeeeeeee!!!!!!!!!!!!!!!!!!!!!"* would echo across the village at all hours. This scream was even spelled out as his WhatsApp handle just so you'd never forget. Gil loved to party, even if it was a party for one, drinks for twelve, and music for the whole village. I kid you not, this was the scene, each and every day, and the more the party ramped up, the more the *"Aiiiiiiiiieeeeeee's"* would ring out across the village.

Gils' property was positioned a short distance from a small freshwater lake just off the Tapajós River. I later learned the lake came up right to the patio in the rainy season that was just around the corner. At this time of year, we were in the final phase of the dry season and there was 400-feet of sand between us and the lake. There were neighbors on each side, but those houses were the holiday homes of people who lived in the city. Gils' place had a two-bedroom house with a toilet, shower, and fridge at the back where his young Swiss business partner would occasionally sleep. In front of it was the treehouse, it was a one-story building with a cement pad about 20x40 feet where my tent and hammock stayed and one floor up in the treehouse was Gil's make-shift office and where his hammock hung. I never once saw Gil or Celso sleep in anything but a hammock, even if it was with another person. In the yard just across from my tent, was a small outhouse I used until I learned of the flush toilet in the house behind me. Out front near the water's edge was an open-air kitchen, basketball net, group dining table, and where the steady flow of people would come to hang out and listen to the deafening party tunes that echoed across the lake from Gil's massive party speaker.

The views of the sandy bay, little fishing boats, and sunsets that sank into the jungle behind the cashew trees where a giant green iguana lived made it feel like I was living in a whole other world, a world that existed long before any other part of the world. I could spend days here swimming, drinking, and relaxing, but I needed to make some miles in order to meet Angie 6-weeks from now and more than 5000-kilometers away in Santiago Chile. After a night of drinks, dinner, and hospitality I thanked Gil & Celso and set off in the morning to head south.

Consulting locals along the way I was told that my route through the clay BR230 road I wanted to ride through the Amazon might take me closer to 10-14 days if the rains began and I should leave well-prepared with supplies for both me and the bike. I again loaded up with fuel and food then headed down the road. The second day into my ride and 60-kilometers down the clay roads of the BR230 the heavens opened up and a tropical storm of biblical proportions began to let loose on KLaiR, Stanley, and I. I knew that escaping it was impossible, setting up a tent would be like setting up a tent on the Titanic, and riding the red clay roads that were turning to rivers would soon become impassable.

While navigating the roads searching for an escape route, it felt like I was peering through a waterfall out the visor of my helmet. I had to tip the visor up just so the water would splash away from me rather than streaming down it so I could see. I finally saw a sign that said something about a National Park. I turned down the road assuming there might be some kind of shelter at the end of the road. KLaiR and I began to crawl down a slick clay hill while I tried to keep her on two wheels. At the bottom of the hill was a fork in the road and I assumed left was the park. Why I assumed I left, I don't know, but left we went.

As you can imagine, right was the National Park. I ended up rolling into a private residence with a little store. I could barely move as the monsoon rains continued to pour and I was revving KLaiR's engine just trying to rumble forward. The clay mud was embedded in KLaiR to the point where you couldn't tell she had spoke rims. I tried to ask the locals here if there was a sheltered area where I could pitch a tent. I was a bit frantic as I was clearly out of options for places to seek refuge. They looked reluctant, but took pity on me and pointed at the car park. Not the patio, not the house, the car park. There was a thatched roof overtop of a space for three small cars, but I'd need to calculate where the water was running through so the tent wouldn't fill with water as the rains washed through the parking area like little rivers running down the road.

I set up the tent, hung up my soaked clothes I knew would never dry in the humidity, and tried to cook dinner. As pasta boiled away in the pot I was trying to scratch out a path with the heel of my boot for the water to run around both sides of the tent as the little road rivers had now split into two and were both coming towards the tent. At least my sleeping mat would give an extra inch of lift if the water levels got any worse.

An hour later, the rains relented and I pulled KLaiR out to get the clay off of her. I knew if the clay hardened it would be like cement and become impossible to remove. With the spokes full and her underbody caked, now when I opened the throttle she would barely move and could only inch ahead before stalling out.

I found a stick and some rocks then began to chip away at the red Amazonian earth that entombed her. Eventually, I had enough clay removed that I was sure she could drive. I hopped on, started her, and rode exactly one foot. Suddenly a puddle of oil pooled in front of the rear tyre. Oh shit, something was broken, I'd never seen oil there before.

I jumped off, parked her, and searched for the source of the problem. The oil was coming from the shock. The Progressive Suspension aftermarket shock that I had faith in to get me across the Americas had crumbled. I believe the mud build up increased the weight beyond the shock's breaking point, but I'm no suspension mechanic. The seals blew and oil had come spewing out the bottom. This was a new problem for me and I wasn't sure exactly what to do. I rode her around in a little circle and it now felt like I was riding an overloaded pogo stick or bucking horse. KLaiR bounced and bounced with every move. Fuck!

At this point, I'm actually in the middle of nowhere at the bottom of a hill, down a muddy track, during the start of monsoon season, with a deadline to make it the same distance I'd previously traveled in 9-months, but now I was planning to do it in 6-weeks. Fuck! Fuck! Fuck!

In the morning I packed up, put my wet riding gear back on, had a coffee with the locals, thanked them, and headed for the hill I rode down to get here. Just as I was giving back the coffee cup a large fuel truck that had been parked here for two days waiting for the roads to dry began to move. He'd come down the hill to deliver fuel to a large boat on the river nearby, because of the rains it had been too slick for him to make it back up and venture on. I thought I'd give him a little head start before I headed out of here. As I rounded the corner 5-minutes later, on my moto-pogo-stick, there was the fuel truck. Halfway up the hill, and jack-knifed across the width of it. There was no way to get past it. Fuck!

If I'd only skipped the coffee chat I'd be out of here by now. Instead, there was a fuel truck blocking my path. Armed with bad Spanish and limited Portuguese, I went and talked to the truck guy. In Portuguese with dramatic hand movements, he explained that if he went ahead anymore he'd slip into the ditch on the right hand side and he'd be stuck. If he went back, he'd slip into the ditch on the left and be even more fucked. However, if he just stayed parked for the rest of the day the road would likely dry up and he might make it out.

I'm not sure if I was pissed, frustrated, or just caught off guard by the endless amount of obstacles I was running into, but I found it nearly impossible to contain my emotions. Fuck, fuck, fuck was the dialogue screaming inside my helmet!

The poor truck driver could see my frustration, likely knew the English swear words I was muttering, and said he'd give it one more try. He put the big rig into gear and began to crawl ahead and he was making ground. Even if it was just a few inches, he was making ground. Finally, we are going to get out of here.

Just then the tyres began to slip and the truck started to slide towards the ditch. I cringed, he stopped, then he got out to explain to me in Portuguese that it was too risky. Instead, we would walk back for another coffee then try again in an hour. And so, back to where we'd come from we went.

Ninety minutes of Amazonian sunshine later and the roads dried lightly. The driver tried again and slowly worked his way up the road as the truck slipped and slid. I was nervous, he was nervous. Just then one of the tyres caught some traction and the truck began to move. Then the other tyre grabbed some ground and the truck inched further ahead. Slowly he was moving, a few slow minutes of sliding around and the truck was free. I excitedly got on KLaiR and headed up the hill.

My heavy, spring-loaded bike with knobby tyres and mud building up again could barely move up the hill. Eventually, I dropped her. I got off, picked her up, and tried again. I dropped her again. The truck driver was watching me. He was as surprised as I was that his truck made it but my bike could not. When she fell again I couldn't amass any more energy to free her from the sticky clay. The driver got out of his truck and came down to help me; this was KLaiR stuck in the mud in Bolivia all over again.

Now the tables had turned and the truck driver was waiting on me to get up the hill so he could continue on without feeling guilty. He gave KLaiR a confident push from behind and slowly we drove up the hill. I yelled out a big "Obrigado" (Thank You) and we both parted ways. Riding my overloaded pogo-stick at 10km/h I made the slow journey back to the city where I'd come from the day before.

I had the bike washed and called the American company who built my shock. They informed me they stopped doing warranty work on these shocks because it was costing them too much money and suggested I buy another. I did appreciate the guy's honesty but explained my situation and where I was in the world. He said the shock could not be rebuilt and there was nothing they would do from America. I was pissed that they knew the shocks had so many problems and that the solution was to discontinue warranty work. Thanks, Progressive, excellent business decision. Don't fix the problem, just avoid further responsibility, it felt like I was part of a bad counseling session.

In the town, I met a local man at a mechanics shop who drove me around looking for a replacement shock for an hour or more. When one could not be found, he eventually fabricated my shock with random parts and fresh oil to get me on my way. He recommended not riding it more than 100-kilometers. After spending several hours on the project, adding a few seals and some oil, he refused payment for all he had done. I knew this fix was only just a band-aid and would require a real solution sooner rather than later. I called the only person I knew in the area and asked for help. I then limped back at 20-30km/h to Gil Seriques' 350-kilometers from here.

The ride took me two days.

I'd tried to arrange a replacement shock from anywhere in North or South America only to realize that getting an item with compressed gas into Brazil was going to be a logistical nightmare. Apparently, bureaucracy along with the complexities of what I needed meant I'd have to pay out the nose to get a shock in a short amount of time.

An endless number of people on KLR650 motorcycle forums offered help by saying they knew a solution or had a friend that could help, but when I went to cash in on these public postings to assist me, the replies went cold. To my disappointment, these were all empty promises made in public then not responded to in private. The closest I got was a guy in Paraguay who would sell me a used KLR shock for $1500USD. In contrast, this same used shock was around $50USD in North America. I could fly home and back with one for less if I wasn't in such a rush to get to Chili and could spare a week or two.

In the end, the Colombian who'd helped me with KLaiR when I burned up my clutch plates near Cali Colombia a year or so earlier found a friend who could get me the part. He said I could trust the man and I transferred him the cash as well as paying a premium for 3-day shipping with UPS from Colombia to Brazil, and patiently awaited for the shocks' arrival. In all it cost me around $500 to get the part.

Three days turned to four, four days to a week, a week into two weeks, and by now I was regularly yelling in English and bad Portuguese to anyone that would answer a phone on Brazil's UPS customer service line, known locally as Deprisa. The trade off was that I was stranded beach-side on the edge of the Amazon with a hospitable host who loved to entertain and party.

Life at the Gil's went something like this; Gil started his day with Cachaça (Ca-Shas-Ah), a Brazilian alcohol made with fermented sugarcane that he mixed with any form of natural fruit juice, usually smashed up cashew fruits that grew on the property. He didn't want to get fat and was mindful of what he used as mix as this was his main source of calories in a day. I found it interesting that he wasn't concerned about drinking from dawn 'till dusk, but concerned if the fruit and sugar might make him fat.

Gil was often the first one up and the last one to bed, though he'd regularly pass out in a hammock at mid-day while little parties carried on around him. Gil would later rise from the dead, unleash the power of his massive speaker that was hooked to a short playlist of international music coming from a rusty old pc hard drive that was continually hauled up and down the stairs from where he slept at night in the treehouse so no one would steal it. From the speaker, music would blast across the village for all to enjoy, or not enjoy. Each and every day.

This cycle continued during my stay and each day I enjoyed a breakfast of tapioca/manioc crepes, then a run by the lake followed by a swim. Lunch was usually BBQ'd by Celso, typically a river fish called Tucunaré or a massive Pirarucu fish over charcoal with farofa, a toasted cassava flour all topped by a spicy sauce also made from manioc. If it hadn't already started, the afternoon was followed by Cachaça cocktails, maybe some quick basketball and the defining music would start.

The more Gil drank the louder he got, the louder the music got, and often the more people that would come to the house for a free lunch and the never ending happy hour. It took me some time to sift through who were the freeloaders in this motley crew of guests and who were truly Gil's friends. Sometimes I wondered which one I was?

The more time I spent in Gil's world the more I learned to both love and loath for the guy. He told me I was maybe the 4th or 5th guest to ever stay at his place and certainly the longest one. We were going on 3-weeks of waiting for my 3-day shock delivery at this point. One day Gil told me a bit about his life and why he was so happy. Gil said he used to be addicted to this Amazon-style cocaine paste and never wanted people around so he could just get high alone. He said one day after what seemed like an eternity of living this addicted nightmare, he woke up and could see where his life was going. Then, just like that, he dropped the habit, cold turkey never looking back. He said that his dealer was even happy for him and was relieved to have Gil off the drugs. Instead he took to drinking, but seemed to more or less function amazingly well.

By now I was part of this motley crew of "friends" and tour guides that helped run Gil's tours around the Amazon. It was me, a few hired hands who could speak English and knew the Amazon well, and his quasi business partner, the young Swiss kid named Loic. Loic was entrancingly handsome and incredibly polite. He looked a lot like Gil when Gil was younger and I felt that Loic was the person Gil saw himself as, but his screaming ego always seemed to take over just at the peak of his incredible hospitality and he'd turn back into the attention-starved Gil.

You could say Gil was a bit infamous. Various television programs from around the planet had done documentaries on Gil and the Amazon region with him as the colorful guide. This also included some guided trips for Alan Dean Foster, author of *Star Wars, Star Trek* and *Alien*. Joe Jackson, author of *The Thief At The End Of The World, Leavenworth Train,* and *Black Elk*. Redmond O'Hanlon host of *O'Hanlons Helden* (O'Hanlons Heroes). Gil was a guy caught between two worlds, the highly hospitable guide / warm loving friend and the unstoppable party-king.

I had the opportunity to help set up a few of his guiding routes through the Amazon with him and Loic, and even acted as a co-tour guide for some trips of his into the jungle with cruise ship clients. From the outside, it seemed like all was going amazing and Gil was racking in the American dollars from the tourists. But this was only on the surface.

One day on our way out to one of the tour routes Gil spotted a massive, probably 20-foot long snake that had been hit and killed on the highway. It had been rotting in the sun for a couple of days and we pulled over to load it into a large garbage bag and take it out for the turkey vultures to feast on. Once the rotting snake was inside the small car, Loic, Gil, and I were all driving down the highway gagging and laughing with our heads out the window as we tried to catch some fresh air rather than the fumes of the carcass in the trunk. Gil would stop at nothing to make sure the tourists had the best experience possible. The vultures were happy and the tourists were in for a treat when they arrived in the jungle with all the birds circling above the rotting snake corpse. But it wasn't the vultures you had to watch out for, it was "the sharks."

After setting up the tour that day, Gil, Loic, and I were driving to Santarém, and Gil said we were stopping to see the sharks. Huh, I said? There are sharks around here? Gil and Loic laughed. Gil said yes, don't you call them "sharks" in North America? I didn't understand what was so funny about sharks.

We then pulled up to a building just outside the middle of the city center in Santarém and Gil grabbed a backpack of American dollars that Loic had from the days guiding. Gil took the backpack and disappeared inside the house for about 20-minutes. When he came back out he was not his usual happy self and explained to me to avoid the fucking sharks if I could. It was here he explained his debts to the local loan sharks who were gouging him with huge interest payments for dollars he owed them. Gils' endless hospitality came with a price tag, and Loics' keen Swiss banking ability didn't like it, he wanted to pay off the sharks and be done with them. I was on the receiving end of this hospitality and I now felt like I was part of the problem.

After another tour some days later Gil, Loic, and I were walking through the city with thousands of USD in this shitty old backpack held closed with two little leather straps. Right in the middle of the same busy city, where I was not allowed off of the boat when we docked until daylight as it was too dangerous when I had originally arrived here a few weeks back. Gil stopped and asked Loic and I to help him count the dollars right there in the busy street. So we each held wads of cash and counted it until we hit something like $6000USD.

From here we walked to the shark's place and Gil went inside to finally pay off the last of his debts. This would make the tour company debt free and Loic & Gil would finally start earning profits. Thirty minutes later Gil emerged wildly upset and swearing up a storm. The shark had not credited his last payment, did not provide Gil with a receipt of that payment, and insisted Gil still owed a considerable balance. Gil could not prove otherwise and the shark still had him by the balls. I knew that Gil put himself in this predicament, but I was feeling for the guy. No one said a word on the drive home that day.

As the days passed and my frustration towards Brazilian bureaucracy grew while waiting for 3-day delivery on my shock, I got to know the real Gil Serique and friends well. Gil would regularly come and get me from my hammock in his drunken excitement, his eyes would be a little glassy from the Cachaça and a little excited to greet me and he would stop, take a breath to calm himself, and in a humble and almost concerned way say to me; *"I would like to go for dinner, and it would be my true honor to have you as my guest."*

Half the day he'd be screaming in excitement with music so loud the other side of town would cringe. He'd be so drunk I'd worry for his health, he'd be pissing off the deck and filming the asses of beautiful Brazilian women walking down the beach. Then he would stop, gather himself, and awkwardly request my presence for a dinner date like I was the most important person on the planet. He would then take me or me and Loic to the most expensive restaurant in town, a little Italian place overlooking the water and town square. Then Gil would try to order the most expensive wine on the menu and whatever the most expensive dishes were. Before we ordered he would call out the owner and the server and explain that I was a world-renowned chef whose opinion mattered greatly and that I would need to confirm the food was worth ordering before he made his final decision. Then the wine would arrive and he'd explain my gifted international pallet and how I'd need to sample the wine before it got approval.

I'd made a few meals around the house and pizza from scratch over the coals of the BBQ for my birthday. However, when I sat down for dinner in one of two pairs of old ripped shorts and one of two sleeveless shirts I had, wearing a Gil Serique tour guide bandana, I hardly felt qualified as the final decision for each item at the table. Nonetheless, they would get me to try this or that and if I approved we'd eat or drink it. I always approved of everything through a half-grin like I was ever going to say no. Loic and I always argued with Gil that we could enjoy $3 beer as much as $80 bottles of wine, but as Gil's esteemed guests we were only enjoying the best when we went for dinner.

Gil's hospitality and rationality were continually conflicted, but it was always very clear that I and anyone else at the table was an honored guest of his.

On a separate occasion, I'd been invited to a dinner in the town's square with Loic and Gil. There were roughly ten of us and the guests ranged in age from Loic in his late twenties to some retirees in their late 60's. It was a mix of mainly Brazilians and a few expats like me and Loic. The guy next to me was a retired doctor and the seat across from me was reserved for his girlfriend whom he suspected would be arriving shortly. I was the only one at the table who couldn't speak Portuguese, yet they all switched to English for my benefit. I came to find out that none of the groups at the table had known each other until that day.

The doctor's girlfriend finally arrived. She was a beautiful blonde woman from Germany about half the doctor's age, who spoke impeccable Portuguese and English. He greeted her warmly and ordered her a very specific meal of grilled meat with no seasoning, a salad with no dressing, and a glass of water. Everyone seemed a bit on the edge of their seats waiting to hear her speak and explain her day.

The table talk quickly switched to discussions about Ayahuasca, and stories about what Ayahuasca was like and how it affected people differently. Then the attention quietly hovered around the German lady. I too was now keenly interested in this woman and wanted to hear what she had to say. I was a bit lost in the mix of Portuguese, German, and English that was now floating around, and finally asked directly what her experience was with Ayahuasca. The doctor laughed a little and answered for her. He said she had just come from an Ayahuasca retreat before joining us.

This was my first encounter with anyone who'd just come from an Ayahuasca retreat and I immediately began peppering her with questions about all things Ayahuasca. She looked overwhelmed and the doctor jumped in to save her from my excited interrogation. She calmly looked at me and said there is no way to explain an Ayahuasca experience, you just need to have one. The conversation continued on around me and I resolved to sit and listen.

That night back at Gil's I sat and talked to Loic and Pierre, his friend who had also grown up between Switzerland and the Amazon region of Brazil. Pierre had explained to me that Ayahuasca was part of the Santo Daime religion that was popular in this region and not a recreational drug like many outside of Brazil thought. In fact, it was legal in Brazil, unlike many other parts of the world. He said he'd tried it close to 30-times and that if I was interested he could point me to some friends of his who regularly held ceremonies close to here. My interest was peeking to a point where I hardly knew what questions to ask anymore, the experience was so close to me and I didn't know what to do. I felt like I was being kissed by a beautiful woman and freezing with excitement not knowing if I should kiss back or walk away.

Pierre then called his friend to ask when the next ceremony was? It was being held the next morning at 10 am and would be about $30 to cover some costs.

Here I was in the Amazon Rainforest in Brazil, there was an Ayahuasca ceremony the next day at 10 am, a friend of my friend was hosting, and the fee was just to cover their costs. It was looking like Ayahuasca had found me and I was too overwhelmed to know what to do. I said I would think about it and let him know in the morning. I already knew the answer.

The day before Celso had made us this soup called Tacaca and after several trips to the bathroom the soup had completely cleaned me out, it was a cleanse of sorts. On top of this, I have a routine every morning where I wake up and immediately prepare or find breakfast and never skip the morning meal. On this day however I oddly had no food or snacks and had not yet gone to the market to get any, I was operating on a clean system and an empty stomach. I talked again to Loic and Pierre about Ayahuasca and they asked me if I wanted to go or not. I said I needed 15-more minutes to think about it. I turned to walk back to my tent. Halfway there I stopped and turned around. Before my thoughts got the better of my decision making I looked at them and said I'd go. Both of the men lit up with excitement for me.

I still hadn't eaten and it was 9:30 am and I knew I had to eat something before I left for the retreat. They put my food hunt to an end and said it's best if I don't eat as I'm likely to puke up or shit out anything I ate. I always ate something, always, but took their advice and added nothing to my freshly cleaned out digestive system.

(The boys and the Pirarucu corpse)

(The calm before the storm that broke KLaiR)

(Pink Dolphin. Photo credit Gil Serique)

(My first Piranha)

Brazil
What Is Ayahuasca?

Ayahuasca (pronounced 'eye-ah-WAH-ska'), also known as yage, is a blend of two plants - the Ayahuasca vine (Banisteriopsis caapi) and a shrub called chacruna (Psychotria viridis), which contains the hallucinogenic drug dimethyltryptamine (DMT). A traditional spiritual medicine used in ceremonies among the indigenous peoples of the Amazon basin.

- Fact

Men shitting their pants, middle-aged women sobbing uncontrollably on the ground, hippies cowering under a tree begging for mercy from some force only visible to them through the emptiness of their vacant eyes, college students screaming into the wind telling "It" to stop.

What I'd vaguely seen of Ayahuasca Retreats from low-grade television documentaries depicted what seemed to be drug-fuelled nightmares of people lost in life and looking to be found by a greater force - often in exchange for money. This is what I knew of Ayahuasca.

If these people were flocking to the jungles of the Amazon region in Peru, Brazil, and Colombia for what looked like a near-death experience and seemingly felt grateful for it, I wanted to know more.

Ayahuasca can be explained in many ways so I'll do my best to subjectively present the complexities of this drug/religion/miracle cure to the best of my unbiased ability.

Ayahuasca is the final stage of an entheogenic brew composed from the Banisteriopsis Caapi Vine, a.k.a. the Ayahuasca plant, along with other herbal ingredients such as dimethyltryptamine (DMT), that contain psychoactive properties known for their hallucinogenic effects on the mind.

In appearance, the Ayahuasca vine looks like a series of ropes interwoven that grow into a neck-thick plant that one could only imagine finding in otherworldly places like the Amazon jungle. Liquid and fiber are derived from this vine and broken down to make the aforementioned Ayahuasca brew.

In regions of the Amazon basin, religious Ayahuasca ceremonies hosted by Shamans have been taking place since 1000 A.D., and have made their way into western practices. Sometimes a western psychologist or religious-oriented person will work with a Shaman to organize "Ayahuasca Retreats". At such retreats, western clients will pay to experience Ayahuasca in a controlled environment in the hopes of resolving some personal issues in their life they feel can only be uncovered at a subconscious level beyond their normal awareness. Current religious groups such as Brazil's *Santo Daime,* use Ayahuasca as part of their common practice rituals.

Summarizing a session that takes place during an Ayahuasca retreat might go something like this; The Shaman concocts a brew one to several days in advance. To do this they include the liquid extracted from the vine of the Ayahuasca plant, then add DMT, some other plants thought to hold sacred properties, water, and additional liquids. The Shaman then boils this mixture down to a honey-thick liquid drink, that becomes the shade of the earthy brown soils where it was taken from. The flavors often reflect an acidic, brash taste that could pucker the face of a vulture.

From here, depending on your session, religion, or general practices of your Shaman, the group would meet, chant, or pray, then set the group or individual's mind toward a point of focus or personal resolution, then consume a controlled amount of the brew. Maybe 2-4 ounces.

Twenty to thirty minutes later, the effects of the brew would begin to enter the mind and body of the consumer, and from here your path unfolds how it should, based on the intention of your mindset prior to consumption.

The Shaman might then guide you along your journey via music, singing & chanting, or let you guide yourself while they watch from a respectful distance. The total journey might take from 6-8 hours with more of the Ayahuasca brew consumed at intervals throughout the experience.

During the journey, those involved might experience a "purging" or "cleansing" of their physical or mental self. A side effect of this full-body cleanse could be uncontrollable crying, puking, defecation, screaming, laughing, and a wide range of exterior and mental emotions that might look like the user is being controlled like a puppet by an unseen force.

Afterward, the Shaman and group might come together to discuss their individual experiences and set an intention for their life going forward. The overall experience has unbelievably extreme emotional highs and lows, like a roller coaster spinning out of control and passing through heaven and hell on the same ride. In the end, the experience is usually a positive one, but that is up to the thoughts of the person having the experience.

So why does this matter? Let's continue on shall we...

Brazil
The Lead Up To The Day

"It's better to have a short life that is full of what you like doing, than a long life spent in a miserable way."

- Alan Watts

More than a year earlier when I was patching up the past with my ex-girlfriend on the patio of her current boyfriend's house, she had told me a few stories of people she knew who found themselves at an Ayahuasca retreat in Mexico.

The stories were similar to those I'd seen on the low-grade documentaries of late-night television in the past. Sure enough, the people she told me about had fallen victim to the effects of "purging". In short, they had shit their pants during the ceremony.

The takeaway, she explained, was that these people had so much metaphorical "shit" built up in their lives that this cleanse was helping them to get rid of the shit that had built up inside of them. Once cleansed, they were now given the opportunity to look at life with a clean slate or fresh starting point in their lives.

Jill also touched on the deeper emotional benefits and how people she knew came out feeling better about themselves and the world they lived in once the retreat was over. I heard what she said and even took into account the warm, fuzzy spin she put on life after the experience was over. Somehow though, the idea of shitting my pants, high as a fucking kite, in front of a group of people I didn't know was the only thing that stuck in my mind.

Maybe that was the point, get over your fear of how the world views you in any situation and take away the positive. Could I do this crying in a pair of shitty shorts? I wasn't sure.

Before parting ways with Jill she had pointed me towards some online groups that met in various parts of the world to be part of these ceremonies. I left her place and set the idea in my mind that if Ayahuasca found me on this motorbike journey then I would go wherever it took me. However, I wouldn't go seeking it out. So, the intention was set and I would pass through Mexico without being found by Ayahuasca or even another mention of it.

Jump ahead six months or so, and as my tyres touched down on Colombian soil I knew that drugs were going to become more readily available. Colombia has a bad reputation for its cocaine past, but I also knew that in the southern regions in the Amazon basin of Colombia, Ayahuasca retreats could be found too. As I rode through Colombia I heard nothing more of Ayahuasca other than a few stories from backpackers I'd met who'd flown into the remote frontier of Leticia, a wild city split between Brazil, Colombia, and Peru. I'd leave Colombia without crossing paths with Ayahuasca.

Later down the road while Angie and I were riding through Peru's Sacred Valley near Machu Picchu, I knew that this area was one of the premier destinations on the planet for Ayahuasca ceremonies. I'd never discussed much in the way of Ayahuasca with Angie, "drugs" in any format aren't really her thing. Of all places in the world, I figured the Ayahuasca topic might come up here though.

On our return from the heroic? failed? inspirational adventure? that was crossing the Andes in a blizzard, crashing the motorbike into the side of a mountain, the most miles I'd put on in two weeks of my entire journey, and hiking into Machu Picchu, we spent a night in the Sacred Valley during a small festival. After checking into our room, Angie was happy to find out that the cheap hostel I'd selected had bedding that smelled like dog piss. Instead of hanging out in the aromatic room, we resolved to head out into the action where we found the village in full party mode and the local women stumbling around trying not to fall over as they squatted to pee in the streets. Maybe it wasn't dog piss we were smelling in the room after all.

In the village, this is where we met "That American Asshole", the one who had earlier been fleeced for $100 when crossing borders in the middle of the night in Central America. He embodied these self-described characteristics. Note; this was his description of himself, not mine. For a guy traveling the world by motorbike, I was surprised at how well he fit his own description.

Dinner that night was under an umbrella of sorts and served from the pot of a Quechua woman whose colorful and elaborate dress reflected those of many women from the area. She was short, round as a barrel, and decorated in elaborate pinks, blues, and blacks topped off with the black *bowler hats* that sit at a precarious seven o'clock position on their heads. I always felt that in Peru the women were proud of their round figures much like women of medieval times and unlike the more sought after stereotypes of the west, where skinny was more the desired look. The large, local ladies always carried themselves quite proudly. Maybe they hadn't yet fallen victim to a copy of Cosmopolitan.

We took a seat on short chair-like stools about a foot off the ground where our noses sat right above an aromatic boiling stew in a cauldron-like pot of local delicacies created by this colorful cook from the Andes. Chicken legs right down to the foot were served next to mixed vegetables and Peruvian potatoes served on little plastic plates. The plates were quickly washed to order in an old basin by the ladies husband between swills from an unmarked bottle.

We sat, pointed, and ordered in Spanish only to find out that she spoke the local dialect of Quechua and not Spanish at all. Good there was only one menu choice.

Next to us on the little stools was an American woman, the Asshole American we'd met who had left as he wanted American food and wasn't interested in chicken parts from a pot and a lady who didn't speak English. The American woman in his place was from California, and Angie and I were delighted to speak English to our new friend while the other American had gone looking for it. The lady would do most of the speaking, she had a lot to share, and we met her at the peak of her needing someone to listen.

The American woman, let's call her "Jane", had come here at the suggestion of her therapist in California. It seems that Jane had been going to a therapist for years to deal with unresolved issues from her childhood. I'm guessing that these issues had never been fully resolved. Jane's therapist had teamed up with a group in the Sacred Valley who were running Ayahuasca retreats and the therapist felt that Jane might find some resolve by partaking in one of these rituals.

Jane said that she came to the retreat along with people from all over the world. It took place in a modified natural setting, designed to house individuals living onsite for these lengthy retreats. Jane's was a week-long and she had gone through several ceremonies during the week.

Jane confirmed that she'd been witness to the crying, shitting, and emotional roller coasters I had heard of. She felt that the session helped her a bit, but never fully resolved her issue. All I could think of is how much pressure poor Jane must have felt at this event. She was investing what I assumed was a large amount of money, feeling pressure to get resolve on a deeper level that could not be resolved with regular western therapy, and here she was in a strange part of the world out of her element. I was mentally questioning the motives of her therapist. Surely this was a commission-based suggestion. Were the therapists' motives purely to help Jane or to help herself while helping Jane?

Jane was once again disappointed with her life and was feeling at a loss by the lack of results of the sessions and all she had gone through to get here. Angie's specialty is listening, mine, not so much, but I was getting the feeling that our unbiased and captive attention was the most therapeutic thing she felt all week.

Before Jane left, I asked the price?

$3000USD plus her flights and whatever she shelled out to get her from the airport in Lima to here. I'm guessing she was close to a $5000 commitment by the time we met her that night. Yikes, Jane's experience was not the Ayahuasca experience I was looking for.

Brazil
The Ayahuasca Experiment

"Rule your mind or it will rule you."
- Buddha

November 1st, 2018

As instructed, I packed a change of clothes, my hammock, a bottle of water, the fee for the retreat, and nothing else. A friendly man on a motorbike picked me up from Gils' and drove me to a home on the edge of the jungle. The scene was a mix between true tropical jungle and urban treehouse residence. Not exactly what I was expecting, though I'm not sure what I was expecting.

I jumped off the motorbike and the driver gave me a warm smile that almost whispered good luck. I turned around and proceeded to make my way through some of the wiry jungle trees and down to a small home. The home was well hidden from the sun under the thick jungle canopy and looked out towards several treehouses built way up in the trees that were only accessible by a wooden ladder built into the tree. Down a few more steps was a meeting area under a thatched roof and out from here were a series of walking trails that snaked their way through the property to various sitting areas cut out from the lush jungle.

I was met by a man in his early 40's who only smiled and said *"Welcome"*, through a thick Brazilian accent. Next to him was a lady of about the same age who was breastfeeding a small child. She too smiled and said

"Welcome". They led me past the home and down the small trail to the meeting area where two other women in their late 40's, clearly foreigners, were already waiting.

The man disappeared back to the house with the child, and I along with the lady who greeted me and the two foreign ladies were left. The lady, Pan (pronounced Paon) introduced me to the ladies who turned out to be friends from Norway. Greeting them with a hello and a handshake I could sense the tense uncomfortableness that comes from meeting people in a situation where you both know why you're there and have plenty to share, but don't know where to start. I broke the ice with some easy questions and asked how long they had been in Brazil and if they were enjoying it?

The ladies and I chatted, both were extremely friendly, however, one of them looked noticeably distraught. Her physical appearance alone emitted the sense of a troubled or rocky life. She had worn eyes like someone who had just come from a red-eye flight and the type of tired skin one might acquire from a lifetime of smoking or living an unhealthy lifestyle. She looked aged beyond her years.

The pair said they had been planning this day for nearly two years, and they had tried to come here once before but the plans fell through. However, they were finally here. The pressure they were putting on themselves to resolve whatever the issue was inside their lives was like a beacon of light flashing around them. I felt their hopes were extremely high for today and what it might change for them.

After a few minutes of discussion amongst our trio of tourists, Pan interjected to say that we should begin. The Norwegians knew impeccable English and next to no Portuguese. I knew some Spanish and could piece together some basic Portuguese. Pan spoke Portuguese, a native language, and the most basic of basic English. Pan tried her best to explain in English what we might expect from the day. Oddly I ended up translating some of the conversation, but much of the intricate points about the full meaning of the day's events were lost on the three of us.

Pan explained that she had held and been part of many Ayahuasca ceremonies, though it was her father that was the highly sought-after Shaman in this part of the world. He was in fact so highly sought after that his deep knowledge of the practice had taken him overseas to help train and consult others on how to guide an Ayahuasca experience. On this day we would be in the trusted hands of his daughter.

She explained that we would first set an intention for the day's events and that as individuals we should decide why we came here and what we were hoping to take away from this experience. She said that there would be music, we would be safe, and that if we needed any assistance she and her husband would be close by. She explained that we might experience a wide range of emotions that we might not be expecting, and that we should not be scared as they were just feelings and not actually happening.

She then explained where the bathrooms were. Funny enough, the one word she did remember quite well was *"shit"* & *"vomit"*. Through a series of thankfully comical and dramatic motions along with continually using the words *shit* & *vomit*, she explained that it was very likely that we could all expect to *shit* & *vomit*. Though if we could get to the bathroom it would be much better than making *shit* or *vomit* in our hammocks. Though if this *shit* & *vomit* did happen it was no problem. I was happy for the comical relief.

After the explanation, she asked if anyone had any questions? Naturally, I did. I put up my hand like a grade four student asking the teacher if I could go to the bathroom and she said, *"Yes Kix what is your question?"* I said that I had not eaten any food yet today and if it was better to eat or not to eat before this experience, citing that my friends said it was better not to.

Pan said no, I should have definitely eaten and drunk something before I got here and that there were bananas on the table & I should eat one. I was feeling conflicted with the information I was given. Was I being told to eat because I was new to this or was I originally being told not to eat because some friends who had done this many times suggested no food was better than food? I split the difference and ate half of a banana.

Just then the husband returned with the baby and a small guitar, a bit like a sitar. From here things got underway. Pan asked if I and the Norwegians could hold hands while she set an intention for the group and each of us set our own intention for the experience. I could sense the two women knew exactly what their intention was, hell they had been planning this for over two years, however, my intention wasn't all that clear to me.

I had always planned to have this experience, but I was never sure why. Why the hell was I here? Was it my failed relationships I was seeking resolve for? Was it to tie up some loose ends that had come unraveled in my childhood and my parents' 25-year divorce? Was it for clarity in my future? Was it for the current girl in my life? Was I hoping to open something up I had buried deep inside and nearly forgotten about? I felt like I had spent the last 2-years alone inside my helmet thinking about all of these "issues" and was now relatively at peace with them and myself. Shit, why was I here? I decided to leave the intention open for possibilities and let whatever came my way happen. If a particular situation or moment in time needed to be touched upon again it would come to me.

With the door of intentions wide open, the four of us began to chant to the soothing rhythms of deep, earthy music that seeped its way out from some small speakers behind us as the man began to play his guitar and lightly sing. The vibe intensified as the chanting continued and the man repeated what felt like a trance of words. After a couple of minutes, Pan asked if we had all set our intention. The Norwegians said yes, I smiled and nodded my head. She then explained how the Ayahuasca was made.

To make the Ayahuasca, Pan said they had mixed the juice from the sacred Ayahuasca vine that grew on the property along with leaves from a shrub (these leaves contained DMT, a.k.a a hallucinogenic) along with various other medicinal herbs I had never heard of, and water. This recipe was then left to simmer over a fire for a couple of days until it thickened. As she spoke she pointed to a thick winding vine creeping its way through the jungle in front of us. She noted that it was the mother vine we'd all come searching for.

What was left from this brew was the thick earthy substance in a clear glass jar before us. The viscosity was like warm honey and the shade of rich brown soil. However, it was the taste I will never forget. Despite possibly resembling the flow of warm honey, it tastes nothing like it. The taste was more like the color, rich and pungent with an acidic bite that embodied all of the flavors of the soils Mother Nature nurtures the world with.

Pan explained that we would break the day into three parts and at each break, we would have the option to have another shot of the Ayahuasca brew.

She said that one shot was likely a good place to start and we would feel the full effects. Though if we'd ever tried anything like magic mushrooms and we were able to positively deal with the experience we may consider having two shots. If for any reason we felt that we had extremely deep or unresolved emotions we were hoping to uncover that we might consider all three shots but did not recommend this for anyone who had never had an Ayahuasca experience before.

The slightly less troubled-looking Norwegian went first. She said that she felt that one shot would be enough to get her to where she felt she needed to be in her life right now. I went next, feeling qualified to check yes to the positive magic mushroom experience. I said that I felt I could handle two shots as I wasn't exactly sure what I was looking for but felt it was a bit deeper than round one. Last was the more worn-looking Norwegian. She said she wanted the full experience and would prefer all three shots. All at once the three of us looked at her with widened eyes and tensed up a little. Pan asked to clarify that she really wanted all three rounds. A simple yes came back at her and off we went.

From this moment things progressed dramatically.

Each of us lined up to take what this mother tree was offering. It wasn't a standard shot glass full, it was more like a 3oz glass as opposed to the typical 1oz shot glass. A 3oz shot glass filled to the rim with a thick earthy substance that sludged its way out of the glass and into our mouths. Unlike a typical shooter, it was impossible to quickly shoot and swallow the drink. You had to slowly ingest the full experience trying to coddle the warm mixture from the glass and force it down your throat while trying to avoid gagging as the pungent flavor fought with your taste buds. After we had fully finished the brew on our own, Pan gave us a drink of water to rinse down the residue.

With round one under our tongues, we were each instructed to find a peaceful place for our hammocks and lie down. The two Norwegians set up near each other just outside of the meeting area. With no one to spend the day with, Pan suggested I go further into the jungle away from the experience of the others and position myself under the tropical canopy below some shady plants. After twenty minutes in my hammock listening to sitars, singing, and the deep tones of heavenly music in the background, I suddenly noticed one of the large green plants up in the canopy look at me, wink and smile then quickly turn back into a plant. I tried to focus on the plant to decide if what I'd just seen had really happened, but it was now just a plant. Then the wind gave it a little push and the plant gave me a little smile again. I stopped and tried to focus on the plant to see if what I'd just seen again had really happened. But as I focused on it, it was just a plant again. Having been down this road in one fashion or another before I knew how to confirm if what I'd just seen had really happened or not. I put my hand up and waved it in front of my face. Sure enough, my hand streaked in front of me into what looked like five or six hands that melted into a wash of bright colors. I smiled and said to myself, here we go.

From this moment the day shifted into a Dr. Seuss meets Dr. Sigmund Freud on the set of the Jungle Book type of day. A warm feeling of joy came over me, as well as the literal intensified warmth of the jungle heat. It was roughly 11:30 am and as my senses heightened everything felt more and more intense. The trees talked to me like we were old friends and said not to worry they would look after me. I could sense that everything around me was here to help me and if I needed anything, anything at all, they would surely help.

I could hear the music in the background getting louder and more intense. As the day progressed it always felt like it was the music that guided the mood. With deep chanting that mainly focused around the word Ayahuasca, a deep throaty base poured out from the speakers along with the snake-charming sounds of an Indian Pungi along with the man's sitar. I got the feeling we were caught between a world of magic carpets & snake charmers set back in biblical times. I felt like I had fallen into another world, another time, another dimension.

The colors of the sky became an endless ocean blue, while the jungle around me came to life in intensified greens, reds, purples, and yellows. It was like a box of Crayola Crayons melted by the sun that had been lightly blown across the canopy by the winds of the world. It all felt very positive, a 5 out of 10 on the intensity scale, and I was starting to feel the uneasiness of my stomach start. I began to gag while I tried to choke down deep breaths of hot, humid tropical air hoping to calm my uneasiness. I kept passing between fits of giggling mixed with gagging and feeling like I was in fact going to shit myself right here in my hammock. I then heard someone's voice behind me but I couldn't tell who it was. As I focused I realized it was Pan explaining that a few hours had passed and if I was still interested, it was time for another round of Ayahuasca. To me, it felt like only minutes. Time had no relevance in my current state.

She watched me as I very slowly and cautiously made my way back to the meeting area like a child learning to walk. The Norwegians were already there along with the man singing and playing the small guitar. I didn't want to take on the energy of anyone else and decided not to make eye contact with anyone. The one Norwegian was asked if she still wanted another shot and she agreed, then sucked round two out from the 3oz shot glass, had a drink of water, and sat down. The other Norwegian was consulted if she still wished to stay with just one shot and she agreed that one was enough for her. Pan then asked if I still wanted another shot and I thought about it for a minute. She said I didn't need to take it but I would need to decide on my own. I pulled myself together, said yes, and slowly another round of the warm thick earthly substance slid slowly inside me. We all returned to our hammocks.

Every emotion, feeling, and color began to intensify even more, as did the music and chanting. I could feel my heart thumping to the beat of the music, and I wasn't sure I was now going to be able to handle round two. I began to gag even more as I tried to force down breaths of the thick tropical air like a cement brick was placed in my beating chest. Thinking about breathing makes it even more difficult to breathe and I could feel the conflict between my mind and my lungs. Next, my bowels groaned and I was sure I was going to shit in my hammock. Then a couple of cartoon monkeys that looked like friends of Stanley appeared along with the smiling plant and said not to worry that they had my back and we're here to help. My very own helper monkeys at a time when I needed help, how fitting I thought.

At what I thought was going to be a bowel-releasing breaking point I knew I had to make my way to the bathroom. I tried to stand up but it felt like my whole body was being pulled down by the weight of the earth. I resolved to let gravity take control and proceeded to melt out of my hammock and crawl to the bathroom. As I got closer I again heard Pan and she asked if

I needed some help? I said I was fine, I just needed to get to the bathroom. The closer I got to the bathroom near the meeting area I could hear the Norwegians off in the trees puking like college girls at the end of 2-for-1 gin night. The sound was not helping my situation.

I made it into the bathroom, closed the door, and lifted the lid of the toilet. I gagged and I gagged but nothing came up. I then very carefully took off my shorts and sat down hoping to shit here rather than back in my hammock. After some time I realized that nothing was coming up or down, I washed my hands and face and made my way back to the hammock, this time on two feet.

As I sat down the situation began to intensify even further. I suddenly found myself on a large ship, but I wasn't sailing the open seas. I was sailing the sand dunes of some far off land and my ship was filled with various cartoon animals, namely three helper monkeys who just kept smiling and saying *"We're here for you man, we got you, anything you need, we'll get it for you"*. I could see myself standing on the bow, the captain of my own ship, with the plants dancing and singing and everyone onboard offering to help with whatever I needed. It was all very positive. We were now sitting at about a 6 out of 10 on the intensity scale.

While I drifted in and out from the world around me to this other world I became increasingly hotter and hotter. The tropical and humid heat of the Brazilian jungle is quite a lot on any given day, but with my senses on overload, I felt like I was being steamed alive. I remember Pan telling us earlier this might happen and if we needed to cool off there was a shower down one of the trails in the jungle we could use. Looking for reprieve I again melted out of the hammock, pulled myself to my feet, and began a distracted search for the shower. It might have taken me 5-minutes or 5-hours to find the shower, time was impossible to gauge.

Eventually, I found this long rope dangling from the treetops high in the jungle canopy that ran alongside a series of bamboo poles put together like a pipe. This was the rope to start the shower. In a state of heat exhaustion, I mustered up all of the energy I could focus on and forced my weight down on the rope while holding on with two hands. Instead of water, hundreds of thousands of large Amazonian ants came raining down over me. I could feel their millions of tiny feet spring to life as they clambered their way across my skin wondering what had just happened. Before I had time to decide what to do, suddenly the water I had come searching for began to pour over me, washing away the ants and cooling my core. I could feel the water washing away the shell of who I once was while the new and reimaged version of myself was finally allowed to shine through. I eventually felt the heat inside of me cool and I released the rope allowing the water to stop. I looked around the jungle floor and didn't see a single ant.

I walked to a sitting area near the shower to sit and ponder all that had happened and what that shower symbolized. With my head in my hands, I fell into deep thought, like a thousand monks meditating on a single point of concern. I felt entranced, I felt like I was searching deep inside myself so intensely focused, thinking about my life and where it was headed. I had never felt so focused on any thought before. I have no idea how much time had passed before my focus was broken by the sound of Pan asking if I was alright and explaining I needed to come back to the meeting area as it was now round three.

One small baby step at a time and I found myself back at the meeting area, where the two Norwegians were along with the man playing the small guitar, the baby, and now a very young boy maybe 6 or 7 years old was waiting. I looked at the man with the two small children, they all said nothing and simply smiled back. I could tell the boy had been in this situation before and knew it was best to only smile.

Pan again asked everyone how they were and explained if we would like another drink from mother Ayahuasca we were welcome to, but we did not need to and this would be the last option to do so. The first Norwegian again declined. I wasn't sure I could take any more intensity and stuck to my original plan of just two rounds. The other Norwegian also stuck to her decision and lined up for her third and final drink. Then, we all retreated back to the comfort of our hammocks.

On this final return to my hammock, the mood shifted again. I could now feel my entire life being lived out inside my head and across my body. I never once saw a single clear image of any particular moment. I only felt the emotions of an entire lifetime. It was like my life was flashing before me, but not in images, in emotions. All 30+ years of good, bad, and one-of-a-kind experiences came rushing through me. The moments I had relived inside my helmet over the last two years, had now transferred into emotional stimulus. The emotions were coming at me so fast and so strong I thought I was going to be blown right out of my hammock. I reached up behind my head with both hands and held onto the ropes of my hammock like a tropical storm was plummeting the jungle. I began to yell, *"Fuuuuuuuuuuck, fuuuuuuuuuck, fuuuuuuuuck"*, *"holy, fuuuuuuuuck, hold on."* We had officially hit an intensity level of 10 out of 10.

As each moment of my magical childhood, diverse teenage years, and adventurous adulthood came through me I felt each and every emotion at machine gun speed. Extreme happiness, confusion, sadness, excitement, joy, surprise, fear, anger, every imaginable emotion times 10,000. I continued to hold on tighter and tighter, screaming louder and louder. My eyes began to stream with liquid. They were clamped shut, I wasn't crying, it felt more like a release. As each emotional feeling ran through me, my body tensed up like I was bracing for impact while falling from the sky, my jaw was clenched but remained slightly open and I continued to scream *"Fuuuuuuuuuck, fuuuuuuuck, fuuuuuuck, holy fuck!"* without moving my mouth and panting like an out of shape hiker at the top of a mountain.

Again I have no idea how long this went on, but I suddenly felt like I had relived my life in an emotional flash. My eyes eventually released and began to open. It was now dark outside, the entire day had passed. The plants that had been cheering me on all day, started to sway slowly like a mother rocking a child to sleep and my eyes drifted open and closed. I found myself back on the ship, with the helper monkeys behind me. My heart slowed to a murmur and I felt free and happy. Then, I suddenly burst into tears.

I sobbed uncontrollably, but now had a better sense of time. I think it was about 20-minutes. I wasn't upset or unhappy. Actually, I'd never felt unhappy the entire day; it all felt quite positive. It just felt like the emotional roller coaster of the day needed an exit point and crying was that point. Then as quickly as the sobbing had started it had stopped and I suddenly began to laugh. I laughed like a small child whose parents were tossing him up in the air, with each giggle I'd get thrown higher and higher. I was now laughing hysterically. Then it all stopped.

At this moment I just lay there and thought. I thought about the day, the wonderful experiences I'd had in my life, and most recently on this grand adventure. I thought about all the amazing people in my life who had helped me to become who I was today. I thought about how grateful I was to be here in this moment. Then with the most perfect of timing, I heard Pan behind me explaining that the day was now finishing up and if I could please bring my hammock back to the meeting area for a discussion.

Back at the meeting area, the music had switched to soft soothing tones, the type that you might hear while getting a massage or during meditation. The whole family was again here and everyone just smiled while I smiled back, the welcoming energy was unmistakable. The two Norwegians were again already here. I smiled at them like you do when you know you and the person you are smiling at have a secret to share that no one else knows. They smiled back the same way. Myself, the Norwegians, and Pan then sat on mats on the floor while Pan led the conversation in broken English.

We were asked to share our experience. The Norwegian who had the single shot went first. She explained she had some pent-up anger and emotional experiences that she had never dealt with and felt like they had come to light and was feeling better about them now. She talked for a moment or two and was feeling like this negativity had been brought to the surface where she now knew what it was and could deal with it in a positive way.

Next went the lady who had three shots. She explained that she had spent a large part of the day puking and in the bathroom on the toilet and this felt like a real release for her. She had felt like she was never able to trust others in her life and that this came from not trusting herself. She said she realized all this negative energy had built up inside of her, mostly in the form of this large roll around her midsection. She had a sort of tire tube of fat that was just sitting around the middle of her but no excess fat bulges anywhere else on her body. She said she had always felt negative energy in this area, but during her experience, she had realized why. At one point during the day, she felt like thousands of black spiders had suddenly begun to crawl over her and eat away at this negative energy stored as fat in the middle of her. She felt like this negative energy had been eaten away and she now trusted herself and that this would translate into trusting others. They each talked about their experiences for two or three minutes.

Next Pan asked me to share. I asked how long I could speak for? She said as long as I needed, but please try to be under 5-minutes. I lit up like a kid on Christmas day and launched into storytelling mode. I explained that my day felt entirely positive. I recounted the emotional hits of my life, the streaming eyes, the helper monkeys, the dancing plants, how I was the captain of my own ship, and on and on. I explained that even when I felt like I was going to be blown away and was screaming fuuuuuuuuck, that I still felt safe and positive. Then Pan burst out laughing. She said when I began to scream she came to check on me and could see my eyes closed and me hanging onto the hammock like I was going to be blown away with my jaw hanging half-opened. She then reenacted what I looked like for what must have been quite a while and laughed even harder. She said she'd never seen anyone who looked or acted like this. We all laughed and it felt good.

I then told the group that I felt like I had been given an extremely unique opportunity prior to arriving here. I had been mostly alone for the last two years, alone inside my helmet, alone inside my head. This whole time I had nothing to distract me from my thoughts. No timeline, no friends, no events, no invented distractions to keep me from myself, the people I spent the most time with were a metal motorcycle and a plastic helper monkey who only listened. I told them that I had literally thought through and had to mentally deal with each and every moment of my life, every relationship, childhood moment, business decision, money decision, friendship, time with my family, everything. I'd relived them all, alone inside my helmet, alone inside my head. An opportunity I felt wasn't granted to many people and that I arrived here feeling like I had nothing to resolve, I only wanted a deeper experience of my life. I felt it was a polarizing difference from why most people came here. I felt free, I felt happy and I felt like this moment had indeed found me in the most ideal setting at the most ideal time in my life. Does a motorcycle break down in the middle of nowhere in the Amazon rainforest by accident or by intention?

I made my way back to Gil's where I was greeted by Celso who smiled, told me I should relax, and handed me a freshly pressed juice. He had organized my camping area with the fan, some fruits, and some water. He smiled and hugged me. The whole place was dark and no one else was around. They all knew what type of day I had just had and made the effort to allow me a quiet evening in their home that was typically alive with music and people.

Like most experiences on this trip, I was basically having them alone. I decided to message Angie. I don't know what she must have thought when those messages came pouring in. The last she had heard from me I was having the usual cocktails with Gil and friends and enjoying beach life. These new messages I was sending likely sounded like they were sent from someone else or from me if I'd completely lost my mind. Maybe I had lost my mind, or maybe I'd found it.

With no reference to where I'd just come from, Angie opened her phone to read messages like this:

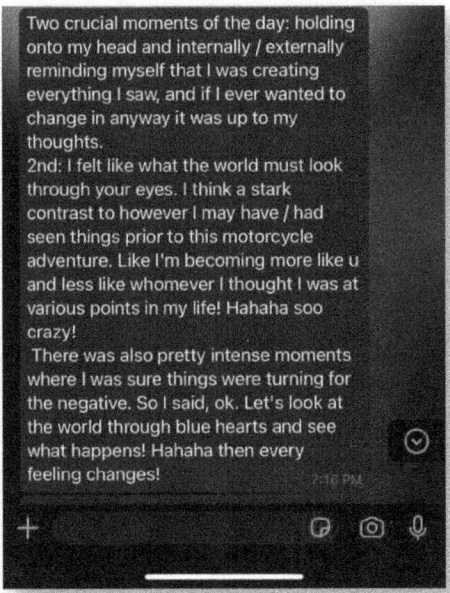

(One of a long list of post-Ayahuasca messages to Angie)

Brazil / Bolivia / Chile
The Race To The Girl

The Canadian Monarch Butterfly migrates an impressive 4800-kilometers from Canada to Mexico then back again continually chasing summer.

- Fact

(Perhaps I was once a Monarch Butterfly)

Roughly one month after the shock had broken and a replacement had been sent with 3-day expedited shipping from Colombia, it had arrived. In under an hour, I had the part changed, packed my tent and clothes, and presented Gil with a buffet of beers, wine, and cachaça for his endless hospitality. It was December 13th, and I needed to meet Angie for Christmas in Santiago Chile 5,500 kilometers from here, as well as source a few parts for KLaiR before everything closed for the holidays. To put this 2-week marathon into perspective, this is roughly the same distance from Cartagena Colombia to Santa Cruz Bolivia, a journey that had taken me closer to 10-months. Hell, even the 4000-kilometer ride from Lima Peru to Campo Grande Brazil had taken me over 4-months. I didn't think I was going to make it.

I cut through Bolivia on the way to Chile and for the third time, stopped back at Bolivia Motorcycle Tours to say hello to Chris and his family and again have him help me with motorcycle maintenance. I wanted to take the superior spring from my old shock and put it on the used factory shock that was now on KLaiR. I was now carrying a spare shock just for parts. To accomplish the spring changeover Chris fashioned together an antique ratchet and strap system to compress the spring so we could work on the shock held down by a vice that we were borrowing from a street side repair shop. Both of us knew if something on this rickety system gave out the spring would be set free and likely take with it one of our fingers or an eye. After some nervous laughter and holding our breath, we changed the springs, and surprisingly, we both walked away unscathed.

A few weeks prior to this I'd also made a deal with Chris where I had some brand new soft motorcycle luggage muled from Peru to his place in Bolivia. This weight reduction from hard to soft luggage would help KLaiR from blowing another shock under all my weight. Chris would then buy a couple of the hard Pelican cases off of me to use for his growing motorcycle tour company. The Pelican cases were covered in stickers outlining my various stops and accomplishments along the trip. These stickers were the biggest conversation pieces with everyone I met. People would see my adventure setup then look over the stickers and ask about each location and I would then answer their questions about what country was the scariest. The stickers were essentially all my souvenirs and treasured moments as I had no room to carry anything else.

Chris is an extremely efficient and effective mechanic and this translated to everything he did. Once Chris had the luggage off of my bike he began to peel all the stickers off one by one to make the luggage his own. I knew I'd never see these stickers again, but I could feel my trip being erased before my eyes as each hard-earned sticker came peeling off the cases. I think this is something only an overlander would understand. When he noticed my eyes widened and smile fade away he laughed, said sorry, and continued to peel away the memories.

10-minutes into his inspection of KLaiR he noticed a small bend in her front rim, then another one, then he spun the wheel and spotted an even bigger bend! He asked what the hell I'd been riding on. I'd been driving like mad across the jungle roads to try and beat the clock to Santiago and hit plenty of potholes and rocks at faster speeds than I normally rode. In all, I had bent the rim in five locations. To eradicate this, Chris took me back to a guy who'd done some work on KLaiR last time I was here as the guy had some "special tools" to fix the rim. When we arrived the rim guy had just broken his leg earlier that day and was in a great deal of pain. He instead directed us to his special tools and through fits of agony explained what we needed to do to fix the bends.

The "special tools" included several large blocks of wood, cut at the exact same thickness, and another block of wood, cut a bit thicker. The idea was that you placed the bend in the rim on one part of the wood and the other piece of wood on the opposite side of the rim. Then you took the larger piece of wood and tactfully smashed the rim until it flattened out like it was before the bend. Sweaty, laughing, and as the two North American apprentices of the Bolivian mechanic with a broken leg, we crouched down and smashed KLaiR's rim back into shape.

On top of this, I had Chris help me to swap out all of my bearings. I had the same bearings since I left and now that KLaiR was at 74,601kms, I thought it best to change them. I had quality replacements for four out of five of the required bearings. One day about a year earlier I had met two men with a small boy broken down on the side of the road in the Amazon region of Bolivia. It was incredibly hot and their bike was in pieces on the side of the road. To their amazement, I had enough tools to take apart the bike and a selection of bearings that I could fix their bike on the side of this dusty Amazonian road. To replace this bearing I had given away, I purchased a Chinese replacement bearing off of eBay when I was back in Canada. This turned out to be a fatal error.

Once again Chris had gotten KLaiR back up and running and showed me how to change the bearings. I can honestly say that I don't know if I'd have made it to Ushuaia in one piece if I hadn't met Chris. He had saved my ass more times from current or future motorcycle breakdowns than I could have ever asked for. To find people like him and his family on the road was literally a life saver.

With the clock still against me, I set off after a couple of nights and headed south towards the Salar de Uyuni salt flats, a must-stop on my list of South American sights. The road trip from Chris' turned out to be short-lived. The very next day, an unplanned stop found me just outside of Sucre, a city high in the Andes. Riding down the paved road I suddenly began to feel like I was riding in slick mud as KLaiR started to slip and slide on the back end. I pulled over and sure enough, I had a rear flat tyre. I pulled off the road into a small area that resembled more of a garbage dumping area than a green space, not uncommon in a country with limited sanitation solutions. I got out my small air compressor and tried to fill the tube. The tube would fill slightly but would not hold any air. I decided to take off the tyre and hopefully patch the tube.

Before I originally headed into the Amazon in Brazil I had wanted the best possible setup to make sure I'd make it through the potentially muddy roads without issue. I had purchased a set of aggressive off-road tyres and put on an extra thick tube to avoid any problems. Naturally, the opposite had happened. With a limited selection, I ended up purchasing tyres at the Paraguay/Brazil border and bought what they had as opposed to what would usually fit. Where KLaiR might typically have a rear tyre like a 130/80/17 tyre with an aspect ratio of 80, or 80mm on the sidewall from rim to tread, what they had was considerably more narrow, closer to 50mm. The guy warned me it would be smaller but would work fine for a short time.

Next, when I went to get these tyres changed just before heading onto the BR319 to Manaus, I asked the guy to install the thicker tubes I had been carrying to avoid any punctures. He looked at the tube and said we can do it, but it's a bit too big and thick for this tyre. However, it would do for a short time.

Now I was on a race against the clock and there wasn't time to shop for another set of tyres in Brazil. I knew the next place I'd be able to source decent or any tyres and tubes was going to be in Santiago Chile. With a thick tube crammed into a narrow tyre I rode like hell through the hot Amazon region and day after day a hot rim and a hot tyre rubbed against each other. When I pulled the tyre off the rim in the cool mountains just outside of Sucre I could see this problem glaring back at me. I didn't have one hole, I had more like thirty holes! The tube had been folded to fit inside the tyre and had rubbed together creating an abundance of holes. I think the tube had actually melted together under the heat and pressure concealing any obvious problems for quite some time. After my first chilly night up in the mountains I felt like this rubber on rubber glue had come unstuck and suddenly I had more holes than tube. I'm not a rubber expert but this is how the situation looked, staring back at me on the side of the road with the scent of rotting garbage wafting up over the hill.

I did have a spare front tube and decided I'd try to use that in the back to get me going. I'd changed or repaired the front tube plenty of times. The rear had thankfully given me next to no problems and I had only successfully managed to change the rear tyre on my own once. Today would not be the second time, unfortunately. After a couple of hours of trying to manipulate the front tube on the rear tyre and get it back on the rim I finally gave up and decided to get a ride to the city and hopefully source the right sized tube and have it changed over by someone with proper tools.

I no longer had the protection of locked luggage on the bike to hold all of my things. Instead, I gathered all of my belongings including the rear tyre and rim, three bags, and threw them over my shoulder, on my back, under my arms, and hitchhiked to Sucre. The first person around the corner picked me up. Luckily he knew of a motorcycle shop and tyre shop. In 15-minutes we were at the motorcycle shop. However, when I explained the situation to the shop owner they only had cheap Chinese tubes for small motorcycles and knew it would pop as soon as it was on big old KLaiR. What this man thought would be a quick rescue turned into several hours of driving me from bike shop to bike shop around Sucre until we found a suitable tube. Then he drove me from tyre shop to tyre shop until we found someone who would work on a motorcycle rim as most shops here were for large transport trucks. While KLaiR waited in pieces on the side of the highway, myself and the driver sorted out the tyre and eventually he dropped me off requesting a slightly larger tip than was first expected. Soon I was back on the road, but this is not where the road trip obstacles ended. Next stop, Salar de Uyuni.

(Repairs done Bolivia-style with Chris at Bolivia Motorcycle Tours)

(Local mechanic checking for balance) (Tyre repair just outside of Sucre)

Bolivia
Salar de Uyuni. Pass The Salt Please

"So, stay tuned to Long Way Up, two guys lost in South America."
- Long Way Up Episode 3. Ewan commentating his own trip.

Salar de Uyuni is one of the most visually magical spectacles on the planet. This is the world's largest salt flat and was once several lakes covering an area of over 10,000 square kilometers back in a time when you'd see Abelisaurus walking through here looking for a drink. The crusty salt bed is rich with lithium and home to an array of colorful flamingos. The area is so unique that the movie Star Wars The Last Jedi, had scenes filmed here. Sitting at close to 12,000-feet above sea level, it's an entrancing and cool place to visit and spend the night.

Once you are out on the flats, the area has almost no land in sight aside from a few islands making it nearly impossible to judge distances. With no reference points for height or distance, the landscape makes for great photos. You can artificially set distances by placing an object in the foreground and another in the background to increase or decrease their size making it look like the two objects are side by side. Manipulating objects can make it look like you are eating your friends alive or like a plastic monster is attacking you and so on. Well, at least you can do this when you're with a couple of friends. The shots are a touch more difficult when your friends are a plastic monkey and a steel motorbike. When it rains the surface becomes a giant mirror reflecting the world around you and at night the lack of light pollution brings the stars to what feels like an otherworldly vibrant life where you can reach out and touch them.

You can hire jeeps to take you out on tours, or if you're lucky enough to have your own motorcycle you can ride around the salt flats and camp out under the stars on the salt or on one of the few islands that pop up from out of nowhere on occasion. The real dangers here are hidden. There are pools of water hidden under various points of the salt that are nearly impossible to see. If you hit one of these you risk breaking through the salt and getting stuck in the muddy saltwater. The other danger is if it rains while you are out in the flats. The ground becomes an impassable sticky clay, locking vehicles into the earth. It's easy to get lost, hard to be found, and there is literally no one around for miles.

KLaiR, Stanley, and I opted to follow the tracks you can see worn in the salt from the tour jeeps. I knew if we got lost or stuck, I'd be even more screwed than someone stuck inside the safety of a campervan who could survive the elements and likely had more than a day's supply of food and water. That night I pitched my tent on an island and set my alarm for 1 am to see the starry skies. I awoke to what felt like daylight as the stars danced, shone, and shot across the sky as if to put on a show for us.

I'd originally planned to spend a few days here, but things had changed with the delay from the shock dramas, and the next day I continued on towards Chile taking a few shortcuts to save time. One of these shortcuts took me across a more remote section of the salt flats further south. Naturally, I got lost, ended up in some village that didn't see many tourists, and had to venture back onto and off of unmarked sections of the flats to get around unmanned checkpoints that had roads blocked off for reasons I was unaware of.

Eventually, I found the final town on this road out of Bolivia. I did some quick calculations based on how much fuel I had left compared to how much Bolivian currency I had left to buy fuel. My shortcut had taken up more miles and fuel than if I'd taken the pavement and now the math to make it to Chile on this tank of fuel wasn't quite adding up. In this part of the world, there were no banks or ATMs and I knew they would never accept credit cards around here. I found a small fuel station, negotiated for the local rate, and exchanged the last of my Bolivianos for some low-grade fuel I was hoping would last me until I could make it over the border.

Riding south, the setting turned from a town to village, then to a few misplaced homes as the pavement crumbled into a well-beaten path and eventually into a dirt track. With the RPMs running high in 2nd gear to get us through the dirt path and loose ground, I watched KLaiRs fuel gauge slowly sink lower and lower. The thought of if we'd make it to the border or not was eating away in the back of my mind, but I was continually distracted by the incredible scenery. The earth was reddish-brown like what I felt the surface of Mars must look like in person and off in the distance sat a smoking volcano jetting up from the vast and empty land.

Eventually, I arrived at the border where a couple of makeshift living quarters and small buildings sat in the middle of nowhere. On either side of a long pole that divided the road from Bolivia to Chile. The man inside the first building was quite friendly and said he could process my motorcycle papers but to get a stamp for my passport I needed to see another guy who had just gone over to another little building for lunch. My border crossings seemed to magically line up with at least one person's lunch break. I asked the man who else used this border? He said not many people and no one else today had come through here. I felt like the other man likely wasn't that busy and decided to walk over to the other building to get him. This greeting didn't go as well.

The door was locked, so I banged on it. No one answered. I then banged a little louder and yelled "Hola, Hola!". Still no answer. I took to the technique that worked at the Peru to Bolivia border and began to bang and yell louder. Finally, the door swung open and a man dressed in military-style clothing with no boots on looked at me, and in a very unpleasant tone explained it was his lunch break and he would be done in an hour, then he slammed the door shut.

I decided to knock again and explain that I had already finished all my other paperwork and just needed the passport stamp. No reply. I continued this technique and after a couple of minutes, the door opened again. This time the guy looked even less happy, but he was wearing boots. I explained I would only need a moment of his time. He relented, and we went to the other office. I talked the entire time explaining how beautiful this location was and how lucky he must be to work here and how he had such an important job. I didn't lay off the compliments until I had the stamp. Success, the gate opened and we were back on the road.

I had rounded the smoking volcano and within moments the road on the Chilean side turned to pristine pavement. I was quickly greeted by a herd of guanacos, a relative of the llama, and right behind them, a blue lake emerged in the mountains that was dotted with vibrant pink flamingos. If this was the back way out of Bolivia and into Chile it was worth it. The scenery was unbelievably alive with color and life.

Soon I arrived at the Chilean border patrol, where things were much more rigid. I was met with forms to fill out, a series of men wanting to inspect my luggage, signs explaining what fruits and vegetables were not allowed in, and a row of officials behind computers processing documents. I got the impression banging on the door and yelling would not have ended well here. After completing the paperwork I jumped on KLaiR and hit the starter. She sputtered and sputtered, but wouldn't start. Shit, she was out of fuel. There was a reserve and that would get us about another 30-kilometers, but not all the way to the next town. I went back and asked where I could find fuel. This led me to a set of hotel doors that were locked but dotted with stickers from other travelers. With no one around I switched back to the banging and yelling technique and eventually someone appeared and led me down an alley to a house where a man sold me fuel from a shed for roughly 5-times the price I paid in Bolivia. He did happily accept American dollars but was unable to produce change in any currency.

December 23rd, 2018. Welcome to Chile!

(Train graveyard)   (Salar de Uyuni)

Chile
W.T.F.! & Other Swear Words Screamed Inside A Helmet

"The best way to spread Christmas cheer is singing loud for all to hear."
– Buddy The Elf

Christmas eve, two days before Angie was set to meet me in Santiago. I was riding the Chilean coastline heading south and running out of daylight fast. I'd been searching for a place to camp for the night and with rocky cliffs on one side and ocean on the other, the options were limited. Once the sun finally set and I was navigating by the moonlight, I spotted a track running off the road and down over the edge to what looked like a flat spot on the sand below. I stopped, turned KLaiR around, and slowly we made our way down the steep sandy hill trying not to slip and skid towards the ocean. When I finally stopped and could focus on where I was, the location was beautiful. It overlooked the ocean, was far enough down the hill no one could see me and I could fall asleep to the crashing waves below. Amazing.

In the broad daylight of the morning, the glaring obstacles were now staring back at me and all the positives from the night before quickly turned into challenges. What was a nice sandy track down to this flat camping spot was made by well-equipped four-wheel-drive vehicles, the sand was too soft to ride back up on two skinny wheels. This combined with my well-hidden position meant that no one from the road could see me or see that I might be stranded.

I sat and ate the standard oatmeal biker breakfast, wished Stanley and KLaiR Merry Kixmas, then promptly buried KLaiR up to her luggage in the sand trying to ride out. I was stuck down the bottom of a sandy hill with the sun coming up on Christmas day and no one could see me. Judging by the lack of gifts under my sand dune shrubs, not even Santa knew where I was. I spent hours trying to get KLaiRs heavy ass back up that hill; it was a nearly impossible struggle that always ended in her buried up to the boxes in the sand.

Finally, I stripped KLaiR down to the metal and plastics, removing anything with weight. Then I let most of the air out of her tyres for more traction on the sand. From here I had to lay her on her side and pull the front tyre across the hill, then stand her up and drive as far as I could at an angle across the hill while pushing her along. Then I would lay her down and drag her front tyre the other way across the hill, heave her back up then push-drive her as far as I could. I'd never wished to get to the top of a hill for Christmas before, but this wasn't your usual Christmas morning and since Santa hadn't come yet I was putting in a late request. On and on we went with the push-pull, heave-ho, scenario until finally in a sticky mess of dripping sweat with blowing sand sticking to it, we hit the pavement! This was just KLaiR & Stanley though, I then walked back down and brought up the luggage and camping gear bit by bit through the soft sand. Then I put KLaiR back together, pumped up the tyres, and rode until finding an open fuel station where I could revive myself with sugary drinks and coffee.

Christmas night was equally as memorable as I pitched a tent at a noisy rest area on the side of the highway where I was treated to a warm shower in a dirty public bathroom in the company of some lonely truckers. Ahh, Christmas memories.

With one day to go until Angie's arrival, I was so close to seeing her I could practically smell her above-average grooming standard mixing with my dirty biker lifestyle. But I wasn't in Santiago quite yet. I was just passing by the city of Los Vilos on the coast about 2.5-hours from Santiago on boxing day, things again came unwound. Sitting at a red light, it eventually turned to green and as I went to take off I could feel KLaiR's backend had a slight delay from the rest of the bike. The next light it happened again, then again. I stopped on the side of the highway to inspect the issue. It wasn't pretty.

The one fucking eBay bearing from China I had put on KLaiR had crumbled. Where the original Kawasaki bearings had lasted nearly 75,000-kilometers, this no name bearing had lasted less than 3,000-kilometers. It had broken, and all of the little balls inside had come rolling out. For God knows how long, my rear axle had been spinning directly on the metal spacers and interior where the axles slid through. The metal on metal had worn down both parts and I knew I was going nowhere. I took the rear tyre off, dismantled the parts from KLaiR, grabbed a few bags from my bike with the most important documents, and walked back 30-minutes to a small town looking for a replacement part.

Finding it nearly impossible to articulate my problem, I tried to explain that I needed a bearing for the bike and that any quality bearing would do so as long as I could just get to Santiago and sort it out there. For an hour, various men in a parts shop tried to solve my problem, but my Spanish communication wasn't clear enough to understand what they were trying to explain. Finally, a man walked in, got a part for himself, asked about my problem and said to come with him, he would help me. Like a lost puppy looking for his mum, I followed him home.

Eric Hawk, a fellow biker in his 40's walked back to his house with me and showed me his motorcycles and small workshop. He said we should hurry as it was very unsafe to leave my bike on the highway here. Great I thought, first the bearing goes, next the whole fucking bike will be gone. Eric said it would take some time to fix the problem, but not to worry we could go get the bike and I could spend the night at his home while he worked on KLaiR. I explained I was very grateful, though I needed to be in Santiago today. He said that would be nearly impossible in this situation as we did not have the correct parts here. This wasn't Eric's first time trying to fit a round peg in a square hole though.

With some various parts from the store and another bearing he had, he carefully worked away at the problem. I couldn't understand why it was so difficult to swap a bearing when Chris had changed them in 45-minutes back in Bolivia. Eric eventually showed me what the men were trying to explain. There was a small piece of flat metal that sat perfectly outside the bearing to hold it into place, a clip of sorts. This needed to come out to remove what was left of the old bearing, then go back in with a new bearing to hold it in place. Something Chris has explained to me in English back at his place. However, with my axle rubbing against the metal mine had gotten so hot they had welded together making it impossible to change. Eric worked and worked until he eventually removed all the plastic and metal from around this small metal clip and eventually fabricated a solution for me in a few hours. He said it was only a short-term band aid and I would need to replace everything in Santiago before I rode any further. I felt like I'd heard this line before.

With Angie set to arrive later that day, I arrived exhausted to a very nice AirBnB she had rented in the center of posh Santiago. I'd slept in my tent nearly every night for months, and now here I was in my own suite. It's hard to wrap your head around this unless you'd been blessed with months of waterfall showers, two meals a day from the same pot and another meal of mystery meat from a cart, fleeting cell phone service, and night after night in a tent surrounded by all your sweaty possessions. The rental had hot water, wifi, flushing toilets, a bed with a mattress, running water, a fridge, and on and on. I thought I'd died and gone to camping heaven!

After over 5,500-kilometers in 13-days, a bent rim, shock repairs, the flat tyre, nearly running out of fuel, burying myself in the sand on Christmas, the unraveling of my bearing on the highway, and the endless calamities of trying to make this deadline I was finally here and even on time! However, this moment of bliss ended as soon as it started.

I received a message from Angie. How great I thought, she must be at her USA stopover just about to board her final flight. That was half accurate.

Lining up nicely with the rest of the calamity, her message said that she would not be arriving today. Her flight had been delayed and she was spending her first day of Christmas vacation at the airport in Dallas as American Airlines was having some issues and had not landed on time to meet the connecting flight. This was not a shocker as I'd flown with A.A. a number of times and each flight had either a delay, appalling customer service, or never left the ground at all. Her personal disappointment about the delay was echoing through the phone.

This did however provide me with a one-day window of opportunity to try and fix the bike in the hopes of not delaying our trip any further. I scoured the travel forums and asked various friends on the road where I might be able to solve my motorbike problem on short notice. I was pointed to a colorful mechanics shop that was able to source the part and change it in record time. Being in Chile meant we were back in the world of for-profit efficiency like I was used to in Canada, though the customer service was a notch higher and they even fed me bbq and beers while I waited. This record time problem solving during the holidays did however cost me about 3x what it might cost in North America. Yet the problem was solved, and like another magical alignment of all the stars in the world, I met Angie at the airport the next morning, freshly showered, shaved, and with a well-running KLaiR.

(Christmas morning fun)

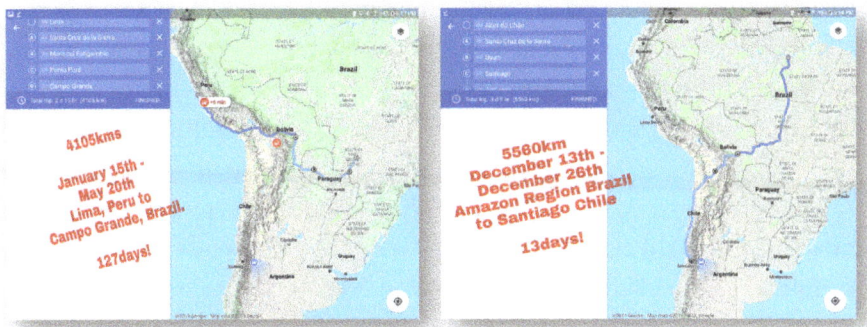

(A comparison of distance and time)

Chile / Argentina
Feening For Friends

"The connoisseur does not drink wine but tastes of its secrets."
- Salvador Dali

With the girl back on the backseat, the standard of the trip had risen once again. I went from camping in the forest and eating one pot chicken soup alone under the stars, to AirBnB's, wine tours, and dinners where you were expected to not smell like where the meat on your plate had come from. I did plead my adventure case a little and we ended up at several shitty hotels and questionable campgrounds during our two-week tour of northern Chile and Argentina. I figured since the last time Angie had come on this trip I'd driven her through a snowstorm and crashed us into the side of a mountain, that it might be better to try and keep her alive in the event this bizarre multi-country relationship lasted further than South America.

After our two weeks of touring northern Chile & Argentina, we exchanged a few airport tears and Angie was back on a plane to the Canadian winter. I was now trying to beat the clock of hitting Argentinian winter at the end of the world in Ushuaia. I again had a deadline. If I couldn't make it to Ushuaia by May I would likely never make it and would need to forfeit my goal entirely. I had roughly 3,500-kilometers to go, which I now knew I could ride in a couple of weeks, but there were more than a couple of weeks of sights to see. Between the finish line and where I was now, I knew I'd be passing through Patagonia, one of the most beautiful places on the planet and the one section of this road trip that resembles the landscape where I was from in Canada. I was dying to explore the region in-depth.

There would be desolate stretches of open road, stunning wilderness camping options, trout fishing, endless asados, glaciers, national parks, fjords, penguins, some of the best wine in the world, 3000-year old forests, and on and on. I didn't want to miss any of it, but I couldn't risk running into winter at the southern tip of South America. Antarctica is just a two-day boat ride from Ushuaia and arriving here in winter would be equivalent to riding a motorbike through Alaska in December.

Alone, I again had time to contemplate life. It's hard to know what you might miss while alone on the road. Sometimes you never even know what you've missed until it finds you. When I was in Peru and was adopted by Ruban & Karina's family for a month I had no idea I was so starved for family time. Once they swallowed me up like a long-lost brother I finally realized that so much time away from my own family had left a void in my head and heart that needed filling. Now that Angie was gone I had realized that I had been missing having any real friends to connect with. Naturally, you meet people often, but only having a short time with everyone and typically fighting language barriers it's hard to form any kind of deeper relationship.

Back in Colombia nearly a year and a half ago, I'd met some other Canadians while camping in one of Colombia's rich coffee regions. Don & Sam were a couple from Ontario who were blazing a trail down the same road as me, the difference being they were in a truck and camper with room to carry wine, weights for working out, clothes for every occasion, and even a pair of inflatable kayaks.

When I first met them it felt like Manny meets Elli in Ice Age The Movie. I finally felt like I'd met my own kind again, like we understood what it was like to be each other. I knew if I put on a Tragically Hip song, they would sing along or if I call them a hoser they'd laugh. No other country in the world would understand this bond. Canadians are like no one else on the planet. You could say this about any culture, I just understood my own kind the best.

I had kept in contact with them during the trip and now they were in Argentina and I was in Argentina, though they were a few days further south from me. Aside from Angie, Chris and bumping into Philippe a few times, I had not had another friend that I'd seen more than once, since I was back in Canada. Alone inside my helmet talking to myself and sharing moment after moment with a plastic monkey and a steel motorbike I was starving for friendship, to hang out with people I could laugh with and seamlessly relate to. Don messaged me and casually said if I was coming this way to stop by and see them. It might have been a friendly gesture like *"Hey let's go for a beer sometime",* but I was dying to have friends again. I rode like hell and met them two days later, showing up at a posh restaurant and bar in my sweaty bandana and dusty biker gear. That night we sat and drank bottle after bottle of Cafayate Malbec while savoring gigantic cuts of Ojo de Biefe (rib eye) and sucking back spoonfuls of rich dulce de leche. I left there absolutely smashed and with aching abs from an evening of laughter. They refused to let me pay for anything, though with the Argentinian currency collapsing we were delightfully surprised by how cheap top cuts of beef and world class wine were right from the source.

I spent a few days with Don & Sam and we'd met up again a few more times as we both headed south to Ushuaia. I'd spent most of my life easily making friends here and there around the planet, but over the last two years, I'd definitely spent more time alone than at any point in my life. It was just dinner and drinks with friends like I'd had with others thousands of times before this. The mental shift is so fucking crazy when you spend this much time alone though. Never in my life did I think that casual drinks with friends would be such a monumental moment, though I'd never really seen the world through lonely eyes before. I'd found an entirely new value for friendship I'd never had in my life. In reality, I'm not sure I'd ever valued friendship before this trip. It had always come too easily to consider putting any value on it as something worth treasuring. This Manny meets Elli moment meant so much to me that before finally leaving Argentina for good, I bought a bottle of that same Cafayate Malbec to commemorate the event and remind myself about what's really important in life. It still sits in my cupboard collecting dust to this day.

Don & Sam weren't the only colorful characters I met in Argentina though. Meet (insert name of new friend with no name).

Back when Angie was visiting we'd stayed in a municipal campground in the small town of Mallargue, Argentina. Just across from us was a man staying in a tent that looked like it had been there for quite a while. He had a single electrical cord from a nearby pole running to his weathered tent with a tarp over top. I'd said hello, we chatted a little and that was it. I had now circled back to this spot heading south again, but this time it was some kind of holiday and the campground was packed. With nowhere to camp I found the man and asked if I could put my tent in his space. He agreed & two kindred spirits found each other.

That night we had dinner together and the man explained his life to me. He had been living in this tent, year-round, for 7 years. Year-round, right through the snowy winters and windy summers. Before this, he spent close to a decade living on a small yacht on a river near Buenos Aires. Eventually, the 75-year-old yacht was beyond repair and he needed to abandon it to avoid waking up at the bottom of the river one day. He explained with a tear in his eye, that on the final night he and his friends chopped up the boat and had a party while he burned it and a decade of memories wooden plank by wooden plank.

Now he was living in this campground and teaching art and outdoor education to children at a small village in the mountains nearby. Wow, I thought, what a teacher to have, to learn from someone with such experience and passion, not from what the teacher had learned in books, but from what they had lived. That night we had a heavily Malbec-induced dinner together and chatted for hours with me telling him about my motorcycle adventures and my life before this. Despite my lackluster Spanish, the conversation rolled on late into the night, thanks Malbec you've taught me so much. In the morning we hugged and parted ways having never actually shaken hands or exchanged names.

Before I left he stopped me and asked me if the way I saw the world had changed on this journey? Before I had the chance to try and explain myself, he happily laughed and said he knew the answer...

(7 years in this tent. We understood each others freedom)

(Dinner for 3, wine for 13)

Argentina
The Asador

Argentina has the world's second-highest consumption rate of beef, with yearly consumption at 55 kg (121lbs) per person

- Wikipedia

Meet the Renards.

In an effort to camp my way across the Americas, I found a riverside campsite just outside the town Junin in the northern part of Patagonia Argentina, tucked just off a side road, that was just off another side road, next to a crystal-clear river on a little patch of grass, shaded by lush green trees. It was almost mythical, this oasis-like camping spot that sprung up from the barren lands before here.

Previous to this, I'd spent three weeks riding through the windy deserts and dry, eye-burning sands north of this town. I was shocked to see trees, grass, and all things green again. The main selling feature of this site is that it had enough shrubs to help block the infamous Patagonia winds, a rare and highly sought-after feature in this part of the planet. The bonus was that off to one side, someone had utilized a bank and a rock face to construct a large cooking area. No wind, excellent cooking, and pristine fishing; if Bass Pro Shops were looking for an ideal location to shoot a commercial for all things outdoor adventure, this was the photogenic backdrop.

After two nights here fishing, drinking wine, and cooking by the campfire, I packed up and went into the town of Junin some 20-30kms away. In town, I used the tourist office's ultra-slow internet to post a photo of the day and let the world know I was alive. I then picked up some biker-budget wine, tried to book myself into a sold-out guesthouse, and investigated a local campground. The campground wasn't nearly as nice as the riverside camping spot. I decided that great camping was more important than shitty wifi and turned around and drove back to the pristine river site. After re-setting up my camp, I settled back into drinking alone while catching trout and mini river crabs for dinner before passing out in a blurry haze of Malbec bliss.

The next day I was packing up just before noon to make my way further south and heard a vehicle coming down the little road towards my camp. Someone in a dusty old silver pick-up truck pulled in, noticed me, then reversed out. Stopping just a moment to yell to the car behind them; *"Too bad someone is already there, we'll go up further."* To my delight and surprise, they shouted back in plain English. Well kind of plain, it did have that American twang to it.

Two vehicles passed, waved, and slowly clogged along on the bumpy track. The third vehicle, however, pulled right down into the site and asked me some questions in fast Argentinian Spanish with elaborate hand signals to make their point more clear. In Spanish he said to me; *You are leaving, or you are setting up?* He asked again more slowly so I could understand him and I explained I was leaving and they could have the spot. I would be gone in 20-minutes or so. The driver noticed my accent and switched from Spanish to English, then asked me if I spoke English? I said yes, a lot better than Spanish! He laughed and continued talking with a more midwest American accent that was peppered with slight Spanish undertones. If I'd closed my eyes, I'd never have guessed he was Argentinian.

The midwest accent Argentinian with busy hands kept chatting and explained he and his family in this car, along with the two other groups of friends that drove by, were coming to have an Asado at this beautiful spot and would I mind if they set up while I was packing. I said it was no problem and he signaled to the other two groups to come back. First, in came this funny little van with an older American couple and next was the small silver truck that had first appeared with another, American couple. American appetites and Argentinian hospitality had both stumbled into my riverside spot for an afternoon get-together.

The Argentinian, Juan, and his wife had lived in New York state for several years. Not exactly midwest, but they could speak English as well as any

North American immigrant, and I soon found out why. Juan actually didn't stop talking for the rest of the day. He spoke English, Spanish, and with his hands to explain his point. Lucky me, as I was about to get an education on the infamous Argentinian Asado in every possible way Juan could explain it.

As everyone rolled in and set up camp with tables, chairs, snacks, and drinks, I learned they had all become friends through fly fishing. With Juan's American friends back in town, he was having a little get-together to show his appreciation for them. The couple in the silver truck, David and Joanne, introduced themselves and Joanne suggested I stick around for lunch. I think my heart skipped a beat when I was asked to be part of the bountiful meat Asado with English-speaking friends. I finished packing my camp, then positioned myself right beside Juan for the next 90-minutes.

I don't mention to Juan that I have any previous cooking experience. I don't want him to think I might know anything and therefore leave out any details he might assume I already knew. It works, and Juan talks to me like it's the first time I'd seen a fire or meat. He then proceeds to explain the whole process with his mouth, while bringing it all together with his hands. Later I find out he doubles as a teacher for one of his jobs. This would explain the clarity and precision of how he is explaining the Asado to me.

Standing in front of the cooking area carved out of the rocky bank, Juan explained he had been up at 6 am to marinate the meat in fresh lemon juice and salt, nothing else. He said that if you marinate it the night before, the salt will dry out the meat. If you marinate the meat too close to lunch, well, it won't have time to soak up the flavors. For the ten or so people attending the lunch, Juan had over 20-pounds of meat! Roughly 2-pounds per person, for men, women, and children. By Argentinian standards this was probably average, by the American Heart Association's standards, I'm sure our names should have been pre-registered for an artery cleaning the following week.

Over the next 90-minutes, the Argentinian Asado class takes shape. I slide in the occasional question about meat cuts and heat control, all while Juan keeps up the steady pace of fire construction and cooking. First, we build a fire on one side of the pit from local hardwoods. On the other side of the pit, Juan positions a grill that sits 8" off the ground. While the fire burns, Juan walks me through the various cuts of meat. A selection of beef ribs, pork ribs, brisket, loins, sweetbreads (organ part around the cow's neck in this case), blood sausage, pork sausage stuffed with cheese, and a few other cuts of less importance. He wants to put everything on at once.

Putting all the meat on at once will;

A- give some cuts a chance to rest.

B- prove how fucking good Juan is at bringing all the meats to completion at once even though they all take different amounts of time to cook.

To me, this is more exciting than watching porn.

The fire burns until the first set of coals has been created. Then Juan slides these coals under the grate-style grill to heat it up, all while the next round of wood starts burning off to the side. Once the first coals have smouldered down, and the grill has heated up, Juan pulls in the next round of coals under the grate, all while starting the process over again with the fire off to the side. Next, Juan lays out the various meat cuts across the grate, above the second round of coals. As there is no flame under the grate, there are no flare-ups, instead, you get aromatic smoke from the coals as the fat from the meat and marinade melts onto the hot bed below. Basically, Juan has taken an excellent way to cook the meat without flame and made it better by adding in the flavor of smoke.

While dealing with the sweat, smoke, and various sears, Juan explains how he sought out the butcher for these cuts based on where the butcher gets his animals, and how much he trusts the guys' expertise in general. No self-respecting Argentinian is impressing his friends at an Asado with cuts of industrial meat from a grocery store, or an underrated butcher for that matter.

Throughout the Asdao class, everyone at the party slips in for a little chat about the meat but doesn't offer up any advice or criticism. The guests explain that if it were all Argentinian men at the Asado, each one being an expert in his own right, the men would be hovering about like I am. But instead of listening, they would be offering up their personal opinions about how the cooking should be done. They would also go out of their way to heckle the Asador for things overlooked or done incorrectly based on their personal scale of expertise. I hover around Juan like he's a grilling God, this is the ideal scenario to maximize his expertise.

I meet Juan's wife, a lovely lady with shimmering dark hair, dark eyes, and dark Argentinian features. Juan's kids, the younger one about 10, who forces out a few English pleasantries to me but clearly feels more comfortable with his native Spanish. Juan's older son, about 15, who feels more confident in his English and asks me some questions about who I am and my motorcycle journey. The older son pops in and out regularly during the Asado class to watch what his dad is up to and take a few mental notes about the process. The son even spends some time right in the smoke above the fire pit coughing while he explains that he understands the process better when he's right in the smoky action. I laugh while the kid coughs and rubs his eyes, smiling the whole time.

The older American couple drops by on occasion, the husband asking a few cooking questions then disappearing. I get the impression cooking isn't his primary interest. His wife comes and offers us some snacks while we work. Then David, from the silver truck, pops in and explains he's keeping an eye on the Asador and me to make sure we look confident/competent in what's going on. Then, Joanne, his wife comes by. She seems very interested in my trip but doesn't want to come across like she's interfering with the cooking class. She asks me several times to come and join them at the table but realized I was actually interested in the cooking and not just trying to be nice. Finally Juan's cousin, a young lady whom I thought was in her 20's, who turns out to be a touch younger than me and has four kids, explains she is in town visiting for the weekend and also enjoys the Asado class.

As the 90-minutes tick by, Juan's hands, body, and mouth continue to flow efficiently and effectively back and forth from the task at hand to the instructions being given to me. But could he pull off the timing of things perfectly? The sausage was first to be put to the side only to sit and soak in some more smoke for the final 15-minutes. The sweetbreads would come off once the outside was crispy, then Juan cut them in half to get the last seer right through the middle. He said he wanted a crisp exterior and a juicy interior, but that the interior was too thick, so he let it cook as long as possible before finally cutting and quickly searing it off in the final few minutes.

Pork ribs were laid to rest above beef ribs, loins turned one final time, and blood sausage pressed firmly with a finger to check for doneness. Finally the last of the meats were treated with a splash of the remaining marinade.

Then, like a dramatic build up to the final encore of Juan's culinary orchestra, meats were removed, precisely cut, and hand-delivered table-side with a smile. The audience cheered and there wasn't a dry eye in attendance (possibly from the smoke).

We ate, we drank, and someone even made a sort of salad no one touched to pretend there were vegetables at the meal. After lunch Joanne invited me over to their place to use the wifi, take a shower, and figure out where I was going to go from here. That casual invitation turned into a bottle of wine, which turned into another bottle of wine, which turned into a night in their guest room. The other guest room had another guest, their red-headed Rastafarian fishing friend, Edwah. Much like the wine, the next night turned into dinner, which turned into a street festival of girls wearing sparkly bikinis dancing in the frigid streets, which then turned into a visit from the Mormons (another story), which lead to a dinner party upon my departure from town several days later.

I made the mistake of letting their salt and pepper hair color fool me and found that I was easily out-partied night after night by my newly found hosts. David even laughed and called me a poser as I couldn't keep up with his partying and he was nearly twice my age. This couple was in their years of retiring from work, but clearly not in their years of retiring from fun. Eventually, I acquired the title of long-lost son and left knowing when we met again I'd need to step up my game.

(The son and the Asador)

(Fine wine & fishing at the oasis camp spot.)

(The festival of sparkly bikinis?)

Argentina
Francis Mallmann

When you cook with fire, when you build a fire, it's a bit like making love. It could be huge, strong. Or it could go very slowly an ashes and little coals. And that's the biggest beauty of fire...

- Francis Mallmann

Juan wasn't the only Asador I was hoping to meet. Way back when I was camping out under the stars on the Baja in Mexico two years earlier, my friend Kyle had sent me a note. He'd seen some photos I posted one day after catching fish in the ocean then bbq-ing them on driftwood along with corn tortillas to make fish tacos on the beach.

He said he'd watched a Netflix special about this chef from Argentina. It depicted the life of an eccentric chef where they showcased shots of him cooking trout he'd caught in a lake in remote Patagonia over an open fire along with plenty of colorful cooking moments that could only have been brought to life by a masterful culinary artist. He'd said I should try and meet him. I looked up this guy's name and made a note on my list; *To Do-Meet Francis Mallmann when I get to Patagonia. The same list I had things written like; *Meet Chris when I get to Bolivia. *Find Liz' aunt in Nicaragua,* and various other sites I was told to see along the way. I'd never heard of Francis, but if he was on Netflix, someone in Argentina must know where I could find this man.

As I rode through the country I continually asked the locals if they knew of this Francis guy and where I could find him. What I didn't know was that he was an Argentinian culinary God, basically what Juan was to me, but on a national scale. In a land where they consume more meat per capita than almost anywhere else on the planet, Mallmann was the Asador Assassin. People laughed when I asked where to find him and if they knew him. After enough jokes about whether or not I was serious came back in my face, I got the impression it was going to take a bit more effort to track Mallmann down. So here's what we did…

Kyle posed as my representative as if I was some grand adventurer who was touring the world and would not have time to personally contact Mallmann. However, if my people could get in touch with his people, then Kyle would put his people in touch with me personally. Kyle then sent out a series of emails to various contacts of Mallmann's that we found online. Somehow this grand idea failed and my hype guy couldn't get a response from his people, so I went to work on my own.

I tracked down as many contact options as I could through his social media sites & restaurants, then began sending emails in English and Spanish explaining who I was and that I was passing through Patagonia on my motorcycle right now. If someone could arrange a meeting for the two of us, I'd ride over and meet him at his remote Patagonian cabin in the woods for a day or two. I pictured showing up with a few rabbits in a cage strapped to the back of KLaiR or maybe a live goat tied to the seat as an offering. I figured my global arrival along with the gift of live meat would naturally entice the cooking God; we'd hit it off and become great friends all while he showed me his master skills from the bounty I'd arrived with. I'd likely capture this all on my GoPro and turn it into a short film.

Well fuck, as you might imagine there is no feature film in the works.

Instead, I eventually hit the roadblock of his assistant Maria de Luynes (if that is her real name) who simply explained to me that Francis was not awaiting my arrival at his cabin in the woods. Instead, he would be out visiting his various restaurants around the world. If you're reading this Mallmann, the invitation is still on the table…

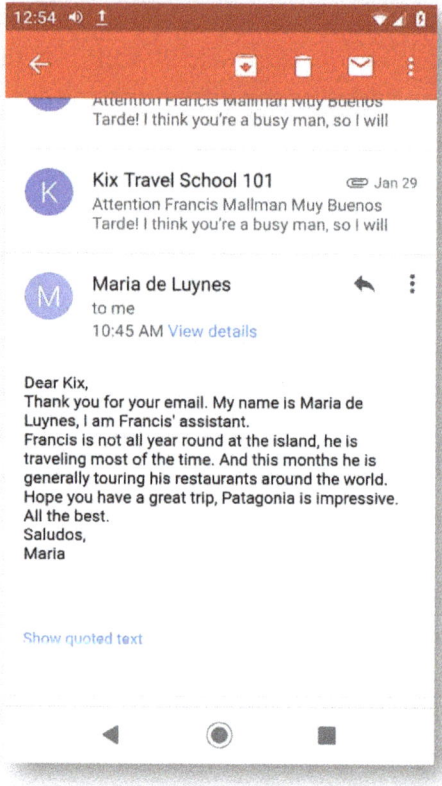

(Francis' gatekeeper, Maria)

Chile
Japanese Running Shoes

"Life is too short to be living somebody else's dream"
-Hugh Hefner

Patagonia will blow your head right off your fucking shoulders. I say this figuratively and literally. An area of over one million square kilometers, I focused on the most majestic strip that spills over both Chile and Argentina along the Andes mountain range. This section is visually stunning and holds some of South America's most treasured gems like the majestic Torres del Paine National Park, the crumbling Perito Moreno Glacier, and the 3000-year old forests near the fjords of Puerto Montt. There are not enough adjectives in the English language to accurately describe the scenery here, but breathtaking is a good place to start.

Mother nature doesn't just give up her treasures without a fight though. Not only are many areas here completely desolate and difficult to reach, but the winds in this part of the world are unearthly. A narrow strip of land dividing the South Pacific Ocean from the South Atlantic Ocean that is void of trees in many areas, the winds have nothing to slow them down. The winds hover around 20kmph most of the time, but can easily get well over 100kmph in the summer months. I spent most days leaning KLaiR into the wind just trying to keep her on two wheels. When the wind would relent for a quick breath or a large truck would pass me, our trio would nearly fall over. I heard plenty of stories from other bikers who'd been blown right off their bikes and into the ditch as well as others who had to stop and park directly into the wind and wait for things to calm before they could continue on.

Just riding for a few hours in the wind was exhausting. Then trying to find a spot to camp where it was possible to set up a tent before it was blown away or somehow keep a flame going to cook dinner became a daily challenge. If by some great miracle the wind was at our back then we made good time with great fuel mileage. When the wind was at our face it would come whistling through my helmet and clothes chilling me to the bone while trying to blow me off KLaiR's back. I could often watch the fuel gauge steadily drop as we fought our way forward. In an area where fuel stations were often non-existent for hundreds of kilometers, it was becoming less of a relaxing ride and more of a challenging mission to make it to the finish line. Some days I'd stop for a snack break and pee on the side of the road and when I'd turn my back and open my zipper I'd suddenly hear KLaiR crash to the ground as the winds had blown her over.

All the fighting to stay upright, scrambling to find fuel, camping amongst rocks and in valleys, sleeping in the frigid nights with my gas-burning stove running inside my tent for heat way up in the mountains were all worth it though. There is no place on earth quite like Patagonia and you run into the most adventurous people in this part of the globe.

I wasn't the only one headed to the end of the world, so was Sasaki Norio, but he was doing it on foot!

One night I had found a spot in some trees on the edge of a dusty road and set up my tent. In the morning I was walking to a nearby creek to wash my dishes. Here I was in the middle of who knows where and out from the trees walks a Japanese couple in well-worn hiking gear. They were taking a break from the dust and wind, a break that was required often in this area.

The girl spoke good English and the man knew some basic English phrases. I asked what they were up to and what this aluminum cart was for behind them. The lady explained that Sasaki had left Alaska 3-years earlier and was walking his way to Ushuaia. Umm, what?

She said they had met near the start of his trip in the Yukon where she was working as a tour guide for Japanese tourists who came to view the northern lights. Suddenly the tables had turned and all the strange and/or typical questions I got about my trip when I met people were launched at Sasaki.

My first question;

-How many pairs of shoes did you go through?

-Answer: I don't know, maybe 30 or 40.

Second question;

-How heavy is your cart?

-Answer: A bit heavy. It's made of aluminium though.

I kept on grilling him. Did you get robbed? How far can you walk in a day? Did you really walk the whole way? Did you get injured? I could tell he'd heard it all before. He said the biggest issue was his aluminum cart and getting it welded when it breaks or finding tyres for it. As well as carrying food, as sometimes it might be close to a week before he would come across a store.

Wow, here I was thinking I was on this trying adventure on two-wheels, then as I neared the finish line out from the woods pops a small Japanese man and his friend who had walked the same route as me in just a few months longer than I had taken to ride it. If I were to add Alaska to my trip they would have been faster than me. Somehow the world has a way of reminding me that I am not a special snowflake like I will often allow myself to believe.

(Sasaki Norio & the aluminum cart that outpaced my motorbike)

(Patagonia. The land of fire, ice, and everything nice)

Chile / Argentina
Screaming At Sunrise

"The farther one gets into the wilderness, the greater is the attraction of its lonely freedom."

- Theodore Roosevelt

Criss-crossing the Andes I ended up with 32 passport stamps from the borders of Chile & Argentina. Though both sides are beautiful for their own reasons, climates and budget would depict where I spent most of my time. For me Chile was stunning, but I enjoyed the people, scenery, and discount pricing of Argentina far better. The countries reminded me of the contrasts of neighboring Canada & America. The Chileans were more wound up and intense like Americans compared to the relaxed, Canadian-like Argentinians. I also felt like there were less stringent rules in Argentina or maybe that's because I saw fewer authorities enforcing the rules. I spent most of my days wandering the Argentinian side until the roads forced us over the border or when there were some must-see stops along the way. One such site was Torres Del Paine National Park.

I wanted to see the beautiful gems nature was hiding inside the park, but the cost of entry and spending the night (if you could find a vacancy) was the equivalent of a week or more of traveling in Argentina. I wasn't convinced it was worth it. I did learn that if you could somehow camp near the park entrance and just happened to arrive before 6 am when the workers would be starting their day at the park gates, you might miss them and unfortunately, not have the option to pay to get in. It just so happened that I found a track up into the bushes overlooking a lake near one of the park gates and set up camp there for the night.

In this part of the world it's cold, really fucking cold, especially at night. Armed with only my tent, cooking stove, and biker gear, I built a fire with bush wood, made dinner, and crawled into bed around 7 pm once the sun had set for the day. Inside the tent my whole body was shaking, It was too cold to sleep. I opted to break every rule in the safety bear camping book and strategically set up my gas-fueled stove in the vestibule of the tent where it could consume some fresh outside air while pumping heat into the tent. Naturally, if I fell asleep and it consumed more inside air while pumping out gas fumes I'd likely not wake up at all. Or if I got really lucky and the fly of the tent caught fire I might wake up in a fiery blaze!

I decided to start the stove and set my alarm for 30-minutes in case I fell asleep while it was running. The tent warmed up and I fell asleep. I slept right through the alarm and awoke two-hours later, shivering like a wet dog on a winter's night as the stove had burnt itself out from the winds. I started the stove again and set the alarm for 45-minutes. When the alarm went off, this time I woke up and turned the stove off until I awoke later in my shivering wet dog state. This cycle continued on until 5 am when it was time to roll out of my icy coffin. What I didn't anticipate is that I'd be moving like an old man with frozen joints when it was time to get up. Just taking down the tent and trying to get my cold hands to work to pack up KLaiR became a grueling task. I eventually started KLaiR and let her run until I could warm my hands on her engine and get them moving enough to continue packing up camp. Eventually, we set off to the park gates, but packing up in my frozen state had taken so long that the workers were waiting for me on arrival.

Feeling like an idiot for all my pre-planning failures, I walked inside and asked some questions about where I could find fuel. They said the closest place was way back in town far from here and there was no fuel in the park. I already knew this and had plenty of fuel. I was looking for an excuse as to why I would need to leave rather than turning around at the entrance looking like a criminal.

I wanted to spend a few days in the park and still couldn't justify to myself that trading a week's budget in Argentina was worth it to look at mountains and lakes behind an imaginary line with a cover charge. Looking like the dumbest tourist to ride a bike 50,000kms only to turn around because he missed the fuel stop, I spent the day around the nearby lakes chatting to tourists and the night at my cold bush camp. The freezing camping cycle of life-risking sleep continued and this time I woke up around 4:30 am and made my way into the park before sunrise. Unfortunately, there was no one working at this time and I was unable to pay the park fee.

Before you get all "I'd never do such a thing", I might point out this idea was definitely not my personal masterminding and if I had to decide between extending the budget of my trip or handing over my money to see a roped-off part of mother nature that was made to only be accessible to those who could afford it, I'd do it all again. If you feel otherwise, please forward me your comments as armchair activists are some of my favorite people to respond too :)

I spent the morning with the heated grips on high and trying to navigate where some of the best spots to watch the sunrise would be. Eventually, I discovered there was a walking trail that started near the back of a camping area. With all the campers still tucked inside their tents or inside cabins, I tried to ride quietly past everyone to the back where the trail began. When I arrived there was a bathroom right across from me and having not seen a flushing toilet in days, I grabbed my toothbrush and wet wipes and headed over. Once inside I found a full-blown bathroom block. I tested the shower and sure enough, hot water came pouring from the taps. Starving for sanitation I ran back to the bike and grabbed my towel, sandals, and soap. I spent the next 20-minutes in hot shower heaven. When I came back out the sun was just starting to rise.

Some of the campers had gotten up to see the sun and this beautiful pink ball of glowing sunshine started to appear between the snowy mountain peaks, up over the turquoise lake. A guy in his twenties wearing shorts and a jacket with his sleeping bag wrapped around his shoulders was so excited he started to yell and shout about how beautiful it was. He was absolutely ecstatic and I think he was even crying; he must have lived his life in a city condo. He was yelling so loud all the campers began to emerge from tents and cabins to see the sunrise. It was a comically magical moment. Freshly showered and having already been up for a couple of hours I was feeling pretty good about life too and could see what all the national park hype was about.

I ended up running into some friends I'd met a week earlier in Chile and spent the night camping with them in some bushes at the base of a mountain before continuing south towards the finish line. Torres Del Paine is definitely worth the stop. You'll need to decide for yourself if it's worth the standard cover charge or the less glamorous adventure biker entry.

(The screaming sunrise at Torres Del Paine)

(Taking a bite out of Perito Moreno Glacier)

(Can you spot the Guanaco?)

(Getting to know the locals)

Argentina
61,264kms. The End Of The Earth

"The one great thing is, I hope it will inspire people that it's possible. A lot of things in life people don't do because of the what if's... The what if's and the might be's are what make it so exciting..."

- Ewan McGregor. Long Way Round, Calgary to New York.

Are goals imaginary? Do we set them to give ourselves a sense of purpose? Do we set them to justify to others our sense of purpose? I mean really, what's the difference between the power-enraged ruler hell-bent on world domination and the guy simply existing with no hopes and no dreams? They may well both achieve their respective goals, but are eventually going to end up with one dog or another pissing on their tombstone. Is any of it worth it?

This was it, this was the crowning moment of accomplishment I'd been chasing for nearly 2.5-years from North, through Central and South America. I'd turned a 20,000-kilometer drive into a 60,000-kilometer odyssey and along the way, created more monumental stories than campfire time I will ever have to tell them. 2.5 years alone on a motorbike with a monkey leaves you with an entirely new perspective on life. The timing could not have been more or less perfect.

While crisscrossing the Andean mountains of Argentina and Chile, I was continually in negotiations with customs officials as to where to place the passport stamp. Thirty two negotiations had taken place in an effort to preserve my disappearing passport pages. Taking in as much of Patagonia as possible had its challenges.

The wind would blow in the snow, then the sun would appear, then rains would blow in, and often it would just blow in no particular direction. It had been about 7-weeks of sleepless nights shivering in my tent to get here. I'd continued to use the stove as a source of heat, shutting off the warmth and CO_2's before finally nodding off for the night. Usually waking up hours later up under my biker gear and rain pants, fully clothed, only to light the stove again to stop from shivering. At least the CO_2 was helping me to fall asleep fast.

The death of those, hopefully, replaceable brain cells was worth it though. This amazing land of stunning mountains, wild animals, bountiful fishing, and clear emerald waters whose surface was only identifiable when the winds would ripple across it. The area still felt slightly untouched as the region's infamous winds and brash winters would only allow adventurers a brief-seasonal glimpse of its beauty.

Starting in Canada those two and a half years earlier I can honestly say I was shit scared about a number of things I wasn't sure I'd be able to overcome;

Being alone - I would usually surround myself with people, parties, and activities. I had never really spent much time alone. Could I do a solo motorbike trip?

Language - I only knew enough Spanish to count to ten and thank someone for a beer. This would quickly become the primary language of my excursion.

Safety – Were all the stories I'd heard true? I wasn't convinced about the stability of the countries I'd be crossing. Would I survive?

The motorcycle - That poor motorcycle would need to deal with an inexperienced rider heading down roads that would require a cliff-face learning curve. To magnify the potential problems, my mechanical skills could be outsmarted by anyone who knew the difference between a metric and an imperial socket. Now was that a 1/2" or 13mm bolt?

Despite what had felt like a task too big to bite off with even the prehistoric teeth of my surroundings, on March 14th, at exactly 3:33 pm I arrived at the entrance of Ushuaia Argentina, the most southerly city on the planet. Actually, I arrived there after I drove through the entrance expecting a more dreamy point of entry. Then I drove around the edge of the city only to realize I'd overlooked the entrance. Then drove back. Much like a thousand destinations before it, even at the finish line I would get lost.

I'd brought a bottle of wine for the celebration, popped the cork, then promptly dropped the corkscrew I'd had for 2.5-years through some wooden planks where it will forever remain. I then requested the assistance of some scruffy hitchhikers to take my photo. Dressed in several layers of anti-wind and rain clothing that was restricting my movement to a penguin's waddle, I would savor the moment straight from the bottle of the first Malbec I'd ever purchased from a shop in my life. It seems some of my tastes had changed along the way too.

As my 5-minutes of monumental glory slipped through the hourglass, and my forced photo shoot was over, I felt empty. I mean nothing. Not a tear, not a laugh, not relief, not anything. I felt like a decorated Easter Egg, who'd had his yolky soul sucked out and the exterior painted to look like the festive part everyone was expecting.

I wasn't depressed or anything, I just wasn't feeling the sense of accomplishment one might expect after what was positioned to be a crowning achievement in one's present life. Now what? Now what the fuck do I do? After so much personal growth, I didn't want to go back to who I was. I went from being the restricted caterpillar crawling around on the ground and morphed into the beautiful butterfly floating on the wild winds over the last two years. Now I was worried that from here I might fade into the musky moth chasing a dim light in the darkness to nowhere.

I'd read this feeling, of no feeling, had been experienced by others who'd survived this multi-Americas journey before me. Really, once you've negotiated with enough shiesty police officers, walked away from crashing into a mountain, survived being hit by a dump truck, shit your pants from questionable meals, been bitten by stray Colombian dogs, had gunshots ring off outside your tent, cried your way out of the Amazon, and lost countless sleep over a girl, arriving in a scruffy tourist town that sells postcards and offers English menus felt more like a participation ribbon than all the trophies I'd been given along the way.

I needed a final sense of achievement; I needed to make it feel like I'd actually "made it".

I'd met some friends in town later that week. We went for King Crab dinner and drinks by the ocean to celebrate and share some laughs. I enjoyed sleeping in a garage turned AirBnB with CO_2-free heat that I was renting for a few nights, but it wasn't enough.

The day after the King Crab celebration I promptly left town on a cold, drizzly day and ventured a further 130kms or so southeast of the city down a questionable gravel road. The wind blew and the weather was wet and unbearable. The roads were washed out at several points. On any scale of sales pitches, this one-way road that would end at the gates of an Argentinian naval base would not interest any touristy onlooker, for any reason. Well, unless that onlooker was looking for a sense of achievement to say he'd in fact, driven as far as he could to the end of the world. For me, I was shivering with smiles the whole time!

With no one around, nothing in sight but the wind-battered flag of Argentina, and the blinking communications towers of the naval base, myself, Stanley on the handlebars, and KLaiR my trusty motorbike, were celebrating a successful journey to the end of the world. Well, maybe not KLaiR, because that bitch has put up with a lot!

That night I'd found an abandoned cabin in the woods, set up my tent inside, and froze my ass off just like old times. To think it had all started in a shed behind my house with some insulation boards glued to tin walls, an extension cord ran to a light, and a propane heater for warmth; all so I could dismantle a motorcycle I knew nothing about just to understand how it worked. Some false reassurance to know I could get there safely. Now it had ended in an old cabin in the woods with a tent pitched inside, a headlamp for light, and a gasoline-powered heater for warmth. With the motorcycle sitting out front that I had dismantled hundreds of times while still trying to understand how it worked. Maybe that motorcycle was a metaphor for my life; how many times could I take it apart just to see how it works.

October 29th, 2016 – March 14th, 2019, 61,264kms. Alberta Canada to Tierra del Fuego Argentina.

(Wine at the finish line)

(Stuffed with an old tyre tube, wrapped in tape & filled with motor oil.
Desperate times)

(Filling the shock with motor oil, again)

(Abandoned cabin in the woods at the end of the world)

Tears & Tattoos
PanAm's Final Chapter

"The plan? Drive across the Americas on my motorcycle."
- My response to my mother when questioned about what I was doing.

We met on May 1st of 2014. It wasn't her first relationship. She'd been living with a guy who completely neglected her. I mean he seemed to really like her, but just didn't have time for her.

I'd heard about her online, and when I saw a picture of her, I immediately fell in love. I mean, she's ugly, and her DNA makes her a bit lazy & slow, but it just felt right and I could see us having a great life together.

She was a 2009 Kawasaki KLR650, purchased new by a guy who had aspirations to ride off into the sunset chasing down wild adventures and living free. At 5-years old, and only 4100kms, the neglect of under 1000kms/year was wearing on him. His dreams had faded, and the motorcycle was for sale.

I knew nothing about motorcycles and tried to lowball him on the price. He was asking around $1/km driven. The ad had been up for one day. He didn't take my bait. He said to sweeten the deal he'd include an Arai helmet. I'd never heard of the brand Arai (one of the more popular/expensive helmet brands) and said I didn't care for the helmet. He was also including Pelican case luggage and mounting bars, a type of luggage I wasn't aware would fit on a motorcycle.

In the end, I bought the bike with the kit and the helmet for near asking price and loaded her into the back of my truck. The first corner I turned the bike fell over in the truck bed and cracked the front plastics. It seemed that step one should be to learn about transporting motorcycles and step two should be to purchase a set of crash bars.

That was almost 5-years ago to the day. KLaiR, as she affectionately became known, is now getting closer to maxing out her 5-digit odometer. She's had a change of luggage, holes in the plastics, a broken shock, signal light tied on with string, zip ties holding the dash on, broken speedo cable, hole in the radiator, broken thermostat, busted tank bag, frayed clutch cable, countless weld jobs, one missing cruiser footpeg, cracked windscreen, various rust, one side of the decals worn off, and a hell of a lot of stories!

From Canada to Ushuaia Argentina myself, KLaiR, & Stanley had become great friends, partners in crime, a place to vent, someone to rely on, someone to get excited with, and the way I kept referring to KLaiR as my girlfriend to everyone I met, you'd think we'd fallen in love.

From the outside looking in, I'm sure a grown man talking to a plastic monkey and a metal bike probably sounds more like I may have fallen off the bike one too many times without a helmet on and bumped my head. Life had become a little bit like Cast Away with Tom Hanks over the last couple of years, and there were days on end when I'd talk to no one other than KLaiR & Stanley. I swear, before this solo expedition had started I was cool. Now my friends were either plastic, metal, or online.

Considering the Andes crash, the Panama crash, the various places she'd fallen upside down puking gasoline across her, the bent rims in Bolivia, the blown clutch plates in the deserts of Colombia, the time I'd filled her airbox with sand in Mexico, the time I used two-stroke oil rather than engine oil in her engine in Guatemala, and endless other atrocities. She had come out of the whole ordeal with the engine running unbelievably well.

After departing from Ushuaia I had for the first time in 2.5-years, no goal. I had been toying with the idea of going to Africa and was trying to plan this around a life that had magically become intertwined with Angie who was living an entirely different life in an entirely different continent. The fact that this relationship with a real live female even existed was probably a greater triumph than reaching Ushiua on a used KLR from Canada.

Up to this point, you could say that every relationship I'd had was eventually a failure. One might argue this is the case for every relationship prior to the one you are currently in; I could argue anything about anything if I wanted. Things with the girl had developed mostly over video chats, emails, and Angie spending her time and money to come and visit me in numerous countries along the way. Our relationship was exactly the opposite of most modern relationships. Instead of meeting online and then dating, we had met in person and then started dating online.

By now I was "dating" one of the most attractive women on the planet. She had long brown hair, deep hazel eyes, the most incredible body, a warm welcoming smile, an intoxicating sense of humor, witty, and had a respectable tolerance for my bullshit but had no problem calling me out when it started to cross the line.

To outsiders, there was no debate about what choice to make. You turn and head straight for the girl that'll you'll never find in any part of the world and thank your lucky stars you found her. To the guy who's willing to abandon all worldly possessions just to live in a tent with his freedom, I was grappling with how I might continue to have both worlds, without losing the girl or the freedom.

I'd been talking about riding through Africa since the day I left. In a newspaper interview on my day of departure from Canada in 2016, I was quoted as saying *"If I can find a sponsor or a job along the way I'll go to Africa, Europe and then home again. If not, I'll turn around and drive right back."* Africa had been calling me for 60,000kms, but had never actually shown up on a plane with fresh baked cookies and a bikini to ride around on the backseat in rain, snow, and sunshine to show me just how much I meant to it.

Now some mythical force had taken over my thinking and I was trying to fight it off, much like I had for the last thirty-some-years. This time, however, I was actually considering someone else other than myself for decisions in my life. This way of thinking did not line up with any relationship previous to this. Leaving an amazing girlfriend in one country or another while I set off on a plane for a different country was not an unusual experience in my life.

Angie had been defending her relationship with the underemployed dirty biker who lived in a tent for a couple of years now and I think her justification for not settling into a more traditional relationship with a person whose family & friends might actually be able to meet or talk to was starting to wear thin.

KLaiR had suddenly begun to lose faith in our relationship too and was starting to continually break down. It was becoming equally as evident that her patience was thinning too. To piss off one girlfriend at a time is daunting, pissing-off two might be more than one man should attempt.

To say KLaiR had done more than her fair share of holding this team together since Canada would be an exorbitant understatement. The more we detoured up and down the coast on the 3000-kilometer journey from Ushuaia to Buenos Aires, the closer she was getting to the 100,000-kilometer mark, and was certainly showing her age.

At one point along the route, I'd checked my stats on the GPS and they showed an average speed of 45kms/h. This wasn't far off as I think the only time I'd ridden faster than 80km/h was in Mexico. I was the slowest person on a motorbike in North, Central, and South America.

However, KLaiR's exterior didn't look like grandma Kix had been riding her at 45kms/hr; rather it looked more like Evel Knievel had been using her as a stunt bike. The fairing was now held up on one side and lashed together with string that was fraying more each day. Various pieces of plastics and rubber were clinging to life with J-B Weld. The frame had countless weld points from countless countries holding it together. More than half of her bolts had rattled out and were replaced with various other bolts and screws. And now there were enough patched holes in her to sink a ship. Aside from the various patch jobs, the main thing holding us together was luck and I could sense a dark cloud looming overhead.

I felt like as soon as we turned north from Ushuaia to Buenos Aires that my whole mental stamina had shifted from a clear focus on reaching the end of the world to not really knowing what I was going to do or where I was headed. Everything was now a blur of indecision.

No matter what had happened leading up to Ushuaia I still had the imaginary finish line to reach and felt confident with that goal and where it would take us. Now I was sputtering around with no real direction. KLaiR felt this blurry indecision and was starting to become unraveled too. Check your thoughts people, as they magically become your reality.

Here is a copy of a Facebook post I'd made on the road up to Buenos Aires when things were spiraling out of control:

April 3rd- Radiator suddenly springs a leak. I "fix" it on two separate occasions and finally resolve that adding coolant every 3 days is easier than taking the bike apart to "fix" it again

April 6th- Thermostat stops working so I no longer have a warning as to when the bike might get too hot and start puking coolant. Surprises are fun.

April 9th- Stop for a roadside pee. Crazy Patagonia winds blow my bike over and break my GPS case. It's now taped shut and no longer waterproof.

April 11th- Rear shock starts to leak oil (the one I bought 4-months ago).

April 12th (11am-4pm)- My AirBnB host spends the day driving me around to find someone willing to work on a Kawasaki, not a popular bike brand in this part of the world. We find a guy named Trucha (Trout) with a shop full of half-dead bikes and for a $100 he "fixes" KLaiR.

April 12th (11:30pm)- Freshly fixed shock is leaking oil on the driveway of AirBnB hosts house. I feel like an ass.

April 13th- I am back at the mechanic for 12 full hours of shock repair in a smoky garage where random seals from other bikes are used to patch my leak. Trout also makes me a rebuilt backup shock made from a Chinese side-by-side. Yes, I am now carrying a full spare shock again!

April 14th (3:30 pm)- 300kms down the road and shock repair #2 begins to fail. Now oil is running on my rear tyre and splattering across all my gear as I ride.

April 14th (4:30 pm)- I turn a corner to pull over, and my water bottle holder has finally called it quits after 65,000kms and goes rolling on the ground. The aluminum has finally rubbed through.

April 14th (4:32pm) - Trying to tie the water bottle holder back on, I notice the clutch cable is frayed. It's hard to know exactly when this is going to break. Hopefully, I get lucky and it's when I go to shift gears to pass someone.

April 14th (5 pm)- My trip-meter hits 90,000kms, at that very moment the voltmeter begins to flash and no longer works properly

April 14th (5:21 pm)- My speedometer cable snaps and I no longer know my speed or how far until my fuel tank is empty.

April 14th (5:57 pm)- I decide that's enough for the day and camp in the closest sand dune I can find near the ocean.

April 15th- I realize I don't have the right tool to finish the Chinese shock conversion to put it on the bike. Instead, I repaired my current shock in the dark with an old tyre tube I acquired from the garbage of a tyre shop, tape, and the only bottle of oil I could find for sale in this vacant ghost town I'm in. Self-repair $8.

April 16th- I buy two bags of cookies and a bottle of wine then take to venting on Facebook about how hard life is!

There was a point on this trip where I was basically eating tacos, fishing, and drinking beer every day. What the hell happened?

The shock repair was done by shoving the old tyre tube in and around the spring of the rear shock to provide some type of dampening. I then wrapped it in tape in an attempt to hold the tube in place. The problem is, if I get going too fast with this hack job repair and hit a bump on the road, the rear end starts bucking like a rodeo bull and I know that at the right speed this might launch me off the bike and skidding down the highway. I have now implemented a personal top speed of 40km/h. Not one driver on the highway is impressed with me.

After a few days I'm now into a routine where I fill the leaking radiator one day, then the next day I'd spend a couple of hours taking the shock off and filling it with cheap motor oil. Then I fill the engine with the remaining oil as the faulty thermostat is causing her to drink motor oil like it's an open bar at a wedding.

The shock will hold oil for roughly 24hrs depending on how bumpy the road is, then I usually camp for a day and fill it the next day. As the oil seeps, it then drips across the rear tyre and splatters up and across all my gear as the cycle repeats itself. The more the rear end starts to bounce the closer I know we are getting to running out of oil. The catch is that to refill the shock with oil I need to find a rock or flat piece of wood big enough to slide under the center stand so when I take the bolts out of the shock, the bike doesn't collapse and fall over on top of me. This doesn't always work out as I want it to and I'm occasionally cradling KLaiR like a baby elephant when she splits down the middle while trying to move a big rock back under her that has slipped out.

The final night before reaching Buenos Aires I am flagged down by several people at red lights who are frantically waving at me. Once they have my attention they point to the pool of green coolant building up below KLaiR from the leaking radiator. I look down each time as though I'm not aware of this environmental catastrophe and pretend to look surprised. I then point out to them the pool of oil that is also leaking out the back end, as if to one-up them.

People's eyes widen as they look at the green pool, then at the black pool, then run their eyes across KLaiR's crumbling exterior and my taped together orange and yellow rain suit made from other various pieces of rain gear I once had. I nod my helmet, wave, then open the throttle until I hit my top speed of 40km/h. I've now become the Swiss rider on the crumbling BMW motorcycle I'd met just before entering Belize two years ago. Aside from the earth-killing chemicals puking out onto the ground, I'm actually quite proud of my appearance.

The more I fret over what to do about the two girlfriends the more extreme my problem-solving becomes. To keep KLaiR going I was sure I could rebuild her if I could get the parts mailed into Spain then ride off through Africa. I contacted several shipping companies, looked into options to get parts to Spain, put together an expense sheet for visas and plane tickets, and sorted out a timeline where if I landed in Spain around July, I could ride Portugal & Spain for a couple of months before arriving in Morocco after the heat of summer let up a little. To me, this was to be the adventure I was still starving for after what felt like the addictive appetizer of the Americas.

After months of planning and agonizing over what direction to take our traveling trio, I finally tossed the coin of life and set a reservation with a shipping agent to fly KLaiR back to Canada. I'd been emailing him and various other agents for over a year for the pricing on shipping into Spain or South Africa. Then I pushed all of that to the side and asked him about shipping into the USA, where I could spend a final month riding back to Canada for summer. On this day, I finally realized that shifting plans to get KLaiR back to Canada and surprise Angie at the same time might be the best of both worlds. KLaiR wouldn't be limping across the states, and Angie would likely be surprised when I randomly showed up on her doorstep after not seeing her for months.

I sent the shipping company my documents, and he was able to secure a spot on a plane to fly KLaiR into Calgary, just 300kms from where Angie was in Edmonton. That night would mark my final night of camping after living an average of five days a week in a tent for a couple of years. I was hoping it would also mark my final night of roadside repairs for a while.

That night I set up in a lakeside campground where I turned my camping stall into a mechanic shop. While other families enjoyed games and BBQ's, by the lake, I sprawled tools, parts, and oil across my table. A steady stream of campers stopped by to ask about my trip and offer assistance. Each time I explained the route and each time they looked over my patched-together life and said "WOW!", as though they really didn't believe me, then continued on. By now I can swap out a shock on a rock and patch a hole in a coolant tank with my eyes closed. I'm not overly impressed that I've had to learn to do these repairs so well.

The weather was warm again, and things were looking good as our trio made the final push into Buenos Aires. Stopping for a roadside pee & snack, I'd received an email from the shipper. He noted that my motorcycle documents were filled out incorrectly. At the last border crossing from Chile into Argentina, they had left off half of KLaiR's VIN number. The importation documents did not reflect my ownership documents and this would be a huge problem when trying to fly KLaiR out of the country. I'd dealt with incorrect paperwork at borders before, and it was always a pain in the ass. The shipper noted I would not be allowed by customs to ship the bike by plane with incorrect documents. I'd need to cross into another country, cancel the documents, then turn around and come back into Argentina getting new proper documents.

The options were:

A: Try to negotiate with the customs officials at the ferry port in Buenos Aires to change my documents. The task seemed easy enough. Just drive to the ferry dock and request to get them changed.

B: Take the ferry from Buenos Aires into Montevideo Uruguay last minute, have the documents changed at the port and come back to Argentina the next day and ship out by plane the following day.

C: Drive 320kms to the border town Colon and cross into Uruguay then cross back. This would be a pain in the ass as I was now traveling at a top speed of around 40km/h on the highway with the broken shock wrapped in a tire tube.

D: Show up at the airport with the documents as is, and see what happens. I was told they might still refuse me as they had others with the same problem. Though a $100USD bill in new condition tucked in an envelope had also been known to expedite the process.

I had 48-hours to solve the problem before confirming shipping and dropping KLaiR off at the airport.

I first went to the ferry port to check the price of tickets for the return ferry. I assumed about $20-$30, and I would get to see the city of Montevideo as a bonus. A last-minute return ticket with the monopoly ferry company would be about $400! As this was my original monthly budget for this trip, I was having a rough time swallowing the figure.

OK, the customs guys would be my next best option. They are usually friendly and helpful in this part of the world. The workers at the ferry port found one guy who could translate Spanish for me with the big boss. They said my documents didn't matter and if it were them, they'd let me in. I explained I was flying the bike out of Argentina into Canada and the rules were more strict. Either way, they said no they would not change my documents without leaving the country. I begged them to help me, they said no. I was crushed. I walked away with tears in my eyes as I knew my time and options were limited and if this didn't work I'd potentially lose KLaiR or miss the booked flights for her and me.

I resolved to spend the $70 on fuel rather than $400 on the ferry and drive to Uruguay. It was too late to set off for the day, and I headed back to my dank hotel to pack for one last road trip and another final, final night of camping. 48-hours until bike departure.

That night I'd met with Luis, a voluntary parts mule I'd met online who'd smuggled KLaiR in a thermostat, clutch cable, filters, and bearings from the USA to Argentina on his vacation. This was going to help me get started riding through Africa, the plan I'd originally decided on when I contacted the parts mule a few months back. You meet the most helpful people on the internet!

Luis and I had dinner, drinks, and shared stories, but I felt too guilty to tell him my plans had changed to ship back to Canada after all his hard work smuggling in parts for KLaiR to continue the road trip.

The next day I set off for the 320-kilometer border run at an average speed of 40kmph. My slow ass speed, plus pee breaks, plus snack breaks, plus stopping to top up the motor oil and check the shock oil and coolant, meant the 320-kilometer drive took me 8.5 hours. By the time the border formalities were finished, I had decided to camp the night in Uruguay. I set up camp at dusk, then cooked dinner and drained KLaiRs coolant to replace the thermostat in the dark of night using the light from my phone. This would solve the burning engine oil problem.

Making my way back to Buenos Aires the next day with the correct documents, I received a message from a man who'd seen a Facebook Marketplace advertisement I'd posted three months ago to see if there would be interest in buying KLaiR for a reasonable price. I'd forgotten all about the ad as no one had responded. I jokingly told the guy the truth about her condition, shock, leaks, and teething problems knowing that she was too far gone for anyone to purchase her, and explained I would be shipping her out in the morning. He seemed unphased by her dilapidated state and still wanted to see her. Shocked, we arranged to meet when I got back to the city that night.

Back in Buenos Aires I quickly washed off the oil splatters and dust from the road and met the man explaining everything about the bike. He was impressed with my journey and to my surprise, he was impressed with KLaiR. He could clearly see the tire tube wrapped around the shock, the liquids on the ground, and had read through my Facebook posts noting my list of recent ailments. Still, he was intrigued by her stamina and putrid beauty. He said to me in English, *"If I understand correctly, the motorcycle is like your girlfriend?"*. I laughed and said yes.

I had listed her at the price of $2800USD, not much less than the purchase price in Canadian dollars 5-years and 90,000kms earlier. I really didn't want to sell her, but with the inflation crisis and import taxes in Argentina, I knew most imported goods were selling for 4-5x the price they would in North America where KLaiR was worth nothing more than memories.

After 2-hours of explanation and negotiation, he offered me $1500USD, or $300 less than my shipping cost and $1500 more than she could be sold for in Canada. Not that I was ever planning to sell her once she was home. It was more likely she would become a large centerpiece in my living room.

I said no on the premise that the emotional value was far greater than his offer and I'd rather ship her home than sell her cheap. We talked some more and eventually parted ways.

It was now 16-hours until the shipping confirmation deadline and 36-hours until KLaiR would be on the plane.

I went up to my Airbnb to organize my gear for the flights. Later, around 11 pm, the man messaged me with one sentence, "I'm in love with your motorcycle." I laughed, and we bantered back and forth about KLaiR until 2 am. I dismissed his final offer of $1900USD — more than my cost of shipping, and more than she would ever fetch in North America.

At 10 am, just as I was starting my day, I sent him a note saying I was meeting the shipper in 4-hours to give him my money for the shipping fee. The man said if he could come up with another $100, he would meet me at 12 pm. I said no, and thanked him.

That fired up some more negotiations, and for another hour we talked and talked, until the axe finally fell. I agreed that if he arrived by 1 pm with $2200USD I would sell him KLaiR.

I went outside at 1 pm and found a note on a pink piece of paper taped to KLaiR's fairing that was written in English. Someone else had heard she was for sale and wanted me to contact them right away. I sent a photo of it to the potential buyer I'd been talking to. He said it wasn't anyone he knew and someone must have seen us talking the day before. He said I could call them if I thought I'd get a better price. I said this was all too emotionally taxing for me, and I didn't want to go through negotiations again. At 1:30 pm (I've never met an Argentinian on time) the man arrived at my Airbnb. True to his word had $2200USD or roughly $3000 Canadian at the time of exchange, all in marked bills noting each serial number right from the bank to prove that they were real.

I put on my helmet and hopped on KLaiR one final time to ride her the two blocks to his friend's garage. At the garage, two men greeted me and were impressed by what they had heard about my adventure and the look of KLaiR. They began asking the usual travel questions. I stopped them and said I was unable to discuss the trip right now. I took a photo with the purchaser, handed him the keys, and burst into a mess of streaming tears and dramatic sobbing. It looked like I was attending my own funeral, in a sense, it was the death of a part of me.

The three grown men looked at me amazed, though they seemed to understand my attachment. I felt awful. I felt disgusted with myself. I felt like I had literally taken my best friend and sold her to the highest bidder. I'd bought and sold dozens of vehicles before this, but never a friend, never like this. I could have been hit by a bus right there on the road and had them steal KLaiR from me in an unconscious state and I would have felt better about the situation.

I said I had to leave and the men just looked at me and said nothing. The guy who bought KLaiR explained to me that she would be with a good family and he would look after her. I hugged KLaiR, kissed her faring, and walked away with my helmet sobbing uncontrollably. I felt ashamed. I felt like I had abandoned her. It was the most awful moment I could ever remember. I felt like I had betrayed one of the most important people in my life. I was no longer human. I had sold my soul.

On my sobbing walk back as I got close to the Airbnb, a man had looked me in the eyes as I passed him as if he knew me. Then as I passed, he called out my name. I knew no one in the city; it was all very bizarre. He said; *"Hey, you're Kix. I was to meet you today to look at a tent you are selling."* In my emotional disarray, I'd forgotten all about the meeting. He asked if I was OK? I explained I'd just sold my motorcycle. He looked sympathetic and said he felt the same about his motorcycle.

That night I purchased a bottle of motorcycle branded wine and bought three empanadas. One for me, one for KLaiR, and one for Stanley. Then I sat in my room and got drunk with Stanley while I ate everyone's empanadas. I was texting Angie while Stan and I were hanging out, but I couldn't tell her about what had happened. To her, I sounded upbeat like everything was fine. Just like so many nights before this, I would share some of the most intimate moments of my life alone with plastic friends and a bottle of wine.

A few days later, before kissing this adventure goodbye, I found a tattoo shop, explained in my best Spanish what I had been up to and that I would like a tattoo to commemorate the events. A couple hundred dollars were handed over along with an hour of my life spent wincing and trying to take a few quality selfies and I was on my way with a map of the Americas and 61,264 etched down the middle of the landmass.

Having booked my flight last minute to fly into Calgary with a no luggage promotional fare, I now needed to switch and purchase oversized luggage and arrange a rental car from Calgary to Edmonton. That week I was living a lie about where I was and what I was doing. Then the time had come and the following week I flew across the Atlantic to London England, then turned around and flew back across the Atlantic to Canada, to pick up my rental car and drive across the province to surprise Angie that evening. This multi-continent route was the fastest way I could get home for under $1000.

As you can imagine, the plane was delayed, the rental car wasn't there when I arrived, and my plans to see Angie by dinner had faded to trying to make it before she went to bed. Some 33-hours of travel time later I arrived on her doorstep.

I slid KLaiRs license plate under the door and knocked. No response, I knocked louder. Still nothing. With my camera ready, I banged on the door one final time and with KLaiR's license plate in hand, jaw hanging from her face, and pajamas on. She stood confused, or maybe that was excited? at the doorway. I handed her Stanley and said she could have my heart.

(The last supper)

(The license plate…)

The Bonus Chapter
I Wasn't Going To Write

Motorcycle Crash
Back To Whose Reality?

"It's a funny thing coming home. Nothing changes. Everything looks the same, feels the same, even smells the same. You realize what's changed is you."
- Benjamin. *The Curious Case Of Benjamin Button*

I wasn't going to write one single word about the "motorcycle crash". I figured it was all in my head and no one could relate. Then one day feeling trapped in a condo in the middle of cold Canadian winter with no sign of freedom in sight, I was reading an article written by a guy who'd done the same trip as me through the Americas, then he finished off my dream of riding a motorcycle through Africa too. What he wrote about coming back to life in America echoed what was going on inside my head and world back in Canada. He was finding it extremely difficult to reintegrate into society, so it wasn't just me? Another day I had read a post on the popular international motorcycle travel forum Horizons Unlimited. Someone was conducting a survey about the after effects of long-term travel, some of the questions included looked like this;

Which situations or feelings do you feel contributed to your depression? (Select all that apply)
- Once my trip was over, I didn't have anything to look forward to
- I had a hard time reintegrating into society
- I had a hard time reintegrating into my old life
- My trip made me feel as if I had been wasting my life

- *I was upset I had waited so long to travel*
- *My trip induced a severe shift in the way I viewed the world and made me question people's priorities*
- *My trip induced a severe shift in the way I viewed myself and made me question my priorities*
- *My old priorities seemed pointless / like a waste of time*
- *I no longer related to my friends / family / partner*
- *My old life seemed stale and uninteresting*
- *I felt as if no one cared or missed me when I was gone*
- *I felt as if everyone else "changed" while I was gone, but I was still the same*
- *I felt as if I "changed" while I was gone, but everyone else was still the same*
- *All I could do was think about my trip / traveling and was unable to function "normally"*
- *None of the above*
- *Other*

There were over 110 comments on that post. Responses like:

"RTW the last 6 years and counting. Heading down to Mexico next month on a different motorcycle... This sounds interesting and definitely not brought up in normal travel conversation."

"We don't talk enough about what happens after travel. I wasn't quite the same after 2 years on the road."

"Spent a year on the road, riding from the UK to Australia ... am happy to help as I know from first-hand experience, that post-travel syndrome is a 'thing'."

It was mildly comforting to know it wasn't just me who could not fit in back at home, but so what, that doesn't make the empty feeling of fleeting dreams go away.

Physically I'd had two significant motorcycle crashes between Canada & Argentina. The first was en route to catch the boat that would ship KLaiR from Panama to Colombia when I tried to pass a slowing dump truck with no tail lights on the inside shoulder just outside of Panama City. The second was with Angie on the backseat after traversing a snowy mountain pass in the Andes of Peru. After all that madness, it was once the snow finally melted away on mostly dry roads that the three of us met the pavement before KLaiR went skidding off into the mountainside.

Each of these crashes scared the shit out of me and I thought they were each the end of the trip, though they could have been worse, they could have been the end of a life. These events could have easily been chalked up to part of the adventure, or even assumed that they would eventually happen during such a long trip through roads slightly less desirable than those in North America.

The final motorcycle crash had a deeper and more lasting effect than the first two. Again I was completely caught off guard, again I wasn't prepared, and again I was lucky to escape with my life.

In the summer of 2016, I was running a half marathon every weekend trying to get myself in optimum shape for the road trip challenges ahead. I'd lost almost every possession I owned that was related to my businesses and sold off almost all of my personal belongings. I was sleeping on a blow-up mattress in an empty house, and spending most of my free time in the make-shift shed turned motorcycle workspace behind my house. My life had become incredibly focused on one task – making it to the end of the earth by motorcycle.

There were maps of the world in every room of my house and on one large laminated map in my bedroom, I had a vague route drawn in felt marker from Canada to Argentina. Taped to this map were newspaper articles of people who'd done similar adventures. One article was from the September 3rd, 2014 issue of the Canadian Press. It was about a Brazilian man who'd done a similar route on horseback. Filipe Masetti Leite rode a horse along with a packhorse from the Calgary Stampede fairgrounds in Calgary Alberta all the way to his home in Espirito Santo do Pinhal, São Paulo Brazil. He made it home with those two horses plus one more he'd acquired, in two years. Incredible!

I was so intently focused on the goal of riding my motorcycle across the planet that all of my energy was going into the project and I was looking for all the evidence I could on how to make it possible.

I wanted to be fit enough to endure long days, have enough money to fund the travels, and have a good enough understanding of KLaiR to know how to deal with most issues that would arise. Looking back, it's shocking how obsessively focused I was on bringing this goal to fruition. I would have moved into the shed with KLaiR if I had to.

Within a few weeks of departure, I was already sleeping in my tent on the beaches of Mexico fishing for dinner and scavenging for driftwood to build a fire and cook with. The further south I went, the more the challenges came; the more I learned how to deal with them as each one presented itself. Life was too unpredictable to worry about anything further than a few days ahead.

At any moment along the course of this incredible adventure, I might be scuba diving in crystal clear waters off the Colombian coast, working on an organic coffee farm in El Salvador, trout fishing in the wilds of Patagonia, hiking into historic Machu Picchu, taking selfies with penguins not far from Antarctica, spending Christmas Eve liquored-up with the locals at a Mexican strip bar, waking up in the hillside homes of humble farmers in Bolivia, fending off corrupt officials in Nicaragua or hugged by welcoming officials in Bolivia. I might be sleeping beside a lava-spewing volcano in Nicaragua, rediscovering myself on the other side of Ayahuasca in the magic of the Amazon rainforest in Brazil, farming rice and picking nuts with indigenous families in the Amazon rainforest of Ecuador, being nursed back to health by my new family in Peru, eating cow intestines from a bucket on the roadside in Bolivia, or negotiating each day in a foreign language. Hell, even when I thought I had half-ass mastered Spanish, I'd find myself trying to talk to locals who were speaking Quechua or another regional dialect and I'd need to start from zero again. Everything, every single day was its own challenge.

The everyday tasks of just buying groceries or finding fuel were a small challenge of their own. Not knowing the currency, not knowing the fruits & vegetables I was purchasing, or not knowing if I was allowed to buy fuel because I was a foreigner. Just having a friend to meet up with and visit on the road was becoming an exciting and monumental moment. Nothing was as easy as the life of "*Free Two Day Shipping*" and instant gratification in the life I'd wandered far away from. I had started to resent aspects of the world I'd left behind and the people who were so blessed to live blissfully in such an easy life, being completely unaware of it. Though I knew it was me who had changed, not them.

One of my biggest fears pre-departure was if I could spend so much time by myself. It's one thing to meet new people and share small snippets of your trip in a broken language but to have an actual friend in the flesh, now that was a welcome treasure. By now most of my "friends" were entirely online. I worked online, I got my travel information online, and I shared stories online.

This sought after human connection was growing stronger and Angie's bi-yearly arrivals became well planned for events that I was crossing continents for. Even reuniting with people I'd connected with on the road was becoming more looked forward to than Christmas. I'd literally driven across the country to meet up with Chris at Bolivia Motorcycle Tours or to reunite with people like Don & Sam. When was the last time you entertained the idea of driving across the country to go for dinner with a friend?

Each of life's days on the road was met with an adrenaline hit of excitement. Moments like eating dinner with a local or seeing a pink river dolphin that I think would be the pinnacle of any incredible story for most travelers on a two-week escape; this was now my everyday life. I was overwhelmingly hooked on the lust of continual adventure and it was being spoon-fed to me in doses that had me forever craving it more and more. I was a junkie, a road junkie, with an insatiable lust for adventure.

Then, like that life-threatening moment in Peru when KLaiR was sent skidding into the mountainside, life stopped, dropped, and it felt like I had crashed into a mountainside again.

The second day I was back in Canada, I was at Angie's house and was already freaking out about what to do with my life. I purchased a whiteboard and called an emergency meeting with her. I scribbled out my goals for the future and asked Angie what hers were? Then we talked about what our goals were and proceeded to write them all down. Two days earlier she thought I was Tango Dancing in Argentina, and now I was standing in her kitchen telling her we needed to write down our goals and make a plan!

Mine were a series of challenges I'd been thinking about on the road and now wanted to make real. It read something like this:

- Write a best selling book
- Create a Netflix show about global motorbike travel

- Drive across Africa
- Own a house in Baja Mexico
- Start a travel stories podcast
- Start doing speaking gigs
- Start an online business selling wine, travel gear, coffee, clearance items, or whatever I could to fund adventures

Angie's a touch more private than me so I'll leave her goals and our goals off the list.

I was feeling quite certain that I would be able to write a book in a few months, source funding for a Netflix show, and be on the way to Africa by the next fall. This would give me about a year to get organized. I had been feeling a bit lost without goals since Ushuaia and was now scrambling to get to work on what was next for me and next for us.

I arrived back in Canada in May, by September the goals I'd confidently written on the whiteboard were floundering and my main new goal was to look for some sort of non-committal employment. By November I'd gained about 15 pounds. In December I'd flown to Portugal to hang out and hopefully do some motorbiking, then meet up with Angie for Christmas in Italy where she was working at the Deaflympics. On December 27th we were engaged on Juliet's balcony in Verona Italy. By February I officially had credit card debt again for the first time in years. I'd managed to live off a poverty budget for nearly 3-years and have the time of my life, now I was struggling just to pay rent. Angie would try to cheer me up any way she could and one way was by finding things on T.V. I might be interested in watching. One show she suggested was called "The Kindness Diaries". It was about a guy who drives a VW Bug from Alaska to Argentina. I could only watch one episode a week as I found it too hard to relive the moments through someone else's eyes and could typically be found crying through the last half of each show. Ohh man, I couldn't even sit through a travel show on NetFlix without having a mental meltdown, let alone try to focus on creating a travel show they might buy.

The doldrums of mundane life had hit me hard in the mid-Canadian winter, a winter I'd managed to avoid for three years now. Living in a small city condo and staring out into winter every day were quite literally killing me and I was at the point where I was finding it difficult to relate to people in my day-to-day world. I picked up odd jobs and felt like I had nothing in common with anyone I'd meet. There is nothing wrong with having a family, settling into a career, enjoying going to your job, investing in your retirement savings plan, or meeting up with friends for cocktails after a long week at the office. This life can be amazing and people are so happy doing it. This life just wasn't for me.

Every time I talked to anyone, I felt like I was trying to downplay my previous couple years of excitement and tried to act excited to talk about the weather, the news and regular topics people converse over. I kept this mind-numbing lifestyle change to myself and said nothing about it to anyone. I feel that either telling your friends how boring you think this life is or bitching because you were no longer navigating the planet on two wheels would have not been met with warm and welcome understanding. I believe these friends are referred to as assholes. I'd just keep my mouth shut, write my book, and each time I write my book, I'd die a little more inside.

In the months leading up to my original departure, I began to list each day three things I was grateful for. I'd never done this before with much success because it would last for a few weeks and I'd slowly forget to write them down each day. On the road, I found three things every day that I was grateful for and when my phone reminder would go off each day at 8 pm reminding me to write them down I'd do it. If I was asleep, busy or my phone was dead, I'd make up for it a day or two later and fill them in. Sometimes I'd wake up in the middle of the night and roll over in my tent, grab my phone and write them down before falling back asleep. I never missed writing down three things I was grateful for, for nearly three years. The day I landed in Canada I'd somehow forgotten all about this grateful act and one day realized I hadn't written down anything in months. Such a subtle mental shift in life, but I never did it again.

On the road, I might meet up with someone and share a bottle of $2 wine around a campfire and discuss how they'd been blown off the road in Patagonia, or where they'd broken down in the jungles of Brazil and been rescued by the locals. We would discuss how they'd negotiated with border officials for entry, how they'd slept under the light stars in the wilds of El Salvador and navigated the roads around earthquakes and protests in Central America, these were my people. Life was so good it had been published in various magazines and online publications, it finally felt like I was living my dream life. To me living in a tent, fishing for dinner, and shitting in the woods was magic, to others, it was a living nightmare.

I'd suddenly lost all of that and my spoon-fed travel addiction had been cut off, cold turkey. Or in this case, cold Canada. Even the European Christmas adventure couldn't fix me. I had experienced such a steady state of challenges and highs that an amazing European adventure for 3-weeks felt too easy. Where was the challenge, what was wrong with me?

Picturing scootering through Portugal, waking up in beautiful oceanside villages of Italy, getting engaged on Juliet's balcony in Verona, and waking up to the most beautiful woman on the planet near Lake Como for Christmas and not filling with an overwhelming sense of excitement. I was by all standards of measurement, post-travel depressed.

Mid-winter I'd spend most days walking down the road to the local coffee shop to write adventure motorcycle articles for my quazi-employer for the last year or two in Vietnam. Once a week I'd go help move furniture for a company to get me out of the house. Angie would usually come home and I'd be on my computer in the same place I was when she'd left. By now I wasn't even looking up when she left or when she came home. I felt like the shell of the excited person she'd met several years earlier. It was terrible.

Now picture trying to explain to your perfectly fantastic fiancé that you want to be 3000-miles away in a tent eating ants you found on the ground (this happened) while shivering yourself to sleep as opposed to right here next to her each day. I could literally see her heart break and come melting from her eyes almost every week when the cycle of my newfound misery would bubble to the surface again. I was addicted to the road and trying to wean myself into a life I'd spent the last several years running from; it was now more than just my quiet little problem. It felt awful; I think it was worse for her.

I can't foresee what the future has to offer, and I'm happy for that. By the time you will have read this book, the world will have changed entirely. The planet will have experienced a global pandemic halting life and travel for the entire populated globe, something that is likely to change the way the world interacts with each other for quite some time.

I will have finally finished this book and become a published author. I'll have started a successful new company. I'll have gotten a new motorbike and planned new adventures. I'll have married the girl who left her heels and king-sized bed behind for boots covered in baggies to keep the rain out and nights on a blowup air mat just to see a volcano spew lava in the dark of night. I'll have another new outlook on life and probably be looking to reinvent myself again. Most importantly of all, I'll have hopefully inspired you or others like you to take a chance on a big goal or achieving something important to you whether travel-related or not. Knowing that you can take comfort in seeing that budgets are the least of your worries and people are good everywhere.

The public goal was always Ushuaia, "The End Of The Earth". Secretly though, I just needed to prove to myself that I could do it, that I could make it. The goal could have been a master's degree, a healthy family, a wealthy global company, running further than anyone before me, a Guinness record, retiring at 30. For me, for now, it was "The End Of The Earth". I'm happy the earth is a circle because you can never reach the end...

Bonus Stories

Trip Stats, And Other Notable People

I couldn't resist contacting this guy.

I couldn't resist trying to get in contact with the guy who'd originally sold me KLaiR. I wanted to tell him I was able to fulfill his dream of riding that KLR off for an adventure. And so, I tracked him down. Here is the email I sent him:

Hey Chris, I'm hoping that this is still your email address.

I bought your KLR back in 2014 & if I recall, you had watched the Long Way Round documentary and were inspired to buy the KLR and ride the world.

Well, Sir, you made an excellent purchasing decision.

I'm just writing my final story about riding your bike from Canada to Argentina and felt compelled to email you!

She made it to every country in the Americas except Venezuela (they are having some problems right now). She was also featured in various online articles from ADV Magazine, to NerdMotorcycle.com, a German motorcycle calendar, a Couple of Canadian newspapers, and Our Canada next month.

I affectionately named her KLaiR and at just under 100,000kms she retired to a nice family in Argentina a couple of months ago.

Thanks for the great motorcycle, she did an AMAZING JOB!

Kix Marshall

*I attached a few photos as evidence :)

REPLY: *Thanks for the update. That is possibly the coolest thing I have ever seen. That must have been such a great trip, and I'm glad she found a new home.*

BTW. I have an 06 BMW 330i I'm willing to sell if you want to drive it the other way around the world.

Take care

Chris

Maintenance List:

- Front Tyre Changed to "Vee Rubber" from factory one at 17,006kms.
- Front brake pads changed at 17,006kms,
- Doohicky Done 20835 kms
- Frame Bolt Upgrade (drill through) 20903 kms
- Air filter cleaned 20,900kms
- Rear Tyre changed from Shinko 705 to Shinko 705. 21,144kms (do the part at the valve stem 1st, lined up with the orange circle)
- Rear tail light changed to LED 21329kms (running light was burnt out)
- Skid Plate installed 22850kms
- Handguards installed 23001 kms
- Rear shock Progressive 465 installed 23210 kms
- Back up clutch cable ran, not installed for use 23210 kms
- Dash Lights LED $14 Princess Auto installed 23290 kms
- Speedo Cable $20 Universal Cycle installed 23290 kms
- Center Stand Installed 24120 kms
- Progressive front suspension and Fork Oil change (10 grade) 25006kms
- Back Up Clutch Cable Installed 25140kms
- Cup Holder 25196 kms
- Fuel Holder Mounted In Case 25205 kms
- Oil Holder Mounted Outside Case 25205 kms
- Front 15T Sprocket, Rear 43T Sprocket, Chain 25321kms

- Oil changes 19400kms, 21144, 24657kms, 29012kms, 33184kms, 37591kms (wrong oil), 38371kms , 41646 kms, 46138kms, 48500, 52357, 57400kms, 61836kms, 65903kms (no doohicky), 70860kms (did doohicky), 746001kms, 80578kms, 86287kms
- Front tyre 31725kms "Pirelli Scorpion". Replaces "Vee Rubber".
- Broken luggage holder welded and missing bolt 34685kms
- Rear Tyre 36326kms "Vee Rubber" Replaces Shinko 705
- 42573kms shim check 3x good, rear left max tight.
- Rear tyre 43723kms Shinko 705 (Cartagena Colombia) replaces Vee Rubber
- Rear braided brake line 45191kms
- Clutch cable, carb cleaned, air filter 48200kms
- 48500 kms new clutch, oil changed, coolant changed, raising link install
- 52357 kms front tyre change to Pirelli MT60 from Pirelli MT60, oil changed
- 55136 kms: rear tyre changed from Shinko 705 to Michelin Sirac. Handlebars new, oil seal in water pump changed.
- 60200 kms shims adjusted to spec
- 61542 kms rear sprocket changed for new crappy one
- 64236 kms front sprocket changed for new crappy one
- 67003 kms NEW x-ring chain 520 EX (AM brand). 16T front sprocket (Sunstar). 43T rear sprocket (Sunstar).
- 67008 kms Uni Air Filter installed
- 67026 kms 12V/USB front power & inside the box rear USB installed.
- 70014 kms rear tyre changed from Michelin Sirac to Rinaldi Knobby & new 4mm Fly racing tube.
- 70014 kms front tyre Pereli changed (still good) to Rinaldi knobby.
- 71783 kms Refurbished rear shock with previous progressive spring
- 74601 kms Air filter, front tyre switched from Rinaldi back to used Perelli, bearings all around

- 75094 kms rear tyre from Rinaldi to Leverin Dual Sport, Rinaldi tube
- 80578 kms Front tyre changed from Perelli to Bridgestone Trailmax, New Front Brake Pads
- 82907 kms. Brake fluid changed front & rear
- 83330 km clutch cable changed
- 84538kms Spark Plug Changed
- 86286kms rear tyre changed from Leverion to Kenda.
- 86287kms Chain, sprockets, coolant
- 91485kms Thermostat
- 91678kms? (Gauge broke) 2200kms?
- Around 96,000kms when sold, gauge was broke for awhile, hard to know exact number

Less-Documented Maintenance

- Sandals #1 glued with J-B weld. Mexico.
- Camera #1 placed on a tripod on the beach for a group photo is hit by a wave and succumbs to a saltwater death. Mexico.
- Broken tent poles taped and re-taped. Nicaragua.
- Phone #1 suffers a sudden power outage then a surge. Phones fried, losing all my photos, data & contacts.
- Boot soles screwed together. Colombia
- Sandals #2 taped together. Peru.
- MSR stove catches on fire in my room and the fuel line attachment breaks while I throw it out the door. I find tiny broken plastic bits in the dirt after 2-days of searching and "fix" with J-B Weld. Peru.
- I'm now keeping twist ties and string I find to repair things, Peru.
- A cheap sprocket welded to a washer then bolted on the bike, Bolivia
- Camera #2 is the victim of a pickpocket theft in a busy market. Bolivia.

- Countless frame and luggage mounts welds in various countries
- GPS held together by tape starting in Ecuador
- Sandals #3 fell off the bike on the highway, Argentina
- Tent door number 1 was now splitting at the seams. Only using tent door #2. Chile.
- Sandals #4, camera #3, phone #3, & jacket #2 arrive at the end of the world and back to Canada.

The Point

You made it to the end, again, congratulations! I was never fully sure that I was going to make it to the end of writing this book. However, I had one main goal in mind that I'd hoped to pepper throughout these pages. The point, the reason, the why, the drive, the underlying assignment of it all.

Why did I write this book, really, why?

Sure, it was a goal of mine to write a book. Sure, there are a lot of great stories I love to share and I enjoy highlighting the characters of the world. That wasn't the main point of penning this all together though.

At one point while writing this I was listening to a YouTube series of motivational people giving speeches and interviews about their lives and some of the incredible accomplishments they had achieved. Some people had build up incredible sums of money, some had conquered a number of the worlds greatest fitness or exploratory challenges, others had been able to take themselves from nothing or the edge of suicide to reinventing themselves into greatness and helping others to do the same.

As these stories and interviews wrapped up I was always left with the warm fuzzy feeling that anything was possible. Then, at the end of one incredible story the video cut to a commercial break where YouTube then generates a commercial based on the audience. The commercial audio suddenly became louder and those in the commercial were displayed in short video clips doing incredibly exciting activities and briefly talking about how their wishes were finally coming to reality. *We can do anything we want... We can finally relax... We can travel the world... We can live life to the max... Now that we won the lottery.* What a bunch of fucking bullshit.

The message hit me like a wet fish in the face. This was a reminder that if you are waiting on some outside force or vast amounts of money to one day capitalize on your dreams, those dreams are already dead.

If I could lay out one main point of importance here that I truly hope you picked up on as the pages turned, it's that dollars do not translate into dreams, action does. Pick the goal, work on it, and magically the money or whatever else you need will appear. I don't know why, I can't explain it, it just happens. If you're looking to send me hate mail because you closed your eyes and wished for a trip that never came, you can get bent and mail the letter to yourself. If you're looking to take action with the unwavering doubt that it can be done, then I look forward to hearing about it.

For me it was a road trip to the end of the world. To get there I just needed to lose nearly everything I owned, then set off with an old bike, used gear, a $20 tent & an $12/day budget. But I made it & so can you. I have "won the lottery" several times in my life, but it did not translate into $43-million suddenly making everything I ever wanted possible. It meant a wildly unimaginable event became possible and that the world occasionally saved my ass.

What's your goal? What's standing in your way? What do you need to do to achieve it?

Just write it down, pick a date, and work out these steps to achieve it. No one has ever reached their end goal by starting in the middle and worrying too much about the end. Did your parents start raising you like you were eight years old when you were born and start picking out your graduation shoes when you were 12? Probably not, because they just knew you needed to make it to adulthood and hopefully graduate school along the way.

You're going to die. Are you hoping everyone at your funeral is going to talk about how great of an employee you were? About the expensive car you drove to impress the people you didn't like? About the vanilla-life you lived? Who fucking cares! Everyone else, that's who. I'd rather have an old van rotting behind my house while I'm out living, then have a new truck living outside my house while I'm rotting away inside. Don't let them toast to the dreams that die along with you.

The 10-steps to freedom listed below might change your life forever. Or forever they will remain blank, it's up to you. I've filled in the first two to help point you in the right direction. Try it and see what happens.

Name:_____

Date:_____

Travel goal or otherwise that I want to achieve _____
_____

Date I'd like to achieve it by:_____

When am I leaving/starting:_____

Steps I need to take to get started:

    1- Tell everyone I know about my goal so they hold me to it.

    2- Take one action each day towards my goal.

    3- _____

    4- _____

    5- _____

    6- _____

    7- _____

    8- _____

    9- _____

    10- _____

Overlanding Vehicles – $1000 to $1,000,000

What's the right Overlanding vehicle/motorbike for the job? You'll be crossing countries and terrain unlike the pretty pavement and graded gravel roads where you came from and probably want to make sure both you and the vehicle survive. For such an event you'll be getting into a long-term relationship with whatever option you choose. The difference to that of a human relationship is that you can modify (ethically) until you've Frankinstined up "The One" for this travel marriage to be.

Much like life, some people choose their partner based solely on good looks. "Looks People" can be seen riding motorcycles they bought second hand with 100,000kms on them because they liked the paint, luggage, and how clean the bike looked. I saw this poor fellow posting endless photos of black smoke from a tailpipe and all the time he spent in garages for buying a motorcycle on looks alone. This same group might also be found driving brand new flashy RV's with duct tape over one of the rear windows from being broken into. I ran into this nice family in Mexico after they parked their "target tourist vehicle" on the street for the day and went on a day trip. They came back to a smashed window and empty RV, ouch! "Looks" tend to draw attention and end up turning the heads of people you'd rather not be noticed by becoming very high maintenance. Have you ever been out with a friend for dinner who has a high-maintenance girlfriend? They're expensive and hard to please. Steer clear of these types in the vehicular format too.

Price People. These people choose based strictly on price. You'll see want ads posted on traveling forums that read "Looking for an amazing travel van/car/or truck that you can sleep in, looks cool, and is less than $2000". I would say this is just asking for trouble, but I will need to qualify that by saying, I once bought a 1969 camperized Ford van for $1800 and drove it from Canada to Guatemala and back, but I feel like that was an extreme exception. These dream travel vehicles for under $2000 can often be found behind tow trucks or parked for weeks in hostel parking lots while the owners try to raise funds to get them fixed. A nice brownish/yellow VW Vanagon topped my travel newsfeed from a fellow traveler who found his ride getting towed from one location to the next, but it looked so cool he had to have it.

Personal Prison People. This is a tough crowd to nail down. On the one hand, they are traveling the world by vehicle, so you should assume they are friendly, interested people with a love for others. Now, on the other hand, they are typically driving massive military-looking Unimogs with prison bars on the windows, armored-style exteriors, and seem entirely unapproachable in their self-contained prisons. If you did want to approach them, you'd need to scale up the side of the Unimog and bang on the bars. Not quite as easy to meet the locals as say on a motorbike. You can find these listed from the high five-figure price range to the high six-figure price range.

Practical People. This group I found had the best overall shot at making it with the least amount of vehicle problems and had the best chances of being approached by locals & getting to know the cultures. These types can usually be found driving older well-known Ford, Toyota, and internationally recognized brands of vans & camper-style trucks. In the motorbike division they are riding a 5+ year old popular Honda, Suzuki, Yamaha, maybe a BMW or Kawasaki. Whatever the ride, the modifications are usually simple enough to fix and the vehicle looks average, dumpy, or "normal" at best. You'd never know they probably have $5000-$10,000 of cameras and computers inside that old thing.

I'd like to think I fall into the practical category, and although that certainly didn't omit me from having any mechanical issues. I definitely didn't give off the impression that I had any more wealth than the next guy who could afford a 650cc or higher motorcycle in countries where 150cc was the norm.

The reality is that you could drive literally anything down the Pan American highway and probably arrive in no worse shape than when you set off. Hell, you'd probably get more positive attention in a less likely vehicle and you might even make it too! Let's take a quick look at some impractical ways to make it around the world.

- **@sasakinorio** the guy from Japan who was walking his way around the world pulling an aluminum cart. I was walking to the river to get water one cool morning in Patagonia and ran into him and a friend.
- **ViaPANAM.be** two Belgian men RUNNING from Alaska to Ushuaia, that's roughly 590 marathons! I met them and their spouses in Cartagena while we were all waiting for our vehicles to arrive from Panama.
- **Worldonboard.wordpress.com** a dude from Singapore who has a knack for skateboarding. So he decided to ride around the world, he calls it "Skate Packing". Oddly I couldn't catch this guy and missed running into him.
- **TukTukTravels.com** are two teachers who decided they would drive around the world in a Tuk Tuk. Why not really?
- Glen Turple. https://youtu.be/rMQhOpSybHM if you just like to ride. I've ridden with and done an interview with 93+ year old Glen Turple who still rides his motorcycle year round.
- I met the family consisting of a German father, Russian mother, and two small children who'd grown up on bicycles. They camped up the hill from me in Costa Rica, and I almost fell over when I saw

- the little pedal modifications for the kids' feet so they could sit and read while their parents peddled them around the planet! I can't remember their website, but Googling "around the world by bicycle" will give you plenty of inspiration.
- I also met an Argentinian couple in their 60's & 70's who were on what they called *"The Final Travel"*. I met them camping on the Argentina side of Patagonia where they were taking a year to ride folding bikes around their native country. Who says you're too old! I could never find their website, but once you hit the open road you will discover many people well into their "Golden Years", out adventuring.

The Money

Outside of "What was your favorite country?" A question that's as easy to answer as asking a parent "Who's your favorite child?". The most popular question I get asked is "How did you afford to pay for all of this?".

That answer comes in many forms and I think I've made it fairly clear how I paid for this little excursion. However, I usually try to gauge who I'm speaking to and if they really want to know how to fund such a trip or if they are looking for a reason why it's unobtainable for them to achieve. Honestly, most people are looking for evidence as to why it's not possible for them, it's so evident by what comes out of their mouth right after someone explains exactly how to buy a house, go on a trip or earn 6-figures. Often, people listen intently to my response until they find something in my answer that they can use to realign their beliefs that they can't make a trip like this happen. They are always looking for impossibility reassurance.

I'll explain to the question-asker in great detail how I sold my possessions or how I learned a new skill to earn money online or how I had to return to Canada to replenish my funds. Then, after all of the how-to's are explained they'll ask something like. "So, do you own a house?" and I'll say; "Yes, I own a house." Then they immediately dismiss everything I said and note how they do not own a house, therefore, can not rent it out to fund the trip.

I'd heard of others who'd sold their houses to fund their travels. I knew if I sold mine I'd never be approved for a mortgage anytime soon and vouched to hang onto it instead. I made a deal with my x-girlfriend to look after my place.

If my house had full occupancy, no repairs, and zero issues during the entire period of my absence I would net roughly $136/month in profits. If anything broke, the tenants didn't pay the rent, or if so much as a microwave blew up, I'd be at a loss that month. By month 5 I had to repair then replace the washer and dryer. You do the math on a brand new washer and dryer and tell me what you think the net profits were that year. Do you think I was going to end the trip over a washer and dryer?

Like I pointed out at the beginning, my goals to open a number of businesses and have that fund my travels soon turned to financial ruin, and instead, I was $100,000 in debt pre-departure rather than $20,000 in the black with money to burn. Ask yourself, are you looking for how or how not to?

The irony of my personal situation, and I'm sure there is a metaphor for life here, is that I could never justify that anything was enough of an emergency to spend my stash of USD. I carried around a few hundred dollars in USD for the whole trip stashed in the bike. When I finally went to exchange it just to spend it, the money had become so moldy from humidity, they wouldn't even accept it.

The Equipment

With the endless options of transportation for this trip, for me, it was the motorcycle. For one, I prefer the adventure and a motorcycle seemed like the right choice. Two, it's significantly cheaper than a vehicle is to operate. It also makes me feel more alive. I choose to buy one of the cheapest adventure motorcycles in my part of the world. To compound these savings, I bought a used one.

I departed on a 2009 KLR650 with nearly 25,000kms on it. I paid $4000 Canadian for the bike and it came with a free helmet. Then I bought and sold similar bikes taking the accessories off and putting them on my bike until I had the parts I needed for free. At one point I had three identical motorcycles in my backyard half-stripped apart. It was looking like a KLR chop shop.

I bought a used jacket and pants that were too big for me and had the pants altered to fit. I also took an old pair of riding boots I had because they were already paid for. These were glued and eventually screwed back together a number of times on the road, but the price was right.

A few winters earlier I'd bought a tent on sale in the middle of winter for $19.99, we took that tent on safari in Africa for a month then I took it on the road to the end of the world. For everything else I searched and bargained my way into anything and everything I thought I might need for the trip.

Having the best Klim riding jacket for $1200 and all-weather Klim riding pants for $900 would certainly be more comfortable. As well, having the best lightweight backpacking tent would have been more ideal, but I wasn't willing to keep inventing reasons why I couldn't leave. There is no lack of people with the best bike, all the right gear, and top-of-the-line camping equipment all collecting dust along with their dreams.

Pick the best gear you can afford and go. If you think one particular item is more important to you than another, splurge on that. For me it was a cooking stove, I wanted the best stove for the job and chose one that could burn any fuel and was extremely reliable. It cost more than my tent, helmet, and biker gear combined. Spend extravagantly on what you enjoy, save mercilessly on what doesn't matter to you. I'd rather be cooking meals in the mountains than trying to impress people that I don't even know in a brand-name jacket.

When's The Best Time To Go?

I met a guy in Botswana once who'd ridden his motorbike from Germany to where I met him, he was planning to end his trip in South Africa. I asked what the hardest part of his journey was? His reply: "Leaving my house".

I set a departure date and said no matter what funds I had, I'd leave by the end of October. On October 29th 2016 I left. Not with $20,000 in the bank like I'd hoped, but with $7,000.

Set a date of departure with no option to negotiate. If you find that you can't follow through with meeting your obligations then you might want to work on this area of your life before failing again with a departure date.

I might warn you that there is never, "The best time to go". On a long enough timeline you will be making memories with missing moments you can never replace. I missed Christmases with family, a grandparents funeral, my father's heart surgery, countless birthdays, births, and celebrations. You will feel guilty. Be prepared.

The Budget

I assumed the trip would take roughly 18-months. With my new budget of $7000 I then ran the numbers on this. 18-months or 547-days divided by $7000. $7000/547= $12. My new travel budget was $12/day, including all costs as well as paying for the washer dryer set.

By Colombia, I ran out of money.

In Colombia, I knew I could either ride like hell to complete the trip and come back in debt or find a solution. I opted to call a friend back home I'd worked for before leaving and ask if I flew back for the summer, would he employ me. He seemed happy with the offer and tucking my tail between my legs, I came back to Canada feeling like a failure to work for just under 3-months. This was my new seed money to fund my further travels.

From here I continued to tent it, cooked most of my meals, showered in waterfalls, lived with and like the locals, and learned to exist off of the bare minimum.

The following summer I was meant to be in a friend's wedding and made the same deal with my previous employer. This time I wasn't so ashamed to be home and was happy to again stay in the basement of my father's house for the summer, rent-free, while I worked.

Budgets- Budgets can run anywhere from $12/day to $120/day and beyond. There is no magic number, no exact budget, and no excel spreadsheet to determine a universal budget. However, you may want to consider the following;

The Vehicle- The larger the vehicle the more fuel you will use. The more rare or newer, the more expensive parts will be. Even taking a new vehicle will not save you from repairs. Something will break and it will break at the most inconvenient moment. If you drive what the locals drive it will be easier and cheaper to fix.

Time- The age-old conundrum of time vs money. It could not be more true on lengthy road trips. To get from point A to point B will require the exact same fuel and equipment. The longer you spread this out the lower your costs. Just picture a two-week vacation to the beach. The plane ticket to get there cost the same if you go for two weeks or two months. The hotel likely cost the same for two weeks as if you were renting a house for two months. Buying groceries for two months cost the same as eating out for three meals a day for two weeks. Would you rather vacation for two weeks or two months?

Fun- What do you like to do for fun? If you need a steady stream of tours, organized hikes, dives, boat rides, and someone to hold your hand along the way, the price adds up. If you take pleasure in taking photos, hanging with the locals, and exploring, it will likely cost a lot less.

Take your total assumed days on the road and divide it by the funds you have to find your daily allowable budget.

Days divided by funds= Daily Budget.

Then kiss this figure goodbye as soon as something breaks or you decide that you must detour to the Galapagos or whatever strikes your fancy.

Tips

- Crossing the Gap: You can fly a motorbike by DHL. Put the bike on a sailboat like the Stahlratte, though the global pandemic likely ruined him. You can use various shipping companies, we used Evergreen, but there are other options you can find once you get closer. The total cost for the shipping container divided by two SUV's and a motorbike was around $2800USD. Ouch!
- Apps: iOverlander (the problem is everyone uses it, the good is it saved my ass).
- Facebook groups. My personal favorite was the Panamerican Travelers Association, but there are plenty. Everyone's an "expert", so take what you hear with a grain of salt.
- Cell phones. Bring an unlocked phone and get sim cards in each country or have an international plan. I used Google Fi as it offered internet for a flat rate no matter where I was in the world.

- Looking for work online? UpWork, eLance, or ask around or travel forums.
- Practical information on each country; Wikitravel has far better information than government travel sites. Read up on a country before you go, not knowing the rules could be costly. For example, overstaying a TIP in Nicaragua is a cheap fine, in Peru is vehicle confiscation.
- Take two wallets, one that you carry that only holds cash and you are prepared to lose. The other you leave behind. The same might go for cellphones, cameras etc.
- Find a bankcard with free or great international exchange rates. Bring two of them. I used Transferwise/Wise transfers.
- Find a hiding spot for money and spare keys. I met one guy who had $500 stashed in his handlebars.

Shout-Outs! / Acknowledgments

This is a monumental and impossible task to do properly. I mean, really, at different points, it felt like everyone was rooting for me or helping me out.

There were my parents who I can always feel biting their tongues while I hop in this plane or that boat or motorcycle to piss off to one remote part of the planet or another where they think my life is in grave danger. If my father hadn't thrown me headfirst into various childhood adventures like taking a shower in the back of a horse trailer in the middle of winter in a campground or sending me off at 13 to lead a group of people on horseback up of a mountain where I'd get us all lost I'd likely be scared shitless to venture out into the unknown.

My mother was always a blunt reminder of what to and what not to consider real problems. She always sent me off with inspirational quotes that left me guessing if I was meant to laugh, cringe or take them to heart. At 18 just before wandering off to the opposite side of the planet for a year after giving her three weeks' notice of the adventure, she looked me in the eyes at the airport and said; "Men will go places with a hard-on they wouldn't go with a loaded shotgun. Keep your wits about you." And so, left me to wonder why a man might find himself in one questionable situation or another.

There was my sister who painted my home between renters while my x-girlfriend dealt with tenant bullshit to keep me from losing my house. My friend Andrew would endlessly answer questions about how to fix this broken part or that missing piece on KLaiR. Friends would offer up homes of family and put in a good word when I was passing through their area. I think my friend Liz had a family member in every country I visited in Central America and could always convince them to let me stop by for a night or two. Thank you to Nat Sapach. Previously known as my high school English teacher whom I'd rarely spoken to in 20-years. Much like high school he appeared when I needed him, presented me with some suggestions about what to do with life & literature, then sat back and let me make my own choices. He was the first person to read this book in its raw format and was happy to explain over and over again what a good and bad sentence fragment looks like :) My now wife Angie who continually cheered me on both behind the scenes and showed up in person to do so in a number of less than ideal situations. She even saved me from a grammatical blunder moments before publishing this book. I've thrown more hair-brained schemes and curve ball ideas at her than she has likely had to consider in her life. Somehow she just smiles and acts like I'm not about to max out her patience :)

Hell, nearly everyone I met wished me well or said a prayer for my journey.

There are an endless amount of people who literally went out of their way to feed me, fix me, entertain me, make me feel like family, cure my illnesses, and save my fuking ass from going missing or losing faith in myself.

I'll never be able to capture them all, but if I can do a shout-out to some of the businesses along the way that others might have the chance to visit and throw some tourism dollars their way I will try to add a few of them here.

- **Turple Brothers** in Red Deer Alberta. TurpleBros.ca Talk to Glen, the 90+ year old motorcycle legend who still rides his trike to work, year-round!
- **Bolivia Motorcycle Tours**. Located just outside of Santa Cruz in El Torno. Owner Chris, his wife Rebeca, and two kids are incredible. Chris seriously saved my ass more times than anyone else in the Americas and he can take you on one hell of a tour of Bolivia!

- **Gil Serique Tours**. I spent a month with Gil while my bike was broken down. To say he is a character would be to say that Santa reminds you of Christmas. Gil is bat shit crazy and one of the most hospitable people on the planet. His love of the Rainforest and its creatures is incredible.

- Ruban and Karina at **Los Ositos in Villa Rica Peru**. Proprietors of a small restaurant and boat touring business on the edge of a tilapia-rich lake. I'd planned to spend a night and ended up staying for a month.

- **Lechuza Cafe** and hotel in Juayua El Salvador. An amazing little hotel and one of the best hands-on tours of coffee from bean to cup in the world. Again a night here turned into a month and Javier changed my life forever.

- **Las Pozas Campground** located at N 16.39392 W 89.49816 in Guatemala. Jose is an unbelievable host.

- **MotoPhil.ch** for the back cover photo and other images in the book.

There are more people, countless people, endless people that I met along the way or who were back in Canada that helped out in one way or another.

All I can say is, THANK YOU!

Writers Notes:

Of all the chapters in this entire book, I found the part on Ayahuasca the most difficult to write. I skimmed past it twice, went back and wrote it a couple of times and ignored it all together for most of the time during the two years I spent writing this book. While most of these stories flew from my mind to my fingertips and onto the page, the Ayahuasca chapter felt like a fight to the finish line. Perhaps it is the most personal story of all the stories, perhaps it's because the Amazon and the Ayahuasca experience were goals I thought I'd never see come to life. I'm happy to share fun stories and good times face to face with people, otherwise I'm wildly secretive about the real me with nearly anyone. On paper or on stage it feels quite the opposite and nearly effortless to divulge the details of my life, nearly. An x-girlfriend looked at me once and said *"You're like an open book, with the most important pages ripped out"*. Hopefully most of the important pages were included here.

I'd Like To Hear From You:

I hope you enjoy this book, if so I'd like to hear from you. Please feel free to write a review on whatever site you acquired this book

www.ingramcontent.com/pod-product-compliance
Lightning Source LLC
Chambersburg PA
CBHW041303110526
44590CB00028B/4231